YELLS FOR OURSELVES

New York City and the New York Mets
at the dawn of the millennium

MATTHEW CALLAN

Copyright © 2019 Matthew Callan
All rights reserved.

No part of this book may be reproduced, or stored in a retrieval system, or transmitted in any form or by any means, electronic, mechanical, photocopying, recording, or otherwise, without express written permission of the publisher.

Published by Inkshares, Inc., Oakland, California
www.inkshares.com

Cover design by Rafael Andres
Interior design by Kevin G. Summers

ISBN: 9781947848801
e-ISBN: 9781947848498

First edition

Printed in the United States of America

ACKNOWLEDGMENTS

The genesis of *Yells For Ourselves* dates back to 2009 and a day-to-day chronicle of the 1999 Mets written at my own blog, Scratchbomb.com. A year later, I worked on a similar project chronicling the 2000 team for Amazin' Avenue; I also wrote a more concise retrospective series on the 1999 Mets for the same site in 2014. The bulk of the research for *Yells For Ourselves* has its origins in these posts, and vestigial tails thereof can, I'm sure, be spotted within the final product. I'm grateful to Eric Simon of Amazin' Avenue for indulging my obsession with these teams, and equally grateful to Chris McShane, Jeffrey Paternostro, and the many other AA writers and editors (past and present) who both encouraged this project and helped promote it during its funding stage by having me on their podcasts and RTing my many pleas for preorders.

In addition to this, Amazin' Avenue published my long-form study of Robin Ventura and the Grand Slam Single game in 1999 ("The Grand Slam Single," October 9, 2014), as well as a journey into the heart of darkness that was the 1993 Mets ("1993: The Year the Mets Broke," April 9, 2013). Both pieces have been mined heavily for the sections of this book dealing with Robin Ventura, the Grand Slam Single, and the ugly 1993 Mets team, though they have been rewritten and rearranged to suit the narrative. Amazin' Avenue also featured a pair of excerpts from earlier incarnations of this book prior to publication ("October 4, 1999: Game 163, Mets vs. Reds," October 4, 2016; "Looking back at Todd Pratt's legendary home run in the '99 NLDS," May 18, 2017).

A piece I wrote on the disastrous 1999 umpires' strike for The Classical ("Called Out: The Forgotten Umpires' Strike of 1999," October 2, 2012) has been integrated into this book where relevant to the story. I'm grateful to David Roth for editing and running that piece, as well as for sharing with his readers at The Classical a very early version of chapter 3 of this book, and for also giving a shout-out to the preorder campaign in his Vice Sports piece about another relic of 1999/2000, Rey Ordóñez.

The previously published pieces cited above are acknowledged as examples of integrating work that originally appeared elsewhere into *Yells For Ourselves*, or where in-progress pieces of this book were previewed prior to publication. If the reader has read these pieces previously, parts of this book may have a familiar ring. However, it is my belief that *Yells For Ourselves* is a work of original research and scholarship, and I hope the reader will agree.

I am extremely grateful to Andrew Lowden for sharing with me video of several crucial games from 1999 and 2000, which were invaluable in informing the descriptions of those games in this book. Perhaps Andrew's greatest contribution to *Yells For Ourselves* was loaning me a VHS tape of the (in)famous Mercury Mets game of 1999, thus allowing posterity to know Rickey Henderson's exact reaction to seeing himself rendered as a three-eyed alien on Shea Stadium's Diamond Vision.

I am also grateful to Dan McQuade, who lent archives of Wharton's student newspaper, *The Daily Pennsylvanian*, which shed light on the Bobby Valentine "Wharton-gate" incident of 2000.

Early versions of this manuscript were read by Greg Prince, Dave Zirin, and Will Akers, all of whom provided invaluable feedback and encouragement.

Tom Scharpling was generous enough to take time out of his weekly radio program *The Best Show* to promote the book and direct people to the fundraising campaign. In addition to being one of the funniest people on the planet, he is a champion of the highest order.

Lou and Stephanie Rebecchi helped my wife and I "street team" to promote the book one rainy June Sunday at Citi Field, accosting strangers as they stepped off the 7 train to hand them postcards about the book (postcards that Lou spiffed up dramatically from my initial proto-minimalist design). It was a blast and I can never thank them enough for all they did to help promote the book. Tip for future crowdfunders that I learned from Stephanie: If someone doesn't want to take a postcard about your book, you can always shame them with a quick "Whatsa matter, can't you read?"

So many people on Twitter and Facebook shared the Inkshares link with their followers that I am sure I would slight some of them in my attempts to name them all. If you did, just know that I owe you in perpetuity and you may collect on that debt at any time.

My wife listened to me moan about trying to get this book published for years, as I lamented my inability to interest any agent or publisher in the charms of Edgardo Alfonzo. She encouraged me nonetheless, never more so than when she told me (not in so many words) that I would probably have to bring this thing direct to an audience if I ever wanted it to see the light of day. She believed I could do that, long before I ever thought I could. That you hold this book in your hands now, in whatever form you are holding it, is thanks to her.

My daughter told me, "If the book meets its goal, we should go out to dinner. And if it doesn't, we should still go out to dinner." So it looks like we're going out to dinner.

A Note on Sources

The statistics contained in this book—everything from batting average and ERA to attendance records and time of games—have been verified via Baseball-Reference.com. Descriptions of in-game action are derived from original radio and television broadcasts where available, via my own collection of video, media generously shared with me (see above), and the ever-expanding library of video found on YouTube and other online outlets. In general, I have only cited such video in the sources if it contains a quote or some other "off field" detail—say, information shared by a broadcaster or sideline reporter about a pregame conversation with a player.

Where audio or video are unavailable, descriptions of games rely on the "gamers" published in New York's local newspapers. As with audio and video sources, newspaper sources are provided to denote origins of quotes, background information, whispers of clubhouse intrigue, trade rumors, and all other details that can be said to occur "outside the lines" of normal game action.

In the case of quotes where a reporter censored an expletive, and context makes it obvious what offending word was used, I've restored it. This was done to reproduce (as much as possible) locker room atmosphere and to reassure readers that ballplayers in 1999 and 2000 did not use muted vocabulary like "stinkin'" and "gosh darn it."

Most of the background information for this book comes from New York's daily newspapers, with much of that research conducted in these dailies' respective online archives. All cited URLs are valid as of this writing, though it should be mentioned that daily newspapers are fickle in the maintenance of their online archives. Both the *Post* and the *Daily News* changed the style and format of their archived content multiple times during the writing of this book and failed to provide redirects from the old links to the new. During the 1999 and 2000 MLB playoffs, CNNSI—a cable channel formed by a partnership between the cable news network and *Sports Illustrated*—performed original onsite reporting, and though the channel itself folded in 2002, much of its online coverage remained available for more than a decade (including video and audio clips from interviews with players and managers that could be found nowhere else). This coverage proved invaluable to the writing of this book, but when CNN and *Sports Illustrated* formally ended their online relationship in 2013, all of it disappeared. In cases of these and other resources that have been consigned to the internet graveyard, cached links from the Wayback Machine have been provided.

A full list of sequential sources is available at: scratchbomb.com/yfosources.pdf

Corrections for links and other information welcomed at: yellsforourselves@gmail.com.

INTRODUCTION

'Round Midnight

WHEN BERNIE WILLIAMS gloved Mike Piazza's long fly ball for the final out of the 2000 World Series, sealing the Yankees' third consecutive championship, the only official sign that the game had ended came from Shea Stadium's giant videoboard towering high above the outfielder's head. It flashed a polite notice asking fans to drive home safely. In their most recent playoff games, the Mets had pumped up their own fans and annoyed the opposition with a jacked-up public address system that literally shook the seats. Now, as their conquerors dogpiled and whooped and hollered on their home field, those same speakers purred a gentle organ rendition of the jazz standard "'Round Midnight."

In the moment, Thelonious Monk's languid composition seemed nothing more than a literal choice, since the final out was recorded near 12:00 a.m. The passing of time has given another meaning to the accompaniment. When the Mets lost the 2000 World Series, the clock struck midnight for them in many senses. Their dreams of overtaking the Yankees in the hearts and minds of New York were dashed. Gone as well was a notion that New York City itself had a place for noble defeat, for the valiant but doomed effort.

After the conclusion of the 2000 World Series, it would be said the Yankees "owned" the city while the Mets played the little brother role. It would be said that things had always been this way. The press would forget that for much of the two years leading up to that Subway Series, they had proclaimed the little brother team was the hungrier one and thus could and should rival the Yankees for the city's affections. The press would forget that they, and many of the fans they served, had fallen in love with an idea of the Mets, which stood in for a love for their rapidly changing city, a love for a romantic notion of what New York had once been, and a subconscious fear of what it had become.

* * *

In the 1990s, both New York City and the Yankees experienced remarkable renaissances, transforming themselves from scrap heaps into well-oiled machines. Both city and team professed they would accept nothing less than total domination. Both preferred to write the 1980s out of their histories because that era represented chaos and rotten excess and dysfunction and . . . *the Mets*.

If you were a Mets fan, though, you saw the 1980s as a time when everyone said *your* favorite team "owned" the city. You might even agree with Mets co-owner Fred Wilpon, who held on to an antiquated notion from the days of the Brooklyn Dodgers and New York Giants, which proclaimed that deep within its soul New York was, and always would be, "a National League town." In those days, there were three teams to suit the city's affections, each with folkways suited for its respective constituents. You saw no reason why the Mets could not likewise carve out its own niche, no matter what New York had become.

The simplest way to do this was, of course, to win again. After years of prospect hoarding produced no appreciable results, in the late 1990s the Mets set about assembling a championship caliber ballclub in a very Yankee-like fashion: they bought it. They were enabled in this endeavor by general manager Steve Phillips, who eschewed the glacial and imprecise process of player development in favor of big deals that could be splashed across the tabloid's back pages.

Despite imitating their crosstown rivals when it came to roster construction, the Mets' 1999 season proceeded in a very Mets-like fashion. They wielded a dangerous offense anchored by Mike Piazza, Edgardo Alfonzo, and Robin Ventura, yet the lineup was prone to bipolar waves of blazing-hot streaks and terrifying slumps. They possessed an ironclad infield defense and a shutdown bullpen, and they leaned heavily on both to compensate for inconsistent starting pitching. Manager Bobby Valentine was regarded by some baseball pundits as one of the best minds in the game. He was also loathed by nearly every opponent and many in his own dugout—and on most days, his standing in the Mets' front office was hardly better.

At times, it appeared nothing could stop the 1999 Mets. At other times, it appeared the 1999 Mets were determined to stop themselves. Twice the team settled into lengthy losing streaks of seven or more games that threatened to end their season. Each time, they righted the ship in the nick of time. They possessed an uncanny knack for backing themselves into must-win situations, whereupon they won in improbable fashion. They danced with danger at every turn, pulled themselves from the brink time and again, stared death in the face, and all but dared it to claim them.

When the Mets fell short in a hard-fought National League Championship Series against the Atlanta Braves, no one dared call the season a failure. Throughout October of 1999, the team's travails dominated the city's back pages and drowned out another methodical Yankee march to a championship. There emerged an idea that the Mets could capture New York's focus and affections, not necessarily through a championship, but through being so resolutely *Mets*.

The press allowed the Mets to play the 2000 season with the glow of noble defeat and saved their harshest glare for the Yankees. Throughout that year, New York's back pages judged the Yankees harshly against a Mets team they considered hungrier, grittier, and more exciting. This fomented a resentment that exhibited itself in several ugly incidents during the regular season and culminated in a tense World Series, in which the Mets proved powerless to prevent their rivals from exacting revenge on the press by proxy. The result seemed to seal once and for all not only the question of which team was better, but to define the very soul of the city for another generation. It was an answer so loud it drowned out any lingering echoes of the question.

Yells for Ourselves tells this story. It draws exclusively on contemporary sources and concentrates on how the media's perceptions of New York's baseball landscape evolved over the 1999 and 2000 seasons to create the narrative that exists to this day. It places these perceptions within the context of the rapid changes then taking place in Major League Baseball: the unprecedented explosions in offensive numbers and free agent salaries and the ever-widening divisions between the sport's haves and have-nots that threatened its precarious labor peace. It also examines the Mets and Yankees within the evolving landscape of New York City and the immense impact the city's turnaround in the 1990s had on both teams, and how these perceptions paralleled a debate about the direction of the metropolis. Like the rivalry between the teams, this debate demanded a definitive resolution, one that declared what type of city New York would be in the dawning millennium.

Yells for Ourselves takes pains to not project the shadow of future events onto this story by reminding the reader what a player would do in the years to come or what we would later learn about his exploits on or off the field. Instead, it recounts events as they unfolded and confines itself as much as possible to the information fans would have learned from reading the newspapers or tuning in to sports talk radio in 1999 and 2000. The goal of this book is to re-create the atmosphere those same fans experienced during these seasons—perhaps the last moments in history when fan opinion was dictated from on high by sportswriters who purported to speak for them, and whose writing captured far more than even the chroniclers realized at the time.

* * *

When the Mets first arrived on the scene in the early 1960s, their mere existence was enough for heartbroken former fans of the Dodgers and Giants who ached for anything to fill the void these teams left behind. Once the Mets started playing and proved to be historically awful, these same fans had to concoct reasons beyond nostalgia that would justify attending the crumbling Polo Grounds to watch one of the worst teams ever assembled by the hand of man. The original Mets did nothing worth celebrating. Fans celebrated them anyway. Something about the Mets spoke to their souls in a way the Yankees never could.

This phenomenon was captured by Roger Angell, who penned one of the first studies of the Mets and their fans in his 1962 piece for the *New Yorker*, "The 'Go!' Shouters." Angell observed the inaugural Mets and the people who felt compelled to shout, sing, and wave signs cheering their every pitiful achievement.

> This was a new recognition that perfection is admirable but a trifle inhuman, and that a stumbling kind of semi-success can be much more warming. Most of all, perhaps, these exultant yells for the Mets were also yells for ourselves, and came from a wry, half-understood recognition that there is more Met than Yankee in every one of us.

Whenever the Mets have captured the hearts of New York City, it was by exhibiting this "stumbling kind of semi-success." The Miracle Mets of 1969. The "Ya gotta believe" squad of 1973. Even the 1986 team that dominated in the regular season fought tooth and nail throughout the playoffs. The near triumph in 1999 fit perfectly within this difficult history, and the public knew it. That is what brought the Mets within a hair's breadth of capturing the city again, or at least capturing their share of it. The Yankees themselves sensed this, and so made it their mission to crush the idea that "semi-success" could prevail in the new New York. Like the Yankees, the city had evolved in the last decade of the twentieth century into a humorless powerhouse. They, and their city, aimed to keep it that way.

Future Mets teams would spend furiously under the misapprehension that fans wanted another championship. And of course they did, because that is what all fans want. But more than anything, what Mets fans really wanted was another 1999.

PROLOGUE

"Great for the City": The Rise and Fall of Bobby Valentine and the New York Mets, 1962–1998

I JUST ENDED MR. BASEBALL'S CAREER.

The boy was roughhousing and it was all fun and games until he landed a shot to his friend's eye. The boy's heart sank because his friend wasn't just any teenager. His friend was Mr. Baseball, aka Bobby Valentine. This was the 1960s, in Stamford, Connecticut, a time and place in which Bobby Valentine was everything.

As a high school athlete, Bobby Valentine dominated all sports. His skill as a running back garnered comparisons to O. J. Simpson from Simpson's own coach at USC. He was so good at basketball that for years local coaches could chide a showboating youngster by yelling, "Who do you think you are, Bobby Valentine?" He excelled at more esoteric endeavors too, winning pancake-eating contests and ballroom dancing competitions with equal gusto. If an event ended with crowning a winner, Bobby Valentine would find some way to be that winner.

Above all, Bobby Valentine preferred to win at baseball, his one true love. The lights outside his house were covered in baseball-shaped globes, lovingly painted by a carpenter father who shared Stamford's belief that Bobby Valentine could do no wrong. He was son to them all, a local treasure to be cherished and protected. That's why, when a boy landed an accidental elbow to Bobby Valentine's eye, that boy feared that he might have destroyed the hope of an entire city.

Bobby Valentine shrugged off this blow. Nothing could stop Bobby Valentine. If your entire hometown called you Mr. Baseball before you reached adulthood, you would believe you were bulletproof, too. The problems would only come when you left that town and entered a world that didn't see you glowing with the same angelic light. That world might never make any sense to you at all. You might never make any sense to that world.

* * *

Bobby Valentine was the Los Angeles Dodgers' first-round draft choice in 1968. His athletic range was matched only by his relentless enthusiasm and his inability to repress a high-octane personality. His rookie league manager—a baseball lifer named Tommy Lasorda, who would become a mentor and lifelong defender—described him as "insufferable, but in a good way." Valentine hit his way through the Dodger organization with breakneck speed, inspiring the big league club to call him up during the 1969 season.

Then Valentine was forced to slow down for the first time in his life by Walter Alston, human speed bump. Alston had managed the Dodgers since they called Flatbush home and had no patience for Valentine's impatience. Each year, Alston accepted a one-year contract offered by the Dodgers' parsimonious owner, Walter O'Malley, and he expected his charges to display comparable humility. Alston used Valentine all over the field, treating him more like a utility player than a budding star. Mr. Baseball responded by openly lobbying for Tommy Lasorda to take Alston's place, then gave the current manager more ammo to use against him when he injured his knee in an intramural football game before the 1972 season. A mediocre season at the plate and continued clashes with Alston prompted a trade to the Angels at year's end.

On May 17, 1973, while patrolling center field at Anaheim Stadium, Valentine pursued a long fly—at full speed, of course. As the ball sailed over the fence, he crashed into its unyielding expanse of chain link. Valentine caught a cleat in the fence and snapped his right leg in two places, so horrifically that bone poked through the skin. The break was then set improperly, causing his right leg to heal slightly shorter than the left. The legs that had once powered Valentine to break state rushing records now tripped underneath him as he ran out grounders.

Finished as an everyday player, Valentine settled into life as a benchwarmer with the Angels and Padres before being dealt to the Mets midway through the 1977 season. He performed well enough the following year to receive assurances from his manager that he would make the opening day roster in 1979. Then, with only a week left in spring training, the team released him, citing the need to give chances to younger players with more potential. The manager who delivered the bad news did his best to be civil, but it was obvious that Valentine's career was all but over. Once assured a roster spot and steady paycheck, all Valentine had left was a shrug of the shoulders and best wishes from his now-former manager, Joe Torre.

Valentine muddled through sixty-two more major league games before hanging up his spikes at the ripe old age of twenty-nine. Then he returned to Stamford to open a sports bar that bore his name. Though the town had filled with new pieds-à-terre for the Wall Street crowd, Valentine opened his bar south of I-95, where the town retained some of the working-class character it held in his youth, where the memories were longer and he was still greeted as Mr. Baseball.

On the walls of his bar, Valentine hung his prized collection of baseball memorabilia alongside a morbid memento: pictures of that fateful night in Anaheim, strobed one frame at a time. You see him approaching the wall, getting closer with each blink. You can tell he won't be able to stop himself. His momentum is too great. A terrible finish is in store. And then you see it. You see Mr. Baseball sprawled out on the turf in agony, his leg shattered, his old life already over.

* * *

After one year as a saloonkeeper, Bobby Valentine accepted a minor league instructional assignment with the Mets in 1981. Once again, he worked his way to the bigs at fevered pace. By 1983, he was on the Mets' big league coaching staff. By 1985, he was tapped to manage the Texas Rangers. Under Valentine's stewardship, the moribund franchise experienced a rare brush with contention, finishing second in the American League West in 1986, its best showing ever. But no matter where the Rangers were in the standings in any given season, the spotlight would always focus on their excitable manager.

Bobby Valentine refused to keep still in the dugout, shifting from one bad leg to the other, pacing, shaking his head, throwing up his hands. He would often position himself on the dugout railing to berate all of his presumed enemies, earning him the nickname Top Step and the ire of opposing managers. He was more popular with his own team, but not by much. Kevin Brown, the Rangers' ace, grumbled that when Valentine's players went through slumps, the manager shut them out, as if their bad luck would infect the rest of the team. The local press could sympathize with Brown's feelings. Simple queries from the beat writers provoked answers that ranged in tone from dismissive to combative, delivered in a voice that came from the back of the throat, guttural, mocking.

Such sins could have been excused if Valentine's teams succeeded, but the runner-up finish in 1986 proved his high-water mark in Texas. He received his pink slip in July 1992, the bad news delivered at a dour press conference led by Rangers team president George W. Bush.

Valentine managed the Mets' triple-A affiliate for one season before the 1995 season brought him an offer to become the first manager recruited directly from America to lead a team in the Japanese major leagues (Nippon Professional Baseball, or NPB). The offer came from the Chiba Lotte Marines, a down-on-its-luck franchise willing to try anything to win, or at least gain some attention. Despite the glaring cultural differences and the Marines' lowly status, Valentine jumped at the challenge.

That challenge came at a crucial time for Japanese baseball, for 1995 was also the year of Hideo Nomo's historic "rookie" campaign. The star pitcher for the Kinetsu Buffaloes "retired" from NPB so he could sign with the Dodgers, making him the first Japanese player to make a jump to the American major leagues in almost thirty years. Nomo's immediate stateside success made him a source of great pride to a baseball-obsessed nation, and the ensuing Nomo-mania inspired American teams to send scouts overseas in the hopes of finding the next Japanese superstar. Though Valentine was new to Japanese baseball himself, he became the go-to quote for Americans hoping to make sense of it all.

Such hubris grated on Valentine's bosses, and before long, team officials were undermining their new manager at every turn. First, the Marines fired the interpreter and head coach who had tutored him on NPB's players, with no explanation, and instructed Valentine to read up on "the book" of NPB players and their stats instead. When reminded that said book was only available in Japanese, a language Valentine could not yet speak or read fluently, Valentine was told to study harder. After receiving verbal promises for a three-year contract, he was offered a paper contract for two years.

Despite these considerable hurdles, Valentine piloted the Marines to a second-place finish and their best record in eleven years, which only infuriated his bosses further. At season's end, the Marines' front office publicly called out Valentine for his training methods. (Japanese teams traditionally relied on rigorous individual drills, whereas Valentine preferred team practices.) The Marines' general manager contended they finished second in spite of Valentine, not because of him, while an assistant general manager said Valentine "was judged deficient in baseball ability." Fans gathered twenty-four thousand signatures on a petition demanding Valentine's return. He was fired regardless.

The Mets welcomed Valentine back to manage their triple-A team again in 1996. In spite of the Marines' best efforts, his misadventure in Japan hadn't humbled him in the least. As far as he could see, he was still Mr. Baseball. It was only a matter of time before the Mets would see it that way too.

* * *

When Valentine returned to the Mets, the franchise was in the midst of one of its periodic ruts while the Yankees were on the rise. In isolation, this state of affairs was not unusual, as the two teams' fortunes had traditionally moved in complementary waves. In the mid-1960s, the Mets were regarded as more in touch with the dynamic go-go New Frontier feeling of the era than the Eisenhower-gray Yankees. The Mets' brand-new home, Shea Stadium—convenient to several new highways and the Long Island suburbs to which so many New Yorkers had fled—was far preferred over the Yankees' outdated home in the South Bronx, ground zero for Robert Moses–induced white flight. The contrast only grew sharper when the Mets won a shocking championship in 1969, then scrambled from last place to first in the final months of the 1973 season and came within one game of another World Series trophy. Beginning in 1964 (the year Shea Stadium opened), the Mets outdrew the Yankees for eleven straight seasons, and the tallies were seldom close.

The tide began turning in 1975 with the death of baseball's reserve clause, which opened the door to free agency. The resulting explosion of player salaries was too much for the Mets' owners, the de Roulet family, so parsimonious they once considered collecting foul balls and scrubbing them for reuse. At the 1977 trade deadline, team president M. Donald Grant shipped the team's two brightest stars, ace Tom Seaver and slugger Dave Kingman, out of Queens in a shortsighted effort to keep down payroll. These moves came to be known as the Midnight Massacre, for to Mets fans they were about as shocking as their namesake Watergate firings, and would doom the team to irrelevance for years to come.

Meanwhile, the Yankees took up residence in a renovated Yankee Stadium in 1976, while their new owner, George Steinbrenner, embraced free agency as much as the Mets ran from it and inked stars like Reggie Jackon and Catfish Hunter to large contracts. The resulting clubhouse mix was a volatile one dubbed The Bronx Zoo, but these Yankees nonetheless won two consecutive championships in 1977 and 1978 and drew crowds that abandoned the hopeless Mets. Once-packed Shea Stadium became known to embittered fans as Grant's Tomb.

The next reversal of fortune began in 1980, when the Mets were sold to a group headed by publishing heir Nelson Doubleday, who then hired Frank Cashen as his general manager. Architect of the great Orioles teams of the 1960s and 1970s, Cashen rebuilt a decimated farm system and concocted savvy trades to fulfill his promise to make the Mets contenders again in five years' time. By 1986, another championship was theirs. By 1988, over three million fans were showing up at Shea each season. As for the Yankees, they lapsed into mediocrity and could find little traction with a sports press fixated on the more exciting and successful Mets, unless it was news about George Steinbrenner's ineffectual and embarrassing meddling.

The 1986 championship looked like the first leg of a Mets dynasty, but that magical season proved to be the era's crest. The Mets' decline proceeded slowly at first, one small slip at a time. Another run at the crown in 1988 was snuffed by a seemingly inferior Los Angeles Dodgers team, which beat the Mets in a seven-game championship series behind a magical year from pitcher Orel Hershiser. Staff ace Doc Gooden struggled with substance abuse and drew multiple suspensions for violating the league's drug policy. Darryl Strawberry feuded with management and left for Los Angeles. Frank Cashen traded away valuable budding stars like Kevin Mitchell, Lenny Dykstra, and Randy Myers and watched all of them power other teams into the playoffs. Manager Davey Johnson continually clashed with the front office until he was canned in 1990. Johnson's replacement, Buddy Harrelson, made it clear he was not made of managerial timber when he withered under criticism and literally hid from the press. Before long, he too was gone.

Then assistant general manager Joe McIlvaine, Cashen's heir apparent, blindsided the team by leaving for the San Diego front office after the 1990 season. Another assistant GM, Al Harazin, ascended to second in command by default when Frank Cashen retired after the 1991 season. Harazin had previously dealt exclusively with the money side of the business and was judged "dangerously shallow" in baseball knowledge by co-owner Fred Wilpon. What Harazin lacked in baseball acumen he hoped to make up for with spending power. Both as Cashen's lieutenant and as GM himself, he successfully lobbied the team to sign pricey stars like Vince Coleman, Eddie Murray, Bobby Bonilla, and Bret Saberhagen. These acquisitions made the Mets a chic pick to return to their former glory, but the 1992 season (Harazin's first at the helm) was doomed by injuries, underperforming, and strife on and off the field. Of the latter, the most heinous incidents were rape charges against three Mets players and bizarre rumors that pitcher David Cone had lured women into the Shea Stadium bullpen with promises of autographed baseballs in order to masturbate in front of them. Charges were dropped in the rape case, and a lawsuit against Cone went nowhere (he vigorously denied the accusations), but the cases tarnished the sullen Mets' reputation even further.

Even so, many observers were willing to give the Mets a mulligan due to the spate of injuries they suffered in 1992 and assumed a healthy team would perform well the next year. As it turned out, the Mets did not endure nearly as much time on the DL in 1993. What they *did* endure was far, far worse.

From mid-April until the end of June, the 1993 Mets failed to put together a winning streak of any length. Over this stretch, what the team did on the baseball field resembled baseball only in the strictly academic sense. Manager Jeff Torborg received his walking papers by May and was replaced by Dallas Green, whose previous managerial work with the Phillies and Yankees labeled him as a drill sergeant type who could whip the Mets back into shape. Soon, Al Harazin was gone as well, replaced by Joe McIlvaine, who'd resigned his own post in San Diego. It was already far too late for Green's tough love to have any effect in the dugout, or for McIlvaine's front office skills to cure a poisoned clubhouse. The moves were little more than deck chair rearrangement on the *Titanic*. Even worse, the ugliness of the Mets on the diamond was only exceeded by their ugliness off it.

Said ugliness began a mere four games into the season, when outfielder Bobby Bonilla confronted *Daily News* beat writer Bob Klapisch, who had coauthored a book about the mess of 1992 with the provocative title *The Worst Team Money Could Buy*. After calling the author a homophobic slur, Bonilla promised Klapisch, "I'll show you the Bronx," then smacked away a microphone belonging to a camera crew capturing the whole thing on tape.

On July 7, with the media in the clubhouse for postgame coverage, one Met tossed a lit firecracker behind a group of reporters. No injuries resulted, but skittish reporters demanded to know who was responsible. The offending pyromaniac kept his identity hidden for three weeks until pitcher Bret Saberhagen defiantly confessed to the act. "It was a practical joke," he sneered. "I wanted to get people's attention. There are always tons of reporters here when something bad is happening. I don't like a lot of them." Asked if he'd been disciplined by the team, Saberhagen all but laughed in his questioner's face. "What are they going to do, fine me?"

A few weeks later, Saberhagen executed an encore by spraying reporters with bleach from a squirt gun. When caught this time, the pitcher was more contrite, telling the press he'd doused them with bleach "accidentally" and professed no intention of hurting anyone. The shift in tone was due to another horrible incident that had happened in the interim, one that turned the Mets' season from an ugly farce to a detestable one.

On July 24, after a game at Dodger Stadium, Vince Coleman tossed a lit explosive from the window of a car in the general direction of a group of fans in the stadium parking lot. This was no mere Saberhagen firecracker. The Los Angeles District Attorney's office later compared it to "a quarter-stick of dynamite." The ensuing blast injured three people, including a two-year-old girl who suffered corneal lacerations. No one but the victims and the LAPD took the attack seriously at first. Coleman shooed reporters away from his locker the next day with a profanity-filled rant. The Mets waited seventy-two hours before issuing an official response, in which they labeled Coleman's acts as "regrettable and reprehensible" but also made sure to classify them, with an implied shrug of the shoulders, as "off-field activities." Dallas Green, reputed bad cop, inserted Coleman into his lineup for three straight games following the incident before public outcry forced a benching. Once he faced felony charges carrying a prison sentence of up to three years, however, Coleman called a press conference to beg forgiveness, his wife and kids in tow for maximum effect. (His eventual punishment would be a one-year suspended sentence plus a civil suit settled for an undisclosed amount.)

These baby steps toward good citizenship proved insufficient for one growing and vocal member of team ownership. New York real estate mogul Fred Wilpon had been a tiny portion of the partnership that purchased the Mets in 1980. Over the following decade, he angled his way into 50/50 control of the team with Nelson Doubleday. Like Doubleday, who was virtually invisible compared to his counterpart in the Bronx, he maintained a low public profile for most of that time, but the Coleman incident changed all that. On August 24, Wilpon called his first-ever team meeting and chewed out his employees for embarrassing the Mets and their city. "You should feel privileged to be able to play baseball in New York," he told them. "If you don't feel that way and you want out, let us know. We'll get you the hell out of here."

Wilpon then scheduled a press conference to inform the gathered media that Coleman would never play for the Mets again. That the outfielder was owed $3 million the next year and that Wilpon neglected to clear this edict with his front office were deemed unimportant details. "I reached a point where I had to say enough is enough," Wilpon said.

The Mets had picked a terrible time to be terrible. While they had quite literally made themselves a tabloid punch line—comparing them to another walking embarrassment of the era, Tom Verducci of *Sports Illustrated* declared the Mets "baseball's Buttafuocos"—the Yankees had begun their slow climb back to the top, thanks in large part to the most humiliating Steinbrenner blowup of all.

In 1990, news broke that George Steinbrenner had paid a mob-connected FBI informant to dig up dirt on Yankee slugger Dave Winfield and his personal charity. Following an investigation by the commissioner's office, the owner received a "lifetime ban" from the game. Steinbrenner's meddling had become so reviled that when breaking news of his ban was broadcast over the Yankee Stadium PA system during a game, the fans in attendance responded with a standing ovation. The Boss's enforced absence allowed the Yankee front office one brief, blessed respite in which to retain talent in the team's farm system rather than trading it away for overpriced veterans, and to supplement emerging prospects with judicious free agent signings—two things Steinbrenner's incessant interference never allowed.

In this manner did the Yankees began to win again, and to reclaim the ground ceded by the awful Mets. In 1993, the Yankees passed the Mets in attendance for the first time since the early 1980s. They would not relinquish that crown for the rest of the decade.

In 1990, almost three times as many New Yorkers professed to be Mets fans than Yankees fans, according to a *New York Times*/WCBS-TV poll, and many respondents named George Steinbrenner as the reason for their preference. "I always enjoyed the Yankees, but George turned me off," said one fan who saw the Mets as "a quieter, more classy team." The team from Queens was not exactly renowned for being quiet or classy during their 1980s heyday—they were, in fact, widely reviled outside New York as the playground bullies of the league—but they were paragons of class compared to George Steinbrenner.

Then Steinbrenner's team began to win, and perceptions began to change. In 1993, another *New York Times*/CBS poll showed the Yankees held the edge, claiming 6 percent more fans than the Mets. This gap widened each year that followed as the Yankees first won a thrilling World Series in 1996, then loaded up on even more free agents, created a juggernaut, and decimated all competition in a season for the ages in 1998. By that point, there was no question as to which was the top team in town. The only debate concerned how far the Yankees towered above the competition, or if the Mets offered them any competition at all.

* * *

That one team was up and the other was down was nothing new. What had truly changed was the city itself. In 1993, while the Mets were imploding and the Yankees were reviving, Rudy Giuliani was elected mayor. In the years that followed, New York went through a radical transformation that placed the two teams' respective places in the city's affections into a brand new context that threatened to solidify those positions into bitter permanence.

Like many New Yorkers of his generation, Giuliani cited the city's ugly descent into rampant crime and near bankruptcy as the reason for his conversion from JFK Democrat to a law-and-order Republican. Appointed as US attorney in 1981, he rose to fame by prosecuting mobsters and Wall Street insider traders with equal levels of pit bull tenacity. The president who appointed Giuliani, Ronald Reagan, would be his explicit political model. He never had The Gipper's way with a crowd or an anecdote, but Giuliani believed deeply in Reagan's uncomplicated with-us-or-against-us view of the world and understood the appeal this view had to the electorate. Americans turned to Reagan because his good guys/bad guys delineations removed complication from a complicated age. Giuliani believed this view could work even in ultra-liberal New York.

When Giuliani first campaigned for the mayorship in 1989, he rested his hopes on a pledge to restore "quality of life." The political novice lost a hotly contested race against David Dinkins, an African American Democrat who hoped to be a balm for the city's simmering racial tensions. Four years under Dinkins brought little relief to crime and even more racial unrest, however, and when the incumbent mayor and the prosecutor locked horns again in 1993, Giuliani squeaked out a narrow victory.

Rudy Giuliani embraced the "broken windows" theory of policing, which urged an aggressive pursuit of small violations under the premise this rendered the commission of all crimes more difficult. His initial targets were hardly master criminals: squeegee men, subway graffiti artists, cars that didn't move for street cleaning, an overloaded social welfare system. In the grand scheme of things, the laws being broken in all these instances were minor. That was exactly the reason why he chose to prosecute them. *Let no one think they can get away with anything in this town anymore*, was Giuliani's unspoken edict.

Not everyone was pleased with the new zero-tolerance New York. Many of Giuliani's critics declared the "broken windows" methods employed by the NYPD—stop-and-frisk, ticketing, instructions to move along under threat of arrest—were used primarily to harass minorities for the "crime" of walking city streets. The city's African American community felt strong-arm police tactics were employed harshest of all in their neighborhoods, that his slashing of the city's welfare system was aimed squarely at them, and that he considered their mere existence in New York to be a criminal act. But there were also many who applauded Giuliani because his administration ushered in the most precipitous drop in crime in the city's history, an accomplishment that, to them, rendered all other considerations moot. The latter group supported Mayor Giuliani when he defended the NYPD in every alleged instance of brutality, and they agreed when he defined freedom as "the willingness of every single human being to cede to lawful authority a great deal of discretion about what you do and how you do it."

Whatever one's feelings about his tactics, it was undeniable that under Giuliani's watch the numbers of serious crimes—especially murder—fell off a cliff. Giuliani had indeed transformed a city considered unmanageable since its economy cratered in the mid-1970s, with a speed that was stunning to behold. In short, Rudy Giuliani's way *worked*. The new mayor and his supporters considered quibbles about the harshness of his methods to be pointless, if not dangerous.

After decades of danger had repelled visitors, tourists began to flock to New York in droves. Developers gobbled up newly valuable real estate, nowhere more dramatically than Times Square, a once seedy outpost of peep shows and porno theaters reborn as a family-friendly center for tourist attractions and corporate headquarters. Manhattan neighborhoods ravaged by drugs and crime in the 1980s became high-rent districts almost overnight. Even outer-borough living became fashionable. Two years into the Giuliani administration, the *Times* touted Brooklyn's Williamsburg as "a new Bohemia" where a two-family home now cost the princely sum of $175,000.

To the world beyond New York, Rudy Giuliani was seen as the man who brought America's largest city back from its darkest hour. And when America saw Giuliani outside of City Hall, the place they most often saw him was Yankee Stadium, watching his beloved Bronx Bombers lay waste to yet another inferior opponent, wearing his lucky team jacket, celebrating as if he too had won.

In the two-team era, whenever New York boasted a baseball champion, that champion uncannily reflected the city's self-image. The Miracle Mets of 1969 provided a stirring underdog story for a city beginning to unravel. The Bronx Zoo Yankees were a mirror image of a city that in the late 1970s was, quite literally, on fire. The 1986 Mets were also like their era in New York's history: cocky, drug fueled, dangerous, and doomed to end in tears.

The championship team of the new New York was the 1998 Yankees. Including a run through the postseason that played out as a mere formality, this behemoth won an astounding one hundred and twenty-five games and experienced no hint of adversity along the way. The entire roster was loaded, right down to a bench that sported expensive part-timers poached from poorer teams. For some outside the city, it seemed unfair that the Yankees could afford to stack an entire roster with superstars, that they could pay their sluggers more than the entire payroll of the some of the league's poorest teams. Inside the city, though, such questions of fairness were considered quaint, if considered at all. The 1998 Yankees were exactly what New York felt it *deserved* as it barreled toward the twenty-first century. No more struggles. No more lovable losers. Winning and winners only.

New York and its Yankees had risen from the ashes. To question how either had done so was to question excellence itself. It implied you believed things were better the way they used to be, that you might even want to return to those awful days. To root for the Mets now carried a similar implication that you might pine for the violent, coke-dusted New York that tolerated drug abuse and sexual assault and firecrackers and bleach squirtings; the New York that Rudy Giuliani broken-windowed into obscurity with brutal efficiency.

* * *

For much of the 1990s, the Mets seemed to have no entryway into this new world. The man who thought otherwise, who believed a path could be found and that he could chart it, was Fred Wilpon. The press conference during which Wilpon "fired" Vince Coleman was more than a wake-up call to his players. It was a wake-up call to himself and to the world. It was the first public sign that, for good or ill, he would run the Mets' show from this point forward.

Both Fred Wilpon and Nelson Doubleday were dedicated baseball fans devastated when the Giants and Dodgers moved west in 1958, but the two men had little else in common. Doubleday inherited a fortune from his family's namesake publishing house. His approach to team ownership fit his background: assemble a solid portfolio and let your assets do the work. He bore a vague resemblance to former New York Governor Nelson Rockefeller, his distinguished silver hair and his respectable yachtsman's tan betraying his background as a well-off man of leisure. Meanwhile, Fred Wilpon grew up as the son of a funeral director in Bensonhurst and mined his own fortune in the cutthroat world of real estate. He had not inherited his fortune, but hustled and scrapped his way to it, as Doubleday would soon find out.

When Wilpon bought into the Mets in 1980, he owned a mere 5 percent of the team, but he had his eyes on much more and quickly found the means to get it. In 1986, Nelson Doubleday sold Doubleday Publishing to the German conglomerate Bertelsmann but intended to retain control of the Mets. (On paper, his stake in the team was owned by the publishing company, not Doubleday himself.) He foresaw no barriers to doing so until he encountered a contractual complication: Wilpon possessed first right of refusal in any sale of the team and could make the resale process difficult and protracted for all parties involved. Though Doubleday had no idea when or how Wilpon had done this, he was forced to come to a settlement whereby the two of them would purchase the Mets from Bertelsmann for $81 million. They would be equal partners, and barely on speaking terms, from that day forward.

Around the same time as his shape-up-or-ship-out presser in 1993, Wilpon felt confident enough to reveal his grand vision for the Mets to *Sports Illustrated*. He wanted to send Shea Stadium's employees to the same rigorous hospitality training as Disney World employees, the gold standard of customer service. He dreamed of replacing the Mets' ballpark with a sprawling entertainment complex topped by a gleaming retractable dome, surrounded by pavilions housing a permanent world's fair resembling the one that Robert Moses placed alongside Shea Stadium in Flushing Meadows Park back in 1964. To New Yorkers of a certain age, that world's fair still evoked New York's prelapsarian glory, its exhibits of the glories of space age technology and better living through science a symbol of a simpler, more hopeful age. In the late 1990s such notions seemed quaint to many, but not to Fred Wilpon.

Wilpon was sure the Yankees had not taken the city for good. His new facility plans were an expression of this faith, a belief that harkened back to the long-gone days of that world's fair, when the world came to Flushing, when Queens was a place where you could dream of the future, when Shea was a crown jewel, when the Mets were kings.

* * *

After Bobby Valentine's brief sojourn to the Far East in 1995, a small miracle was required for him to return to the major leagues. That miracle occurred when another manager was somehow judged more controversial than him.

While Valentine was toiling away in Japan, the attention-starved Mets promoted a trio of hard-throwing pitchers from their farm system and dubbed them Generation K, a play on the Generation X label that was already several years out of style by that point. The belly laughs induced by the phrase "Generation K" notwithstanding, all three hurlers were ranked among the best prospects in baseball and rightly stirred excitement for the future from Mets fans desperate for hope. All three had also shouldered tremendous workloads as minor leaguers. This gave the Mets no cause for alarm because it wouldn't have alarmed any front office in the mid-1990s, when pitch counts were not yet tallied like the ticks of a time bomb. The Mets were far from the only team that would lose promising young arms to the surgeon's knife. The Mets *were*, however, the only team proclaiming they possessed three aces and daring to call them (*snicker*) Generation K. Each member of the ill-fated trio—Bill Pulsipher, Paul Wilson, and Jason Isringhausen—pitched indifferently after their promotions when not lost to the disabled list (which happened often). Generation K's failure to be phenoms right out of the gate proved a PR disaster, one that was exacerbated by manager Dallas Green calling out his team for rushing the young pitchers to the bigs. "These guys don't really belong in the big leagues," he griped in August of 1996. "It's that simple. It sounds very harsh and very negative. But what have they done to get here?"

With the Mets muddling through another disappointing year, Green's ill-advised criticism of Generation K (accurate though it may have been) led to his dismissal with thirty-one games left in the 1996 season and the promotion of Bobby Valentine to the big league job. Upon receiving the news, Valentine rented a car to make the long drive from Pawtucket, Rhode Island, where the triple-A team was playing at the time, to Queens. Once he got within range of New York's sports talk radio station, WFAN, Valentine tuned in to see if word of his hiring had leaked out yet.

It had. Valentine was treated to an endless string of callers moaning about the new Mets manager. *Valentine's an idiot. How can the Mets do this? Bad decision* . . . Somehow he endured two hours of such masochism before shutting the radio off.

Fans weren't the only ones skeptical of the choice. Dallas Green was seen as the tobacco-juice-spattered old-school skipper, while Bobby Valentine was considered his spiritual opposite: worldly, sophistic, cerebral. His stint with the Rangers was regarded as undistinguished at best, his time in Japan a demerit for its utter foreignness. Traditional sportswriters couldn't understand why he asked his pitchers to watch video of opposing hitters during batting practice rather than shag flies. They understood even less when Valentine admitted he learned Japanese using a computer program and developed a liking for the internet because of it. In the mid-1990s, when cyberspace was the exclusive province of nerds, what kind of manager thought he could learn anything about baseball from the *internet*?

In 1997, Valentine dismissed some of these doubts by captaining the Mets to their first winning record in seven years, despite having few stars on his roster. The two exceptions were switch-hitting slugger Todd Hundley, owner of the single-season home run record for his franchise and for all major league catchers (41 in 1996), and John Olerud, a surprise off-season pickup who would anchor the Mets' lineup and rejuvenate their infield for three seasons.

Though he'd won two championships and a batting title in Toronto, John Olerud's batting average took enough of a dip after the 1993 season that the Blue Jays feared his best days were behind him. He was a quiet man, given the ironic nickname Gabby because he rarely spoke at all, the type of athlete New York is supposed to devour whole. The fact that he wore a batting helmet in the field—a precaution he adopted after an aneurysm nearly killed him as a minor leaguer—struck some as a sign of deeper fragility. His manager in Toronto, Cito Gaston, couldn't imagine Olerud would cotton to Gotham, and vice versa. "I wouldn't be surprised if he walks away from baseball at the end of the season," Gaston predicted after Olerud was traded to Gotham.

Defying this pessimism, Olerud found that New York fit him like a glove. More intellectually inclined than the average ballplayer, he took advantage of all the culture New York had to offer. He eschewed the suburbs of Long Island or Connecticut for an apartment in Manhattan and even took the 7 train to the ballpark for many home games. His cultural yearnings and proletarian transportation choices would have meant little if he hadn't performed, however, and in 1997 Olerud knocked in 102 runs, belted 22 homers, and logged an on-base percentage of .400. He was rewarded with a two-year contract extension the following winter.

As surprising as his resurgence at the plate was, his performance on the infield was even more shocking. In Toronto, Olerud's lack of speed made it difficult for him to handle the balls that zipped across the SkyDome's artificial turf, but on the slower natural surface of Shea Stadium, he became a wizard with the glove and a weapon at first, charging in on bunts and cutting down lead runners with a strong arm he'd never had a chance to display on Toronto's unforgiving carpet.

Olerud's example would prove the catalyst for one of the team's biggest assets in the coming years. Taking his cue from the new infielder, third baseman Edgardo Alfonzo began to play his position with similar aggressiveness. Meanwhile, shortstop Rey Ordóñez emerged as one of the most dazzling players to ever man his position. The Mets' starting pitchers at the time were mostly control artists who logged far more grounders than strikeouts. Fielders like Olerud, Alfonzo, and Ordóñez compensated for this lack of firepower by making sure those grounders became outs. Thanks to Olerud, the Mets had improved their pitching without acquiring a single new pitcher.

When a ball did manage to sneak past the infield, Olerud made the batter's time on the basepaths uncomfortable. Rather than play on the bag or behind the runner, Olerud stood in front of him, screening him from the action, stalking his every move. Opposing teams believed Valentine asked Olerud to play first base this way for the same reason they assumed he did everything else—to be a jerk—but when pressed, Valentine said he was simply letting Olerud be himself. New York and Bobby Valentine found a way for Gabby to speak loudly.

* * *

On June 16, 1997, the advent of interleague play brought with it the first regular-season Subway Series game. In front of a sellout Yankee Stadium crowd, the Mets shocked their hosts with a 6–0 victory. Starting pitcher Dave Mlicki—a man even most Mets fans couldn't pick out of a lineup—went the distance, scattering nine hits and striking out eight Yankees, six of them looking (including Derek Jeter), to end the game.

By the ninth inning, with most Yankees fans having long since left, the House That Ruth Built rang with foreign chants of "Let's go Mets!" Stung by this humiliation, the Yankees rebounded to win the last two games of the series. The final contest was particularly contentious, as the Mets rallied late from a 2–0 deficit and scored the tying run when David Cone (by that point a Yankee, and regarded as an elder statesman by local press who never mentioned his earlier indiscretions) balked home a runner in the top of the eighth. Yankee manager Joe Torre later complained, "Bobby tried to plant the seed early," claiming that Valentine pointed out an odd hitch in Cone's delivery to the home plate umpire. Mr. Baseball countered that he was doing a favor for the less perceptive by pointing out a balk move when he saw one. Valentine's eagle eye merely prolonged the game for the Mets, however, as the Yankees prevailed in walk-off fashion in the bottom of the tenth.

The first Subway Series in 1997 established the pattern that would continue for Met-Yankee summit meetings in the following years. The Mets would receive kudos for giving the Yankees a good fight if they lost, while reserving the right to treat each victory like a mini World Series if they won. "It was a great three days, wasn't it?" said Edgardo Alfonzo at the conclusion of the inaugural series. His team had lost two of three games in the Bronx, yet he could proclaim the series "great" with no fear of drawing criticism.

The Yankees, expected to win the *real* World Series, would treat the affair with a mixture of contempt and dread. Playing the Mets in contrived circumstances offered them little to win and everything to lose. David Cone told reporters that dropping two of three to the Mets would have sent him scrambling for a cyanide tablet. Derek Jeter said such an outcome would have forced him to move to New Jersey. (He would repeat variations on this odd "threat" often in the years to come, apparently believing there were no fans to hassle him in the Garden State.) After Tino Martinez sealed a Yankee win in the first series finale with a walk-off RBI single, he said it lifted a ton of bricks from his back. Former Mets who had migrated across town, like Cone and Doc Gooden, were constantly polled about the differences between the squads and chafed at the constant questioning. One reporter noted that upon being called up to the Yankees on the eve of the first Subway Series, Wally Whitehurst (another ex-Met) asked his old teammate Gooden when pizza would be delivered to the clubhouse. He'd asked this in jest, but Doc answered it with deathly seriousness. "We don't do that stuff here, Wally," he warned, looking over his shoulder to make sure no team officials had heard the impudence. "This ain't the Mets."

There was no better demonstration of the tension between the two camps than the scene at Shea Stadium on April 15, 1998. Two days earlier, a five-hundred-pound support beam collapsed at Yankee Stadium, shutting down the House That Ruth Built until city inspectors could ensure the facility's safety. The Mets were scheduled to play a game that evening but invited the Yankees to use Shea Stadium for the afternoon to complete their series against the Angels.

It was a neighborly gesture that satisfied no one. Mets players fretted that welcoming the Yankees into their stadium would have the same effect as inviting vampires into one's home. Yankee players called the temporary relocation a "distraction" and dressed in the Bronx rather than dare use the facilities at Shea. Yankees fans who descended on Flushing that afternoon compared the temporary digs unfavorably to the self-proclaimed Cathedral of Baseball ("NOT BAD FOR A MINOR LEAGUE PARK" read one wag's sign). Mets partisans who arrived that evening said the place would need fumigation after being invaded by *those* fans and bristled over team ownership accommodating their most hated rival.

The first Subway Series had been marked by full-blown fistfights in the Yankee Stadium stands. Players contemplated popping cyanide tablets if they lost. One fan base compared the arrival of the other team's fans in their stadium to an infestation of pests. A local sports radio personality dismissed the idea that New Yorkers could root for both teams by proclaiming, with the fervor of a Baptist preacher, "You can't be for God and the Devil!"

The media made note of all this animosity, but only to dismiss it. In their estimation, the Subway Series was a unifying civic event that uplifted the entire city. Everyone said so, from the mayor on down. "It's wonderful for the city," Rudy Giuliani said of the event. Every outlet of officialdom adopted this line as their own, ignoring Giuliani's own recollection of a youth when Dodgers and Giants fans couldn't be in the same room together without fighting. Brawls in the stands were labeled "skirmishes." Hate-filled volleys from one team's fans toward another's were placed under the umbrella of playful exuberance.

The press ran with the mayor's contention and took it one step further. Now that New York had returned to its former glory, the only thing it was missing was a *real* Subway Series. If midsummer games between the Mets and Yankees were a civic boon, then an October showdown would be even more of one. *Wouldn't that be great for the city?* the scribes would coo, blind to all the evidence they gathered that said otherwise. Or as if such a contest would settle a question presented by the teams' continued coexistence: If the city could only be owned by one team, which team would lay claim?

* * *

1997 was an eventful season for the Mets, both for the advent of the Subway Series and for the ascension of a long-promised wunderkind to the head of the front office food chain. In July, thirty-four-year-old Steve Phillips was given the general manager's chair, making him baseball's second-youngest top executive. (Detroit's Randy Smith edged him out by a month.)

After a brief minor league career in the Mets organization, Phillips joined the executive set when Joe McIlvaine offered him his first front office job in January of 1990. From the start, it was clear the Mets eyed Phillips as their executive of the future. For years, his quotes could be found throughout the city's back pages with a frequency belying his obscure (if important) position as director of minor league operations. After the 1995 season, when Phillips was named assistant general manager, his name was being whispered as the imminent replacement for McIlvaine, whose relationship with team ownership had deteriorated beyond repair. McIlvaine's preference for team building via the slow and unglamorous player development process had already produced one major flameout in Generation K before it was undone completely by the failure of Ryan Jaroncyk, a Mets first-round draft pick who quit the game altogether early in the 1997 season while confessing that he'd always thought baseball was boring. There were many factors prompting Jaroncyk's premature retirement, most so personal they would have escaped any executive's notice, but Mets ownership drew one simple conclusion from his example: Joe McIlvaine's way didn't work. The newest iteration of the

Mets would therefore not construct itself through sober accumulation of young talent, but through flashy quick fixes. Six weeks after the Ryan Jaroncyk debacle came to light, Joe McIlvaine was "reassigned" in the Mets' front office and replaced with his protégé Phillips. Upon introducing his new general manager to the press, Fred Wilpon—in a line destined to be repeated back at him for years to come—insisted Steve Phillips possessed executive "skills sets" that his predecessor lacked.

For much of the twentieth century, a general manager's job was closer to that of chummy middle managers in the *Gray Flannel Suit* era, deals settled over three-martini lunches by execs who rarely worked beyond 5:00 p.m. By the late 1990s, however, the position was fully corporatized and held the expectation of being perpetually on the clock and under the microscope. Phillips embraced this view and marveled over reminiscences of times early in his executive career when he witnessed Frank Cashen and Al Harazin sitting in their Shea Stadium suite *reading*, discussing not trades or free agents but *current events*. Imagine, he would recount with a shake of his head, a general manager who had time in his daily schedule to contemplate a world outside of baseball.

Bobby Valentine and Steve Phillips were like two notes a semitone apart, too similar to ever form pleasant harmony. Like Valentine, Phillips relished the spotlight. Like Valentine, Phillips had a high opinion of his own baseball knowledge. (Phillips's insistence on visiting his manager's office before and after almost every game to discuss strategy would prove a pain point.) Like Valentine, Phillips possessed a myriad of foibles that tended to land him in trouble (though Phillips's foibles were of a different stripe; more on that later).

As for their differences, Phillips possessed a more selective filter between his brain and mouth. ("Sometimes I wish I had the 'no comment' in me," Valentine confessed in grudging admiration.) Whereas Valentine's relationship with reporters was strained at best, Phillips played New York's sports press corps like a fiddle, providing quotes, access, and background to all comers. His sartorial sense and articulation allowed him to adopt the part of the young go-getter: impeccably dressed, perfect coif of sandy hair, accented by wire-rim glasses whenever it was time to look *serious*. He possessed the air of the spokesman an embattled corporation would send before the cameras to assure the public that, despite all the nasty rumors, their product was perfectly safe.

Joe McIlvaine had brought Bobby Valentine back into the Mets organization for his ability to teach the game to young players, calling him "one of the best teachers of baseball there is." Such skills were not treasured by a front office headed by Steve Phillips, however. Phillips referred to the overachieving Mets of 1997 as "a good little team with good little players." If that reads like condescension, he surely intended it as such. When McIlvaine was demoted, then departed for the Minnesota Twins—a small-market team whose only hope at competing was to develop good little players—Valentine was left behind to wonder how he fit into the Mets' new equation.

Phillips began his first off-season by taking advantage of the Marlins, as many teams did that winter. Florida loaded up on high-priced superstars in 1997 to fuel a stunning World Series victory, then dismantled themselves before the victory parade confetti had settled. Phillips got in on the fire sale by shipping three minor leaguers to the Marlins in exchange for left-handed pitcher Al Leiter.

A New Jersey native, Leiter enjoyed up-and-down years with the Yankees and Blue Jays before finding his form with Florida, where he played a key role in the Marlins' championship. Though a veteran, he more resembled a Little Leaguer who took the game a bit too seriously. He was prone to both losing his focus and criticizing himself to worrisome extremes. He had idiosyncratic on-field habits, such as jumping in the air and clicking his heels to clear mud from his spikes. More troubling was Leiter's propensity to argue with his managers to remain on the mound far beyond the point most pitchers would, which sometimes saved a call to the bullpen but just as often led to a blown lead.

These shortcomings could be tolerated because Leiter was a very good left-handed starter who could often fight his way to greatness. When he joined the Mets' starting rotation, he became its best member by a wide margin. He was thrilled to join the team he grew up rooting for as a kid from Toms River, even if he would have to play for a manager who once tried to psych him out from the opposing dugout by screaming, "You'll never make it out of the fourth inning!" As big as the Leiter trade was, though, Steve Phillips's biggest deal was yet to come.

Out in Los Angeles, free agency loomed for Mike Piazza, who had already established himself as one of the best-hitting catchers in baseball history. His desire to remain with the Dodgers began to sour when the team rejected his agent's contract terms, then curdled even more after the *Los Angeles Times* conducted an interview with Brett Butler, an ex-teammate, who painted the catcher as "a moody, self-centered '90s player" and insisted "you can't build around Piazza because he's not a leader." It was a not-too-subtle hint that the team believed it could get by just fine without him, and Piazza chose to take the Dodgers at their word. As the 1998 season began, divorce proceedings progressed quickly, and a trade was executed on May 14 that shipped Piazza off to Florida. The payroll-hemorrhaging Marlins were a mere layover for the catcher. The only question was where he would fly to next.

On the back pages and sports talk radio airwaves in New York, the chatter screamed for him to land with the Mets as a replacement for Todd Hundley, who would miss much of 1998 recovering from Tommy John surgery. For days, WFAN's drive-time duo Mike and the Mad Dog fielded almost nothing but frantic calls from Mets fans demanding that the team make a deal for Piazza. Though team ownership was reluctant to replace Todd Hundley, one of their few genuine stars, Fred Wilpon became convinced that this was a deal that had to be made after hearing the fervor of the fans screaming for action on the radio.

Eight days after Piazza left LA, Steve Phillips made the trade that brought him to New York and immediately made him the best hitter to ever wear a Mets uniform. He started slowly in New York before stepping on the gas, hitting .351 in the second half of the season and .378 in September. As soon as he took off, so did the rest of the Mets. John Olerud flirted with a batting title, Edgardo Alfonzo complemented his slick fielding at third base with strong production at the plate, Rey Ordóñez acted as a human vacuum at shortstop, and Al Leiter was as good as advertised. On September 20, the Mets' win-loss record stood at 88–69. They held a half-game lead in the wild card standings, just ahead of the surging Cubs and Giants, with five games left to play.

And then, as if someone flipped a switch, everything stopped working all at once.

In their last two home games of the year, the Mets faced a middling Montréal Expos team that had inexplicably given them fits all season. The Expos lost ninety-seven games in 1998, yet won eight of twelve games against the Mets, and none were more damaging than this last pair. On the evening of September 22, Mets starter Armando Reynoso—perturbed by unseasonably cool temperatures that "seemed to signal the onset of autumn," in the ominous words of the *Daily News*—allowed a lead to evaporate as New York went down in defeat, 5–3. The next night, the Mets were shut out by rookie hurler Carl Pavano.

To finish out the year, the Mets traveled to Atlanta to play three games against the Braves. There was no rivalry between the two teams at that time, unless an insect can be said to have a rivalry with a bug zapper. While Atlanta captured division titles through the 1990s, New York offered no threat to their dominance whatsoever. When the Mets arrived at Turner Field on September 25, the Braves had clinched yet another division crown almost two weeks prior and had won 103 games. The visiting team had everything to play for. The home nine had no concerns but the upcoming playoffs.

And yet, the Braves were the ones who played like a team on a mission, while the Mets played like a team just learning the game. In the first Atlanta contest, as the Mets trailed by two runs in the top of the eighth inning, Bobby Valentine used speedy September call-up Jay Payton as a pinch runner, hoping he could jet home from first on an extra-base hit and score the tying run. The move backfired when Payton attempted to advance to third on a two-out single and challenged the powerful arm of Atlanta center fielder Andruw Jones. The rookie was gunned down by a good five feet, having committed the two cardinal baseball sins of making the last out of the inning at third and doing so while Mike Piazza stood on deck. The end result was a 6–5 heartbreaker of a defeat. The Mets would come no closer to winning for the rest of the season.

In the second game in Atlanta, Al Leiter held off the Braves for five innings but faltered in the sixth, ceding more than enough runs to ensure defeat at the hands of Atlanta ace Tom Glavine. For the final scheduled game, Bobby Valentine was forced to send the shaky Armando Reynoso to the mound because his preferred starter, Hideo Nomo, had pitched poorly since a midseason trade to New York and begged off the assignment, citing pride, despite excellent career numbers against Atlanta. Reynoso was shelled for five runs before the end of the second inning and the Mets went on to lose yet again. Atlanta manager Bobby Cox seemed to relish the conquest when he compared sweeping Valentine to defeating Casey Stengel and John McGraw, a contention that had the ring of sarcasm to it. (Valentine chose to take this as a compliment.)

To pour extra salt on the Mets' wounds, the Cubs and Giants finished the season in a tie for the wild card, necessitating a one-game playoff. If the Mets had won a single game of the five they dropped to close out the season, they would have found themselves in a three-way wild card tie. If they'd won two, they would have captured a playoff spot outright. Instead, they won a premature trip to the golf course.

The entire organization took the loss hard, but no one took it harder than Bobby Valentine. Normally impossible to shut up, the manager was at a loss for words. "I don't know what happened," Valentine told reporters. "If I knew, I would have done something about it. That's my frustration about it. Everything I tried didn't work."

If Steve Phillips felt the same devastation, he did a better job of hiding it. "My hopes were grander than just getting to the playoffs," he admitted after the Mets' final, brutal loss. "But I'm also excited about putting a team together for 1999. And that's what's getting me through today."

Steve Phillips was never a man for the long view. As he set about the business of assembling the next season's roster, it is unlikely he gave much thought to one minute beyond 1999. And yet, almost despite himself, Phillips would assemble one of the most beloved teams in franchise history.

PART I: 1999

CHAPTER 1

Some Assembly Required

IN THE WINTER of 1998-1999, all eyes are on Steve Phillips. The brutal collapse that ended the Mets' season prompts New York's sports press to call for immediate moves to ensure next year will end better than the last one did. And with the NBA in a lockout that will last until the end of January, even more back-page real estate is free for scribes to fill with their demands.

The first item on Steve Phillips's agenda is to re-sign both Al Leiter and Mike Piazza, who became free agents at season's end. "Losing either of them would serve as an enormous public relations blow at a time when the club can ill afford negative publicity," the *Daily News* warns. The excitable Leiter, incapable of a poker face, telegraphs his desire to return to New York, though he also hints that a return of Piazza would sweeten the pot for him. But his battery mate is much harder to read, and the signals Piazza gave during his initial year in New York were mixed at best.

When the catcher struggled in his first month as a Met, he drew boos from fans and pop psychology from the press who feared Piazza was too much of a laid-back "California guy"—the worst insult imaginable, to New York's sports press—to adapt to New York's pace. Piazza actually grew up near Philadelphia, but to the media his years as a Dodger have tainted him with the mellowness of Tinseltown. In August, after a report "circulated widely on the internet" (a novel concept in 1998) said Piazza had already decided he would not return, he called a press conference to announce that he would not negotiate a new contract during the season and would refuse to answer any questions on the subject until year's end. Piazza would tear the cover off the ball in the following months, but his refusal to speak about his future added fuel to the theory that he couldn't handle New York's relentless media coverage.

Piazza himself isn't sure where he wants to be until the off-season, when he leaves New York and finds that he misses that unnamable thing about the city, that energy that drives some mad and drives others to greatness. If he ever was a "California guy," he is one no longer. On October 25, 1998, Piazza inks a seven-year, $91 million deal, making him the richest Met ever and the highest-paid player in the game. Nelson Doubleday goes so far as to refer to the deal as "a bargain," possibly because it virtually guarantees a return for Al Leiter, who soon inks a four-year, $32 million contract.

The Piazza pact will raise the market price of all players, much to the dismay of George Steinbrenner, who fears sticker shock when signing his own free agents. "I think that all of baseball has been a bit shocked," Steinbrenner tells reporters upon hearing the news of Piazza's record contract. "I hear that others are quite upset." It is a classic slice of Steinbrennerian transference, proclaiming his own displeasure as the displeasure of the game in general. In his own mind, George Steinbrenner *is* baseball.

Of all people, Steinbrenner should know that the Mets are assembling their team in the accepted manner of the age. The artificially suppressed salaries that prevailed before the 1994 players' strike (the result of owners' collusion that led to the strike in the first place) have given way to rampant inflation. Piazza's contract is soon eclipsed when pitcher Kevin Brown signs with the Dodgers to the tune of seven years and $105 million. When the checkbooks are put back in their holsters, MLB commits a grand total of $481.5 million to six lucky players this off-season—Piazza, Brown, Bernie Williams of the Yankees, sluggers Mo Vaughn (Angels) and Albert Belle (Orioles), and fearsome southpaw Randy Johnson (Diamondbacks).

The franchises with money to burn are from large media markets, their willingness to spend spurred by the boatloads of cash generated by regional sports networks and brand-new stadiums built in imitation of the Baltimore Orioles' game-changing Camden Yards. At the same time, teams from smaller markets, which can't avail themselves of such revenue streams, must slash payroll. This sets in motion a vicious cycle wherein disgruntled fans refuse to show up at the ballpark or watch at home, diminishing such teams' revenues even further. Witness the Montréal Expos, whose lack of a new arena and regional sports network forces them to make due with a payroll of $8.3 million, less than one full season's salary for Mike Piazza. The Minnesota Twins begin the winter by declaring their payroll will be slashed into the $10–15 million range. The Kansas City Royals cut an already modest payroll of $32 million in half.

A few efforts have been made to bridge this disparity, but most have been toothless. MLB enacted a properties agreement after the resolution of the 1994 strike that would distribute revenue from merchandise sales evenly among all teams, but this initiative, which would have greatly benefited the have-nots, was quickly undermined by the biggest haves of all. In 1997, the Yankees brokered their own exclusive ten-year merchandising pact with Adidas for close to $100 million, or more cash than most other teams garnered from their broadcast rights, all of it theirs to keep. Through carefully executed legal jujitsu, the Yankees argued this deal didn't violate the strict letter of the league's properties agreement. When commissioner Bud Selig demanded the Yankees cancel their pact, George Steinbrenner sued his fellow owners, effectively accusing them of being parasitic losers leeching off his success. And just to show everyone who was baseball's real boss, he pointed to the Brewers—the team Selig once owned—as one of the league's more pronounced failures. Small-market teams begged Selig to fight back on their behalf, but the commissioner merely lobbed a few symbolic sanctions at the Yankees, then negotiated a settlement that gave Steinbrenner exactly what he wanted.

Incidents like these cause small-market teams to believe their days are numbered—Padres executive Larry Lucchino literally refers to Kevin Brown's enormous contract as "the apocalypse"—unless something drastic is done to help them. Jim Bowden, general manager of the Cincinnati Reds, suggests realigning the divisions by economics rather than geography to guarantee playoff slots to poorer teams, a nigh socialist redistribution of postseason wealth. With MLB's labor agreement set to expire after the 2001 season, Bowden believes such radical change is necessary to save small-market teams before another job action finishes them off for good.

Half of MLB is swimming in vats of cash like Scrooge McDuck. The other half declares, "The end is nigh." Beyond the slap on the wrist he gives to the Yankees over their back-stabbing Adidas deal, Bud Selig's only response is to announce the formation of the Blue Ribbon Task Force on Baseball Economics, a committee that will study the problem and make recommendations. The task force has no firm deadline to submit its conclusions, nor does it have any power to enact or enforce its recommendations. After losing his fight with Steinbrenner, the commissioner has no stomach for this battle, even if huge portions of his league are sure they're living on borrowed time.

* * *

The Mets, who are flush with cash compared to the likes of the Expos and Twins, have the luxury of paying this doomsaying little mind. Steve Phillips proclaims re-signing Al Leiter and Mike Piazza is just the beginning of his off-season plan, while the media proclaim these contracts had *better* be just the beginning, since they simply restore the roster that turfed out to finish 1998.

At the exact moment the front office must get to work, however, Steve Phillips is hit with a sexual harassment suit filed by an employee of the Mets' spring training facility in Port St. Lucie, Florida. Though this would have been huge news at any time, it is even more so in 1998, when the Bill Clinton-Monica Lewinsky scandal has dominated national headlines for months. The charges are also a disturbing reminder of the awful early 1990s, when several Mets were accused of rape and multiple incidents of sexual harassment. After Phillips publicly confesses to an extramarital affair while denying the charges, the Mets suspend him "indefinitely." They undermine that punishment by choosing the semi-retired Frank Cashen to fill the slot in Phillips's absence, a signal that his hiatus will be brief.

Most coverage of the accusations concentrates on how Steve Phillips's suspension will affect the Mets' off-season plans. Very few local sportswriters raise the question of whether someone accused of sexual harassment should be allowed to keep his job at all. Even fewer question it when the Mets judge Phillips reformed after "extensive personal counseling" that lasts eight days. A lengthy, sympathetic profile of Phillips in the *Times* compares his press conference confession to a public flogging. In the coming years, when the subject of the lawsuit is raised at all, emphasis will be placed on how much pain the incident caused Phillips. That someone else might have been victimized by his actions—say, the woman he allegedly harassed—goes unconsidered.

Frank Cashen's only move during his brief time in the captain's chair is to ship relief pitcher Mel Rojas to the Dodgers. Few Mets fans are sad to see the pricey and ineffective Rojas go on November 11, but many are distressed to see who returns in the deal: Bobby Bonilla. Cashen emphasizes the decent numbers Bonilla posted since leaving the Worst Team Money Could Buy and insists the outfielder has matured since those unpleasant days. Bonilla goes out of his way to prove Cashen wrong by uttering derogatory comments about former Dodger manager Tommy Lasorda, then apologizes for the same while insisting he was misquoted.

Once back in the driver's seat, Phillips makes a move to shore up the outfield further while also strengthening the bullpen via a three-way deal with the Dodgers and Orioles. On December 1, Todd Hundley—who'd locked horns with Bobby Valentine before being rendered redundant by Mike Piazza—goes to Los Angeles in exchange for outfielder Roger Cedeño. The twenty-four-year-old Venezuelan has tons of raw ability, but the Dodgers' haste to contend superseded Cedeño's need for on-the-job training. The Mets imagine him as a pinch runner and fourth outfielder, figuring that the veteran Bonilla will draw far more playing time than the youngster.

In the same deal, the Mets acquire Baltimore closer Armando Benítez, whose blazing fastball and astronomic strikeout rate should be in high demand. But Benítez is available because he has issues, immaturity chief among them. On the field, he triangulates between chest-thumping bravado, blackest despair, and unchecked anger. His temper flared most infamously in a game at Yankee Stadium on May 19, 1998, when he responded to the humiliation of giving up a home run by drilling the next batter, and was fortunate to escape with his life when the entire Yankee bench stormed onto the field in search of revenge. His teammates' efforts to protect him were perfunctory at best, and Baltimore manager Ray Miller went so far as to apologize to the Yankees for Benítez's actions. This incident, and multiple playoff meltdowns in 1996 and 1997, punched Benítez's ticket out of Baltimore.

For all his faults, Benítez's blazing fastball has the potential to make the Mets' bullpen one of the best in the majors. Phillips bolsters it by re-signing well-traveled southpaw Dennis Cook, who baffled hitters during the Marlins' postseason run in 1997, and eccentric righty Turk Wendell. In the grand tradition of quirky firemen, Wendell favors a shark-tooth necklace, slams a rosin bag to the ground before throwing his first pitch, and has a preoccupation with the number nine that compels him to ensure all dollar amounts in his contract contain as many nines as possible.

The same day Armando Benítez and Roger Cedeño arrive in Queens, the Mets finalize a four-year deal with free agent third baseman Robin Ventura. Ventura's biggest claim to fame is ownership of the longest hitting streak in NCAA history. He manned the hot corner for the Chicago White Sox for nine seasons, collecting five Gold Gloves over that span while showing an uncanny knack for hitting grand slams. Much like

John Olerud, a slight downturn in production caused his employers to sour on his future. When Ventura became a free agent, Chicago made no effort to retain him.

There are other similarities between the two corner infielders. As with Olerud, Ventura is not an obvious fit for New York. He possesses a penchant for self-deprecating humor, a red flag to those who attempt to suss out which players will be crushed under Gotham's weight. He certainly didn't have New York at the top of his wish list. The California native hoped he could return to the West Coast, preferably to San Diego, but the Padres are shedding payroll drastically, and though the Dodgers and Angels are both spending like mad, neither showed any interest. The Orioles make an earnest play for Ventura's services but want him to play first base until ironman Cal Ripken abandons third. Ventura declines this thankless task and chooses the Big Apple instead.

Ventura's somewhat reluctant arrival in New York will push aside Edgardo Alfonzo, who had settled at third base after years of shuffling between that position and second base for years, in deference to more established teammates. At first, signs point to trading Alfonzo in a deal for a starting pitcher, but the Mets nip these rumors in the bud by announcing their intention to hold on to Alfonzo and move him to second base.

Alfonzo agrees to switch positions without a word of protest, declaring he's looking forward to being double-play partners with shortstop Rey Ordóñez, defensive magician. He is the consummate team player, at times to his own detriment. During Venezuelan winter league action, when Alfonzo should be logging time at what he calls his "new old position," he remains at third base because his winter league squad has already penciled in a hotshot prospect from the Astros' organization to play second. Far too polite to pull rank, Alfonzo takes workouts at second before and after games instead.

Two weeks after Ventura hops on board, Phillips signs future Hall of Famer Rickey Henderson, the greatest base stealer and leadoff hitter of all time. In an age when offense is predicated on home runs and little else, Henderson is a throwback to the speed-and-discipline days of the 1980s. In his fourth tour with the A's in 1998, he led the American League in walks and stolen bases at the ripe old age of thirty-nine. Upon signing his new deal, he declares, "I would say the Mets are going to be the best team in New York right now. The Yankees have been carrying the crown for a long time. It's about time for the Mets to take over." A bold claim, and most likely an attempt to needle George Steinbrenner, with whom Henderson clashed during his tumultuous years as a Yankee in the 1980s.

This is no "good little team," but it is a team whose window for competing will be small. The 1999 Mets roster will be long in the tooth, and the flurry of free agent signings have cost the team draft picks, slicing an already thin farm system even thinner. And for all the moves Phillips has made, only the Al Leiter re-signing addresses the Mets' starting pitching. Behind their ace lefty is soft-tossing righty Bobby Jones, control artist Rick Reed, and the erratic Masato Yoshii. Beyond these men, a series of question marks stretch off into the horizon.

The Mets are mentioned whenever one of the have-not teams is said to be shopping its ace, but one possibility, however slim it might have been, is taken off the table as spring training begins. On February 18, after a long winter of wild speculation, baseball is stunned when the Blue Jays trade Roger Clemens to the Yankees. Steve Phillips made a few stabs over the winter to acquire The Rocket, but the Mets' unwillingness to part with Edgardo Alfonzo prevented talks from progressing beyond the *what if...* stage. Smart money had Clemens landing in his home state of Texas, but both the Astros and Rangers hemmed and hawed on the issue, leaving the Yankees room to swoop in with a package headed by lefty pitcher David Wells.

Beyond the Yankees and their fans, few are thrilled with the move. (That includes Wells, who wept upon learning he would no longer wear pinstripes.) For the Yankees to make this trade after one of the most dominant seasons in baseball history underscores the feeling among baseball's poorer teams that they exist solely to feed the rich. *Sports Illustrated*, in a piece that mildly criticizes the deal, points out the Twins have parted ways with their shortstop, Pat Meares, because they cannot afford to pay him $3.4 million, the same amount the Yankees spend on their backup catcher. In a fit of sour grapes, Houston's general manager, Gerry Hunsicker, grumbles, "That's the most important message here: Regardless of who the Yankees want, they are in a position to outbid virtually any other franchise in the game."

If there is any possible way for the Yankees to improve on their 1998 season, Clemens might provide it. There is, however, one piece of the Rocket's résumé that remains lacking. For all of Clemens's dominance on the mound in the regular season, it has yet to translate to postseason success. On his ledger are one lone playoff win and several ugly October meltdowns. It remains to be seen whether the Yankees' luck or his own will prevail.

* * *

As news of the Clemens trade and its resulting backlash die down, the Mets get down to the springtime business of exuding optimism for the upcoming season. Clouds don't emerge until March 22, when Paul Wilson, luckless Generation K member, suffers a "significant and partial tear" of a ligament in his pitching elbow. Tommy John surgery will knock him out of action for all of 1999. Wilson's fellow victim, Jason Isringhausen, enlists state-of-the-art digital technology to identify the mechanical issues that have led to so many injuries, but it's not enough to prevent him from starting the year at triple-A.

With both Wilson and Isringhausen out of the starting rotation discussion, the Mets turn to an old nemesis for help. At age forty, Orel Hershiser is not the dominating pitcher who smothered the nascent Mets dynasty in its crib during the 1988 playoffs. He can still grit his way through a game, however, thanks to a sinker ball that results in a high number of grounders, a useful attribute when employed in front of the Mets' infield. So when Hershiser is released by the Indians at the tail end of spring training, the pitching-starved Mets scoop him up.

The addition of Hershiser stabilizes the Mets' rotation somewhat, but their outlook appears anything but stable when all of their starters pitch poorly in spring action. Ostensible number four starter Masato Yoshii is the worst offender, pitching to an ERA close to 10, but he will remain in the rotation because no other pitcher in camp performs well enough to take his place. Rumors bubble up that the Mets still aim to deal for a top-line starter, but the general manager dismisses these as wishful thinking. "I'm not all that hopeful for a trade before the end of spring training," Phillips admits with less than a week until opening day, and his pessimism prevails. No trades are made. The Mets will go to war with the pitchers they have and hope the addition of Robin Ventura and the shift of Alfonzo to second base will provide enough defense to compensate for the rotation's deficiencies.

There's little left for the Mets to do at this point but round out their twenty-five-man roster. Youngsters and long shots slough off the list, headed for the minors and the sunset. With the aging legs of Rickey Henderson and Bobby Bonilla in mind, most of the bench spots go to outfielders. This gives hope to Melvin Mora, who has spent equal time in the infield and outfield and turns heads by hitting .421 during Grapefruit League action, but he will start the year in triple-A. Tough choices are a manager's lot this time of year, but Bobby Valentine compounds Mora's misfortune by committing the same sin Joe Torre once committed against him: he fails to tell Mora of his fate until the last possible moment. Mora's bags are on a truck bound for Queens, along with the other major leaguers' gear, when Valentine breaks the bad news.

The news hits Mora so hard he contemplates jumping off a bridge. His only recourse is that of any other jilted big league hopeful: wait for the crush of disappointment to fade into a dull throb, then vow to make his name known before the year is out.

CHAPTER 2

Si No Gana, Empata

THE METS BEGIN their season with seven road games against the Marlins and Expos, two teams whose modest records in 1998 belied their ability to play like All-Stars whenever they faced the Mets. New York racked up a winning record against Florida by the slimmest of margins (7–5), even though the Marlins tallied a pathetic forty-nine wins against all other contenders. With Florida's payroll still as low as it was following their post-championship sell-off, they project to be no better this year.

When Al Leiter exits the bullpen in the campaign opener on April 5 to make his first appearance in Miami since game seven of the 1997 World Series, the home team shows its appreciation to the former Marlin by playing "Born to Run" for the huge Springsteen fan. The crowd accords him an impressive ovation, even if the throng itself is less than impressive, as the Marlins have covered huge swaths of unsellable upper-deck seating with tarp. For their own starter, the home team chooses Alex Fernandez, a pitcher who hasn't climbed a major league mound in over eighteen months while recovering from rotator cuff surgery.

Though conditions are set up to hand the visitors a tidy victory, the Mets drop a frustrating, error-filled mess of a game by the score of 6–2. New York hitters strand fourteen men while batting 0 for 9 with runners in scoring position. Robin Ventura gift-wraps three first-inning runs for the Marlins with shockingly sloppy play. Leiter, the supposed ace, allows five runs in five grueling innings.

In the eyes of the media, the deadly losing streak that closed out 1998 has not yet been broken. One badly played game is sufficient cause to point out the Mets' precarious grip on relevance, and also serves as a reason for their general manager to fire a warning flare in the *Times*:

> Unlike the Marlins, the Mets are built to win now. Their starting lineup averages 31 years of age, their starting rotation 34; their closer is 38. Phillips had talked before the game about his only expectation being that his players perform to their average capabilities.
>
> If that happens, the general manager was asked, is this a playoff team? "It should be," Phillips said, well aware that the Mets have not qualified for the post-season since 1988. "It better be."

With this rebuke in mind, the Mets rebound to take the next two games against the Marlins in convincing fashion. For the reporters who were so quick to doubt the team after a disappointing opening day, Steve Phillips quips, "We're pretty good in must-win games," and suggests the headline "Money Well Spent."

From Miami, the Mets travel to Montréal for four games. The Expos lost ninety-seven games in 1998, yet won eight of their twelve matchups against the Mets, including the first two contests of New York's disastrous five-game end-of-year losing streak. Little else has gone well for Montréal in recent years, as they've traded away numerous superstars to save money, causing attendance at debt-ridden, claustrophobic Olympic Stadium to rank among the lowest in the majors and throwing the franchise's future into jeopardy. When the Mets arrive for Montréal's home opener on April 8, rumors swirl that the team will be relocated as early as next season. Almost forty-four thousand Expos fans show up for the first game against the Mets in a defiant show of support. Amid a surprisingly raucous atmosphere, the Expos take advantage of a laboring Orel Hershiser, hanging five runs on him in four innings and cruising to a win.

Attendance dips to barely five-digit levels for the remainder of the series, however, and the Mets take the next three games from the home team, though each win is tempered with a sliver of bad news. In the second game, Mike Piazza knocks in five runs but also injures his knee during a pick-off play at second base and flies back to New York for an MRI while the team holds its collective breath. By the time the Mets complete a come-from-behind win in game three, they learn the injury is only a mild sprain, but one that will put Piazza out of action for the Mets' home opener. With the lineup already depleted, the team's pitching takes a hit in the series finale when starter Rick Reed tears a calf muscle trying to leg out a double, putting another strain on an already strained starting rotation. The Mets prevail in the game anyway, which means their record thus far looks good on paper, where injuries and crushing pressure are not registered.

* * *

Shea Stadium has had some work done. Among the $250,000 worth of off-season clubhouse renovations are a revamped manager's office fitted with an enormous desk leaving little room for visitors. Considering Steve Phillips's propensity to drop by after games to discuss strategy, Bobby Valentine doesn't consider this aesthetic choice a drawback.

As for external improvements, 221 new high-priced seats have been placed above a maintenance tunnel behind home plate and dubbed the Metropolitan Club, tickets for which cost a whopping $35. New permanent box seats have been placed next to each dugout and a set of bleachers installed beyond the left-field fence as well. All of these upgrades are intended to offset the cost of the Mets' off-season spending in general and Mike Piazza's seven-year deal in particular. Fans satisfied with sitting in the nosebleed sections discover that the cost of the cheapest upper deck tickets is now $9, two whole dollars more than 1998.

For those who can afford to attend, the home opener on April 12 goes swimmingly between the lines. Blue skies prevail. Virtuoso violinist Itzhak Perlman plays the national anthem. Tom Seaver tosses out the first pitch to Mike Piazza, who receives it ably despite his balky knee. Mayor Giuliani attends and even dares to exchange his "lucky" Yankee jacket for some Met gear, though Steve Phillips notes Hizzoner "looked like he was in pain" as he donned it. Starter Bobby Jones holds the Marlins to one run and four hits in seven strong innings and even hits a home run in the fifth en route to an easy 8–1 victory.

The win is literally dampened when a sewer pump fails in the Mets' shower room, filling the newly renovated clubhouse with a lake of foul-smelling water. Bobby Valentine finds his new office flooded, his boxes of prized baseball memorabilia ruined. His team is forced to relocate to the old Jets dressing room, left over from Shea's years hosting the

NFL, facilities that haven't been used in fifteen years and which lack running water.

Scribes can't resist the temptation to compare the Mets' home opener to the Yankees'. Three days earlier, the first game in the Bronx began with the welcome return of Yogi Berra, who'd stayed away for fourteen years over a slight from George Steinbrenner. After soliciting prayers for Joe Torre, on leave from his managerial post as he battles cancer, the team hoisted another championship flag. Harvey Araton of the *Times* notes, "The Yankees played under an appropriately somber sky, in a persistent, divine rain." There is no better reflection of the teams' respective status than this. The Mets can ruin a sunny home opener by flooding their clubhouse with raw sewage. The Yankees can play under gray clouds and precipitation described as *divine*.

* * *

In the Mets' second home game of the season, Orel Hershiser, Turk Wendell, and Armando Benítez victimize an overanxious young Marlins lineup and hand a 4–1 lead to John Franco in the ninth. It proves an atypical Franco appearance, as it is completely lacking for drama. The lefty strikes out the side to record his four hundredth career save, a milestone reached by only one other pitcher in baseball history. After the game, a joyous Franco distributes plastic flutes of Dom Pérignon to his teammates, along with the promise, "This is the first of many celebrations, boys."

Franco arrived in New York prior to the 1990 season. He blew three key saves that September and pitched to a 5.91 ERA as the Mets finished in second place behind the Pirates. The man he was traded for, fellow southpaw Randy Myers, helped power the Reds to a stunning World Series title that same season, then went on to pitch in the postseason for Baltimore and San Diego. Franco has never made a playoff appearance, because the Mets have failed to reach October since he arrived.

For the entirety of the 1990s, Franco has climbed the mound for the Mets. His contract ensures, health willing, he will climb the mound for them into the next millennium. Throughout the decade, Franco has racked up saves but infuriated fans with his tendency to flirt with disaster. "I have a weird hate-love relationship with the fans," he tells *Sports Illustrated*. (Note the order of the emotions.) "There were a few nights when I thought I would need a ride home with the National Guard."

John Franco grew up in Bensonhurst and speaks often of his father, a sanitation worker who literally worked himself to death to provide for his family, passing away of a heart attack at the wheel of a dump truck. (Franco still wears an orange sanitation department shirt under his jersey in tribute.) He remembers the circuitous trips he took from his neighborhood to Shea Stadium along with friends named Bucktooth and Lumpy, exchanging coupons from Borden's milk cartons for upper-deck tickets. He worshipped Tug McGraw, another left-handed Mets fireman with a penchant for making save opportunities a little too interesting. (When the Mets bestow a custom motorcycle on Franco as reward for his four hundredth save, the gift is delivered by McGraw, wearing a helmet emblazoned with the number they share, 45.) As a go-to postgame quote in the clubhouse, Franco's accent—indistinguishable from a character who'd be called Brooklyn in an old World War II movie, or from that of many an aggrieved WFAN caller—is heard on the local news almost every night, all summer long, win or lose. And for most of his tenure in New York, it's been lose.

He hails from a world familiar to many Mets fans of his generation: raised in a housing project, sustained by the city's municipal safety net that promised no luxuries but guaranteed a city worker wouldn't starve. Franco echoes their feelings when he proclaims, "New York is the greatest city in the country, in the world." But these days, he can sound like a man out of time. His home borough has been transformed by an influx of brownstoning homesteaders, bohemian types, and, amazingly, the uber-rich. Now, the place named Brooklyn no longer stands for guys whose dads drove dump trucks, or who grew up in public housing, or who had friends named Lumpy.

Two weeks after reaching his milestone, John Franco receives an honorary key to the city from the mayor in a ceremony at City Hall. Rudy Giuliani declares, "He has never given Mets fans a dull moment," a play on his penchant for giving the Flushing faithful agita. The ceremony is packed with members of the press who have very little interest in the pitcher and instead are waiting to grill the mayor on his latest controversy. A few days prior, Giuliani proclaimed the city's school system "should be blown up." For years, Giuliani has agitated for direct city control of the schools and bristled over his inability to gain that power. The record shows Giuliani has threatened to metaphorically "blow up" the school system for years, using those exact words in speeches even before he became mayor. This time, he used these words less than a week after the school shooting horror in Columbine, Colorado, a moment when placing the words "school" and "blow up" too close to one another both evokes and trivializes that tragedy.

And so, John Franco's big day at City Hall takes a backseat to a flurry of questions over the mayor's poorly timed turn of phrase. While Giuliani refuses to apologize and insists his rhetoric merely reflects his unrelenting dedication to school reform, reporters find this ceaseless combativeness tiresome, if not baffling. Rather than celebrate the accomplishments of his administration, Giuliani wastes his time picking fights as if the city were still a war zone. Former mayor Ed Koch, an erstwhile supporter, can only shake his head at the mayor's behavior. "It's like his goal in life is to spear people, destroy them, go for the jugular," Koch says.

Giuliani would no doubt agree, and wonder why destruction was such a bad thing. If the press sees a transformed New York City as one quirky *Friends* episode after another, Giuliani still sees it as the endless loop of *Taxi Driver* it once was, a state it could easily devolve back into if he lets up for one moment. His favorite attack to launch against anyone who dares question him is to say they are being *political*. He considers himself a politician only in the technical sense. His aims are above mere politics and closer to a crusade, rendering anyone who opposes him an infidel.

Like John Franco, Giuliani spent much of his childhood in Brooklyn, raised with his generation's almost religious belief in the city's greatness. The price of greatness was the unending pressure to stay great. Surrender an inch and watch the other guy take a mile. That belief is perhaps why a kid who grew up in the shadow of Ebbets Field would nonetheless become the loudest and proudest Yankee fan of them all.

* * *

The series against the Marlins at Shea concludes with an embarrassing, error-filled loss and is followed by yet another series against the Expos, during which the Mets appear more eager for a change of scenery than victories after thirteen straight games against the same opponents. "I think they were sick of seeing us and we were sick of seeing them," Bobby Valentine concedes.

The Mets' first look at the rest of the league begins with a series in Cincinnati on April 20, as the visitors take two of three and Al Leiter earns his first win of the year. They then move on to Chicago via a tempest-tossed plane ride Valentine dubs "The Knuckleball Express."

Conditions barely improve once they touch the ground, as game-time temperature for the series opener on April 23 stands at 44 degrees, with 36 mph winds swirling around Wrigley Field. (Robin Ventura, South Side vet, dares to call such weather "mild" for a Chicago April.) Despite Mother Nature's best efforts, the Mets rally to overcome a deficit and are propelled to a 6–5 victory on the modest heroics of a pinch-hit sac fly from Rey Ordóñez. The shortstop's performance come after sitting out the two previous games. His first day on the bench arose from his paltry .172 batting average, while the second was prompted by the temper tantrum he threw after the first benching.

Rey Ordóñez's inability to hit with any consistency is matched only by his infuriating lack of maturity. He goes out of his way to annoy teammates, sneaking up on them to make buzzing sounds in their ears, mugging in their line of sight while they're being grilled by reporters. Luis López, a benchwarmer who occasionally spells Ordóñez at shortstop, has complained the taunting comes close to bullying. His immaturity is also reflected in his discipline at the plate, or lack thereof. In 1998, he collected only twenty-three walks in 548 plate appearances.

Ordóñez almost compensates for this with his wizardry in the field. He is a dynamic fielder who can make difficult plays look easy and execute them with the grace of a ballet dancer. His signature move: sliding on his knees to field a grounder, then popping up, wheeling around, and firing a throw in plenty of time to nail the runner at first. Such a move would be a career highlight for some shortstops. Ordóñez performs it almost daily.

Teams once demanded little more of their shortstops than defensive excellence. Then came Cal Ripken and Robin Yount, shortstops who won MVP awards in the 1980s more for their bats than their gloves. The 1990s brought even more offense-first players at the position, and no amount of leather-based magic can make Ordóñez stand above this new breed of slugging shortstop. In 1997, he was featured in a shirtless photo shoot for *Sports Illustrated* with shortstop contemporaries like Derek Jeter and Nomar Garciaparra, whose chiseled physiques made Ordóñez look like a proverbial ninety-eight-pound weakling in comparison.

Being overshadowed was a familiar feeling for Ordóñez. As a player for the Havana Industriales, a top Cuban squad, he couldn't break into the starting lineup because his team already employed the nation's best shortstop. When he defected and signed with the Mets organization, he became only the second Cuban baseball player since Fidel Castro's revolution to attempt a career in the American major leagues. Compatriots soon followed his lead, however, and most of these Cuban players garnered much more acclaim than him (like Orlando and Liván Hernández, half brothers and ace pitchers who won championships with the Yankees and Marlins, respectively).

When he does draw the attention of the press, it is for all the wrong reasons. Many Cuban defectors send money and other aid back to their impoverished homeland, but Rey Ordóñez has sent no such help, according to relatives polled by a *New York Times* reporter who made a trip to Havana to ask them—not even to the wife and six-year-old son he left behind. The *Times* captures the scene of his son, Reynaldo, showing off a brand-new fielder's mitt he believes was sent to him by the major leaguer himself but was actually a gift from relatives in Miami sent to soothe the boy's feelings. "He has never taken any interest at all in the boy," Reynaldo's mother says. When planning his defection, Ordóñez made vague promises to send for his wife and child. Once in the States, he remarried instead.

The *Times* story is set to hit the newsstands a few days after Ordóñez's game-winning plate appearance in Chicago, which might explain why he reacts to being benched with such childish indignation. Echoing the criticisms of Kevin Brown a decade earlier, he complains that Bobby Valentine is isolating him because he has hit a rough patch, quarantining him from the rest of the team. "He's the boss. He's the one who gives the orders. I'm the only one he does it to. Maybe it's because I don't talk to him or say hi." He sounds almost hopeless when discussing his relationship with the manager. "*Si no gana, empata*," he says of Valentine: If he doesn't win, he ties. "You can't beat him."

Valentine responds, "I like when guys are upset about not playing—in a very professional manner."

***

Rey Ordóñez's pinch-hit heroics prove the zenith of the Mets' trip to Chicago, as they drop the last two games of their set at Wrigley Field before returning to Shea for a nine-game homestand. The first opponents to arrive are the San Diego Padres, sacrificial lambs for the Yankees in last year's World Series. Little more than the name remains from those pennant winners, as the team let most of its free agents walk and traded away other pricey stars. With the dismantling coming hot on the heels of their postseason success, *Sports Illustrated* dubs the Padres "Marlins West" in their season preview. The selloff did wait, however, until after San Diego voters approved a bond issue for a new stadium, leaving some fans to feel their surprising playoff run was little more than a long con.

This makes the Mets' pathetic 6–2 loss in the series opener—during which a small army of baserunners are left stranded—all the more galling. The Mets look poised to rebound the next night, thanks to seven innings of one-run ball from Al Leiter, until Armando Benítez—who'd fanned seventeen batters in his first ten appearances as a Met—allows the Padres to take the lead. When the Mets bat down by a run in the ninth, there is little reason to think they will prevail. San Diego owns a streak of 181 straight games in which they have not relinquished a lead after the eighth inning, a historic mark due in large part to closer Trevor Hoffman, who saved 53 games for the National League champs in 1998. Hoffman is so sure of his abilities that he's spent much of the season confronting baseball writers who dared leave him off their Cy Young Award ballots. (He lost the trophy narrowly to Atlanta's Tom Glavine, due in large part to voters who disdained the emergence of the one-inning fireman.)

On this night, however, Hoffman retires no one. Leading off the bottom of the ninth, John Olerud reaches on an infield single aided by a shortstop's bobble, bringing Mike Piazza to the plate. The catcher has gone 1-for-13 at the plate since returning from the disabled list and left three more men on base this evening, after stranding an astonishing seven runners the night before. Hoffman does him a favor by offering a high, outside fastball, the kind of pitch Piazza has made a career of rocketing to the opposite-field stands. This is exactly what he does, depositing Hoffman's offering into the Mets' bullpen for a game-winning two-run homer. His teammates flood the field, anxious to mob him with joyous pogoing once he touches home.

After the Mets win their last game against San Diego, the San Francisco Giants arrive and bring with them unfavorable comparisons of Bobby Valentine to their manager, Dusty Baker. While the Mets collapsed and missed the postseason at the close of the 1998 season, the Giants surged to win four of their last five and tie the Cubs for the wild card berth, thus displaying grit and determination the Mets (and their skipper) are said to lack. When a rival executive describes Baker as a man who can motivate his players to overachieve, the *Times* tartly notes, "Similar comments are not heard about Bobby Valentine."

This makes the ensuing sweep of the Giants quite satisfying, with the series finale on May 2 especially sweet. To that point in the season, Masato Yoshii had pitched miserably, booed off the mound in his last start after giving up four runs to an anemic Padres lineup in less than five innings. Following this debacle, Valentine claims Yoshii's struggles were all his fault, because he'd instructed Yoshii to move toward the first base side of the rubber, robbing the hurler's trademark *shuto* (a reverse slider thrown by many Japanese pitchers) of its effectiveness. Valentine is so impressed by this discovery that he demands the press corps watch video evidence of his theory, playing it on a loop for them as if it were the Zapruder film. The tape plays dividends when Yoshii proceeds to toss six shutout innings against San Francisco, while his teammates eke out a win, breaking a scoreless tie when the Giants' infield flubs a towering windblown pop-up.

The inspiring sweep of San Francisco is followed by a deflating series against the Houston Astros, a powerful squad driven by its Killer B's lineup of Jeff Bagwell and Craig Biggio, who take two of three from their hosts. The last loss is especially troubling, as Armando Benítez allows a long go-ahead homer to Bagwell that proves the difference in a 5–4 loss. The Mets' latest stay at Shea should have been a successful one, and on paper it was (six wins to three losses), but the sting of the final game appends it with an ugly coda. Throughout 1999, the Mets will be judged not merely by how many games they win, but when and in what fashion, a sliding scale set by the men paid to judge them.

* * *

The disappointing end to the Houston series carries over into the Mets' next road trip, a disastrous swing out west that begins with a stop in Phoenix to play the Arizona Diamondbacks, now in their sophomore season. Determined to shake off expansion team growing pains in record time, Arizona engaged in an off-season spending spree that left New York's in the dust, their biggest acquisition (both figuratively and literally) being Randy Johnson, a lefty with a triple-digit fastball and an NBA center's wingspan. When the Mets arrive at Bank One Ballpark on May 5, the Diamondbacks stand one game over .500 and are poised to take off in a big way. Arizona's ascent to the stratosphere commences by launching off of the Mets, as the home team deals them two defeats in this three-game series, both by blowout margins.

The beleaguered Mets pitching staff is abused even further by their next hosts, the Colorado Rockies. In the frigid atmosphere of Denver, game-time temperatures hover in the mid-forties each night and one game is nearly delayed by a snowstorm. The bar for acceptable pitching at these mile-high elevations is set quite low, but the visiting hurlers find a way to crawl under that bar as they are pounded in the first two games. When the Rockies torch Bobby Jones for eight runs on May 11, it continues an ignoble streak of three straight games in which a Mets starter allows the most runs of his career. Following Jones's ugly outing, Mets starters have accumulated an 11–14 record and an ERA of 5.30. When the team broke camp, starting pitching was envisioned as its weakest link, but this stat line proves more ghastly than anyone's worst nightmares. In the colorful words of the *Daily News*, the Mets' starting staff "continued to possess the hue and smell of sewer water."

While Mets pitchers serve up gopher balls, the Mets outfield crumbles bit by elderly bit. During the series against the Giants at Shea, Rickey Henderson suffers a knee injury that lands him on the disabled list. Then, in Denver, Bobby Bonilla is hit by a pitch in the left knee that has bothered him since spring training, sending him to the DL as well. Though termed a disaster in the moment, the injuries of Henderson and Bonilla are in fact a boon to the team, as they force the Mets to rely on two young outfielders who will power them for the rest of the season.

First comes the call-up of perpetual minor leaguer Benny Agbayani, a desperate measure borne of desperate times. The Hawaiian was held in such little regard by his own organization that he wasn't invited to major league camp during spring training. At age twenty-seven, this served as an unsubtle hint that he might want to consider another line of work. His only saving grace to this point is the fact that Bobby Valentine, a former manager at Norfolk, remembers him fondly. At first sight, Agbayani's most glaring shortcoming is his weekend softballer's physique. Once circumstance forces Agbayani into the everyday lineup, however, he makes the opposing pitchers look like the beer leaguers. He belts his first major league home run during the series in Denver, then crushes ten more before the All-Star break in only ninety-six at bats.

While Benny Agbayani goes deep with Ruthian frequency, Roger Cedeño steps up to fill the role vacated by the injured Rickey Henderson. Having worshipped Henderson's speed and base thievery as a youth in Venezuela, Cedeño is both overjoyed and amply prepared to stage Henderson-like performances in his absence. He first raises eyebrows against the Astros on May 3, stealing two bases, scoring two runs, and turning a single into a double against a Houston outfield unprepared for his speed. But his true breakout performance comes when the Mets slink out of Denver and touch down in Philadelphia. During the first game at Veterans Stadium on May 14, Cedeño victimizes the Phillies with four stolen bases, scoring three times. "He should go every time he gets on," Bobby Valentine says, advice Cedeño takes to heart. "Roger is in a groove. I don't think they can throw him out on a pitchout."

Valentine talks up the talents of Agbayani and Cedeño, but his enthusiasm prompts regular queries from the beat reporters about who will receive the bulk of playing time once Rickey Henderson and Bobby Bonilla return. Every time the Mets are powered to victory by Agbayani or sped to a win by Cedeño, one of the first postgame questions the manager fields is inevitably, *Who will play when the veterans return?* Valentine deflects these queries as premature, on one occasion snapping back at a reporter, "Don't ruin a good day with a silly question."

* * *

Questions, silly and otherwise, continue to nag the Mets. First, they drop the final contest in Philadelphia, then return to Shea Stadium and drop the first two of a four-game set against the lowly Milwaukee Brewers. Bobby Valentine seethes over a called third strike that ends the series opener on May 17, then receives more fodder for complaint the next night when Brewer manager Phil Garner demands the umpires examine Rick Reed's glove. Valentine accuses Garner of doing this not to uncover cheating but to rankle his pitcher, whereupon Milwaukee's manager sniffs, "I don't play those games," implying that Valentine does. The Mets go on to lose when Armando Benítez allows a three-run homer to Marquis Grissom in the top of the eighth, an eerie replay of a crushing homer the closer allowed to the slugger in the 1997 playoffs. It is their ninth loss in the last thirteen games.

A rainout necessitates a doubleheader on May 20, which also enables Robin Ventura to achieve a curious baseball milestone by becoming the first player in history to hit one grand slam in each half of a twin bill. Apart from this historic anomaly and the fact that the Mets win both games, the proceedings are not pretty to watch, as Al Leiter struggles with his control in the first contest and exits after five innings with six runs to his discredit. The Mets' bullpen nearly gives up a hefty lead, and the last out of the game is only secured when the man representing the tying run loses a shoe on the basepaths and is thrown out at the plate, a suitable end to an unsightly win for the home team.

Once the Brewers depart, the Mets host the Phillies for three games. After splitting the first two, the rubber game on May 24 is preceded by a two-hour rain delay, but Mets management is loath to cancel the game outright with close to thirty-five thousand tickets sold for a Sunday afternoon giveaway (kids' jersey day). When the game finally starts, the Mets' bats never leave the dugout, stymied by the wizardry of pitcher Curt Schilling.

The Phillies' ace pitches this game like a man on a mission, a reflection of the battle he's been waging against his own front office for years. In 1997, he signed a modest contract extension rather than seek bigger bucks in free agency, a display of loyalty fans forever seek from players but rarely see. He assumed the Phillies would use the savings on his contract to pursue reinforcements, but the team responded by slashing payroll down to a miniscule $26 million. Schilling has become increasingly vocal with his gripes of late. Right before the Phillies arrive in Queens, he tells an interviewer unequivocally that if Philadelphia won't spend the money necessary to compete, he'd prefer to play for a team that will.

The *New York Times* fetes Schilling with a glowing profile published the day of his start at Shea, one that plays up the technophile's use of a laptop to keep eight years' worth of notes on opposing batters, while also praising him for his old-school tendency to "finish what he started," pitching many complete games when bullpen specialization has made the feat more rare with each passing season. On this occasion, Schilling does indeed go the distance, though not in the manner he would have liked.

As the ninth inning begins, Schilling has a reasonable 107 pitches under his belt and a healthy 4–0 lead to his credit. A two-run homer from Robin Ventura to start that frame indicates he may be tiring, yet no one stirs in Philadelphia's bullpen. The Phillies' closer is not available, and even if he was, manager Terry Francona has no intention of removing his ace. "Regardless of who was available, that was his game," Francona says later.

One out and one single later, Schilling nails weak-hitting bench player Luis López with a pitch, then cedes an RBI hit that trims the Phillies' lead down to one slim run. Still, Schilling remains on the mound, and it looks as if he might escape danger when Roger Cedeño hits a ball right back to him. But the screamer clanks off the pitcher's glove, so Schilling can only toss to second for a force out as Cedeño reaches first safely. The speedy outfielder then swipes second to put the winning run in scoring position. The Phillies oblige him by not offering a throw to halt his progress.

And still, Schilling remains on the mound. He even backs Edgardo Alfonzo into a two-strike count, but pitches too aggressively inside with a ball that grazes Alfonzo on the forearm, loading the bases. It is the second hit batter of the inning by a pitcher who hasn't hit anyone in his previous eighty-one innings.

"That's the game," Schilling concedes afterward.

Momentum has swung so far in the Mets' favor by this point that what follows seems a mere formality. John Olerud lines Schilling's first offering into shallow left field for a single. López scampers home to tie the game and Cedeño follows right behind, sliding on his back, beating a throw to the plate by a step. As he looks up and sees the umpire signal safe, Cedeño pumps his arms and legs in celebration from a prone position on top of home plate. A sure 4–0 loss has turned into a 5–4 win, a stunning five-run ninth-inning rally executed against one of the best pitchers in the game.

Save the first Subway Series win in 1997, this might be the most thrilling and unlikely win the Mets have enjoyed so far this decade. The team is permitted to revel in it for only a few moments before the cruel light of reality intrudes.

Bobby Jones was the team's most reliable starting pitcher at the beginning of the season, but after weeks of middling starts and an especially ugly outing against the Phillies, he confesses to feeling shoulder pain. Moments after this heart-pounding comeback, the Mets announce Jones will be placed on the disabled list. Shortly after the bad news about Jones drops, Bobby Valentine discloses that Al Leiter will have his next start pushed back a day to accommodate a sore left bicep.

This quickly developing disaster is what it takes to force the recall of Jason Isringhausen, a man well acquainted with disaster. Arguably the most star-crossed of all the Generation K members, he sat out all of 1998 recovering from elbow surgery, once dealt himself a broken wrist by punching a dugout garbage can, and even spent time on the shelf due to tuberculosis. So when Isringhausen starts the opener of a brief three-game road trip to Pittsburgh on May 24, it is quite predictable that his first major league pitch in twenty months would be knocked for a double, and followed shortly thereafter by a three-run homer. He shows signs of his promise by striking out seven batters, but the five runs and hard-hit balls he allows in his 1999 debut do not convince the Mets that Isringhausen is the answer to their pitching woes.

And then there are personnel issues of a different kind. When the season began, Bobby Bonilla deflected skepticism about his abilities with self-deprecating humor, an attempt at image rehabilitation that seemed genuine. His good humor disappears with his trip to the disabled list, as the whispers say this time on the shelf is a painless means for the Mets to bench him and his anemic bat. The team adds fuel to this theory by insisting the veteran make some rehab starts in the minors before he is reactivated. Bonilla counters by asking the Mets to fly minor league pitchers to New York to face him, because the Mets accommodated Mike Piazza in this fashion when the catcher was recovering from his own knee injury. When queried about this diva-like demand, Bonilla blows up at reporters before threatening the silent treatment. "Every time I try to be nice to you guys," he growls. "Now, I'm just going to play ball. I'm not going to even talk about it anymore."

The new Bonilla, if he ever existed at all, is gone. In his place, an unwelcome return of the "I'll show you the Bronx" Bonilla. To many in the media, Bonilla's mere presence on the roster prevents the Mets from scrubbing away the stain of the early 1990s. Wallace Matthews of the *Post*—local sports media's most ardent scold—compares the team from Queens unfavorably to the Yankees thusly: "The fact that Bonilla is still a check-cashing member of the New York Mets is all you need to know about the class gap between this town's two ballclubs."

* * *

Pessimists can point to a torrent of injuries and the grousing of Bobby Bonilla, but the Mets have fodder for the glass-half-full crowd as well. Benny Agbayani and Roger Cedeño have picked up the slack in a hobbled outfield. The infield has remained healthy while transforming many a potential hit into an out, and nearly every member of that infield is hitting the cover off the ball (Rey Ordóñez being the lone exception). His knee injury and the brief slump that followed it aside, Mike Piazza has been Mike Piazza. Masato Yoshii has rebounded from the awful start to his season to become the team's best starter. Apart from a few hiccups, the bullpen has been outstanding, as Armando Benítez, Dennis Cook, and Turk Wendell have formed an impregnable bridge to John Franco—who, amazingly, has converted all of his save chances so far.

As the Mets return from Pittsburgh and May slips toward June, the team, its fans, and even the media can all dare to feel good about the team if they wish to. Within a week, no one will.

CHAPTER 3

The Pretender

JUNE 9, 1999, the day Bobby Valentine writes a whole paragraph in his obituary, is a strange day even by his own standards. It begins with a Shea clubhouse shouting match with *Newsday* reporter Marty Noble, who is upset over Valentine's accusation that the newsman hasn't spoken to him in over a year. Shortly thereafter, Benny Agbayani suffers a freak injury during batting practice when he foul tips a ball into his right eye. The lineup is further compromised because disgruntled outfielder Bobby Bonilla, though recently restored from the disabled list, is unavailable, even if Valentine won't (or can't) say why. Signs point to the front office having ordered a Bonilla benching, but Steve Phillips has no comment, and Bonilla—never inclined to make a reporter's job easy—tells the scribes he has nothing to say and makes good on his word.

Adding to the evening's odd vibe is the presence of Venezuelan president Hugo Chávez, in town to visit the United Nations, who throws out the ceremonial first pitch while draped in a billowy warm-up jacket adorned with the colors of his nation's flag and wearing a full Mets uniform, including pinstriped pants. In deference to this guest, the Venezuelan national anthem is played prior to the start of the game, in addition to the standard "Star-Spangled Banner" and the "O Canada" necessitated by the visiting Toronto Blue Jays.

David Wells takes the mound for Toronto to make his first start in New York since the Yankees dealt him northward for Roger Clemens. Shea hosts many Yankees fans who have no qualms about cheering for a divisional rival at the expense of the Mets. Boomer's return to the Big Apple coincides with his birthday, and a postgame shindig awaits him at trendy Soho nightclub Veruka. Club owner Noel Ashman patrols Shea's Diamond Club throughout the game, checking in with his doorman via cell phone to decree who shall be permitted to enter.

Wells looks like a man ready to celebrate as he mows down the Mets' batting order with little effort through the first eight innings. A complete game is a seeming formality until the Mets rally to tie the score in the ninth against Wells and Toronto's bullpen. A frustrating extra-inning slog follows. Shea's giant right-field scoreboard flashes periodic updates from game five of the NBA Eastern Conference finals, which ends with the Knicks triumphant over the Indiana Pacers while this game plods on.

In the top of the twelfth inning, when Mike Piazza appears to have thrown out a would-be base stealer, the umpire signals that Piazza interfered with the batter. Bobby Valentine storms out of the dugout to make his displeasure known and is ejected for his insolence. He should not have been in the dugout to witness the Mets pull out a victory, and a series sweep, by means of a bloop RBI single from Rey Ordóñez in the bottom of the fourteenth. And indeed Valentine is not present when all this happens, at least not entirely.

No one will ever know why Valentine does what he does next, and in the end, his act is so ridiculous that assigning reason to it is all but pointless. Much the same could be said of what he and the Mets did in the agonizing eleven days that precede this one.

* * *

Turn back the calendar to May 28. The Mets are trailing by one run and down to their last out against the visiting Diamondbacks. With the bases loaded and a 3-1 count to the batter, pinch hitter Luis López looks at a pitch that sails across the plate, ankle-high. It should be ball four, resulting in a walk to force in the tying run. The home plate umpire calls it strike two. Rattled, López watches another pitch for strike three, ending the threat and the game. The Mets lose by the excruciating score of 2–1.

Thus begins a week of tough luck, near misses, and bad blood, a dark period when no calls or bounces go the Mets' way. Game two against the Diamondbacks is a three-hour, forty-minute trial in which their bullpen is roughed up and they again lose by one run. The next day, Randy Johnson strikes out ten Mets while Masato Yoshii watches his *shuto* get shuttled from one side of the park to the other. A sizeable crowd arrives at Shea for a Sunday matinee that also happens to be Beanie Baby Day, but few remain to see the conclusion of the 10–1 drubbing.

Three rough losses in a row are enough to prompt murmurings of mutiny. An unnamed veteran complains to the *Times* about Bobby Valentine's volatile lineup choices. "There are a lot of guys who are upset that there is no set lineup," gripes the mystery man. "Look around at the other teams. They have the same lineup every day." A baffled Bobby Valentine proffers statistics to show that the team is hitting well regardless of his machinations. When this does nothing to diminish the controversy, he informs Roger Cedeño and Benny Agbayani they will receive fewer starts, despite the injection of life both players have given to the Mets, because Bobby Bonilla and Rickey Henderson and their fragile veteran egos (and hefty salaries) must be accommodated. "The two young guys are, as they should be, a little confused," Valentine reports to the press, no happier about the move than Cedeño and Agbayani themselves.

When the Reds come to Queens on May 31 and take the opener of their three-game series, Bobby Valentine chooses to accentuate the positive. He declares that Al Leiter—making his first start in seven days due to a persistent knee issue—was "four or five pitches away from a complete game shutout." Those four or five pitches presumably include a two-run homer by Pokey Reese and a 423-foot bomb off the bat of Greg Vaughn.

Leiter also feels he pitched better than his line would indicate, which comes as little surprise. After every mediocre start he's made to this point in the season—and he's made many—Leiter has been quick with an excuse. When he struggled through five grueling innings in Miami on opening day, he dismissed the results as a delayed reaction to being hit in the hip by a bat during a spring training game. When he lost to the Expos at Shea a week later, he placed the blame on bad hops, not bad pitching, and implied a rainy spring had affected him worse than any other pitcher. When weather couldn't be blamed, he insisted the problems originated in his mind rather than his arm, as he did following a 6–1 loss to the Astros. "I've got to stop the negative thoughts," he counseled himself. "I've got to stop listening to 'What's wrong with Al?' There's nothing wrong with Al." After he squandered several leads in an unsightly start against the Brewers on May 20, he said it was due to the pressures of pitching for the Mets. "I happen to find playing in New York with the team I rooted for exciting, good or bad," Leiter said. "I just have to filter a lot of the exterior distraction out."

So when Al Leiter follows his loss to the Reds on May 30 with excuses like, "I felt good, just a few pitches that didn't go my way . . ." the press can mouth along with every word. They've heard this song many times before, and it's growing old.

On May 31, the Mets field their full projected opening day lineup—including an outfield of Bobby Bonilla, Rickey Henderson, and center fielder Brian McRae—for the first time since early April. That lineup is shut out 4–0 by Pete Harnisch, an ex-Met who, upon his release in 1997, couldn't wait to call WFAN and tell the world that no one in the Shea clubhouse respected Bobby Valentine. Two balls hit into the right-field corner go for triples when Bonilla is slow to track them down. Chants of "BOBBY SUCKS!" resound throughout the stands, supplanted by cheers when Roger Cedeño jogs out to take Bonilla's place for defense in the ninth inning. Mike Piazza confesses he is "trying to put the ball over the scoreboard" with every pitch. A players-only meeting is called to relieve the tension.

In a back-and-forth series finale on June 1, the Mets rally for four runs in the bottom of the seventh and carry a one-run lead into the top of the ninth. Two quick outs from John Franco put the Mets in excellent position to grab a morale-boosting win. Then, Franco walks Greg Vaughn, and the crowd begins to stir. Moments later, Barry Larkin hits a ball near the shortstop hole that goes for an infield hit, and the stirring gives way to groans. When Vaughn and Larkin execute a double steal, all the fans who stood in anticipation of the final out feel nervously for their seats. The entire stadium slumps in frustration when Franco allows a single up the middle to the next batter. Franco spins around like a top, watching the ball skip into the outfield as Vaughn and Larkin score the tying and go-ahead runs behind his back. The home team falls yet again, 8–7.

Thus concludes a miserable 0–6 homestand, the first time the Mets have been swept in back-to-back three-game series at home since their dreadful inaugural season of 1962. With the Mets' season hanging in the balance, the pitchforks emerge from the mob, and most point their sharpened tines at Bobby Valentine. In the *Times*, Murray Chass *tsks*, "The Mets once again have promised more than they can deliver. They have fooled their fans and themselves before, and here they have gone and done it again." Long a Valentine nemesis, Chass ascribes the Mets' slide to their manager because "Valentine has more people in baseball pulling against him than any other individual."

What the Mets could use is a low-stress road series far away from New York's glaring spotlight. What the Mets will get instead is the exact opposite: the Subway Series.

* * *

In the first two years of the Subway Series, the Mets had a "golly gee whiz" approach to the affair. In 1999, as the first leg coincides with the nadir of their season, the team is a lot less gung ho. For the first time, they make noise about the unfairness of playing six games against the Yankees (a new wrinkle; in each of the last two seasons, the Mets and Yankees only played one three-game series), while their closest divisional rivals will play the Yankees only three times, if at all. "It's not an equitable schedule," Bobby Valentine grumbles. For once, no one in Shea's clubhouse is too excited to talk about the Subway Series. Following his blown save against the Reds, John Franco is asked a few questions on the subject and responds to each with a terse "I don't care," a remarkable display of churlishness for someone who spent the last decade all but running to the press after each game.

For their part, the Yankees maintain their traditional annoyance at all the artificial hype. "It takes the focus away from where it belongs," George Steinbrenner says, "and that's on the pennant races." His players likewise insist the Subway Series games are no more special than any of the 156 others they must play to reach October. Paul O'Neill, veteran outfielder and cantankerous spiritual leader, insists the Subway Series "isn't that big of a deal." When a reporter asks him about a dramatic game-winning home run he hit at Shea in 1998, O'Neill downplays the memory and contends, "I remember a lot of other games more than that one. It didn't mean that much. They didn't lose by one game, did they?"

O'Neill is reminded that yes, the Mets did miss out on the playoffs by one game in 1998.

"Oh," he mutters.

Four-plus seasons in pinstripes and two World Series rings have wiped out memories of David Cone's days with the Mets—except this time of year, when the scribes still pelt him with questions about the difference between the two teams. "I know after playing three games at Shea last year, our players were glad to see it was over," Cone sighs. "There was intense scrutiny, high stress, and high drama at a time of the season when you're trying to play it day by day." During an interview with ESPN,

Derek Jeter sounds a variation on his traditional take when he insists that if the Yankees don't beat the Mets, he'll be too mortified to leave his Manhattan apartment.

Deep though it may run, the Yankee players' dislike of the Subway Series pales in comparison to that of their manager. "It's a nightmare for us," Joe Torre groans to one reporter. "The fans love it, the whole city is charged, and that part is great, but the outcome of the game is torture. There's so much made out of winning and losing. I've got to pick up my dry cleaning. Those are the guys that torture you."

At the risk of upsetting his dry cleaner, Torre and the Yankees welcome the Mets on the evening of June 4. As the media arrives in the Bronx, reports circulate that the Mets have placed Bobby Bonilla and Brian McRae on waivers, with an eye toward dealing both of them. While McRae has little to say, Bonilla growls, "Ask me if I give a shit," then suggests he'd be happy to spend the rest of the season on his couch as long as he keeps getting paid. Steve Phillips declines comment, which the press interprets as evidence the team would have already dealt the two outfielders if they'd found any takers. Words like "confusion" and "wavering" dominate the reports that follow.

If the waiver wire incident doesn't exude a bumbling atmosphere around the Mets, the game that follows it certainly does. Rey Ordóñez knocks a double to tie the score in the top of the sixth, but the Mets are prevented from sending the go-ahead run home when a spectator leans over one of Yankee Stadium's low field-level walls and interferes with the ball. It is not quite Jeffrey Maier—the young fan who stuck his fielder's mitt over an outfield fence during the 1996 playoffs, turning a potential fly ball out into a Yankeee home run—but it has the similar effect of providing the Yankees with a tenth man on the field.

"Who knows what would have happened had the Mets gotten both runs?" Bill Madden wonders in the *Daily News*, before coming to the conclusion, "They probably would have found some other way to lose the game."

The way they find to lose in this case is via a rare miscue by John Olerud, who dives for a grounder he should have left for Edgardo Alfonzo, resulting in an infield hit. Moments later, the Yankees go back in front when Rickey Henderson misplays a carom off the outfield wall. In the ninth, the Mets nearly recapture the lead as Alfonzo hits a long fly ball to right, tantalizingly close to a two-run homer, but the Mets lead the league in near misses these days. The ball settles into Paul O'Neill's glove a few inches on the wrong side of the wall. The Mets lose again, 4–3, their seventh consecutive defeat.

With all other tactics exhausted, Valentine opts for cockeyed optimism. "I can't be any more proud of a team," he says in the wake of yet another defeat. "We're playing a good brand of baseball . . . Other than a victory, there's nothing negative I can say about my guys." *Other than victory* . . . What a thing for a manager to say, and to say it at Yankee Stadium, where there is *nothing* other than victory. At this desperate juncture, his words have a Panglossian ring.

Rumors begin to swirl that Valentine's days as manager are numbered. Fred Wilpon attempts to deflect such speculation by declaring, "He's the manager." The media's follow-up: *You mean, for the whole year?* "Yes. He's under contract and he's our guy." Steve Phillips also swears Valentine is doing a "good job," but not every Met agrees. While Wilpon and Phillips issue tepid reassurances, John Franco is interviewed at Yankee Stadium by WFAN's Chris "Mad Dog" Russo and confesses that his manager's lineups leave his teammates "scratching their heads." (This admission may help identify the unnamed veteran who complained about lineup inconsistency.) When Russo shares his belief that the Mets don't give their all for Valentine, Franco coyly responds, "You may have something there."

There is no better demonstration of the Mets' recent luck than the moment in the top of the second of Subway Series game two, when Rey Ordóñez hits a sharp grounder right back to pitcher Orlando Hernández, smacking the ball so hard it wedges between the fingers of his glove. Unable to dislodge the ball, Hernández flings his whole glove toward first base overhand to record an unusual force out. Robin Ventura, who ran to third base on the play, is too flabbergasted to try and score while the ball is trapped in leather.

If ever the baseball gods sent the message "This is not your day," surely this was it. Masato Yoshii squanders an early lead and the Mets fall yet again, 6–3. The Mets' eight-game losing streak has dropped the team a game below .500 and into third place in the National League East, behind the poorhouse Phillies.

Before the game, Steve Phillips is blindsided by published rumors he is about to fire pitching coach Bob Apodaca. Whispers of Apodaca's tenuous grip on employment, murmured all year due to the sorry state of the Mets' starting pitching, have gathered steam during their nose dive. The only thing that saved the coach's neck was his close relationship with Bobby Valentine, but that connection means a lot less now than it once did. Phillips neither confirms nor denies such rumors while backpedaling from the tepid "good job" endorsement of Valentine he'd muttered a day ago. When asked if Valentine's status is as shaky as that of his pitching coach, Phillips says tersely, "Draw your own conclusions." Following the game, he is even more brusque, bristling at a reporter's question before using it as an excuse to make an early exit from the Bronx.

Later that evening, Phillips addresses the press via conference call to inform them he has dismissed half of the Mets' coaching staff. Bob Apodaca gets the axe as expected, but so do hitting coach Tom Robson and assistant pitching and bullpen coach Randy Niemann. The dismissals of Robson and Niemann make little sense unless you know that both men, like Apodaca, are close confidants of Bobby Valentine. The trio formed Valentine's brain trust in the Mets' clubhouse. Now, all are gone.

The general manager insists he decided to fire these three coaches the previous Thursday and that the outcome of the Subway Series had no bearing on the move. He offers no explanation as to why a decision he'd made days ago was announced in the dead of night on a Saturday. "The new idea seems to be straight from the Book of Steinbrenner," Joel Sherman writes in the *Post*. He means the *old* Steinbrenner of the 1980s, the one who spent his money on free agent busts and reacted to crises by issuing cruel, indiscriminate pink slips.

Phillips denies the firings are a backhanded attempt to force Valentine to quit. When an ESPN reporter points out that the three coaches who got the axe were Bobby Valentine's *aides de camp*, Phillips tells the reporter, "I wouldn't read anything into it." Few believe him. It is widely assumed that the Mets see Bobby Valentine out on a ledge and are giving him multiple reasons to jump.

If this is in fact the Mets' intent, Valentine refuses to play his part. He insists his fired underlings insisted he stay on and fight rather than quit, though this contention is regarded with all the skepticism it deserves. Shovel in hand, Murray Chass of the *Times* pens a column entitled "To Valentine, It Seems, Loyalty Has Its Limits," in which he calls the manager a coward for not falling on his sword. What kind of person would continue on like this, Chass argues, when his bosses are telegraphing that they want him gone?

The stage is set for a cringe-inducing press conference prior to the Subway Series finale on June 6. Steve Phillips does most of the talking, defending his actions in clipped, measured phrases, expressing remorse that, *sigh*, it has come to this. Bobby Valentine sits at his side, looking like a hyperactive child forced to squirm through Sunday mass, his eyes darting in every direction. He bites his knuckles throughout the grotesque charade, as if afraid his mouth might betray him if it isn't filled with something.

When asked if he's "lost" the team, Valentine responds, "None of my power is gone. I still have total control over things I've always had control over." To Lisa Olson of the *Daily News*, this statement rings with echoes of Al Haig, the bygone secretary of state who screeched, "I'm in charge here!" after an attempt on President Reagan's life and thus proved he was in charge of nothing. In truth, at this point, Valentine has control over nothing but words, so he forms them into a cudgel and wields them on himself. The Mets have played fifty-five games to this point in the season. In his opinion, the Mets have the talent and ability to win forty of the next fifty-five games they play—and if they don't, he deserves to be fired.

A few outlets interpret this as some brilliant three-dimensional chess move. (*Sporting News* calls it "an act of Machiavellian genius" that "set the agenda before [the Mets] could open a smaller window and throw Valentine out of it.") But most report the manager's words with little comment. Given the Mets' struggles, forty out of fifty-five sounds like the ranting of a street corner madman, or of a man who begs to be fired because he's too proud to quit. The *Post* compares Valentine's prediction to putting a gun to his own head and asking the front office to pull the trigger.

The Mets desperately need to salvage a victory in the Subway Series finale but will have to do so against Roger Clemens, winner of twenty decisions in a row, an American League record. The Rocket hasn't been perfect this season, but the potent Yankee offense has bailed him out more than once, proving it is often better to be lucky than good. The Mets will counter with Al Leiter, who has been neither lucky nor good so far in 1999. For an added bit of pressure, the game is broadcast nationally during prime time on ESPN, thus allowing the entire country to take in the Mets' humiliated state.

This confluence of events seems laboratory engineered to end the Mets' season before the All-Star break, which makes what happens during the game even more remarkable. The Mets load the bases against Clemens in the top of the second, setting up back-to-back two-run knocks from Bobby Bonilla and Benny Agbayani, all while an unnerved Clemens stares in at the umpire and stalks the mound when close calls are deemed balls instead of strikes. The Rocket is even more perturbed in the third inning by a two-run homer by Mike Piazza, a monster shot that lands in a narrow corner of the Yankees' bullpen. Moments later,

Agbayani sneaks an RBI single past a diving Derek Jeter, spelling the end for Clemens and giving him one of the ugliest pitching lines of his career: 2 2/3 innings, eight hits, seven runs, all earned. With the home team trailing by seven runs, Bronx Bombers fans head for the exits and hubristic Mets fans, starved for anything to cheer, taunt the ones who remain—including Mayor Giuliani, who hears it from orange-and-blue partisans for the rest of the evening.

As amazing as the Mets' sudden bout of clutch hitting is, Al Leiter's performance is even more so. The Mets' reputed ace finally pitches like one, allowing only one run on four hits in seven innings of work. It is exactly the kind of performance the Mets need, and the kind of performance a number-one starter is paid to deliver. The visitors sail to a stress-free 7–2 victory. With no need to excuse another mediocre outing, Leiter quips, "I'm so relieved just so I don't have to answer your questions of why I'm so shitty."

The Mets follow their win over the Yankees by taking the first two games of a series against Toronto at Shea, including a victory that gives Jason Isringhausen his first major league win in almost two years. "I get teased that every time I go out there, there's a black cloud over the stadium," the weary Isringhausen tells reporters after the game, expressing a sentiment every Met understands after the last week. But a modest three-game winning streak is not sufficient to end the Bobby Valentine Death Watch. Newspapers run opinion pieces with titles like "Mets, Own Up to the Inevitable," urging the team to cut its losses and ditch Valentine for the good of everyone involved. Valentine's survival depends on restoring some sense of normalcy in the Shea clubhouse, but as Jack Curry points out in the *New York Times*, "Exactly what is normal for the Mets is still uncertain."

* * *

Moments after Valentine is given his early exit on the evening of June 9, the television cameras spy a lurker in the Mets' dugout. In the strictest sense, this man is not in the dugout. He stands on the top step connecting the dugout to the clubhouse tunnel. On his head, a black baseball cap with an indecipherable logo. He wears a Mets T-shirt that has the cheap look of a bootleg. His eyes are obscured by a large pair of aviator sunglasses. Below his nose, a laughably fake mustache painted on with eye black. It is the kind of "disguise" a person would wear not to go undetected, but to be noticed.

The lurker's arms are folded. He rocks side to side, performing such a strenuous job of trying to not be seen that no one can fail to miss him. The players on the bench do everything in their power to *not* look at him, which only serves to draw more attention his way. The mystery man in the ridiculous getup remains silent, for his appearance says everything. *Isn't this supposed to be fun?* he says without speaking a word. *Isn't this supposed to be a game?*

For those watching live, he seems to hover there forever. But only a few moments pass before he is gone.

CHAPTER 4

The Drive to Fifty-Five

BOBBY VALENTINE'S DISAPPEARING act is a flop, but his true magic trick fools everyone.

His own view of the "disguise" incident evolves quickly. When first confronted about his costumed chicanery, Bobby Valentine is bold enough to swear the masked man seen on camera wasn't him. After an off day to ponder his strategy, he returns to Shea on June 11 and cops to the crime with a sense of pride. The manager leads a group of eager reporters on a step-by-step recreation of the incident to prove he didn't leave the clubhouse tunnel and therefore hadn't technically broken the rules. He asks the reporters if they believe he was in the dugout. When most raise their hands, Valentine smiles and says, "You're all wrong."

Ultimately, though, Valentine doesn't seem too concerned about being punished. "It's going to cost me a lot of money," he admits. "So what? It was a mistake, but for a moment [in] the emotions of a group of tight people, it was a break, and for me too."

Some see Valentine's act for what the manager says it was, an attempt to inject levity into a clubhouse still tense from a long losing streak and the loss of three coaches. For most reporters, however, it reinforces his reputation as a notorious attention hog. Murray Chass is again the first to pounce on Valentine, blasting the manager as "a legend in his own mind."

The National League office bides its time in reacting, largely because there is little precedent for such a crime, before handing down a two-game suspension and a $5,000 fine, a punishment Valentine vows to appeal. Forced to address the subject during a thirty-minute conference call,

Steve Phillips experiences a rare loss of cool. "When can we talk about baseball?" he gripes.

In light of Valentine's transgressions and his "win forty of fifty-five or I'm fired" promise/threat, any discussion of the Mets must focus on their skipper and his fitness to manage a major league ballclub. All the pressure that weighed on the Mets in the season's initial months—*win or else*—is now placed on the manager. It's doubtful this was Valentine's intention, but his actions nonetheless have the same effect as a magician's misdirection. With the media's focus diverted for a few precious weeks, the Mets follow one of the worst stretches in franchise history with one of the best.

* * *

While Bobby Valentine's antics are still a topic for daily snickering, a Mets executive sighs and wonders aloud to a reporter who once covered The Other Team in Town, "Is this what it was like with the Yankees?" As it happens, the Yankees are embroiled in their own controversy at the moment, even if their role in that controversy is incidental.

On June 11—the same day Bobby Valentine recreates his spy act for the press—first lady Hillary Clinton is interviewed by Katie Couric on *The Today Show*. Most of Couric's questions revolve around Clinton's presumed candidacy for a New York Senate seat in 2000. (The piddling matter of her nonresidency in the state will presumably be handled soon enough.) Clinton fields all questions in the noncommittal manner of a presumptive political candidate, except one. When Couric poses the question of which baseball team she'd root for as a New Yorker, Clinton avers she's "always been a Yankees fan." Heading off those who point out previously declared Chicago Cubs fandom, Clinton maintains the Yankees were "always" her preferred American League team.

Hillary is given a chance to prove her bona fides later that day when the White House hosts the Yankees for the traditional honoring of the reigning World Series champs, and George Steinbrenner presents a Yankees cap to both the president and Mrs. Clinton. Hillary must be aware of the old electioneering rule to "never wear the hat," which holds that no candidate should under any circumstances wear a gifted souvenir cap on camera, or else prepare for swift and brutal ridicule.

The first lady ignores the old saw, not only donning the Yankees cap but wearing it throughout the ceremony. Inside-the-Beltway types assume Clinton does this for the sole purpose of irking her presumed

Republican opponent for the senate, Rudy Giuliani. Though Giuliani's popularity has receded in New York City proper, outside the five boroughs he remains known as the pugnacious mayor who tough-loved New York out of the abyss, and the thought is this may be enough to earn him a senate seat. As is the case with Clinton, Giuliani's senate candidacy is taken as such a given that it is all but official.

The Yankee cap incident proves a major gaffe for a campaign that hasn't even begun yet, because anyone who chooses to do battle with Giuliani over the subject of the Yankees is sure to lose. Asked if he feels "betrayed" that the Yankees were being used as a photo op for a presumed rival candidate, Hizzoner laughs it off. Then he rattles off questions he'd pose to Hillary Clinton, one die-hard Yankees fan to another. *Where were you when Reggie Jackson belted three homers in game six in 1977? Where were you when the Yanks won it all again in 1996? Best center fielder: DiMaggio, Mantle, or Williams?* "Under the right set of circumstances, we could even have a debate about this," Giuliani says, knowing full well he could demolish any challenger in such a contest.

The Yankees, who expected an apolitical afternoon of snapping pictures and shaking hands with the president, are instead grilled on the subject of Hillary vs. Rudy. When asked, David Cone attests to Giuliani's lifelong Yankees fandom. Then, upon realizing that the mere mention of this could now be deemed partisan, Cone insists he'd welcome the Clintons "with open arms" should they ever visit the House That Ruth Built. After this, he says no more, bullet dodged.

* * *

The Mets' resurgence begins when their one face-saving win at Yankee Stadium is followed by their sweep of Toronto, and continues with a series against the Red Sox at Shea Stadium beginning on June 11, in which they win two of three. Al Leiter follows his gem at Yankee Stadium with another ace-like performance in the first victory over Boston. Combined, the lefty's outings against the Yanks and the Sox have lowered his ERA by almost an entire run. "The tides turn," Leiter says, "and right now, I feel like they're turning back in my favor." Benny Agbayani goes deep in both wins, a welcome sight after his batting practice eye injury. Fans have taken such a shine to the Hawaiian that during his every at bat the Shea faithful sing along to Elton John's "Benny and the Jets" (cannibalized into "Benny and the Mets" by most crooners).

The Mets begin their first proper road trip since the Subway Series with three games in Cincinnati beginning on June 14, where they again win two of three while clubbing six homers in one game, a new franchise record. While in Cincinnati, Valentine receives word that his suspension appeal has been denied and he must serve his two-game ban immediately. He takes in the remainder of the series from the stands of Cinergy Field (the new corporate name of the Reds' longtime home, Riverfront Stadium). Forbidden to wear his uniform, Valentine opts for an odd checkered suit that reminds Mike Piazza of old Philadelphia Athletics skipper Connie Mack. The suspended manager sits with Steve Phillips, who is in Cincinnati to prevent further Valentine mischief, with assistant general manager Omar Minaya nearby for backup.

The Mets then travel to St. Louis on June 17 for a four-game set against the Cardinals. Busch Stadium fills to capacity every night as fans bask in the afterglow of Mark McGwire's 1998 home run race with Sammy Sosa, but on the field, an injury-ravaged pitching staff and underperforming lineup has put the Cardinals at the bottom of the standings. McGwire himself sounds exhausted by all the attention and weary of the losing. "I'd like to at least somewhere in the last few years of my career be on a winner," he says on the eve of the Mets series, an eye cast back toward the more successful Oakland teams of his youth. "At least get the taste of it again. It's been quite a few years." New York wins three of four in St. Louis, taking the finale through the unlikely assistance of Rey Ordóñez, who goes 3-for-4 at the plate and, with an assist from an inattentive Cardinal defense, scores twice on infield singles.

If he is still far from an offensive threat, Ordóñez has at least transcended "automatic out" status. During the Mets' disastrous eight-game losing streak, he dyed his hair an eye-catching bright orange as a luck-changing gesture. The ensuing hot streak has raised his batting average to an astonishing (for him) .294. He attributes his offensive surge to feeling better about his job security ("I'm more relaxed now, I'm playing every day.") and his new do ("Maybe the hair changed my mind."). In fan balloting for the midsummer classic, Ordóñez trails only Barry Larkin of the Reds, the National League's All-Star shortstop in perpetuity. When the Mets return to Shea, Ordóñez is greeted with messages on the auxiliary scoreboards urging fans to "VOTE FOR REY." Nonetheless, it will take more than a few good weeks to erase Ordóñez's reputation for weak hitting. When Buster Olney of the *Times* wants to demonstrate how badly the Yankees' offense has sputtered during a recent slump, he notes that six of their everyday starters own batting averages lower than Ordóñez's, a statistical fact that remains indictment enough for any hitter.

If there is any damper to the Mets' Midwest road trip, it comes from the question of what is to be done with Jason Isringhausen. Since his promotion from the minors, Izzy has struggled to pitch well and for the length expected of a starter. In his outing in St. Louis on June 19, he coughs up six runs, is knocked out of the box before the end of the third, and confesses afterward that his throwing arm "feels like a noodle," an ominous sign considering he tossed only seventy-five pitches.

With his strikeout stuff and lack of stamina, Isringhausen should be a prime candidate to convert to relief work. For most of the season, the Mets insist they are dead set against the idea. "You wouldn't use an Indy car as a taxi in New York City," is Bobby Valentine's chosen metaphor. The front office's thinking on the matter evolves, however, with the ugly start against the Cardinals the tipping point for their reversal. After his ugly outing in St. Louis, Isringhausen is told he must return to triple-A to begin the bullpen transition. Upon arriving in Norfolk, he dyes his hair blond, reasoning that if it could work for Rey Ordóñez's bat, then it could be a panacea for any lost cause.

* * *

The Mets return to Shea on June 22 for a brief homestand and execute a quick three-game sweep of the Marlins. The only drama of the series occurs late in the second game, when Mike Piazza is hit in the back of the head by a batter's backswing and suffers a mild concussion. With a twenty-four-game hitting streak on the line (a tie for a franchise record), he toughs it out for one more at bat but does no better than a weak groundout. "I think I swung at one of the balls I saw," he tells the *Daily News*.

The games against Florida are weak undercards to the heavyweight bouts that loom ahead. The Mets will play two series against the Braves in quick succession and will begin the first set in Atlanta on June 25, only three games behind the Braves. When pressed, players insist that fretting over divisional standings in June is an exercise in madness, but their actions speak louder. Throughout the last game in the Marlins series, Mets players run in and out of the Shea clubhouse to transmit updates on the game in Atlanta.

The Braves have held a stranglehold on the division for so long that attempting to topple them seems like challenging a mountain to a fistfight. Bobby Valentine speaks of them in almost supernatural terms, saying on the eve of the Atlanta series, "They're always there. They'll always be there."

For those who dare to dream, however, this is the first time in years that the Braves appear vulnerable, because Atlanta's pitching staff has been dealt a blow by a sudden sea change in strike-calling practices. Co-aces Greg Maddux and Tom Glavine dominated opposing batters for years by dancing on the edges of the strike zone and finding a way to get calls in their favor. This changes when prior to the 1999 season, MLB instructs umpires to employ a narrower interpretation of the strike zone. This causes strife for all pitchers, but the Braves feel as if the edict was specifically designed to knock them down a peg. Atlanta pitching coach Leo Mazzone contends, "It affects the true artists of the game, the guys that live on the edge of the plate." When the Mets visit Atlanta for the first time, both Maddux and Glavine own ERAs above four, and each pitcher is averaging fourteen baserunners per nine innings, astonishing marks for men who were virtually unhittable for years. Maddux's personal catcher, Eddie Pérez, confesses to Tom Verducci of *Sports Illustrated* that he's baffled by how much Maddux is missing with his pitches these days. John Harper of the *Daily News* believes the Mets can overtake the Braves because "hitters no longer need to genuflect before stepping into the batter's box against Greg Maddux or Tom Glavine."

The Mets take Harper's message to heart and display an unwise level of cockiness when they club the Braves in the series opener. Though Mike Piazza sits this one out as he recovers from his concussion, the Mets score early and often and win 10–2. "Times are changing," one *Post* writer dares scribble after the Mets' first win in Atlanta in almost two years.

In the long run, though, the win may serve no purpose but to awaken a sleeping giant, as the Braves take umbrage at the Mets' overconfidence. Rickey Henderson steals a base when the Mets enjoy a five-run lead, and rather than apologize for this unwritten law transgression, Bobby Valentine gives his outfielder full license by saying, "Rickey's been in that situation as much as anyone."

The Mets' mounting sense of hubris is displayed further in the second game, as this is the day they choose for Octavio Dotel's big league debut. The jewel of their farm system, Dotel is a wiry, baby-faced twenty-five-year-old who appears taller than his reported height of six feet when standing on the mound, an optical illusion caused by a devastating fastball that has decimated triple-A batters all season. As with the conversion of Jason Isringhausen to relief duty, the Mets were adamant about not rushing Dotel to the major leagues before executing an abrupt about-face. The team could have scheduled Dotel's coming out during their last series against a much softer Florida lineup, yet penciled in his first major league start for Atlanta, against the dynastic team of the 1990s.

A walking jitter on the mound, Dotel puts the Mets in an early hole with a pair of first inning walks that set up a three-run homer, then cedes three more runs in the fifth. Bobby Valentine admits later that Dotel "was a two-pitch pitcher, and he has to throw more than two pitches here." He does not explain why a "two-pitch pitcher" was allowed to start in such an important series, however. Dotel's opposite number, Tom Glavine, paints the corners and keeps Mets batters off balance all night as the Braves sail to a 7–2 win. With the home team up by five runs in the bottom of the seventh, Chipper Jones steals a base, a clear response to Rickey Henderson's gratuitous swipe the night before.

In the series finale, Greg Maddux shows little sign of the struggles he's experienced this season as he dominates the Mets batters for eight innings, allowing only two hits over that stretch. Masato Yoshii does his best to match Maddux by keeping the Braves mostly quiet for seven innings, but Atlanta scratches out a run in the third, which proves one run too many.

When the top of the ninth arrives, the Braves turn to John Rocker, who took over the closer's role after the Braves' former fireman, Kerry Ligtenberg, went down with Tommy John surgery. An excitable lefty with a bodybuilder's physique and a guttural rebel yell for every strikeout, Rocker bursts from the bullpen in a full sprint before shutting down the Mets. The visitors manage to get the tying run to second base against Rocker with two out and Mike Piazza striding to the plate, but the Braves issue an intentional walk to face Robin Ventura instead. Despite owning an excellent average against southpaws, Ventura looks helpless against Rocker, striking out on a nasty breaking ball. The Braves win 1–0 and take the series. The proceedings are complete in two hours and six minutes.

After exploding for ten runs in the first contest at Turner Field, the Mets scratch out only two runs in the last two games, and do next to nothing against the two Braves starters who were supposed to be ruined by baseball's new strike zone. And yet, the team does not sound cowed at all as they leave Atlanta. Rickey Henderson has the audacity to say,

"From what I see, we have the better club . . . The one thing I've always said about the Atlanta Braves is they're a lucky club."

The Braves do not reciprocate. The team that has taken two out of three, and has taken a division title nearly every year of the decade, need not sully itself with trash talk. Bobby Cox and his charges can afford to be gracious to their supposed competition. For now.

* * *

After the pennant-race pulse of Atlanta, the Mets win three of four in Miami, where muggy conditions and the Marlins' miserable play keep attendance near eleven thousand paying customers each night. Once again, Florida serves as a poor amuse-bouche for the feast that follows: three more games against the Braves at Shea beginning on July 2, with the Mets once again only three games back in the division. The two teams will not face off again until late September, so this marks the last chance for the Mets to inflict damage on the division leaders until then. A sellout crowd arrives in Flushing for the series opener hoping to witness the Mets shave the Braves' divisional lead a little thinner. They are treated instead to a bloodbath.

Greg Maddux continues his mastery of Mets batters, further quelling the idea that 1999 is his Waterloo. Masato Yoshii, who nearly matched the Braves' ace pitch-for-pitch last week, is bludgeoned for eight runs in only three innings. They annihilate every man who follows him as well, scoring twice in the fourth inning and adding one run apiece in the fifth and sixth.

In the top of the ninth inning, an injury is added to these insults. After taking the mound to get some work in, John Franco feels a pop in his middle finger and is forced to leave the game. In the long term, Franco's injury will compromise the Mets' bullpen. In the short term, it leaves Bobby Valentine with little choice but to ask Matt Franco—his go-to lefty bat off the bench, who has two minor league innings on the mound to his credit—to finish this mess. The fans cheer Matt Franco with all their might, but his arrow-straight 84 mph "fastball" requires more than cheers to retire batters. After surrendering a long three-run homer and a triple, he manages to record a strikeout for the final out of the inning, though the batter's swing at a pitch in the dirt comes across as a desperate ploy to end this abomination. "It was fun," Matt Franco tells reporters later, though he hastens to add, "The 16–0 loss wasn't worth it." The pummeling marks the worst shutout loss in team history and the Braves' most one-sided victory since moving to Atlanta.

"There was talk from the Mets that this series with Atlanta would be a barometer," William C. Rhoden writes in the *Times*, "a measuring stick for how far the team had come in the last month. If the game was a stick, Atlanta used it to thrash the Mets back to reality last night."

Harsh reality prevails again on the sweltering afternoon of July 3 as the Mets fail to score against the Braves for their third straight meeting. Al Leiter matches zeroes with Atlanta's young righty Kevin Millwood until the fifth, when he permits a two-out double to Chipper Jones, bringing slugger Brian Jordan to the plate. Last season, a friendly dinner with Bobby Valentine and Steve Phillips led Jordan to believe the Mets would pursue him once he became a free agent at year's end. When no offer came, he signed with Atlanta instead and swore, with the furor of a jilted lover, that he'd make the Mets pay for toying with his emotions.

Leiter gives Jordan his first real chance for revenge by serving him what the hitter later characterizes as "the straightest fastball I've ever seen Leiter throw." Jordan deposits it in the left-field picnic area for a two-run homer. Staked to a 3–0 lead, the Braves again call on John Rocker in the ninth to finish things off, and though he puts runners on the corners with nobody out, the southpaw strands both and ends the game with an impressive three-pitch strikeout of Mike Piazza. It is New York's thirteenth loss to Atlanta in its previous seventeen meetings. Bill Madden writes, "It is as if the Braves have come to treat the Mets like a common housefly that periodically comes around to pester and is then routinely dispatched to the floor with one flail of the fly swatter."

The July 4 series finale marks the Mets' last meeting with the Braves until faraway September. With temperatures reaching ninety-six degrees (the hottest Fourth of July in New York since 1966), the home team generates some heat against John Smoltz, turning an early two-run deficit into a two-run lead. Then Orel Hershiser begins to melt, giving back the advantage as Atlanta takes a 6–4 lead in the third inning. Smoltz stifles the home team until the bottom of the seventh, when he surrenders a cathartic three-run go-ahead home run to Edgardo Alfonzo. Armando Benítez finishes the game off in style by striking out the heart of the Braves' lineup in order.

The Mets are grateful for the win and Benítez's ability to preserve it, because an MRI on John Franco's pitching hand reveals a tear in his left middle finger. All year, there has been a push from fans for Armando Benítez to take over the closer's role, but Bobby Valentine was reluctant to push aside a veteran who held a great deal of sway in his clubhouse. Now injury has intervened to make the move that Valentine wouldn't. The Mets have worked Benítez hard this season as setup man. They will need to work him even harder.

"It was a test if there's ever been a test," Bobby Valentine says after the thrilling win. The main reason it was a test, however, is because the Mets lost the first two games in such ugly fashion, on the heels of losing two of three in Atlanta a week earlier. The team's talk that they are every bit as talented and capable as the Braves remains just that—talk. They will not have a chance to prove otherwise until September.

* * *

The second, dizzying Braves series is followed by a hangover of a four-game set against the Expos beginning July 5. New York is in the midst of a brutal heat wave, with temperatures pushing past one hundred degrees during the day and not ebbing much below that before the evening's first pitch. Despite the broiling heat, most players are forced to conduct their pregame workouts on the field because Shea's clubhouse air conditioning is malfunctioning. In this Dantean atmosphere, the Mets battle Montréal to a disappointing split before welcoming the Yankees to Shea for the second leg of the Subway Series.

The Yankees are no more jazzed to play in Queens in July than they were to face the Mets in the Bronx at the beginning of June. Asked about his plans for the impending All-Star break, Paul O'Neill reports he will visit his father, who is recovering from heart surgery. "But first we have to get through the World Series this weekend," he says, his tone drenched in sarcasm. George Steinbrenner's attitude is similarly dismissive. "We'll help them get a few sellouts this weekend, just like they did for us," he tells reporters. "The fans still seem to be into it, so it can't be all bad. But I think it's still too much." Even Derek Jeter, diplomatic to a fault under normal circumstances, admits, "I enjoy playing the Mets, but it does get a little old. I think three games was perfect."

The first game at Shea will feature a rematch of the finale at Yankee Stadium: Al Leiter versus Roger Clemens. Both Leiter and the Mets have cruised since that matchup, with the team winning twenty-one of their last thirty-one games and the pitcher putting up a 2.90 ERA over that span. Clemens has only suffered one loss since that game against the Mets, but he is nonetheless judged harshly by Yankees fans and the media who serve them. This is of a piece with the perception of the Yankees themselves, who have performed well this year yet are widely regarded as lacking a certain ineffable something that propelled them to historic greatness in 1998. Joel Sherman of the *Post* captures the prevailing mood when he insists the Yankees should be "judged against the incredible high standard they have set for themselves during the better part of this decade . . . We are not looking for perfection, we are looking for the Yankees." Sherman and fans will presumably know what "the Yankees" are when they see them, and thus far in 1999 they feel they haven't seen them.

The strangest criticism of the Yankees might be that they are too focused on the postseason. The team that has always proclaimed nothing is more important than winning a championship is now blasted for focusing exclusively on that goal. William C. Rhoden of the *Times* makes an unfavorable comparison to the juggernaut of 1998 by saying this year's Yanks are "simply marking time until the playoffs," and points to a division lead of "only" four games as evidence.

For those who buy Rhoden's line (and many in the Yankee fan base do), Clemens is their scapegoat. He is far from the first person to catch on with the Yankees in the hope of winning an elusive championship, but the expectation was that Clemens would lead the way to that championship. Instead, he comes into the Mets series with a 4.50 ERA and is arguably the third best pitcher on the team behind Orlando Hernández and David Cone. (A disappointing season from Andy Pettitte protects Clemens from the fourth spot.) Buster Olney of the *Times* faults Clemens for pitching his way into trouble, as opposed to two-time champ David Cone, renowned for his ability to gut his way out of jams. That Cone would, by this definition, *also* have pitched his way into trouble doesn't occur to either Olney or any of Clemens's many detractors and underscores the unfairness of some of these criticisms. Clemens's failure to be the staff ace is interpreted as a willingness to let the team carry him, rather than the other way around. "It seems clear that after years of trying to bring lesser teams to the big show," opines one writer, "he was counting on the Yankees to bring him."

The scrutiny on Clemens intensifies as the Subway Series nears because Shea Stadium has never been kind to him. He made two starts there during the 1986 World Series, both poor for different reasons. In game two, he was knocked around and failed to make it through the fifth inning. In game six, he threw a gem but mysteriously left after seven frames with his team only six outs away from a long-awaited championship. Whether he begged out or was forcibly removed by his manager remains a bone of contention, but in any event the decision would factor into the Mets' unlikely comeback in that game, and that series. While with Toronto, he also made his worst start of an otherwise spectacular 1997 season in an interleague game at Shea. It's highly likely this result stemmed from all the pick-off throws the Mets fired his way when he reached base during that contest ("Once he was out there, we figured he might as well stay out there," manager Bobby Valentine explained in his postgame remarks.) But there were plenty of people who said it was not the pick-off throws, but the mysterious power Shea held over Clemens's psyche that was to blame.

As the first game of the Shea portion of the Subway Series unfolds on July 9, the accumulated weight of this pressure is visible on Clemens's face in every television close-up. MSG Network's play-by-play announcers wonder aloud several times about when they will see "the real Roger Clemens." The pitcher's demeanor suggests he is wondering the same thing, as do his curious decisions during the game. In the bottom of the second, Rey Ordóñez steps up to the plate with two outs, a runner on second, and Al Leiter on deck. Though Leiter is a laughably terrible hitter, even for a pitcher, Clemens chooses to challenge the shortstop. Ordóñez lines Clemens's first-pitch fastball up the middle to bring home the first Mets run. Then in the bottom of the third, moments after the Yankees tie the score, Clemens hangs a splitter right down the middle of the plate to John Olerud, who cranks it off the big scoreboard in right field to put the Mets back in front.

The Yankees rebound to tie the game again in the sixth, but once more Clemens wastes no time in giving the lead right back to the Mets. In the bottom of that inning, Edgardo Alfonzo bloops a leadoff single to shallow right, bringing Olerud to the plate. With the first baseman's earlier moonshot still in mind, Clemens pitches carefully and issues a walk. Unfortunately for The Rocket, this decision brings up Mike Piazza, who whips a diving slider into the left-field bleachers for a home run, giving the Mets a three-run lead. A frustrated Clemens grates against the noise and his own mistakes, marching around the mound like a caged animal before delivering brushback pitches to the next two batters. The one he fires at Roger Cedeño is particularly eye-catching, as the ball sails above the batter's helmet.

Energized by Piazza's home run, Al Leiter cruises through the seventh and eighth innings to complete his longest outing of the year. In the ninth, Armando Benítez invokes his predecessor in the closer's role by allowing a leadoff double and a walk to bring the tying run to the plate, but he fans pinch hitter Chili Davis on a 98 mph fastball to end the ballgame.

"I couldn't sit," Bobby Valentine confesses to reporters after the game. "I was walking along the dugout, telling guys: 'This is exciting. This is exciting.'" Everyone agrees this is the most satisfying win of the Mets' season, but less than twenty-four hours later, it will be eclipsed by one of the wildest games in the history of Shea Stadium.

The tone of the game on the afternoon of July 10 is set immediately when Rick Reed cedes a two-run homer to Paul O'Neill in the opening inning. The Mets rebound to score two runs in both the second and fourth innings against Yankee lefty Andy Pettitte, who is enduring such an awful season that he is widely rumored to be trade bait for a Yankee team with a few holes to fill. The visitors storm back to tie the game on back-to-back homers to start the top of the fifth, then retake the lead via long balls from Paul O'Neill in the sixth and Chuck Knoblauch in the seventh. The Mets retaliate in the bottom of the seventh when Mike Piazza destroys a fastball from reliever Ramiro Mendoza, sending it over the visiting bullpen, even over the tented picnic area beyond the bullpen, for a mind-boggling distance of 482 feet and a go-ahead three-run homer.

Impressive though the shot is, no lead is safe in this game. In the top of the eighth, Dennis Cook allows Jorge Posada's second home run of the game, a two-run shot that returns the lead to the opposition. This translates to a ninth-inning appearance by Yankee closer Mariano Rivera, who put the Mets to bed with little trouble in both their losses in the Bronx. This outing proceeds with more difficulty for Rivera, as he issues a walk to Rickey Henderson and watches center fielder Bernie Williams misplay a fly ball from Edgardo Alfonzo, putting the tying and winning runs in scoring position with one out. He shrugs off the miscue by inducing a sharp grounder to first base from John Olerud that freezes both runners, bringing the Yankees one out from victory.

Mike Piazza is due up next, but with first base open the catcher is walked intentionally to bring up pinch hitter Matt Franco. Before Franco can blink, a called strike and a swing and a miss put him in an 0–2 hole. Rivera's third pitch comes in at Franco's knees, a height that could certainly earn a strike call. The home plate umpire takes a small eternity to make his call before declaring it a hair too low, prompting loud protests from the visitors' dugout. "My heart stopped for half a breath," Franco admits later.

Given a stay of execution, Franco laces Rivera's next pitch into right field. Henderson scores easily, with Alfonzo trailing behind him. Paul O'Neill fields the ball and fires a bullet to home plate, but Alfonzo beats his throw to plate the winning run. The Mets storm from the dugout in jubilation as Alfonzo leaps to his feet in triumph. Franco is mobbed at first base. Police mobilize on the warning track to prevent frenzied fans from running onto the field and tearing it apart. The Mets clinch their first-ever series win over the Yankees with an insane, improbable 9–8 victory.

If the Mets are beside themselves with joy, the mood in the Yankees clubhouse is uneasy, to say the least. The fact that they've dropped the first two games of this set dovetails with the perception that the 1999 team is a pale imitation of last year's. A *Daily News* assessment of the Yankees opens with, "They are flawed. They are human," as if humanity itself were a failing. The papers are filled with headlines like "YANKS COLLAPSE WHEN IT COUNTS," as if they were a luckless team like the Cubs or Red Sox, and not winners of three of the last four World Series. In a fit of misdirected rage, George Steinbrenner executes an ambush roster move, sending one reliever to the minors in exchange for another without informing Joe Torre first, which serves no purpose but to remind his team that he can and will make any personnel moves he damn well pleases.

The next afternoon, delirious Mets fans bring brooms to Shea, hoping to see their team sweep the Yankees. More than two hundred NYPD officers are called to duty—four times the usual number for a game—to handle the largest Shea crowd in twenty-seven years, filled with partisans of both teams in rare moods. The Yankees turn to Japanese pitcher Hideki Irabu—a disappointing post-Hideo Nomo signing, publicly humiliated when George Steinbrenner labeled him "a fat pussy toad" in the press—to reverse their fortunes. Amazingly, Irabu proves up to the task, overcoming some early hiccups to throw seven innings and fan eight batters in a Yankee win.

The Mets receive some criticism for overplaying these victories—"All the Mets proved this weekend is that they are capable of playing up to their payroll," sneers Wallace Matthews in the *Post*—and for seeming to treat the Subway Series finale as a nice-to-have rather than a must-win. "I don't think we came out with any lack of intensity today," Mike Piazza responds after the loss. "'But I think that any game would be anticlimactic compared to yesterday." The Mets' play in the Subway Series did impress one important observer, however. When the series opened,

George Steinbrenner remained a vocal opponent of six games between the Mets and Yankees. Now he says, "The Mets series is great for the fans of New York. I'll admit that. They've sold me on the greatness of the series." After the All-Star break, the Mets will host the Cubs to sellout weekend crowds while the Yankees will sweep a powerful Cleveland Indians squad before a packed stadium, the two teams combining to host over 162,000 fans in the span of one weekend. The sight of so many occupied seats sends The Boss into a rapture, choirs of angels singing in voices that sound much like cash registers. "Where else in the whole world could two teams draw capacity on the same day when they're only four miles apart?" he swoons. (The actual distance is closer to eight miles, but the attendance numbers are impressive nonetheless.)

That Steinbrenner would say anything complimentary of the Mets, however faint, is news in and of itself. So is the fact that he dares to contemplate, out loud, the possibility of a real Subway Series in October. "Wouldn't that be something?" he moons. With the Mets playing blazing-hot baseball since their trip to Yankee Stadium, he is not the only one dreaming.

* * *

The All-Star rosters are announced during the stifling series against the Expos, and the Mets are stunned to find out Mike Piazza is their only player elected by fan ballot. Despite great offensive years from Robin Ventura, John Olerud, and Edgardo Alfonzo, no one in this trio finishes higher than fifth in the voting for their respective positions. Rey Ordóñez, subject of an aggressive get-out-the-vote campaign by his team, is ultimately edged out by Barry Larkin.

Upon hearing the news, Bobby Valentine holds out hope that some deserving Mets will receive spots on the All-Star bench, but Bruce Bochy, skipper of the reigning National League champion Padres, fails to pick a single Met as a reserve. Steve Phillips describes himself as "surprised and disappointed" over the Bochy snub, while Bobby Valentine insists, "We'll throw our non-All-Star team out there and hope we can thrill our fans."

The last All-Star Game of the millennium is held at Fenway Park and is preceded by a ceremony honoring the All-Century Team, gathering together the greatest living players in the game. Roger Clemens, late of the Red Sox and one of the few active players honored with a spot on its roster, is loudly booed by a Boston crowd that resents his new uniform.

The celebration concludes with an emotional appearance from Red Sox legend Ted Williams, who looks distant and frail as he is driven toward the pitcher's mound on a golf cart. His gait is halting when he rises from his seat to throw the ceremonial first pitch to another Boston great, Carlton Fisk. And yet, he manages to hurl the ball on the fly to Fisk's awaiting glove.

When Ted Williams takes the field, all players are drawn toward him. They could not look more different, these modern players with their bulging biceps and body armor, gathering near The Splendid Splinter. They approach Williams with the cast of zealots gathering to catch a glimpse of a fragile, holy relic.

* * *

While MLB's attention is centered on Boston, most of its umpires are focused on Philadelphia, where they are gathered for a union meeting at which they will discuss a season's worth of accumulated slights. They believe their livelihood is being threatened by Bud Selig, who has made direct control of the umpires a goal of his administration.

Through the modern baseball era, Major League Baseball's umpires had been hired and regulated by league presidents, a system that led to the leagues evolving different interpretations of the strike zone. The advent of interleague play has made the idea of two separate but equal teams of umpires with different concepts of what constitutes a strike an anachronism, and Selig aims to eliminate it. He will do so through Sandy Alderson, longtime Oakland general manager who left the Athletics to take an executive vice president position in the commissioner's office.

On February 19, Alderson's office issues a memo dictating that the upper reaches of the strike zone shall be raised to two inches above the top of the uniform pants. Baseball's official rule book shows the upper limit of the strike zone is even higher, but this minor memo is received with major uproar by the men charged with enforcing it. The umpires' response to Alderson's memo boils down to, *Make us*. Bruce Froemming, the National League's senior umpire, declares, "It's a total lack of respect to change something against the rule book definition and not sit down with a group of umpires and say, 'this is what we'd like to do; how do you feel about it?'"

As a former Marine who served in Vietnam, Alderson takes a dim view of insubordination. In April, he asks team officials to chart pitches and file reports with the commissioner on strike zone consistency. This edict is issued only a month after umpires' egos were bruised by a players association rating of arbiters that was leaked to the press. The timing convinces the umpires that Alderson intends to humiliate them before usurping their authority.

When the regular season begins, most umpires don't follow Alderson's orders exactly, but rather shrink their strike zones all around. With pitchers all but forced to serve the ball right over the plate, offense booms even more than it did in 1998. By June, batters have connected on a staggering forty-eight grand slams. The miniscule strike zones and bloated ERAs lead to arguments on the field between pitchers and umpires, further fueling the latter's us-vs.-them mentality. The last straw comes on June 26 when umpire Tom Hallion bumps Rockies catcher Jeff Reed during a confrontation on the mound. Hallion receives a three-game suspension, the first ever given to an umpire in MLB's history. To everyone's shock, that suspension is handed down by National League President Leonard Coleman. The league offices once offered safe haven to their umpires. That protection has disappeared.

During the contentious union meeting on July 14, the umpires first vote to strike, even though their current contract prohibits such job actions. They back down from this threat after more deliberation, but though the tactic they eventually decide on is permissible under their contract, it is infinitely more baffling.

The umps' plan is launched at the behest of Richie Phillips, head of the Major League Umpires Association for over two decades. Since 1979, Phillips has spearheaded three umpires' strikes that successfully raised salaries and won important benefits. The umpires see his combative style as the main reason for the power and respect afforded to their union. Throughout the 1999 season, every time the umpires receive another perceived threat, Phillips is front and center in the press, blasting MLB in loud and often hyperbolic fashion. When Phillips calls his charges to meet in Philadelphia, he is 100 percent sure of two things: that his umpires will follow him to the ends of the earth, and that he can't lose.

Phillips emerges from the meeting with the announcement that rather than strike, fifty-seven of the league's sixty-six umpires will submit their resignations, effective September 1. At that point, the union would be dissolved and a new umpires association would form to begin negotiations anew. This would not only thrust inexperienced replacement umpires into duty during the last month of the regular season, and possibly the playoffs as well, but also put the league on the hook for as much as $15 million in severance pay. "Baseball is in chaos," Phillips declares, almost proudly, when revealing the resignation plan. His opening offer would be the nuclear option.

Many in the game are afraid the umps might make good on their threat, but Sandy Alderson is not among them. "I heard he might make a move like this in the near future," Alderson says coolly while revealing he's been working for two months to line up replacement umps.

The union chief has failed to consider that Selig wants to remake umpiring in his own graven image. There could be no better way to expedite this goal than to replace the umpires wholesale. At the cost of $15 million worth of severance pay, it might even be, as Alderson notes in a cruel bit of accounting, "the cheapest option." Richie Phillips believes he is defying management. In truth, he's giving them exactly what they want.

* * *

The Mets begin the second half of their season on July 15 with an eight-game road trip. Each stop welcomes them with open arms. First, three games at domed Tropicana Field against the struggling sophomore edition of the Tampa Bay Devil Rays, who host a Turn Back the Clock Night featuring many old-time Mets (including a national anthem sung by Tug McGraw and Ron Swoboda). With the presence of Mets legends drawing ex-New Yorkers to the gate, the Devil Rays boast their biggest crowds since opening day. The Mets welcome the hospitality and win two of three inside the dome.

They find themselves even more welcomed in Baltimore, where they travel for a three-game set beginning on July 18. Like the Mets, the Orioles spent a boatload of cash in the off-season. Unlike the Mets, the Orioles have nothing to show for it. The underperforming of slugger Albert Belle, the Steinbrennerian meddling of owner Peter Angelos, and the departure of renowned general manager Pat Gillick have combined to send Baltimore to the bottom of the standings. Now the Mets come to town to pour salt on their wounds, flaunting a powerful bullpen headed by Armando Benítez, a pitcher the Orioles gave up on, and Robin Ventura, the Gold Glove third baseman they might have signed if they hadn't demanded he change his position. Many Mets fans take the trip down I-95 to see what all the Camden Yards fuss is about, and the Orioles' own fans find themselves outnumbered and outshouted. The visitors once again win two of three games, then sweep a brief two-game set in Montréal.

When the Mets return to Shea Stadium and go on another hot tear that pulls them within a half game of first place in the National League East, they might well expect the press to focus on their winning ways. Instead, all the talk centers around a series of ill-conceived promotions that make them feel like visitors at their own ballpark.

The Mets' homecoming on July 23 is Merengue Night at Shea Stadium, conveniently timed to coincide with Sammy Sosa's and the Chicago Cubs' sole trip to Queens this season. Through his chase of the single-season home run record in 1998, Sosa brought a long-delayed recognition of the accomplishments of Latino players in general and Dominican *peloteros* in particular. His return to New York is a three-day celebration for the city's Dominican expatriates, who flock to Flushing to laud their hero. It is less celebratory for the Mets themselves, who feel they've been robbed of home-field advantage.

On Merengue Night, the Mets rally from behind and come out on top in the box score, but it's hard to shake the feeling that Sammy Sosa is the night's real winner. Before the game, he is feted with a pregame ceremony, an unusual honor for a visiting player who is not about to retire. When Sosa connects for a long three-run homer against Masato Yoshii in the first inning, the stands roar as loudly as if the home team had pulled off the feat. With horns, whistles, and cowbells ringing from the first pitch to the last, Shea feels more like the site of a block party than a ballgame. During the postgame merengue concert, Sosa even joins the band onstage as revelers chant his name. In this fiesta atmosphere the Mets are, at best, an afterthought.

After the game, the visiting hero refers to the evening as "Sammy Sosa Night," an understandable mistake given the hero's welcome that continued well after the game's final out. "The hosts did everything but throw rose petals at Sosa to open the series," writes Lisa Olson in the *Daily News*, "while ignoring its own players." The headline in the *New York Times* proclaims, "Mets Win Road Game at Shea."

In his postgame press conference, Bobby Valentine does nothing to hide his anger. "It was a nice night for the fans," Valentine gripes. "But I wish they all were Mets fans. It's a damn shame this team never gets any appreciation, even in our own ballpark." Embarrassed by Valentine's comments, the Mets executives instruct the manager to put a lid on it. Unnamed team officials remind the press that the team said nothing about Valentine's costumed antics back in June and had hoped he would reciprocate when they did something widely seen as a mistake, though none will concede, even anonymously, that the Sosa lovefest was a mistake.

Playing like a team desperate to prove itself, the Mets complete a satisfying sweep of Sosa and the Cubs, then proceed to win two of three from the Pittsburgh Pirates. The one game they lose comes when rookie hurler Kris Benson ties the Mets in knots on July 27, but less credit is given to Benson than to the event the Mets are forced to endure this evening: Turn Ahead the Clock Night.

The idea began innocently enough as a once-off promotion at Seattle's Kingdome in 1998, during which the Mariners and Royals envisioned what the game would look like in the year 2027. (Mariners superstar Ken Griffey Jr., who helped design uniforms for the event, imagined it would involve lots of metallic spray paint and backward caps.) The commissioner's office saw this fun romp and converted it into mandatory corporate synergy. Teaming up with Century 21, MLB enforces Turn Ahead the Clock Night in the summer of 1999 by asking teams to wear "futuristic uniforms." Some, like the Yankees and Cubs, flat out refuse. Others rework their kits with enlarged logos or reimagined color schemes.

As for the Mets, their Turn Ahead the Clock Night celebration comes from another planet. Literally. For one night only, they are known as "the Mercury Mets" and take the field in silver and black duds burned forever after into the nightmares of those forced to view them. Lisa Olson of the *Daily News* describes the scene:

> Baseball wanted us to imagine we were watching a game in the year 2021, and so it outfitted the players in short-sleeved gray-and-black uniforms made of 100% polyester, just in case a cure for sweat still hasn't been discovered in the new millennium. On the front of the jersey was the chemical symbol for mercury, or maybe it meant that the Artist Formerly Known as Prince was the team's new owner . . .
>
> A voice boomed over the loudspeakers, sounding like what we presume was supposed to be a little green Martian. "Greetings, earthlings. Welcome to Shea Station 4C. Blastoff time is 7:40." It also encouraged earthlings to visit the "replenishing depots," which in another life-

time were called concession stands. Over in the opposite dugout, [Pirates manager] Gene Lamont rolled his eyes. Maybe he was miffed that the Mets were the only team from another planet; his Pirates were still from Pittsburgh, not Pluto, and their uniforms weren't nearly as Star Wars cool.

To complete the outer space motif, Mets players are shown on Shea's Diamond Vision video board with "alien" features like green skin and antennae. While at bat, Rickey Henderson spots his face altered to include a third eye and must step out of the box, out of both disbelief and humiliation. The Mercury Mets jerseys are auctioned off for charity after the game, so some good resulted from this ill-conceived event, but the fact remains that for the second time on the homestand, the Mets players are made to feel they are a pawn in someone's marketing game. "We should have had a big top," a miffed Orel Hershiser says after the game. "If we can't sell the product the way it is, maybe we should give it a rest."

"It's been a progression of nonrecognition," Valentine tells the *Daily News*. "No matter what we've done, we've gotten no credit for it . . . We have earned what we've gotten, but we haven't gotten our fair due." When asked what he wants, Valentine responds, "Acknowledgment of the truth of the situation, that we were a dog team three years ago, we've continually gotten better and we've been a good team every day of this season.

"That's fact," he insists, "not perception."

* * *

As the July 31 trade deadline approaches, the Mets have been on fire for almost two months, but this has not blinded anyone to the team's most glaring flaw. Their hot streak has come in spite of a starting rotation whose collective ERA sits disturbingly close to five. The Mets' relievers have picked up the slack and then some, but how long they can continue to do this is questionable. Both Turk Wendell and Dennis Cook have been used nigh daily and are showing the strain, as Wendell's control has begun to desert him and Cook has been allowing long balls with disturbing frequency. Even Armando Benítez has struggled of late, blowing a save in Tampa Bay, then walking four consecutive batters in the ninth inning of the Pirates series opener to turn a laugher into a squeaker. These relievers could use some relief.

The Mets have wanted to deal for a "front-line starter" since their 1998 season came to an abrupt end. Throughout the winter, Steve Phillips told fans he was pursuing several leads. When none materialized by spring training, Phillips assured fans the hunt was still on. He has repeated these assurances even as the time to make good on his promise grows shorter with each passing day, and as the same hurdles to acquiring a pitcher remain—namely, a dearth of valuable prospects. He believes he's finally addressed the issue when he completes a trade on July 23—the same day as the ill-conceived "Sammy Sosa Day" at Shea—that sends two minor leaguers to Oakland in exchange for left-handed starter Kenny Rogers. If Phillips is pleased by his efforts, however, few others in New York are.

On paper, Kenny Rogers is a solid pickup, a hard-throwing lefty who has pitched quite well for Oakland in the last season and a half. Off paper, where most baseball games are played, Rogers has a reputation for inconsistency between the lines and volatility outside them. Despite Oakland's status as a surprise contender this season, rumors of Rogers's departure have raged for months. The southpaw known as The Gambler literally punched his ticket out of the East Bay, first by slugging a teammate over a clubhouse card game, then by throttling a bank of bullpen phones in a fit of rage during an interleague game in San Francisco. "Kenny never really wanted to be here," admits A's general manager Billy Beane once the deal is done. "I had hoped the continued improvement of the team would help rope him into the momentum, but that didn't happen."

It isn't shocking that Rogers would leave Oakland. It *is* shocking that Rogers would leave Oakland for New York. The pitcher spent two indifferent seasons with the Yankees that made him an exemplar of the type of player who can't "handle" the Big Apple. After signing a four-year, $20 million contract with the Yankees prior to the 1996 season, Rogers proved middling at best during the regular season and awful after it, getting shelled in all three of his playoff starts. He was shipped to Oakland after the 1997 season, with the Yankees paying half of his remaining salary just to be rid of him.

Rogers is fully aware that his previous stint in New York was a bust and expresses a competitor's need to prove himself, but his efforts to change the narrative leave something to be desired. More than once during his initial press conference as a Met, he refers to his time with the A's in the present tense. When referring to the Mets' second baseman, he struggles to recall the man's name, spitting out "Edgardo Alfonzo" only after a long, awkward silence. He also names the chance to play closer to his home in Tampa as a major reason why the Mets will be a good fit for him.

The acquisition of Kenny Rogers creates a logjam in the starting rotation, at least until the odd man out is identified. Bobby Valentine professes he will employ a six-man rotation in the immediate future and even leaves the door open to using it for the rest of the season "if everyone has good starts." A quick resolution to the question of who will start and who will be pushed to the bullpen (if anyone) becomes less likely when, during his first throwing session as a Met, Rogers reveals he suffered a right hamstring "twinge" in his final start for the A's. The lefty insists Oakland knew nothing about it because he was traded the day after that outing. A fact check reveals Rogers's last start for Oakland came a full three days before the trade went down. This obfuscation has a familiar ring to it. In his first spring training with the Yankees, Rogers kept quiet about a shoulder injury that would nag him for the rest of the year. The silence put him on bad footing with Joe Torre from day one, and he never regained the manager's trust.

Rogers's first start as a Met is pushed back to the last game against Pittsburgh, and he throws six fantastic innings of one-hit, one-run ball. After the sixth inning, however, he feels his balky hamstring tighten up and leaves the game. Rogers believes he can make his next scheduled start, while Valentine considers that outcome "questionable." Steve Phillips declares himself "unconcerned." That would make him the only one.

* * *

With a day and change left before the deadline, and with the Mets still having many glaring needs, Steve Phillips is anxious to complete a deal, any deal. He is so impatient to meet up with his team as they play in Chicago that he refuses to be delayed by trifles such as the three-car accident he pinballs into on his way to LaGuardia Airport. (He escapes the incident unscathed.)

The Mets' arrival in Chicago coincides with a brutal, historic heat wave. A heat index of 114 degrees knocks out local TV transmission twice during their first game at Wrigley Field, as well as some of the traffic lights outside the ballpark. "Just thank God there was no Astroturf," Mike Piazza says later, "or they would have been taking corpses off the field."

The Mets split the first two games in the steamy Friendly Confines, doing their best to block out the scorching heat and the uncertainty of the trade deadline. This is easier said than done for Jason Isringhausen, whose name has come up in every Mets trade rumor. Isringhausen made the transition from starter to reliever in a bid to save his career and bolster his team's bullpen. Since returning to the majors, however, the team has been reluctant to use him to set up Armando Benítez, as that job is shuttled between Turk Wendell and Dennis Cook. The long-man role is already filled by Pat Mahomes, late of Japan's Orix Blue Wave, who's done yeoman's work with many multi-inning outings that have kept his team in games all season. As a result, Izzy has been used almost exclusively in mop-up duty, as in the second game in Chicago, when he is thrust out on the broiling Wrigley Field mound for three innings of thankless work in a blowout loss. Even if he is confined to garbage time, Isringhausen desperately wants to remain with a winner after so many years of pain and injury and pleads with anyone who will listen, "I don't want to leave this team."

His pleas fall on deaf ears. In one of a flurry of deals the Mets complete hours before the July 31 deadline, Isringhausen is sent to Oakland as part of a package for Billy Taylor, the A's sidearming closer, who Steve Phillips envisions as an insurance plan for Armando Benítez. When announcing the deal, Phillips is careful to emphasize experience, saying he "wanted more veterans to complement our team."

The Mets then reinforce their bullpen and outfield by sending a package headed by forgotten center fielder Brian McRae (odd man out in the outfield shuffle, who'd clashed with Bobby Valentine over his lack of playing time) to the Rockies for lefty reliever Chuck McElroy and Darryl Hamilton, whose slick glove work gives him the ability to sub for any member of the team's defensively challenged outfield. Steve Phillips adds another bench bat by sending a minor leaguer to St. Louis for Shawon Dunston, Brooklyn native and one-time superstar shortstop for the Cubs, now a journeyman part-time outfielder. Dunston, who's swapped uniforms six times in the last five seasons, and who was about to buy a house in the St. Louis area, threatens to not report to the Mets at all. Family in East New York, mostly Mets fans, prevail upon him to change his mind.

No blockbusters can be found in Phillips's deadline moves, but a series of solid veteran pickups to serve as reinforcements for the postseason push. This comes with a cost, of course, namely a payroll now inflated beyond the previously unbroken barrier of $70 million. "We're going for it," Phillips says to reporters before the series finale in Chicago. "Now's the time."

* * *

With the trade deadline now in their rearview mirror, the Mets take their final game in Chicago, then execute a tidy sweep in Milwaukee. Along the way, Bobby Valentine backs away from his six-man rotation threat and demotes a starter to the bullpen. The top candidates were thought to be the aging Orel Hershiser or the inconsistent Rick Reed, but Valentine shocks all by picking Masato Yoshii instead. Reed, who'd been torturing himself for weeks with thoughts of a trade or a relief demotion, throws a gem in the Milwaukee opener on August 2, his first decent start in what feels like years. ("Fuckin' finally," he sighs.)

The Mets return to Shea on August 6 for a four-game series against their mirror image, the Dodgers. The off-season spending spree in Los Angeles was even more extravagant than the one in New York, with ace Kevin Brown's contract dwarfing the one bestowed on Mike Piazza. General manager Kevin Malone looked upon his works and declared the Dodgers would face the Yankees in the World Series come October. Then the season began, and the Dodgers barely got through April before conceding defeat. They arrive in Queens fourteen games under .500, about to battle a Mets team with several former Dodgers making big contributions. The sight of Roger Cedeño, who they all but gave up and who is now leading the league in steals, would be the most galling of all were it not for the loss of Mike Piazza.

Former Met Todd Hundley is symbolic of the Dodgers' woes. The catcher owns a respectable sixteen home runs but is batting only .219 and continues to struggle to throw out runners, an after effect of the elbow surgery that knocked him out for most of 1998. Hundley brings many memories with him to New York, good and bad. He set the single-season home run record for catchers in 1996 and was a bright spot on some mediocre Mets teams during that time. He also felt betrayed by their acquisition of Mike Piazza, especially since that acquisition came within hours of assurances from ownership that they would not make the trade. But most of Hundley's animus stems from his ugly clashes with Bobby Valentine, who almost went out of his way to antagonize him publicly. The manager once cryptically told the press that a slumping Hundley needed "to get more sleep," implying he liked to party too much. When the papers filled with rumors that Hundley had a drinking problem, the catcher assumed Valentine was the source, engendering a feud that lasted long after Hundley had left for Los Angeles. Back in spring training, after

Valentine gave an interview during which he uttered some more oblique criticism of Hundley, the catcher responded, "I'm going to try to meet him in a dark alley and talk to him about it."

The Mets' first game against the Dodgers is an important one for reasons that have little to do with Todd Hundley. It marks the fifty-fifth game after the Mets' disastrous eight-game losing streak that ended in early June. Back then, Bobby Valentine claimed his team was good enough to win forty of its next fifty-five games, and if they didn't, he should be fired.

A lot can happen in baseball over fifty-five games. Over that span, the Mariners relocate from the stuffy confines of the Kingdome into brand-new Safeco Field. David Cone pitches a perfect game against the Expos at Yankee Stadium. (The *Daily News*' Mike Lupica insists this event helped "lift our nation's broken heart" following the sudden death of John F. Kennedy Jr., killed in a plane crash days earlier.) In the span of a few hours, Mark McGwire belts his five hundredth career home run and Tony Gwynn collects his three thousandth career hit. Two days later, Wade Boggs finally records his own three thousandth hit. In the spirit of this power-charged season, he reaches the mark with a home run.

One more thing happens over this fifty-five-game span: Bobby Valentine's prediction comes true. In the Mets' first matchup against the Dodgers, a 2–1 win gives them that promised fortieth victory in the last fifty-five games. Thanks to recent stumbles by the Braves, it also gives them a 1.5-game lead in the National League East. The Braves haven't been out of first place so late in a season since 1994. The Mets haven't been in first place so late in a season since 1990.

"I didn't want my situation to get in the way of us being a good team again," Valentine explains now that his prognostication has proved shockingly on the nose. "I didn't want this to turn into something where every week was a referendum on whether or not I was going to get fired. So it was like, let's have a deadline and see what we all can do . . . Now let's see how we do over the next fifty-five." In order to play fifty-five more games, the Mets will need to make it to the postseason, a place Bobby Valentine has never been.

Before these fifty-five games, the Mets thought they were cursed. Now they believe they are charmed. Wins can look like magic to a team starving for them. There is little harm in allowing yourself to believe in magic, as long as you can keep the magic going.

CHAPTER 5
The Middle Finger Team

THE METS HAVE made good on their manager's promise to win forty of fifty-five games, and the glow of this accomplishment is almost enough to blunt the sting of the final games against the Dodgers, who hand their hosts a trio of ugly losses. The team rebounds with a sweep of the hapless Padres beginning on August 10, the only satisfaction accorded to San Diego being the standing ovation for the legendary Tony Gwynn, who recently collected his three thousandth career hit.

In the season's final weeks, the Mets must make three trips out west, full with the knowledge that many a promising Mets season has crashed against the rocks of a Pacific trip. Just last year, an ugly 6–9 record in California was one of many reasons why they failed to make the playoffs. The Mets' first Pacific swing goes swimmingly, however, beginning in San Francisco on August 13. This will be their final visit to the windy, hated facility once known as Candlestick Park (in keeping with the times, the decrepit facility has been rebranded 3Com Park). Bobby Valentine, who played many games at Candlestick as a young Dodger, admits, "The misery of nighttime games here had few redeeming qualities." But it's the home team who is left miserable when the Mets win two of three from the Giants. On August 14, they're stifled by Orel Hershiser, who pitched for San Francisco in 1998 but opted for the Mets the following year, leaving the Giants to feel snubbed. ("Orel Hershiser never really gave us the time of day," Giants GM Brian Sabean sobs to the *San Jose Mercury News*. "He's that type of animal.") The next afternoon, they are even more perturbed to lose to Kenny Rogers, who destroyed a bank of bullpen phones in their ballpark earlier in the summer as a member of the A's. The Giants attempt to deliver a $1,700 bill for damages to Rogers in person, but he contests the charges. ("They tacked things on," he insists.) The Gambler goes the distance to log the first complete game from a Mets pitcher in over a year, and also drives his hosts up the wall by attempting to bunt for a base hit with his team up by six runs. The Giants can do little more than shake their fists as the Mets depart for San Diego, where they take two of three from the overmatched Padres.

The first West Coast test of the late summer met and conquered, the Mets return to New York on August 21 a full game in first place. Their next opponents, the Cardinals, bring with them the spectacle of Mark McGwire, who has just belted his five hundredth career home run and continues to be a box office draw despite his team's struggles. He also continues to field questions about androstenedione, the designer steroid found in his locker by a reporter last season. (Most of the anger that ensued was directed not at the slugger but the scribe for a presumed invasion of privacy.) The questions contain more curiosity than condemnation, but the slugger has tired of answering them all the same. McGwire recently announced he'd stopped taking the steroid because "I got tired of hearing about young kids under age who were probably taking it improperly." He also insists that steps taken by the Olympics and other sports leagues to ban the substance is "hogwash" and that andro is "all natural," a contention that is strictly true in the biological sense yet stretches the definition of "all natural" to its breaking point.

While in New York, McGwire belts one of the most impressive homers ever hit at Shea Stadium, a titanic blast off of Octavio Dotel that not only knocks out a few lightbulbs in the visiting batting order on the scoreboard but is still arcing upward when it does so. McGwire celebrates little else while in New York, however, as the Mets take two of three from St. Louis. When they win the series finale on a walk-off hit from Edgardo Alfonzo, the *Times* views the Mets mobbing Fonzie and proclaims they are "practicing . . . for celebrations they hope to stage in the final six weeks of the regular season." The celebrations continue when the Astros come to town on August 23 and the Mets again win two of three. Houston seems oddly unnerved by the raucous atmosphere at Shea. Slugger Jeff Bagwell, upon seeing the visiting clubhouse filled with reporters, asks, "What is this, 1986 all over again?" In the series finale, Kenny Rogers nearly goes the distance again, despite suffering back spasms that must be dealt with by the application of hasty between-inning massages. The spasms began when he sneezed a bit too hard and felt a twinge between his shoulder blades, but he tried to gut his way through the discomfort, only to leave before the end of the third inning of his last start. The Mets won that game anyway, but this is only the latest example of the lefty valuing his own macho ideals over the good of his team. "Rogers set out to . . . drop the cloak of mystery that has only grown around him during his second stop in New York," writes Selena Roberts in the *Times*. "Determined and energized, he took the mound in a crucial game, as if to say, 'Trust me.' But can you?"

* * *

The Mets' second western trip of the late summer begins on August 27 with three games against the Arizona Diamondbacks, who have begun to run away with the National League West. New York's helplessness against Arizona continues as they drop two of three in the desert. The Mets' skid, and a torrid streak by Atlanta, combined to give the division lead back to the Braves.

Despite these losses, the Mets don't feel as put out as the umpiring crew assigned to this series, whose equipment was lost by the airline between their last assignment and Phoenix. One resourceful umpire takes the field in a pair of long black shorts and black socks with white tops pulled up to his knees, a failed attempt to mimic pants. The *Daily News* likens him to "an extra from *White Men Can't Jump*."

Little has gone right for the umpires since the defiant stance taken by their union during the All-Star break. On the same afternoon that Richie Phillips's resignation ploy is announced, reports emerge that one faction of umpires is seeking another representative to take his place. All of Phillips's subsequent attempts to open negotiations with the league are rebuffed. It is clear that the umpires' union is not a solid coalition, and Bud Selig is more than happy to watch it self-destruct.

On July 29, Selig's office announces it will begin officially accepting the resignations it has received. A full-blown panic ensues as umpires begin to rescind their resignation letters, while the umpires who continue to back the resignation plan snipe at their vacillating colleagues; one umpire complains to the press that a "dissident" sect of the union is conspiring against him and his orthodox comrades.

In a desperate attempt to save as many jobs as possible, union lawyers tell the National Labor Relations Board that the resignation letters were intended as "a symbolic gesture." This argument goes nowhere with Bud Selig, who insists he will accept the resignations of all twenty-two umpires who have not rescinded them—thirteen in the National League, nine in the American League—and hire replacements from the minor league ranks. In the press, Selig pointedly refers to these replacements as "permanent employees," while the league presidents remind the umpires that anyone who strikes in violation of the collective bargaining agreement "will have his employment terminated." During a 1979 umpires' strike, the arbiters garnered a great deal of public support when they were replaced with incompetent substitutes. But with this latest umpire job action coming so soon after the devastating players' strike of 1994, the public is indifferent, if not hostile, to their cause. Fully aware that fans are unsympathetic toward the umpires, and with only a third of them still sticking to threats of resignation, Selig can sprinkle replacement umpires throughout the league with little pubic outcry and, he imagines, minimal impact on the quality of umpiring.

On September 1, as MLB accepts the resignations of twenty-two umpires, Richie Phillips finds himself not arguing for their reinstatement but negotiating their severance packages. Among the umps who get the axe are veterans like Terry Tata, Frank Pulli, and Joe West, all of whom have been on the job for twenty years or more. Ed Hickox, who toiled in the minor leagues for a decade before getting called up to the bigs in 1999, also receives a pink slip. One vet who gets the boot is Drew Coble, whose wife is dying of cancer. "His family has been abandoned by major league baseball and his bosses," says colleague Richie Garcia, a week after the mass firings, as he serves as a pallbearer for Coble's spouse.

Most of these umpires are scheduled to work games the day they learn they've been canned. Fans barely notice that twenty-two men have lost their jobs in an ill-conceived negotiating folly, nor is there yet much public anxiety that the last month of the baseball season will be decided by the umpiring equivalents of September call-ups.

* * *

Edgardo Alfonzo can be trusted. He was trusted by the Mets' front office to move all over the infield during his initial years in the majors—*play third, no second, no third again*—and not utter a syllable of protest. He found a niche at third base in 1997 and 1998 but was trusted to vacate that position when the Mets acquired Robin Ventura. He was trusted to take small indignities in stride, like the multiple times this season his own team has spelled his name "Alfonso" on its batting practice roster.

Or when he took a midseason trip to Venezuela to attend a family funeral and rejoined the team in San Francisco to find his locker in the visiting clubhouse squeezed behind a large pole.

The question of Alfonzo is like that of the falling tree in the forest. If he did gripe about such slights, would anyone hear him? The back pages are dominated by quotes from Al Leiter, John Franco, Mike Piazza, and Rickey Henderson. Even the camera-shy Robin Ventura and John Olerud are quoted in the papers with a frequency that leaves Alfonzo in the dust. Alfonzo has hidden in plain sight, seldom slumping, never doing anything that might require an apology or spin doctoring.

Alfonzo's offensive stats should be difficult to ignore. Every time the Mets need a rally, he seems to spark it or keep it going. On August 11 at Shea, when a rough start from Octavio Dotel puts the Mets behind early, he hits a two-run double to help defeat the Padres. On August 15 in San Francisco, he bails out another flailing pitcher (Kenny Rogers this time) by igniting a rally and driving in four runs. The next evening in San Diego, when Dotel allows a no-hitter and a lead to slip from his grasp, Alfonzo singles and scores the tying run in the ninth inning, then hits a solo shot in the tenth to single-handedly win the game. On August 22, his walk-off RBI single finishes off the Cardinals in Queens.

By the end of August, Alfonzo has passed career highs in homers and RBIs, while also breaking the mark for most runs driven in by a Mets second baseman. He has also played nearly flawless defense, forming an ironclad double-play combination with Rey Ordóñez. Though he is relearning second base at the big league level, he has committed only two errors all season.

On August 27, the *Times* runs a glowing profile that terms him "The Anonymous Alfonzo." Typical of his luck, it runs at the precise moment when Alfonzo is stuck in his first dry spell of the season. As the Mets leave for Arizona, he is mired in a 3-for-30 slump, and he doesn't hit much better during the team's ugly series in Phoenix. Despite sweltering desert temperatures, Alfonzo takes extra batting practice at Bank One Ballpark, hoping to find his elusive stroke. By the time the Mets arrive in Houston on August 30 for their last scheduled trip to the Astrodome (like the Giants, the Astros will open the new millennium with a new ballpark), he has found it, launching offensive fireworks that are unprecedented in team history.

Every Met destroys Houston pitching this evening as they rout the Astros 17–1, but no one is more thorough or cruel than Alfonzo, who goes 6-for-6 with three home runs, hitting each long ball off of a different pitcher. His feats tie or break several franchise records and challenge a few major league ones as well. His sixteen total bases shatter a club mark set by Darryl Strawberry in 1985 and fall only two bases shy of the all-time record. His six runs scored tie the modern era record for most in a major league game. Alfonzo's bat is so potent that in one game he manages to raise his batting average eight points. When he raps out his sixth hit in the top of the ninth, even Astros fans hand him a standing ovation.

The media's reaction is to write about Alfonzo as someone who should be noticed but isn't, though it is their job to notice such things. Judy Battista's take in the *Times* is typical: "A potential most valuable player candidate? Sure, if anyone in baseball was even aware of him." Overnight, Alfonzo goes from a player nobody talks about to a player everyone talks about not being talked about.

At the end of it all, what does Alfonzo consider his favorite moment of the night?

"The last out," he says, "because we won the game."

* * *

The Mets split the last two games in Houston before a six-game homestand hosting Colorado and San Francisco. Games against these struggling opponents would promise little drama anyway, but they have no way of competing against the drama the Mets stir up upon their return. In the wee hours of September 2, during the bus ride from Newark Airport to Shea Stadium, Rey Ordóñez and backup shortstop Luis López come to blows. Ordóñez suffers a black eye and requires a few stitches, but most of the damage is of the PR variety. What brings the two shortstops to blows is unclear, though it's likely that Ordóñez's relentless taunting of López is the catalyst. Anonymous players confide that they're surprised Ordóñez had to wait until September before he was punched in the face by a teammate.

Steve Phillips does his best "nothing to see here, move along" act with the press. When this proves insufficient for the hungry back pages, he calls on Ordóñez and López to address reporters before the beginning of the Mets' first game back at Shea. The two infielders do not shake hands or show any outward signs of rapprochement while situated on opposite sides of Phillips, who resembles, as the *Times* puts it, "the principal standing between two naughty students, forcing them to apologize to the student body for fidgeting." If not as grotesque as the Yankee Stadium press conference Phillips inflicted on Bobby Valentine in June, it is no more dignified. During the press confab, López is repeatedly addressed as "Rey" by one clueless reporter, forcing him to correct the writer.

The ugly incident unfolds in full view of a crowded clubhouse, as the arrival of September has allowed the Mets to call on a series of reinforcements. Most notable among the additions is Bobby Bonilla, who'd not seen a major league field since accumulated aches and pains sent him to the disabled list in early July. He is reactivated now only because expanded rosters won't force the demotion of a more valuable player. Bonilla openly admits he will devote his diminished talents to the labor of playing cards, much as he's done all this troubled season while Roger Cedeño and Benny Agbayani filled the gap he left behind.

The Mets see the return of a few more welcome players, such as Rick Reed, who spent the past two weeks rehabbing from a strained middle finger while fielding questions about his willingness to transition to relief work once he was healthy. His answer is an emphatic "Hell no"; in response, Bobby Valentine makes a temporary reversion to a six-man rotation that includes Masato Yoshii, who'd returned to starting duty in Reed's absence. Bobby Jones, not seen since going down with shoulder discomfort in May, finally ends months of torturous rehab, but with the starting rotation logjammed, he rejoins the team in the bullpen. The Mets are also able to welcome back John Franco, who's been champing at the bit to return since his own middle finger injury in July. One August afternoon, while rehabbing at Shea, he stalked the Mets' clubhouse wielding the jagged handle of a broken bat, threatening to use it if he was not reactivated. "Just a joke," he said, though he didn't look like a man who was kidding.

The Mets are as anxious to bring back John Franco as he is to return, because their once impenetrable bullpen is dangerously close to becoming a liability. Chuck McElroy and Billy Taylor, acquired at the trade deadline to take the workload off of other relievers, have struggled so badly that they've produced the opposite effect. The team didn't suffer many crushing losses during a blazing-hot August, but McElroy and Taylor coughed up leads in most of them. This utter uselessness has caused Bobby Valentine to lean on Dennis Cook and Turk Wendell even more, exacerbating the very problem the trades were intended to solve.

The issue is underscored during the homestand that begins on September 3. Though the Mets win four out of six games against the Colorado Rockies and San Francisco Giants, both defeats can be attributed to the tired arm of Wendell, who is tattooed in each of them.

The Mets also come close to losing the Giants series finale when Cook and his fellow relievers allow four runs. After this close call, Cook admits he is "worn out." In the season's first sixty-three games, Mets relievers collected a mere five losses. Now they've been responsible for that many defeats in the team's last fourteen games.

Turk Wendell expresses the hope that "I'll get all this out of my system before the end of the season and be ready for the playoff hunt." He is calm when making these pronouncements, a far cry from his last outing against the Giants, when he repeatedly pounded his glove in disgust. The next day, he arrives at Shea with a swollen middle finger—the same unlucky digit that felled Rick Reed and John Franco. Remembering that last season the Mets suffered a preternatural number of injuries to their catchers, Reed dubs the 1999 squad "the middle finger team."

* * *

The last of three westward trips that should have spelled doom for the Mets begins on September 9 and ends without disaster striking, as the team wins five of seven in Los Angeles and Colorado. The Dodgers put up little resistance in the four games played at Chavez Ravine, save for a story planted in the *Los Angeles Times* that alleges the Dodgers attempted to reacquire Mike Piazza via trade earlier this season, a contention so laughable its only purpose could be to irk the catcher. Piazza exacts his revenge between the lines by belting two homers and driving in six runs. Then the Mets move on to Colorado on September 13 and have little trouble against the Rockies. While at Coors Field, Benny Agbayani breaks a troubling home run drought by going deep for the first time in 160 plate appearances. Another solid West Coast swing, combined with some stumbles by the Braves, keeps the Mets one slim game behind Atlanta in the standings.

Despite team bus dustups, middle finger boo-boos, and relief pitching speed bumps, the Mets have enjoyed more good luck than bad over the summer. Robin Ventura attributes their good fortune to "mojo," a timeless term lately revived by its use in the Austin Powers movies. "We've got a nice mojo workin' here," he observes after another midsummer victory. Ventura begins celebrating wins by blasting the "mojo risin'" coda of The Doors' song "L.A. Woman" in the triumphant clubhouse. By September, victories at Shea Stadium receive the same musical accompaniment. "Mojo risin'" becomes the Mets' semi-official slogan for the 1999 stretch run.

The idea that the Mets' surge is attributable to mojo, and Ventura's role in propagating that view, are furthered by Tom Verducci's cover story on the Mets infield in the September 6 issue of *Sports Illustrated*. Though the article talks about the greatness of the infield as a whole, it zeroes in on Ventura's impeccable fielding instincts, motivational tactics, and amazing year at the plate. His every at bat is now accompanied by chants of "M-V-P!" from the Shea faithful. John Franco dares to call Ventura "the best signing in the history of the franchise" within earshot of Mike Piazza. In the *Times*, Jack Curry wonders if Ventura might be the best player in New York, better even than Derek Jeter, who is assembling an MVP-caliber season of his own. Ventura dismisses Curry's likening to Jeter outright—"There's no way that's true"—and responds to questions about how he's enjoying such an amazing season by saying, "It's a lot better than stinking up the place."

Robin Ventura has many strengths, but taking praise well is not among them, nor is a flair for the spotlight. He seems almost embarrassed by his curious penchant for hitting grand slams, calling it a "freak thing," less an accomplishment than the product of dumb luck. Back in August, when Shea was visited by the Cardinals and Mark McGwire, Ventura spotted Big Mac swamped by autograph seekers during batting practice and shuddered at the sight. It was bad enough being the Grand Slam Guy. "I wouldn't want that for anything in the world," he confessed.

Only a few times did Robin Ventura come close to *that*. As a sophomore for Oklahoma State in 1987, he batted .469 and compiled an NCAA-record fifty-eight-game hitting streak, yet found a way to go almost totally unnoticed while doing so. He pulled off the feat with such little flair that, on one occasion during that historic streak, Ventura's coach was about to pull him from a game in which he'd gone hitless until a school official sprinted to the dugout to prevent the switch. Ventura stayed in the game and singled in his final at bat, then confessed embarrassment over the flap. Why such fuss over him?

Ventura's disdain for the spotlight was cemented in 1993, when he was hit by a pitch from Texas Rangers hurler Nolan Ryan and charged the mound, only to have the legendary pitcher grab him in a headlock and punch him repeatedly. Nolan Ryan had been plunking White Sox batters for years with impunity, and at some point during the 1993 season, Chicago's dugout decided the next batter to get hit would have to do *something* to fight back. Ventura drew the short straw. None of this backstory was mentioned when the footage of grandfatherly Nolan Ryan pummeling an infielder twenty years his junior was replayed ad infinitum during every local sportscast's Wacky Highlights Special. Robin Ventura's teammates would laud his guts, but most observers thought the youngster had lost his mind and praised the elder statesman for taking him over his knee. "Remember the Alamo!" yahooed Rangers co-owner George W. Bush.

Ventura retreated to the shadows as much as any All-Star-caliber player could. He was adept at keeping his teammates loose and relieving their anxiety when the going got tough but preferred to keep his clubhouse cheerleading within the clubhouse. In 1997, when the White Sox dealt away three of their best pitchers at the trade deadline despite being within striking distance of the first-place Indians (moves that would enter the annals of baseball infamy as the White Flag Trades), Ventura printed T-shirts for his teammates with the proclamation "CHICAGO LEFTOVERS."

During Ventura's first spring training in Port St. Lucie, grizzled New York scribes probing for signs of this feisty leadership grew frustrated with his terse answers and verbal contortions that pretzeled any question seeking a personal response into an answer about the team as a whole. His unwillingness to talk about himself stopped reporters from asking him anything at all, which was likely his goal. Teammates testify to his quick wit and his ability to keep them loose with well-timed wisecracks, but these performances are not for the public. Only his clubhouse may witness them. If his fellow players see him as a leader, it doesn't matter how anyone else sees him.

The *Sports Illustrated* cover alludes to this ambivalence, beginning with its headline: "THE GREATEST INFIELD EVER?" Not a statement, but an open question. The cover photo is slightly tilted, as if it were shot inside a Batman villain's hideout. Rey Ordóñez and Edgardo Alfonzo are positioned at the left and right extremes, each of them caught on the cusp of a smile but not quite there. John Olerud stands in the middle, sporting the batting helmet he brings with him to the infield. Beneath Olerud, Robin Ventura is perched on a stool, the only player who is seated. His head is clamped in the crook of Olerud's left arm, caught in a position a lot like the one Nolan Ryan inflicted on him.

He is the center of attention, the man pointed to as the source of his team's turnaround, the fount of its mojo. And yet when his big moment on stage arrives, he chooses to remind everyone of the most humiliating moment of his professional life.

* * *

By virtue of fording three West Coast trips and living to tell the tale, the Mets have made believers of the hardest nuts to crack. Writers who once approached the Mets' comeback summer with an attitude of "I'll believe it when I see it" have seen enough.

Typical of the pack is Bill Madden of the *Daily News*. One can almost see him shaking his head in disbelief as he writes, "They are a team put together by a general manager who, nine months ago, was in jeopardy of losing his job, and led by a manager who in ten previous seasons of directing big league clubs had never been in first place after the first week of July." By employing this parallelism, Madden implicitly puts Valentine's failure to reach the playoffs on the same level as Steve Phillips's sexual harassment allegations, making it unclear if he intends to elevate the former or diminish the latter. In the same article, Madden dismissively refers to the reason for Steve Phillips's near firing as his "intern problem"—as if the intern, not the general manager, was the source of that problem.

The reason the Mets won't falter down the stretch this time around, say the scribes, is character. A few short weeks ago, the team was judged lacking in this commodity, but winning can make penance for a multitude of sins. Now, the Mets are seen as having a certain fighting spirit lacked by the 1998 team that collapsed down the stretch. Murray Chass of the *Times* is no fan of Bobby Valentine's, and yet he declares that the Mets' dominant West Coast trips "made the point" that they "are not the team that stumbled along the way to the playoffs last year."

Bobby Valentine allows himself to think things will be different this time, and to discuss openly why he feels 1999 won't end the same way as 1998. He confesses he didn't like his team at the end of that season, calling them a "scrappy" squad that did the best it could through a fog of "inconsistencies and unknowns." (Shades of Steve Phillips's "good little team" here.) The 1999 vintage, he says, is "more mature . . . more professional, more together," all qualities no one would have dared ascribe to Mets at the start of June.

Such a turnaround seems to come from the realm of magic. Robin Ventura calls it mojo, this thing the Mets have, and that may be the best word for it. Before Austin Powers, before Jim Morrison, before even bluesmen like Muddy Waters sang about getting their mojo working, mojo was a word associated with an elusive magic that went by many names. Those who gave this magic credence stuffed a mojo bag with different charms, depending on what kind of good luck was desired. In order for the mojo to work, the user had to hold the bag close at all times, but concealed.

Those who believed in mojo knew that mojo was a tricky thing. You did not speak of it, and you prayed the luck held out until you got what you wanted. Because the mojo was a charm, and charms tend to backfire on those who wield them. Charms can stop working on a whim or begin working in reverse without warning. They might fulfill one's wishes, but with cruel, literal irony.

CHAPTER 6
The Fall

THE BRAVES HAVE reigned atop the National League East for years with little to challenge their dominance. The summer of 1999 gives them a formidable foe in the form of the Mets and also forces them to hurdle one calamity after another. The Braves' pitching takes a big hit when Bud Selig's new strike zone stymies Greg Maddux and Tom Glavine. Their bullpen loses closer Kerry Ligtenberg to Tommy John surgery. Slugger Andrés Galarraga misses the entire year due to cancer treatment. Catcher Javy López undergoes knee surgery in July and is lost for the rest of the season.

The Braves are able to weather these storms as Glavine and Maddux adjust to the new strike zone, Cox pieces together sufficient offense through judicious platooning, and fireballing southpaw John Rocker barrels into the breach left by Ligtenberg. From July 25 through September 10, Atlanta racks up a mind-boggling 31–11 record, twenty-seven of those victories delivered in come-from-behind fashion. They credit the Mets in part for this. "In years past, September was a month when we kind of took it easy and took some days off here and there to get ourselves prepared for the postseason," Chipper Jones admits. "That may have an impact on what happens in the postseason, in that guys have trouble just flipping the switch on and off. I don't foresee us having any problems flipping the switch this year." Chipper makes these remarks more than a week before the Mets arrive at Turner Field for a crucial three-game set, prompting the *Atlanta Journal-Constitution* to warn the Braves to not look so far ahead when they have games scheduled against other opponents.

The Braves find themselves unable to follow the media's warning. In the games leading up to the Mets series, Atlanta stumbles badly, losing five of eight, while the Mets return to Shea for a brief homestand on September 17 and take two of three from a Philadelphia team decimated by injuries, their brief flirtation with contention in the spring a distant memory. This means New York will arrive at Turner Field only one game out of first place. With a healthy lead in the wild card race and a division title within their grasp, the Mets dare to announce a sale date for playoff tickets, while one 7 train conductor takes to calling the Shea Stadium stop the "home of the 1999 World Series."

On the eve of the Atlanta series, Bobby Valentine announces he will revert to a five-man starting rotation and chooses Octavio Dotel for a bullpen demotion, a move that betrays the Mets' mortal fear of untested youth. At times, Dotel has been the Mets' best starting pitcher, racking up strikeouts by the truckload. He has also demonstrated an uncanny ability to alternate stellar performances with troubled ones. The Mets are in no position to gamble on which Dotel might show up at Turner Field and will instead turn to veterans Rick Reed, Orel Hershiser, and Al Leiter in the Atlanta series.

Reed carries his own risks, as he has allowed seven runs and six walks in only ten innings since returning from the disabled list, and is haunted by the memory of the game he lost at Turner Field last September. He pitches like a man eager to prove himself in the series opener on September 21, striking out six batters over the first six innings (a lofty total for him), but he also leaves a fastball up to Chipper Jones in the first inning. In 1999, you cannot make such a mistake. Jones comes into the day with an MVP-worthy stat line of ninety-eight RBIs and forty-one homers and collects one more of each as he knocks Reed's fastball for a solo shot.

Reed is countered with John Smoltz, who all season long has felt ominous elbow discomfort. Rather than seek a medical solution, Smoltz reconfigures his pitching style to sidearm in order to sidestep pain and remain effective. The John Smoltz the Mets face in the Turner Field opener is a completely different pitcher from the one they saw in July, and their bats have no answer for this stranger, apart from one lone run scratched out in the top of the third.

With one out in the bottom of the eighth, the score tied at one, and Chipper Jones due up, Bobby Valentine calls for lefty Dennis Cook, in a gambit to force the switch hitter to bat from his historically weaker right side. Chipper has no weak side this season, however, so when Cook serves up a fat fastball, Chipper is able to club it through the wind and into the left-field seats, putting the Braves back on top. Moments later, John Rocker records the save by striking out Robin Ventura, Shawon Dunston, and Benny Agbayani in order on just eleven pitches, sealing Atlanta's 2–1 win.

The following night, Orel Hershiser also finds himself helpless against the power of Chipper Jones, watching him crush a two-run homer to deep right field in the bottom of the first. Like Reed, Hershiser settles in after this humbling encounter, at one point retiring eleven batters in a row. Tom Glavine does much the same, stifling the Mets' bats until the fourth, when Mike Piazza hits a titanic game-tying two-run shot.

The Braves recapture the lead in the bottom of the seventh via a pair of singles and a sac fly. The Mets also begin the top of the eighth with two singles but are thwarted thanks to the longest, strangest managerial chess game of the season. Bobby Cox and Bobby Valentine counter each other with an endless parade of new pitchers and pinch hitters, Cox summoning relievers, Valentine conjuring pinch hitters to confound those relievers, in endless combinations permitted by expanded September rosters. The interminable series of moves and counter moves requires forty minutes and ten substitutions to play to its conclusion, and the top of the eighth ends with the score remaining the same as it did at the beginning, with the Mets still in arrears. Then Octavio Dotel digs the hole deeper as he makes his relief debut in the bottom half, walking the first two batters he faces and allowing both to score. John Rocker logs another easy save in the ninth as the Mets once again fall to the Braves, 5–2.

At least the Mets can say they played well in the first two games in Atlanta, something they cannot claim after the embarrassing series finale. The game begins with promise as the Mets score twice against Greg Maddux (itself a small miracle) and look poised for more by loading the bases against him with nobody out in the top of the second. When the Mets log three weak at bats and fail to push another runner across the plate, however, it sets the frustrating tone for the rest of the game. In the fifth, Rickey Henderson dooms another potential rally when he runs through a hold sign from third base coach Cookie Rojas—"A lope to death," in the words of the *Daily News*—and is thrown out at the plate by a mile.

And the horror is just beginning. In the bottom of the fifth, Al Leiter fires a pick-off throw to first base that should have the runner dead to rights, except that John Olerud can't pull the ball out of his glove. After a bloop single, Chipper Jones strides to the plate with runners at the corners. Leiter attempts to induce a double-play grounder, but his pitch catches too much of the plate. Chipper parks it into the left-field seats, his third homer of the series and his seventh against Mets pitching this season. Distracted by his mistake pitch to Chipper, Leiter permits more baserunners and tosses another errant pick-off throw to lead to the fourth Atlanta run of the inning.

A Mike Piazza leadoff homer in the top of the sixth gives the Mets some hope that all is not lost, but Turk Wendell literally throws the game away in the seventh by fielding a comebacker and flinging it toward an unmanned second base, yet another pitcher's throwing error leading to yet another Braves run. Another sliver of hope emerges in the top of the ninth, when John Rocker appears to be a bit tired in his third consecutive outing, issuing two walks to allow the tying run to come to the plate. The closer even uncorks a wild pitch to move both runners up a bag, but it is nothing more than a tease. Edgardo Alfonzo flies out for the final out of the series, as the Mets fall, 6–3.

Over their amazing summer, the Mets tore through twenty-one consecutive series without being swept. They have chosen an awful place and an awful time to end that streak. With only nine games left in the regular season and the Mets fallen four games out of first place, these three losses all but concede the division title to Atlanta. As the Braves prep to travel to Montréal for their next series, they make a show of bringing cases of champagne along with them.

In the aftermath, most of the criticism lands squarely on Bobby Valentine for choosing to pitch to Chipper Jones at all. Quietly, some Mets whisper that Chipper is stealing signs, a conspiracy theory Valentine lends credence to by describing Chipper's power against Mets pitching as "uncanny." He immediately regrets the characterization ("Maybe I shouldn't have used that word."), knowing it can only serve as bulletin board material for Atlanta and make his team look like sore losers, but once a Bobby Valentine gaffe is spoken it can never be unsaid.

To the New York press, the sweep in Atlanta can't be credited to the successes of Chipper or his teammates, especially after the error-filled finale and the sour-grapes charges of cheating. This is not a Braves triumph. It has to be a Mets failure.

* * *

As the Mets crawl out of Atlanta, they take solace in knowing their next stop will be Philadelphia, to face a team whose promising season crumbled after the All-Star break. At the trade deadline, when the Phillies were still in wild card contention, they were rumored suitors for Andy Pettitte, but that deal fell through when George Steinbrenner got cold feet over dealing his homegrown lefty, and the resulting disappointment took much of the wind out of the team's sails. Little else has gone right for the Phils since. Star third baseman Scott Rolen suffered a back injury and was shut down for the season in August. Curt Schilling made only five starts after the All-Star break before he too was put on the shelf.

While New York raged throughout the summer, Philadelphia wilted. As the Mets arrive at Veterans Stadium on September 24, the home team has won a pitiful total of four games in the previous month. Last week, they were defeated twice at Shea, in a series where the Mets touched up their pitchers for twenty-one runs. But the pummeling in Atlanta brought on a brutal hangover the Mets can't seem to shake, and the Phillies offer no hair of the dog.

In the series opener, the visitors are limited to two runs over eight innings by Joe Grahe, a pitcher who hasn't logged a start that long in over eight years. Masato Yoshii does his best to make these two runs stand up by allowing only one run and four hits over seven innings, but the Phillies rally against the bullpen in the bottom of the eighth, with an assist from some poor decision making by Bobby Valentine. The manager allows Armando Benítez to face lefty slugger Bobby Abreu, one of the Phils' few remaining threats, even though John Franco is warmed up and ready to provide a lefty-lefty matchup. Abreu ties the game with an RBI single, then scores the go-ahead run when the next batter singles. In the ninth, the Phillies ask for a save from journeyman reliever Scott Aldred. Last week at Shea, Aldred pitched a disastrous inning that ended with a grand slam hit by Rey Ordóñez, the shortstop's lone home run of the season. On this occasion, Aldred somehow gains the strength of Mariano Rivera and sets down the Mets in order, ensuring their 3–2 defeat.

A players-only meeting is held prior to the game on September 25, clubhouse attendants shooing away all interlopers, even coaches. No one shares what is discussed, perhaps because it has zero positive effect on any Met, least of all Kenny Rogers. After allowing back-to-back homers in the bottom of the second, Rogers throws the game away in a wild third inning, loading the bases before issuing a pair of walks to drive in two more runs. All day, Mets batters are thwarted, and when a golden opportunity to tie the game presents itself in the top of the eighth, it is promptly discarded. In that frame, a two-run shot by John Olerud cuts the deficit in half, then a pair of walks put the tying runs on base with nobody out. Bobby Valentine proceeds to commit another unforced error by asking Darryl Hamilton to bunt the runners over against a pitcher who has completely lost the strike zone. Hamilton's effort rolls toward the pitcher, resulting in a force out at third. Benny Agbayani follows by hitting a bullet right at the second baseman, who doubles up the nearest runner. The Mets mount no more threats and go down in defeat yet again, 4–3.

While all this losing has gone on, the Mets' formidable cushion in the wild card race has evaporated completely. Mere days ago, the Mets led the wild card race by four games. Now, they are tied with the surprising Cincinnati Reds, who have come out of nowhere to not only challenge the Mets for the wild card spot, but the powerful Astros for the National League Central title as well. As he did during the Mets' eight-game losing streak in June, Bobby Valentine responds by threatening his own job security. "If we don't get into the playoffs, I shouldn't come back," he tells the press after the second loss in Philadelphia. When Steve Phillips is asked if his manager should get the blame for fading down the stretch two seasons in a row, a reality that appears more imminent with each passing day, Phillips responds with a question of his own: "Has any team ever had collapses two years in a row?"

After their latest defeat, Mets players blast music in the visiting clubhouse and enjoy a luxurious postgame spread of soft-shell crab, showing no outward signs of remorse or worry. This reaction infuriates the press who want to see the slumping players sitting in silence in front of their lockers, heads bowed, or to see their manager cow them into doing so by dumping a buffet table on the floor in childish frustration. "Paul O'Neill gets more worked up over making an out in a meaningless ballgame than any of the Mets have in blowing a half-dozen crucial ones," grumbles Wallace Matthews of the *Post*. That the team and its manager have yet to display any outward signs of panic is itself cause for panic.

Desperate to kick-start the Mets' flatlining offense, Valentine slides a slumping Edgardo Alfonzo down to the sixth hole in the lineup for the series finale on September 26, inserting Roger Cedeño in his usual second spot. The manager insists the switcheroo was Alfonzo's idea, but this assertion is undermined when Alfonzo takes one look at the posted lineup, wheels around red-faced, and kicks a laundry basket in silent protest.

The lineup reshuffle nets zero results. The Phils send to the mound lefty Paul Byrd, a former Met who has pitched to an unsightly 9.39 ERA in his last five starts, including a game at Shea in which the Mets hung six earned runs on him in less than five innings. On this occasion, the Mets can only extract six hits and two runs from him. The Veterans Stadium AV team mocks the visitors' futility by playing "Taps" whenever they are retired. Meanwhile, Rick Reed limits the Phillies to only three hits in six innings of work, but two of those hits are a two-run homer and an RBI single, enough to give Philadelphia a one-run lead.

The Mets still trail by one run in the top of the ninth when they load the bases with one out on three consecutive walks. Rickey Henderson strides to the plate, needing only a fly ball, a well-placed grounder, or simply a walk from the man poised to break the MLB career record for free passes to keep hope alive. Instead, Henderson hits a roller toward second base to start a game-ending double play. While the Mets are swept away in Philadelphia, the Braves complete their own sweep in Montréal to clinch the National League East, and the Reds pull off a thrilling walk-off win to take sole possession of the wild card spot.

Reporters who chastised the Mets for failing to display contrition the day before are rewarded with a funereal atmosphere in the visiting clubhouse. No tunes are cranked as the Mets eat a modest postgame dinner in silence. Rey Ordóñez kicks his way through the dugout at the conclusion of the game and is spotted later at his locker, eyes red, staring a hole through an unseen enemy. To one reporter, he recites a saying from his native Cuba, "So much swimming, only to die on the shore."

* * *

During the Mets' disastrous sweep in Philadelphia, the home office puts on a brave face and proceeds with its division series ticket sale on September 25. Blue wooden NYPD saw horses are set up to corral an expected 2,500 hopeful ticket buyers on a bright Saturday morning, but the resulting crowd is no more than half that many. The prospect of waiting for hours in Shea's parking lot to buy playoff tickets is no longer as appealing as it was a week ago, especially when those tickets top out at a pricey $40 a pop for field-level seats.

"They're watching the scoreboard, these people," notes one Shea employee.

The Mets hand out ticket-buying opportunities via lottery as fans are given wristbands with numbers corresponding to balls drawn from a bin, bingo style. As a further indignity to Mets fans, the first number drawn belongs to a man covered head to toe in Yankee paraphernalia. He returns from the ticket booth clutching seven division series tickets in his hands, proclaiming to local news cameras his plan to flip these for Yankees playoff tickets. The Mets fans behind him react with vocal but subdued vitriol. The hell their team is putting them through has left them with little strength to fight.

Though bowed by the Mets' slide, the fans who show up remain optimistic, after a fashion. "Every fan here has faith that the Mets will make the playoffs," contends one young fan from Brooklyn. "Bobby Valentine might choke, but the Mets won't."

* * *

When the Braves arrive in New York on September 28, their division clinched and another playoff appearance assured, they should have no incentive to put up max effort. But after accusations from various Mets that Chipper Jones had stolen signs from them at Turner Field—accusations fanned by Bobby Valentine—the Braves are prepared to play these games with postseason intensity. "Believe me, they threw some charcoal bricks on the fire when they started mentioning Chipper's cheating," Brian Jordan confesses. "That just pumped us up more." Stinging over Bobby Valentine's use of the word "uncanny," Chipper Jones growls, "If anyone thought we were going to come in and lie down for these games, they have another thing coming." Yankee executive Gene Michael takes this opportunity to scout the Braves in person for a potential World Series matchup. "This is as good a series as any to watch the Braves, even though they've already clinched," Michael says by way of explanation. "They hate the Mets."

Since the team's last disastrous trip to Turner Field, angry WFAN callers have advocated brushing back Chipper Jones to make him uncomfortable at the plate. Orel Hershiser may have this counsel in mind as he climbs the mound, but he gets ahead of himself by plunking the leadoff hitter. The evening goes downhill swiftly from there, as Hershiser allows four hits and three runs in the first inning and is yanked before he can even blink. When Octavio Dotel takes his place, his first pitch squirts past Mike Piazza, allowing a fourth run to score. As for Atlanta's pitching, Tom Glavine dominates the Mets yet again, as he has all season in defiance of the new strike zone that should have broken him.

The home team shows not the slightest fight until the top of the eighth, when reliever Dennis Cook initiates a screaming match with home plate umpire Alfonzo Marquez, one of many rookies called up from the minors after twenty-two umpires got the axe on September 1. Before the series, the Mets made a formal request with the National League office that novice umps be restricted to "meaningless" series, or at the very least be kept away from home plate duty. Both requests were ignored. One Mets suit grumbles to the press that Bobby Cox—whose history of umpire baiting equals if not surpasses Bobby Valentine's—"intimidated" Marquez by barking at the rookie up from the visiting dugout, resulting in calls that went against the Mets. Behind in the standings and behind in the game, the Mets smell conspiracy in all corners.

When Dennis Cook is lifted from the game after an ugly four-pitch walk, he stomps in Marquez's general direction, covers home plate with a handful of dirt, and goes nose-to-nose with him to garner a hard-earned ejection. His tantrum fires up the crowd, who taunt Marquez with screams of "CLEAN HOME PLATE!" and his teammates, who gather at the summit of the dugout, remembering that they are fighting for their playoff hopes. The emotional outburst has no tangible results, however, as the Mets manage no more than a pair of RBI groundouts the rest of the way, while Pat Mahomes allows four runs in relief to put the game out of reach. The Mets lose to Atlanta again, 9–3, their seventh consecutive defeat.

Blame in the latest Mets collapse is assigned to many factors. In the *Times*, George Vecsey suggests the team "got caught in a twilight zone between a pennant race and a wild-card race." Mike Lupica of the *Daily News* points the finger at a high-priced lineup that stopped hitting all at once. "People scream about [Valentine] these days," Lupica writes. "They should scream about the middle of his batting order . . . If they hit, nobody is saying a word about the manager." To many others, the Mets' slide has been so ugly and so disastrous that tracing its source seems pointless, if not cruel. "Mathematically, the Mets live," Murray Chass writes in a piece that reads like an obituary. "But after the first inning at Shea Stadium they would be better off dead. Anyone with the slightest touch of compassion could see that."

Atlanta's manager cuts through it all. Asked for his opinion as to why the Mets are choking down the stretch for a second year in a row, Bobby Cox confesses he doesn't believe in choking. "Teams do not choke," he says. "They just get beat."

***

It is a time to try anything. Rey Ordóñez blows cigar smoke around the bat rack, hoping this bit of pseudo-Santería will awaken their slumbering lumber. Darryl Hamilton visits a fortune teller who predicts all will turn out well for him and his team. The Mets don their traditional pinstripes rather than the solid black or white tops they've worn for most home games in 1999. John Franco insists the pinstripes will bring them good luck, his reasoning being, "something has to."

Something finally seems to work on the evening of September 29, as the Mets rap an improbable eight straight hits against Greg Maddux in the fourth inning and put up a seven-run outburst capped by a John Olerud grand slam. Al Leiter throws seven stellar innings as the Mets collect a desperately needed blowout victory, 9–2. For one blessed night, the Mets can tell themselves the hex is lifted. A team does not abuse Greg Maddux without some help from the supernatural.

Things still seem to be going their way in the Braves series finale on September 30, when Edgardo Alfonzo belts a two-out game-tying homer in the bottom of the eighth that drives the Shea crowd to the brink of insanity. It all seems too magical now, too perfect, too *mojo*. Teams don't pull rabbits out of their hats like this, only to lose.

But an eerie silence descends as the game toddles on into extra innings and the Mets do no damage against the Atlanta bullpen. After using a flurry of pinch hitters and pinch runners to keep the game tied, Bobby Valentine is all but forced to place Shawon Dunston in right field, a position he has only played four times since his trade to the Mets, and not once at Shea Stadium. Sure enough, the ball finds him in the eleventh, as Brian Jordan starts the frame by lofting a long fly his way. Dunston trots in the direction of the warning track to run it down, but when he looks up he realizes to his horror that he's lost sight of the ball. He looks over his shoulder, at odds with the direction of his body, wanting to peer in all directions at once.

The ball drops beyond the reach of Dunston's glove by a hair, a moment before he crashes into the outfield fence. By the time he recovers and heaves the ball into the infield, Jordan stands on third with a triple. One batter later, a long sac fly allows Jordan to trot across the plate with the go-ahead run. Fans can't bring themselves to boo Dunston's misplay. The crowd has nothing left but pity—pity for their team, pity for themselves.

In the bottom of the frame, Bobby Valentine bursts from the dugout to argue with home plate umpire Phil Cuzzi—another rookie inexplicably placed in the most important post on the field during a game with payoff implications—over his refusal to get help on check swings and is subsequently ejected. Thus he is spared the sight of Robin Ventura flying out to left to conclude a crushing 4–3 defeat.

The Mets' latest loss places them two games out of the wild card berth with three games left on the schedule. Only one team has ever vaulted a two-game gap with three games to play, and that was the 1962 San Francisco Giants, who boasted future Hall of Famers Willie Mays, Willie McCovey, and Juan Marichal. The Mets, losers of eight of nine games when it mattered most, do not look like they are made of such timber.

The Mets will need some help from others to have any shot at the playoffs, but the remaining schedule does not portend such assistance. The Reds will travel to Milwaukee to take on the punchless Brewers, and the Astros—tied with Cincinnati for both the National League Central division lead and the wild card slot—will be at home hosting the Dodgers, who have been phoning it in for months. It looks quite likely that Houston and Cincinnati will split their division and the wild card berth, while the Mets will head home early. "Do you believe in miracles?" begins a typical postmortem by Tom Keegan of the *Post*. "I don't."

The utter hopelessness of the Mets' situation inspires the Braves to share their true feelings. Up to this point, they preferred to let their play speak for them. Now, with the Mets all but dead and buried, many of them grab a handful of dirt to toss on their grave.

John Rocker jumps in first. After the final game at Shea, the closer lashes out against Mets fans. "They just don't know when to shut up," Rocker marvels. "I've asked a lot of people all week, 'How many times you got to beat a team before the fans finally shut up?' And I still don't know. We beat them nine out of 12 times and they're still talking trash." But it's Chipper Jones who delivers the harshest blows. After he compares taking two of three from the flailing Mets as "the next best thing to a World Series win," Chipper fires the opposing player's equivalent of a nuclear warhead. "Now all the Mets fans can go home and put their Yankees' stuff on," he says. He feels confident in saying this because he believes neither the Mets nor their fans will have an opportunity to make him eat these words until the year 2000. He will enjoy the playoffs. They will not.

* * *

The Pittsburgh Pirates are baseball's canary in the coalmine in the 1990s. They began the decade by winning three consecutive division titles, but became the first team to suffer the cruelties of baseball's new economic realities when they lost all of their superstars to free agency. Irrelevance soon followed. For several years at decade's end, the Pirates played respectably for the first half of the season, only to be undone by their inability to afford reinforcements. Their 1999 season proceeded in much the same fashion: flickers of hope undone by injuries and a lack of payroll flexibility.

As the Pirates arrive in Queens for the final series of the regular season on October 1, Shea Stadium is almost tomb-like. The stadium's vast upper deck is abandoned, the raucous mood of the Braves games replaced with the air of mourning. Local scribes find the press box spacious again because the national columnists have decamped elsewhere. In the Mets' clubhouse, someone with a taste for gallows humor cues up the theme to *Titanic* on the stereo.

As the game unfolds, a Robin Ventura laser into the hometown bullpen and a four-hundred-foot Mike Piazza solo shot give the Mets a 2–0 lead, precious cargo entrusted to Kenny Rogers. For the first seven innings, Rogers's trademark curveball breaks perfectly, inducing many swings and misses from an overmatched Pirates lineup. Then in the top of the eighth, a walk and a pair of one-out singles drive in a run, cutting the lead in half. Rogers might have been pulled before the Pirates drew blood but for the failure of Shea's dugout phone, and the subsequent failure of a backup set of walkie-talkies, which forces Bobby Valentine to send messages via relay runners back and forth down the tunnel leading to the bullpen.

With the bases loaded and a lefty batter due up next, the call goes to John Franco, whose patented screwball could induce an inning-ending grounder. Instead, the batter taps a ball that hits the pitcher's mound and loses momentum. Edgardo Alfonzo rushes in from his post at second base, barehands the ball, and heaves a throw to first. Too high, too late. A run scores to tie the game at two.

The Mets' outlook dims further when Franco falls behind 3–0 to the next batter. One more ball out of the strike zone will force in the go-ahead run and just might eliminate the Mets from playoff contention altogether. Franco fights back to get two strikes, then fires a pitch that appears low to the naked eye. Home plate umpire John Hirschbeck deems it strike three. During the Atlanta series, the Mets clashed with umpires over close calls that didn't go their way. This time, they tip their caps and count their lucky stars.

For the second night in a row, the Mets find themselves in a tense extra-inning affair. Pat Mahomes, the team's long relief savior all season, keeps Pittsburgh in check by working three scoreless innings. As Shawon Dunston steps to the plate to lead off the bottom of the eleventh, he hears the crowd erupt into a roar. He assumes the cheer is not for him, and discovers its source on the out-of-town scoreboard, which has just noted the Astros have lost to the Dodgers. The scoreboard also tells him that the Brewers are tied with the Reds in the eighth inning of their game. Both scores give the Mets a chance to gain ground in the wild card race—provided they can win this game.

Dunston does his part by singling to center, then moves to third on a sac bunt and a groundout. An intentional walk of Piazza puts the game in the hands of Robin Ventura, whose earlier home run was the one bright spot in a miserable slump that has lasted for weeks. The third baseman suffered a deep bone bruise in July, and though he performed at MVP levels all summer despite the injury, the bill has now come due for playing through this pain and other ailments. While the team was in Houston at the beginning of September, Ventura had his knee drained, a procedure that only came to light weeks later when Bobby Valentine felt compelled to explain Ventura's declining bat, and to blame himself for not resting his third baseman earlier in the season. The draining provided no immediate dividends at the plate. Ventura admits to sleepless nights after his miserable performance in the Braves series at Shea, when he went 2-for-13 and had the added misfortune of making the final out.

There will be no need for Ventura to rue what could have been tonight. As he dunks a single into shallow center field, Dunston trots home to give the Mets a 3–2 victory. Then, the players gather around a TV in the clubhouse to watch the Brewers prevail over the Reds in their final at bat, cheering on Milwaukee's walk-off win as loudly as their own.

The Mets' doomsday clock is arrested for a day. They are now one game out of the wild card with two games left on the calendar, significantly better odds than prevailed when the day began. "Twenty thousand sad people out there somewhere," Valentine says in reference to Shea's empty upper deck. "They missed a good show. They should have waited another day to go to Broadway."

* * *

The mayor is now an art critic. In early October, the Brooklyn Museum is hosting an exhibit entitled *Sensations* that features pieces by Chris Ofili, a thirty-year-old British artist whose work is most notable for its utilization of unusual media like elephant dung. The exhibit includes one of his pieces, *The Holy Virgin Mary*, that depicts a black Madonna surrounded by stills from blaxploitation movies and cutouts from pornographic magazines. New York's tabloid press becomes hung up on the idea of using animal feces in religiously themed artwork and employs words like "stained," "covered," and "smeared" to describe its use, descriptors as sensationalistic as they are inaccurate. Mayor Giuliani reads these reports and becomes convinced dung was actually flung at an image of the Madonna. "The idea of having so-called works of art in which people are throwing elephant dung at a picture of the Virgin Mary is sick," Giuliani bristles. Declaring himself offended on behalf of New York's entire Catholic population, the mayor issues the Brooklyn Museum an ultimatum: shut down the exhibit or forfeit $7 million in city grants.

It is another one of the quixotic crusades that have marked Rudy Giuliani's second term and which betray profound misunderstandings of the city he governs. Witness his doomed quest in 1998 to transform New York into a more "civil" city, a campaign that produced no results beyond widespread derision and a protest strike by cabbies that brought Manhattan to a standstill. Though these baffling moves are often viewed as a way for the mayor to position himself as a culture warrior in opposition to Hillary Clinton, a true political operator should have recognized that asking New Yorkers to be more civil was as pointless as asking the Hudson River to change direction, and that calls for artistic censorship would find no traction in this ultra-liberal city.

But *politics* is still a dirty word to the mayor, and so he plows on with the battle against the Brooklyn Museum exhibit because his offense is genuine. (He swears he is an observant Catholic, though the depth of his observance is hard to pin.) The Brooklyn Museum stands firm and vows to mount *Sensation* with or without city money, infuriating the mayor further. "There's nothing in the First Amendment that supports horrible and disgusting projects!" Giuliani sputters, forgetting two-hundred-plus years of Constitutional law that says otherwise.

Giuliani's protests turn *Sensation* into an actual sensation, as crowds flock to Eastern Parkway to see what all the fuss is about. *The Holy Virgin*

Mary is protected by extra guards and a plexiglass shield, but in the exhibit's crowded opening days, no visitors proclaim to be offended by Ofili's work, not even self-professed Catholics. The *Daily News* catches a few art lovers traveling to the museum to see the work on the lovely Saturday afternoon of October 2. Karen Masterson and her seventeen-year-old daughter are more amused than deterred by the small group of protestors they must wade through to enter the museum, who hand out vomit bags so visitors can cope with the exhibit's presumed "sickness."

Though Masterson is Catholic herself, she doesn't find the artwork offensive, but takes the souvenir sick bag with her anyway. "We can use it later," she tells the *News*, "when the Mets lose."

* * *

Fortunately for Masterson, the events of October 2 give Mets fans no need to test their gag reflexes. That afternoon in Milwaukee, as the sky clouds over and temperatures plunge to a sub-autumnal forty-seven degrees, the Reds freeze up completely and lose once again. The improbable luck that propelled Cincinnati into the playoff pictures appears to be running out. Meanwhile, the Astros provide some clarity by shutting out the Dodgers, retaking the National League Central by a full game. Thanks to Cincinnati's loss, the Mets can end the day in a tie for the wild card berth with a win. Fans arrive at Shea with signs heaping praise on the Brewers, ecstatic that, after all the crushing heartache of the past week, the Mets again have a chance to be in control of their playoff fate.

The results in Milwaukee do not calm down today's starter, Rick Reed. He paces the clubhouse, stalking between the training room and weight room and back again ad infinitum. When he plays long-toss in the outfield, he finds himself unable to locate the catcher's glove for love or money. *This is going to be a long night*, he fears.

But whatever anxiety grips Reed lets go the moment he steps on the mound. Following a one-out double in the top of the first, he retires eight Pirates in a row. A leadoff single breaks the streak in the fourth, so Reed starts another one, setting down the next fifteen batters he faces in order. When the Pirates manage to put the bat on the ball, it doesn't travel far. Apart from one lone pop-up to shallow center, every out Reed records is registered either in the infield or via strikeout. By night's end, he collects a career-high twelve K's, seven of them looking, while walking none. Pittsburgh virulently protests some of the strike calls from home plate umpire Jeff Nelson, but even accounting for the umpire's relative inexperience—Nelson is in his first year in the bigs, though not one of the resignation replacements—it is hard to deny that Reed throws the game of his life.

Reed must be dazzling, because the Met offense continues to sputter for much of the game, scratching out only two runs against rookie hurler Francisco Córdova. Seeking a sturdier cushion, Reed provides it himself in the bottom of the eighth inning by rapping a two-run single. The Mets go on to score five times against Pittsburgh's bullpen, and when Reed catches a batter looking to seal the 7–0 victory, the usually reserved pitcher allows himself a moment of celebration, pumping his fist and screaming a triumphant "fuck yeah!" clearly visible to the lip readers viewing at home.

For the second consecutive year, the Mets will enter the final game of the regular season tied for the National League wild card spot. In 1998, the last day came as their trajectory was pointing downward. In 1999, it seems to be aimed in the opposite direction.

* * *

On October 3, 1951, the Brooklyn Dodgers were fighting for their lives. Over the summer, they'd held first place by as many as 13.5 games until their bitterest rivals, the New York Giants, went off script and refused to lose. The two teams ended the season tied for first place, and a three-game playoff would determine the National League pennant winner. After splitting the first two games, the Dodgers took the lead in the deciding contest at the Polo Grounds with a three-run outburst in the top of the eighth. Brooklyn hurler Don Newcombe pitched brilliantly, allowing only one run through eight innings. The Dodgers would win the pennant after all, it seemed.

But Newcombe faltered in the bottom of the ninth, allowing two singles to open the inning, then a run-scoring double that placed the tying runs in scoring position and brought the winning run to the plate in the person of Bobby Thomson. The call to the bullpen went to Ralph Branca, a righthander who'd struggled in the first game of the series and who would take the mound on only one day's worth of rest. Branca's first pitch was one he deemed a perfect fastball. Thomson took it for strike one. His second pitch was another fastball intended to throw the batter off balance for a curveball that would follow, but there would be no curveball. Thomson pulled Branca's fastball into the Polo Grounds' short left-field grandstand for a walk-off, pennant-winning three-run homer that would come to be known as the Shot Heard Round the World.

Any chance Ralph Branca had for redemption on the field was shattered when he suffered a freak back injury the following spring that was never properly treated. He was never the same pitcher again and had to accept a premature retirement from the game. He did well for himself outside of it, working in finance and later channeling that expertise into the Baseball Assistance Team (BAT), an organization that helped former players who fell on hard times, a vital service for those who played when the average major leaguer earned a workingman's wage. He embraced his role in baseball history as much as he could, making the rounds at memorabilia shows and off-season winter banquets with his one-time tormentor. Thomson would play the conqueror, Branca the lovable loser.

In 1977, Branca's daughter Mary married a ballplayer. Like Branca, this player was a former Dodger phenom who'd fallen on hard times due to an improperly treated injury and had kicked around the league ever since. At the time of the wedding, he was a benchwarmer for a miserable Mets team. His name was Bobby Valentine.

Flash forward to October 3, 1999, and Bobby Valentine is also playing for his life, or at least his job, which is much the same to him. The Mets' fortunes have waxed and waned so much in the last week that the *Daily News* provides a timeline of the previous seven days for dizzied fans. The short version: if the Mets can win today, they will live to play another day. Where and when will depend on the Astros, who are hanging on to a one-game lead in the National League Central, and the Reds, who are tied with the Mets for the wild card spot. Depending on the outcome of these teams' final games and their own, the Mets can either capture the wild card for themselves or be forced into a one-game playoff against either Houston or Cincinnati. The Astros game already seems to be little more than a formality, since their opponents, the Dodgers, will sit slugger Gary Sheffield and ace Kevin Brown, while Houston will counter with Cy Young Award candidate Mike Hampton. As for the Reds, they're just hoping to play at all, as the forecast in Milwaukee calls for temperatures in the forties and persistent rain, if not snow, at the first pitch scheduled for 4:05 p.m. New York time. By that hour, the Mets' own game might be finished already. If they lose it, their season might be finished as well.

Back in Queens, where temperatures are at a springlike seventy degrees, the Mets' hopes rest on the forty-year-old arm of Orel Hershiser. Valentine chose not to start Al Leiter on short rest, reasoning a fresh

Hershiser would provide better results. He does not mention the reason Hershiser is so fresh is because he only threw twenty-four pitches in one-third of an inning in his last start against the Braves before he was yanked.

Though the Pirates batted .179 in the first two games of the series at Shea while recording an astonishing twenty-nine strikeouts, they manage to scratch out a run in the top of the first after Hershiser issues a leadoff walk and a two-out bloop single makes him pay dearly for it. Hershiser limits the damage there, however, and keeps Pittsburgh in check for the rest of his afternoon. The Pirates believe he is receiving undue help from a gigantic strike zone and protest a double play call in the top of the third, when the trailing runner appears to beat the throw to first. These calls, following the twelve-strikeout game on Saturday night, add fuel to Pittsburgh's conspiracy theory that the umps are helping the Mets write a comeback script. Bobby Valentine, who screamed about "unfair" calls during the Braves series, is now silent on the subject of umpire competence.

Umpire aided or not, Hershiser stalls the opposition to one run through five while recording the two thousandth strikeout of his career along the way. But the one run he allows almost seems too much against Pirate pitcher Kris Benson, last seen at Shea on the infamous night when the Mercury Mets made their simultaneous debut and finale. The Mets break through against the rookie in the bottom of the fourth, when a pair of errors put John Olerud into scoring position, and he eventually trots home on a Darryl Hamilton double to tie the game at one. This, however, is all the damage the Mets will do to Benson, as they are continually undone by their preternatural ability to smash hard-hit balls right at opposing fielders. Time after time, the gift of a leadoff single or a Pirate error is returned via a line-drive out, exasperating a near-sellout crowd comprised largely of hopeful walkups, who moan in unison each time another potential rally is squashed. Mets radio play-by-play man Gary Cohen speaks for frustrated fans when he laments, "How many times can the Mets set the table without sitting down to eat?" Benson stalks off the mound after seven innings, 120 pitches thrown, seven hits scattered, the game still tied at one, and Mets batters held to 1-for-11 with runners in scoring position.

The Mets relievers take over for Hershiser in the sixth and fare well until the top of the ninth, when Turk Wendell allows a two-out single. Armando Benítez is called on to record the final out of the inning but pays the runner no mind at all, allowing him to steal second base standing up. Before Benítez can face his next batter, Bobby Valentine jogs out of the dugout to talk to him. This is an event of blue moon rarity. The manager hardly ever approaches a mound during a game, preferring to leave calls to the bullpen and mound conferences to his pitching coach, Dave Wallace. On the radio, Gary Cohen surmises he wants to "make sure Armando has his head screwed on straight." But Benítez's head is sufficiently attached to fan the hitter and prevent the go-ahead run from scoring.

With one out in the bottom of the ninth, the Mets send up Melvin Mora for a rare at bat. The rookie entered the game as a pinch runner, which is about as much big league action as he's seen this season. After failing to make the team out of spring training at the literal last second, Mora has shuttled between Queens and Norfolk all year long. Used largely as a pinch runner or defensive replacement, Mora has logged only thirty major league at bats. It is not faith or a hunch that inspires Bobby Valentine to let Mora bat in this situation, but a lack of options. The manager employed a flurry of pinch hitters and defensive replacements in a vain attempt to break through against Kris Benson and the Pirate bullpen. Even with expanded September rosters, the Mets bench is now close to bare.

Though this is no ringing endorsement, Mora accepts it and reciprocates with a single to right field, only his sixth major league hit. The next batter, Edgardo Alfonzo, lines an 0-1 pitch to almost the same spot. With a hit-and-run called on the pitch, Mora scurries all the way to third base, sliding into the bag headfirst. The Mets' hopes for playing again in 1999 stand ninety feet away from home.

The Pirates opt to intentionally walk John Olerud. This ensures a force at any base but also ensures they will have to face Mike Piazza instead. With the Shea stands thundering, Pittsburgh calls on sidearmer Brad Clontz, a former Mets farmhand who has a history of success against the catcher, in the hopes of inducing an inning-ending double play.

Only one person in the stadium is prepared for what happens next. Fortunately for the Mets, that person is Melvin Mora. As he inches his way off the third base bag, he sneaks a peek at Clontz's grip and realizes his first pitch will be a slider. Mora observed this slider often when he played with Clontz in the minors last season. He knows this pitch tends to bounce. It was utter torture for Mora to be left behind at the end of spring training. And yet, he is here now, when he's needed most.

As Mora predicts, Clontz's first pitch is a slider that keeps sliding and sinking until it lands in the dirt of the batter's box opposite Piazza, bounces off the ground, and scoots toward the backstop. Piazza backs up from the plate and raises his hands in the air, less a triumphant gesture than an exasperated "you gotta be kiddin' me" shrug. Mora runs like mad toward the plate. Then, a few feet before home, he slows down, lowering his stride, almost crouching, touching home in a gait like Groucho Marx duck-walking his way toward a punchline. As he touches the plate, officially securing a 2–1 Mets win, "L.A. Woman" thunders out of the Shea speakers, the Mets' missing mojo found. Mora's teammates pour out of the dugout to engulf him. His manager follows close behind, with the look of a man who has just heard a jury deliver a "not guilty" verdict.

Ralph Branca is in the stands to witness all of this. The night before, he attended mass and said a prayer to St. Anthony, patron saint of miracles. After spending most of his Sunday signing autographs at a baseball card show in New Jersey, he made a beeline toward Queens, his car radio tuned to the game the whole way, and arrived at Shea in time to witness the game's odd but miraculous conclusion.

Branca says this day owed his family one.

* * *

Elation is followed by confusion. The Mets celebrate their walk-off win, hoisting each other in the air, hugging, towel waving, high-fiving, saluting the fans in the crowd. Then they trail off into the clubhouse, realizing they have nowhere to go yet. Depending on the outcome of games yet to be played, they could either proceed straight into the playoffs or into a one-game contest to decide the wild card winner. Al Leiter, who will pitch whatever game the Mets play next, swears to reporters he will watch video of Cincinnati hitters to prepare for a potential play-in game against the Reds. But with his objective unclear and nothing but time on his hands, he haunts the Shea Stadium press box for hours, raring to go but with no destination.

The Astros provide some clarity by easily defeating the Dodgers in their final game to capture the National League Central crown outright. This means the Mets' next move depends on the Reds, as the commissioner's office determined via coin-toss in mid-September that a play-in game for the National League wild card between the Mets and Reds would be played in Cincinnati. The Reds would make that game necessary with a win, but the weather in Milwaukee continues to rain on their parade. Bud Selig is present for the game in Milwaukee, not so much to cheer on the team he once owned as to hope his presence will force a break in the clouds. "We've played games here on fields thirty times worse," Selig insists mid-rain delay. The rain persists, as if taking his boast as a personal challenge.

This was supposed to be the last-ever baseball game played at County Stadium, longtime home of the Brewers and the Milwaukee Braves before them. Then, construction delays for the Brewers' new ballpark ensured it would not be ready for opening day of 2000. This, combined with the weather, leads to many no-shows. When umpires give the signal to start the game at 8:50 local time, almost six hours after the scheduled first pitch, County Stadium's fifty-six thousand seats are occupied by only a few hundred hardy fans who've braved the drizzle and the forty-five-degree temperatures. Eager to get home, the Reds plate five runs in the top of the third while Milwaukee is stifled by Bobby Valentine's old nemesis, Pete Harnisch. Cincinnati cruises to a 7–1 win, if anyone can cruise in a game played in wintry conditions that ends a few minutes short of midnight.

Exhausted, the Reds head home, unaware that tomorrow's opponent has beaten them there. Rather than wait for the weather to decide their fate, the Mets make the decision to fly to Cincinnati, either to be ready for a play-in game played there if the Reds won or to fly on to the first round of the playoffs if the Reds lost. They take off at 10:00 p.m. New York time and are already settled in their hotel before the end of the game in Milwaukee. The Mets would not receive home-field advantage, but they would have the edge afforded by a good night's sleep.

Lack of rest aside, the Reds play game number 163 with house money. Unlike the Mets, they entered the 1999 season without the dictate of Playoffs or Bust, and with less than half the payroll ($33 million). While the Mets spent their Sunday watching the MLB scoreboard, the Reds whiled away a long rain delay by catching up on all the NFL action in County Stadium's visiting clubhouse, as if the baseball outcomes were of no concern to them. After their victory over Milwaukee forces the play-in game, the Reds do not jump up and down on the field of play as the Mets did. "What were we going to celebrate?" manager Jack McKeon shrugged.

While many rival managers could be said to dislike Bobby Valentine, McKeon—considered an old-school type in sharp contrast to the Mets skipper—has made a point of needling him and his team multiple times this season. During one June evening at Shea, in the midst of the Mets' eight-game losing streak, Cincinnati's skipper raised a stink about white lettering on Jason Isringhausen's glove that was supposedly distracting to his hitters, and also demanded the grounds crew dry up the dirt at home plate while the Mets were in the field. ("I was concerned for your catcher," he explained.) Two weeks later in Cincinnati, he objected to the orange undershirt Pat Mahomes sported beneath his black jersey, which differed from the standard black undershirt worn by his teammates. Lacking a black undershirt of his own, the reliever was forced to literally take one off the back of the team's trainer. While Valentine was often accused of raising petty quibbles like these to rankle opposing teams, McKeon seemed to do so as a preemptive strike against such tactics.

For all their differences, the two managers are identical in one sense: Neither has ever made his way to the postseason. Tonight, someone's waiting will end.

A sellout crowd at Cinergy Field is prepared to scream McKeon and the Reds to a win if that's what it takes, but the Mets quickly rob them of this strategy by shutting them up. Leadoff man Rickey Henderson, powering through hamstring aches, reaches on a leadoff single. Then Edgardo Alfonzo belts a long fly ball to straightaway center. Off the bat, it looks like an easy play, and Cincinnati's center fielder takes a leisurely route to track it down. But something grabs the ball mid-flight, and it keeps traveling and traveling. All broadcasters—Jon Miller on ESPN, Bob Murphy on WFAN radio—are stunned when the ball drops behind the outfield fence for a two-run homer. Even the raucous home crowd doesn't realize the ball will leave the yard until it does. As Alfonzo trots around the bases, Reds fans are shocked into near silence.

They are ready to make noise again after Al Leiter issues a walk to the leadoff batter in the bottom of the first. Walks and first-inning meltdowns have gone hand-in-hand for Leiter this season, and the free pass doesn't bode well for his night, especially with the heart of the Reds batting order to follow. Though Leiter induces harmless flies from the next two batters, he then must face Greg Vaughn, the National League's player of the month for September. During Cincinnati's late-season surge, Vaughn collected one huge hit after another, including a three-run blast in Milwaukee last night that made this game possible.

Vaughn works the count full, whipping the Reds fans into a frenzy. Few in the crowd doubt Vaughn will come through again until Leiter freezes him with a curveball. Called strike three, inning over, crisis averted, crowd silenced once more.

The Reds and their fans are scarcely heard from again. Leiter dominates for the rest of the game, at one point setting down thirteen

Cincinnati batters in order. The righties are pounded on the hands mercilessly, the lefties fed wicked breaking pitches. Barely a ball leaves the infield. The crowd sits on its hands, waiting for a reason to cheer that never comes. Though his teammates cobble together three more runs for insurance, these prove unnecessary.

Only in the ninth does Cincinnati show any signs of life, as they collect their first extra-base hit of the game. Though Leiter chastises himself in typical Leiter fashion—stalking the mound, screaming into his glove—he secures the final out, albeit in heart-pounding fashion, as a line drive off the bat of Dmitri Young almost takes his head off. The pitcher whirls around, hoping someone, anyone, will be able to track it down.

That someone is Edgardo Alfonzo, of course. The second baseman scurries to his right, drops to his knees, and spears the liner for the final out. Leiter raises his arms in triumph before being engulfed by his teammates, who pour in from the outfield and out from the dugout to celebrate an actual, for-real trip to the playoffs after two years of doubts and second-guessing, and eleven years in the wilderness for the franchise.

In the triumphant visiting clubhouse, when asked if this trip to the playoffs redeems all that preceded it, Valentine betrays bitterness for a moment. "The last thing I want to do is shed a shadow on what this team has done in the last week," he says. "I'm not going to talk about the garbage written about me." He moves past this, though, and spares a thought for Jack McKeon, whose hand he shook when the game was over, making sure to congratulate him on a great season. "To win ninety-six games and not have a tomorrow," Valentine says. "I probably had that thought run through my body once or twice."

Then he pauses and observes the scene around him, the champagne spraying and screaming and laughter and hugging, and for a moment he feels outside himself. It is so real it looks unreal, like a dream he has had many times, like a dream he is still having.

"I have imagined a room like this," he says.

CHAPTER 7

Delivery

THE DIAMONDBACKS ARE Buck Showalter's team. When George Steinbrenner unceremoniously dismissed him as manager of the Yankees following the 1995 season, Jerry Colangelo, owner of the newly awarded franchise in Arizona, snatched Showalter up and christened him not merely the skipper of the nascent team, but its architect as well. With twenty-seven months on his hands before the team took the field, Showalter busied himself with every aspect of the team's development, from running intense minicamps for prospects to deciding where to situate the family section in an unbuilt ballpark. When architects arrived with plans for that ballpark, Showalter cut the blueprints into pieces to show the planners how it should *really* be done. Showalter turned down broadcast opportunities, comparing these years to the precious developmental moments of a child's infancy that he could never experience again, should he miss them.

Showalter is painted as a man from another time, someone who exhibits intense competitiveness that stands out even in a field that is nothing but competition. During his time as Yankee manager, he inspired respect from the New York press corps with his nose-to-the-grindstone attitude while also infuriating them with a tight-lipped approach to all inquiries. He often spoke as if he were an intelligence official threading the line between not lying and not revealing damaging secrets, even though the first teams under his tutelage weren't exactly world beaters. "We're talking about Mike Gallego and Pat Kelly, not Mantle and DiMaggio," grumbled one frustrated beat reporter.

The curt responses that didn't play in New York fit perfectly in Phoenix. He is still young for a manager (forty-three) when he leads the Diamondbacks to a surprise division title in 1999, yet possesses the mien of a classic Western hero. There could not be more of a contrast, it seems, between Showalter and the manager he will oppose in the first round of the playoffs, Bobby Valentine. No one can imagine Buck Showalter sneaking back into a dugout in disguise after an ejection. No one can imagine a player under Showalter's harsh gaze daring to fade down the stretch. The Diamondbacks enjoyed a healthy division lead in September and could have coasted to a title, yet captured twenty-one of their last twenty-seven games to finish with one hundred wins.

While old-fashioned grit and gumption make for good back-page copy, in truth the Diamondbacks are every bit the checkbook champs that the Mets are. Arizona undertook a complete makeover for its sophomore year, signing center fielder Steve Finley, leadoff sparkplug Tony Womack, and starting pitcher Todd Stottlemyre, then upgraded their bullpen midseason via a trade for Matt Mantei, closer for the championship Marlins team of 1997. They even benefitted from some plain-old dumb luck by picking up undistinguished outfielder Luis Gonzalez, who shocked everyone by exploding for 111 RBIs and a league-leading 206 hits, and also received unprecedented output from second baseman Jay Bell, who'd never hit more than twenty-one homers in a season before clubbing an astonishing thirty-eight in 1999. Protected by these surprise producers, third baseman Matt Williams (a remainder from Arizona's first year) rebounded from a disappointing 1998 to put up MVP-caliber numbers, smacking thirty-two homers and driving in 142 runs.

Arizona's biggest addition, in more ways than one, is Randy Johnson, the six-foot-ten fire-throwing lefty who is able to mow down batters at will. The pitcher known as The Big Unit was one of the most sought-after free agents in the previous off-season, and the Diamondbacks stunned baseball by landing him with a five-year, $52.4 million contract. With a fastball that routinely touches 100 mph and a visage that resembles a grizzled prospector, Johnson ignored the offensive explosion of 1999 by pitching to a 2.48 ERA and holding opposing batters to a .208 average while striking out 364, a single-season total bested only by Sandy Koufax and Nolan Ryan. At a time when fewer pitchers than ever are throwing complete games, Johnson logged over 271 innings and went the distance twelve times.

Facing Johnson is a daunting prospect, a fact pointed out by a few spoilsports while the Mets are still celebrating capturing the wild card berth in Cincinnati. The Mets will counter Randy Johnson with Masato Yoshii, though not because they believe Yoshii matches up to The Big Unit in any sense. After four straight days of must-win games to reach the playoffs and using ace Al Leiter in the play-in game, it's simply Yoshii's turn in the rotation.

Distracted by the arduous business of making the playoffs, the Mets hand in their postseason roster at the last minute the morning after the game in Cincinnati. The biggest surprise is the inclusion of Bobby Bonilla, who has been used sparingly and exclusively as a pinch hitter since his return from the disabled list in early September. It is assumed that Bonilla offers Bobby Valentine another lefty bat, even if Bonilla's heart does not seem to be in October. More than once, he has said he'd be just as happy to stay at home and earn his paycheck from there.

The other surprise inclusion on the Mets' playoff roster is Melvin Mora. Despite his heroics in the last game against the Pirates, Mora possesses a dearth of major league experience. He is chosen because of his versatility, since he can spell both Rey Ordóñez in the infield and Rickey Henderson in the outfield, but it is assumed he will be restricted to pinch running and defensive replacement duties, as he was during his intermittent major league callups throughout the season.

While some in the press quibble with the Mets' roster choices, most of their griping is aimed at MLB's scheduling. A full slate of playoff action is set for October 5, with the Braves playing the Astros and the Yankees playing the Rangers in the first games of their respective series. Someone must draw the late game, and it makes sense the team playing in the Pacific time zone would get the nod. Nonetheless, the New York–based scribes are angered by a first pitch scheduled after 11:00 p.m. Gotham time. "The only people who can stay up for these games are insomniacs or binging crackheads," harrumphs the *Daily News*. By the time the game in Phoenix begins, the Braves-Astros tilt in Atlanta is long over, with Houston a surprise winner over Greg Maddux, while Orlando Hernández and the Yankees are mere outs away from a blowout win over Texas.

The New York writers are perturbed that they must accommodate the local clock for a city that's low on baseball enthusiasm. Matt Williams concedes the locals are "not rabid baseball fans," a brutally honest assessment confirmed by the fact that Phoenix media fails to rake the third baseman across the coals for pronouncing it. Writers from New York's dailies scoff at the atmosphere of Bank One Ballpark, calling out its thundering sound system as overcompensation, mocking the swimming pool beyond the outfield fence. One fan confirms city slickers' prejudices when he tells the Associated Press, "Even if you don't like baseball, there's a lot to do here." Further snobbish provincialism is shown when New York writers refer to Phoenix, a city of over three million, as "Dogpatch," surmise the locals prefer tractor pulls to baseball, and fall over themselves laughing when an Arizona newspaper publishes a fans' guide to the playoffs. "Make noise, don't leave early," are among its instructions, along with a guide on proper etiquette when dealing with ticket scalpers.

Whether they've been tutored in baseball watching or are imbued with genuine excitement, the fans who crowd into the BOB are at full throat when game one begins. Temperatures at game time stand at a tolerable ninety-three degrees, so the stadium's retractable roof remains open, and yet the cheers resound thunderously when Randy Johnson retires his first batter. They are less loud when the second batter, Edgardo Alfonzo, belts a Johnson fastball off the façade of a bunting-laced stanchion in straightaway center for a solo shot. And they are positively silent in the top of the third when John Olerud clubs a Johnson offering ten rows deep into the right-field bleachers for a two-run homer, putting the Mets up by three. The Big Unit hadn't given up a home run to a lefty batter in over two years.

After the Diamondbacks scratch out a run in the bottom of the third, the Mets respond when Robin Ventura hits a double to start the fourth—another big hit by a lefty against a pitcher who allowed nine hits to left-handed batters all season—and soon comes around to score, expanding the Mets' lead to 4–1. But after Johnson escapes the fourth with no more damage done, he pitches like a man possessed, putting up zeroes in each of the next four innings, striking out Mets with devastating ease.

Meanwhile, it becomes clear that the Diamondbacks are taking their measure of Masato Yoshii, as every ball they put in play seems to be hit a little harder than the last. A solo shot in the bottom of the fourth cuts the Mets' lead down to two runs, and in the sixth, a monstrous two-run home run by Luis Gonzalez, crushed 452 feet to dead center, erases that lead altogether.

Johnson enters the ninth inning with 120 pitches under his belt and not the slightest indication he might be tiring or the slightest indication he wants to leave the mound. He has lost his last five postseason starts dating back to 1995, most of those losses being the hard-luck kind. With the score still tied at four, he is bound and determined to see this game to its conclusion. So when Ventura starts the ninth with a single, he shrugs it off. One out later, Rey Ordóñez bounces a single between third and short, the first true sign that Johnson's willing spirit might have to bow to his weakening flesh. This becomes clearer once Melvin Mora, a late substitution in the outfield, works a walk to load the bases.

Buck Showalter doesn't want to remove Johnson any more than Johnson wants to be removed, but the pitcher's sudden fall from grace forces the manager's hand. As Johnson falters, two relievers are warmed up and ready to enter the game. One is Matt Mantei, the closer Arizona nabbed from the Marlins at the deadline, but Showalter is wary of bringing in Mantei with the bases loaded due to his tendency toward wildness. So instead of turning to his best reliever, Showalter instead brings in Bobby Chouinard, who spent large stretches of this year in the minors and made Arizona's postseason roster by the skin of his teeth.

Chouinard falls behind in the count to Rickey Henderson before the all-time steals leader smashes a ball down the third base line. Gold Glover Matt Williams, positioned on the grass for a play at the plate, dives to stop the ball and throws from his knees in time to record a force out at home. An ecstatic crowd chants "M-V-P!" in Williams's direction while a flabbergasted Henderson stands at first, hands on hips, shaking his head in disbelief.

This thrilling reprieve for Arizona lasts all of five pitches. Chouinard looks uncomfortable throwing to the next batter, Edgardo Alfonzo, firing a slew of pitches that come nowhere near the plate. Behind in the count, the pitcher is forced to offer something in the strike zone. Alfonzo crushes his offering down the left-field line, the ball arcing higher and higher as it goes. It is surely ticketed for the upper deck. The only question is what side of the foul pole it will land on. Alfonzo gallops up toward first, clutching the bat in both hands, while Ordóñez spins around at third base to watch its trajectory.

The ball lands to the right of the foul pole by a matter of feet, making it a grand slam. Once the umpires give their signal, Alfonzo drops his bat and allows himself a small fist pump before trotting the bases. Some disappointed Arizona fans are up and out of their seats before Alfonzo's blast lands, hoping to beat traffic. Those who make their way to the exits miss nothing in the bottom half of the inning, as the home team goes quietly before Armando Benítez to seal the Mets' stunning 8–4 victory. Randy Johnson has yet another hard-luck playoff defeat. The Mets have yet another miraculous win, in a week that has brought them nothing else.

* * *

In game two of the divisional series, everything that had gone the Mets' way in their miraculous week reverses course. It does not seem a coincidence that when the Mets' luck changes, Kenny Rogers is on the mound.

Rogers is opposed by Todd Stottlemyre, who is pitching on borrowed time after being diagnosed with a 70 percent tear of his rotator cuff. This normally calls for reconstructive surgery, but that is a risky proposition for someone at the advanced pitcher's age of thirty-four. Stottlemyre chose instead to strengthen his upper body and take pressure off the damaged shoulder. Doctors cautioned this rendered his arm a ticking time bomb, but he still considered the workout regimen the better of two bad options.

Game two starts at the same late hour as game one, 11:00 p.m. eastern time, due to another full day of playoff action. (The Indians take the first game of their series against the Red Sox, while the Braves even up their series against the Astros; both tilts wrap up well before the contest in Phoenix.) The Mets put many runners on base against Stottlemyre, but in a disturbing reminder of their offensive struggles at the end of September, nearly all are stranded. They break through for a moment in the top of the third when Rickey Henderson hits a leadoff single and eventually scores on a sac fly, but this will be the extent of their offense for the evening, and Rogers gives back this advantage and then some in the bottom half.

Rogers records two quick outs in that inning before loading the bases on a hit batsman and a pair of singles, the last of which is a Matt Williams chopper that so perturbs the pitcher, he loses focus and walks the next batter to force in the tying run. He nearly wiggles off the hook by getting ahead in the count against Steve Finley before allowing a single to right. The runner at third scores easily, with Williams hot on his heels. Roger Cedeño fields the ball and fires a bullet to home, and to the naked eye it appears Mike Piazza tags out Williams on his left leg before he touches the plate. The runner is called safe nonetheless, handing Arizona a two-run lead.

In the top of the fourth, a potential Mets rally is doused when Robin Ventura is picked off of second base, though replays show he may not have been tagged at all. Two close calls in two half innings go against the Mets, a sharp reversal of fortune from the many judgments in their favor in the last week.

Rogers staggers as far as the fifth inning before hitting the showers. Pat Mahomes and Octavio Dotel prevent any hope of a comeback by allowing two more runs each, and the Mets make little noise the rest of the way as they go down in defeat, 7–1, to even up the division series at a game apiece.

The Mets don't sound too broken up about the loss afterward. Mike Piazza professes to speak for the clubhouse when he says, "Nobody here is disappointed at all with coming away with a split." Robin Ventura echoes the sentiment: "To win a game in a division series, to split, to go back home, to beat Randy Johnson, where we were last week, we'll take anything," the third baseman says. The press clutches its pearls at such talk. "Is there any sense of urgency," William C. Rhoden of the *Times* wonders, "or do they see anything from this point on as gravy?" But after a week of running on little more than adrenaline, the team is too exhausted to care about quibbles with their attitude. "We've got a day off tomorrow and we'll take it," Valentine says ahead of the team's flight back to New York. "Our guys can use it."

* * *

He can't say when the pain started because there's always *some* pain. If it's not his knees, it's his back. If it's not his back, it's his shoulders. If it's not his shoulders, it's his glove hand, pounded by a million fastballs. If it's not his glove hand, it's his throwing hand, nicked by a million backswings. Mike Piazza is a catcher. Catching means pain.

Had the Mets taken an easier path to the playoffs, Mike Piazza would have been given more time off down the stretch. But the Mets forced themselves to scratch and claw their way into October, and so forced their star catcher to play more than he should have. Anyone with eyes can see he is exhausted after a long season. He went hitless during the play-in game in Cincinnati and collected only two hits in the first two games in Arizona, both singles. He endured the pain because his mere presence forced the opposition to pitch to everyone else. He would rest when everyone else rested, on Thursday, the team's first off day in three weeks. He said little about the pain because he was counted on to play no matter what, so what was the point in complaining?

For reporters covering Piazza, such stoicism is often interpreted as a lack of fire. When Piazza admits to being satisfied with a split of the first two games in Arizona, Mark Kriegel of the *Daily News* accuses him of being too much of a "laid-back Californian," dredging up the criticisms he drew when he first came to Queens. "Sometimes you wonder if he'd rather play drums than baseball," Kriegel wonders. Piazza rarely responds to such pop psychology, and, as with the pain of catching, has grown to accept all but the worst of it.

Then the worst of it comes. The thumb on his glove hand feels like it's on fire. This is the same thumb that was whacked by a backswing during a mid-September game, and the injury was further aggravated by a play at the plate during game two in Phoenix. When that game got away from the Mets in the late innings, his manager gave him the option of sitting out the last few innings. He refused.

Back in New York, Piazza receives a cortisone shot from the team doctor to alleviate the swelling, but the shot has the opposite effect. He wakes up the morning of October 8, hours before game three, to find his thumb swollen even worse than before. An allergic reaction. He can't bend it. Team medical officials can do little but stare at his grotesquely enlarged digit and shrug. The swelling will go down eventually, they say. Bobby Valentine holds off posting his lineup for as long as he can, hoping "eventually" might translate to "before first pitch." When Piazza and Valentine finally yield to the inevitable, the catcher appears at a press conference and attempts to answer questions about his health through the fog of a buffet of anti-inflammatory drugs.

Interviewed for a local news pregame show on NBC-4, Steve Phillips spins things as best he can, insisting he is "pretty confident" Piazza will be ready for game four the following day. This is either a willful misreading of the catcher's diagnosis or a bout of optimism bordering on the delusional. The team trainer's assessment, one more anchored in reality, says Piazza will require forty-eight to seventy-two hours after his cortisone shot to recover, which makes a start in game four doubtful at best. Valentine says Piazza may be available to pinch-hit, but when asked what would prompt an appearance by Piazza in his condition, the manager conjures up the frightening image of Orel Hershiser consulting the bat rack in a hypothetical fourteenth inning. Fans hoping for Piazza to pull a Willis Reed act are disappointed when he greets the Shea crowd during pregame player introductions while wearing a warm-up jacket, his injured thumb swaddled to bowling pin dimensions.

If anyone connected to the Mets is grateful for the Piazza injury, it might be Bobby Valentine. Bad though it is, the news overshadows turmoil of his own making.

The same day as game three, an issue of *Sports Illustrated* with a lengthy profile of Valentine hits the newsstands. Mostly sympathetic, the article concentrates on the many tribulations of Valentine's baseball life and his close connection to Stamford, the city that produced him. But the profile's author, S.L. Price, gathered most of his reporting while following the skipper during his rough weekend in Philadelphia at the end of September, and the quotes he offered prove red meat for New York's carnivorous tabloids. After trashing his predecessor, Dallas Green, as well as Bobby Bonilla and other unnamed malcontents on his roster ("You're not dealing with real intelligent guys for the most part . . . there's about five guys in there right now who basically are losers, who are seeing if they can recruit."), Valentine implied his current pitching coach, Dave Wallace, had leaned on the front office to fire Tom Robson, the team's former hitting coach and a close friend of Valentine's. He said he might quit altogether when the season is over. And just so no one felt left out, Valentine spared some time to threaten a reporter. Following the Mets' brutal loss in the Philadelphia finale, one beat writer dared ask him, "You said you felt good yesterday. How do you feel today?" then followed this zinger with a short laugh. Valentine had little to say in the moment but fumed later when alone with Price. "How about that fuckin' asshole?" he thundered. "I could stand up and say, 'As soon as I whack you and see you on the ground, I'll feel really good.'"

Confronted about his comments, Valentine never approaches apology. He is not sorry for the article's timing, which was beyond his control ("What am I supposed to do, call an editor and tell him when and how to run it?"), and is even less apologetic for what he said. "I'll tell [my players] if the shoe fits, wear it. If not, don't worry about it. Anything I said there I've said a thousand times before."

The players are unfazed, long since numbed to the controversies that flare up with Old Faithful regularity in a Valentine clubhouse. The only one who speaks on the record about it is Bobby Bonilla, who proclaims himself "disappointed" by the remarks, relishing the opportunity to play the injured party while his manager squirms. Everyone else stays quiet or offers anonymous comments. "Guys care about what's in here and doing what we have to do for ourselves," one anonymous player insists. "We don't care about what the manager says."

The game that follows provides ample proof of this contention. Rather than sag under the absence of Mike Piazza and another managerial controversy, the players are energized by their day off and a full Shea Stadium hosting its first playoff game in eleven years. With the Yankees enjoying an off day in their own division series, the Mets are able to start a game at a reasonable hour and with no local competition, all while enjoying brisk autumnal temperatures of fifty-eight degrees at game time.

The Mets build their advantage modestly, scoring once in the second inning and twice in the third. On the mound for the home team, Rick Reed is not quite the dominant pitcher seen in his previous start against the Pirates, but he keeps Arizona off the board with little trouble through the first four innings. Things get a little too close for comfort when Reed allows a two-run blast in the fifth, but he experiences no further issues, while his teammates take advantage of some ugly Arizona fielding to put up a crooked number in the bottom of the sixth. Right fielder Tony Womack, not known as a solid defender, barehands a single into foul territory to allow one run to score and heaves a weak relay throw home to permit another to cross the plate. The shoddy glovework and a barrage of singles conspire to drive in six Mets runs in the fateful sixth, making the rest of the game a purely academic exercise. The home team prevails, 9–2, and are now one win away from a trip to the National League Championship Series.

Though the state of Mike Piazza's thumb still looms large, after the game three win, the only questions posed about Valentine's *Sports Illustrated* profile ask how little mind the players paid them. "Like I said before the game," Valentine says, "they don't care about that nonsense."

* * *

Beats the hell outta delivering pizzas, don't it?
Backup catcher Todd Pratt fields this question more than any other, on those rare occasions when the press bothers to ask him anything. Whenever the question is asked, he must object. He never delivered pizzas. He *managed* a Domino's franchise, thank you very much. That was the kind of work awaiting Pratt when the Mariners released him following the 1996 season, and with his baseball career seemingly over, he was grateful to have any job at all. It was hard work, sweaty and cramped and without a shred of glory. Not too different from catching, really.

Pratt split his time between Domino's and a part-time instructional gig at Bucky Dent's Baseball Academy in Florida until the Mets offered him a minor league deal in 1997. He hit well enough to receive a call-up in July of that year and was given a good number of starts when Todd Hundley was lost to Tommy John surgery. His future was unclear for great stretches of 1998, when the Mets' catching situation was muddied by their acquisition of Mike Piazza and the awkward post-Tommy John surgery return of Todd Hundley, and he spent a good chunk of his year at triple-A Norfolk. By the time the 1999 season began, with Hundley gone off toward the LA sunset, Pratt felt confident he'd established himself as Mike Piazza's one and only understudy.

Such a role calls Todd Pratt to action as often as the Maytag repairman, leaving him time to double as the team's resident cheerleader. In the dugout, no one yells louder, claps harder, or high-fives more forcefully. In the clubhouse, no one defends his teammates more virulently. They call him Tank because he moves like one, rolling over whatever gets in his way. He takes personally every nasty word scribbled about his team. After the Mets' win in Cincinnati sends them into the playoffs, Pratt takes time out from spraying champagne to blast members of the press as "frontrunners," damning them for praising a team they'd buried days earlier.

Pratt plays good soldier when he receives the bulk of attention due to Piazza's thumb injury, yet all the questions he must field are about the man he will replace. *When do you think Piazza will be back? Do you know if he's available to pinch-hit? What did he say to you, Todd?*

"I'm not Mike," Pratt says. As if anyone was in danger of confusing the two.

Al Leiter, who will throw to Todd Pratt in game four, reminds everyone that when he made one of his best starts of the year—a fifteen-strikeout effort at Wrigley Field—Pratt was his receiver. "He really wants to catch a good game," Leiter says, well-meaning but faint praise for the man who is the Mets' equivalent of the dreaded slip inserted into the playbill that regrets to inform ticketholders their beloved star will not be appearing at this performance.

As game four unfolds, Leiter is not the dominator seen in Cincinnati. In that game, the Reds batters barely put the bat on the ball, whereas the Diamondbacks do almost nothing else this afternoon. Leiter leads a charmed life in the initial frames, relying on his defense to turn all the hard-hit shots into loud outs. It's clear that it is only a matter of time before someone gets to him, however, and that someone is first baseman Greg Colbrunn, who hits a wall-scraping homer to left to tie the game at one in the top of the fifth.

Wary of throwing Randy Johnson on short rest after he expended 138 pitches in game one, Buck Showalter rolls the dice and turns instead to Brian Anderson, a lefty control artist who flitted between Arizona's starting rotation and bullpen this season. The Mets break through against him in the bottom of the fourth when Edgardo Alfonzo turns on a knee-high changeup and sends it into the left-field bleachers for a solo shot, but Anderson proves stingy otherwise, negotiating the rest of the inning with no further trouble and tossing a scoreless fifth as well.

When the Mets come to bat in the bottom of the sixth, they've logged a grand total of three baserunners against Anderson. Luckily for them, the inning begins with an at bat by Henderson, a player who has made an art out of reaching base safely. Backed into a two-strike count, Henderson fouls off an Anderson offering. Then he fouls off the next one. And the next one, and the one after that too. Henderson has to lunge to reach some of these pitches, but reach them he does. Anderson is determined to stay around the plate, and Henderson is determined to find something he can hit. On pitch number fourteen, Henderson wins the battle, dunking a single into shallow right, a result that fires up the Shea crowd and leaves Anderson visibly perturbed. One out later, John Olerud lashes a single to left that moves Henderson to third, and Benny Agbayani follows with a double into the right-field gap. Henderson scores to put the Mets back on top, and they appear to be poised to score much more.

With his afternoon on the brink of unraveling completely, Anderson catches a huge break when he induces a comebacker from Robin Ventura that freezes the runners. Arizona escapes the inning without allowing another run and logs another goose egg in the bottom of the seventh. The Mets are left to wonder how they could only scrape together two runs against the crafty but hardly overpowering southpaw.

Given a slim 2–1 lead, Al Leiter attempts to make it stand up by pitching his own scoreless seventh. When he sets down the first two batters in the eighth, the Mets are four outs away from a trip to the next round of the playoffs. Though John Franco and Armando Benítez are warming up in the bullpen, Leiter might be able to finish this one all by himself, loud outs be damned.

Then the Diamondbacks send up pinch hitter Turner Ward, who Leiter inexplicably walks on four pitches. The next batter, speedy leadoff man Tony Womack, has been held in check the entire series and struck out twice today, but he hits a hard grounder that takes a bad hop in front of Alfonzo. The second baseman knocks it down with the heel of his glove, but an extra nanosecond of bobbling is all the time the speedster needs to reach first safely.

Bobby Valentine pulls his ace and calls on Armando Benítez for a four-out save, a feat he was rarely asked to perform during the regular season. Benítez responds by falling behind Jay Bell before giving up a booming drive to left field. The blast nearly clears the fence, bouncing off the top of the wall. By the time Melvin Mora runs down the ball, both Ward and Womack have scored to give Arizona a 3–2 lead, and Bell has cruised into second.

With first base open, the Mets walk dangerous lefty batter Luis Gonzalez to face Matt Williams (also dangerous, but a righty) instead. Benítez backs the third baseman into a two-strike hole, only to give up a sharp line-drive single to left. All in one motion, Melvin Mora scoops up the ball and fires a throw toward the plate. Todd Pratt fields his bullet and sweeps around to tag Bell a hair before he reaches home, keeping the deficit at one run.

Now holding the advantage, Buck Showalter makes a few moves for defense in the bottom of the eighth. Among other transfers, he shifts Tony Womack from shortstop to right field, a move that will come into play almost immediately. After Edgardo Alfonzo earns a leadoff walk, John Olerud sends a fly ball to right that Womack loses in the low late-afternoon sun, allowing Alfonzo to run to third and Olerud to second. Roger Cedeño follows with a long sac fly to tie the game at three. However, the Mets are denied a chance to take the lead when Diamondbacks closer Matt Mantei induces a comebacker from Todd Pratt that renders Olerud a dead duck at home, then strikes out Rey Ordóñez to sidestep further damage.

Benítez and Mantei trade zeroes in the ninth, while John Franco pitches a scoreless top of the tenth. Buck Showalter sticks with Mantei in the bottom of the tenth, and Robin Ventura obliges him by offering at his first pitch and flying out to right. On WFAN, Gary Cohen surmises that Ventura hoped to end the game with one swing. The next batter, Todd Pratt, has no such delusions, having hit only three long balls all year. It's been a frustrating day at the plate for Piazza's backup. Three times he has come to the plate with at least one runner in scoring position. On each occasion, he hit an ineffectual ground ball that produced nothing. Had he come through even once, the Mets might be celebrating instead of playing extra innings.

Matt Mantei's second pitch to Pratt is a fastball that catches too much of the plate to ignore, and the catcher wheels on it, giving the ball a ride to straightaway center. The crowd exhales a rising, hopeful roar. For a moment Pratt allows himself some hope, hopping at home plate with his arms outstretched in a Carlton Fisk impression. Then he remembers that center field is Steve Finley territory. The catcher has seen Finley's act too many times on *SportsCenter*, the Gold Glover speeding to the wall to rob an extra-base hit. Pratt executes a perfunctory jog to first base, sighing, muttering to himself over his lousy day at the plate.

Finley beats the fly to the wall by a few precious seconds, but has little time to find his footing near the 410-foot marker and execute a desperate leap. His jump is awkward, his body leaning rightward at a forty-five-degree angle, his feet barely leaving the ground. But Finley stands at six feet, two inches, and he doesn't need much air to keep a ball from leaving the yard. He has done this hundreds of times before. His leather clears the top of the fence, barely. He closes his glove.

The first person to realize what Todd Pratt has done is Charlie Rappa of Bay Fireworks, who is situated behind the center-field fence, readying a pyrotechnical display that will celebrate a series-clinching victory, should the Mets pull one off. As the roars from the stands swell, Rappa looks up from his post and sees something bouncing his way. It is a baseball. That baseball means Todd Pratt has homered. It means the Mets have won the game, and the series.

The second person to realize what Pratt has done is Steve Finley. He touches back to the ground and peers into his glove, expecting to see a ball there, and finds nothing. Finley places his hands on his hips, slumps them to his side, and darts his head left and right for a cue about what to do with himself now that it's all over.

Seeing Finley's reaction, the Mets run onto the field, screaming and towel waving, as John Franco executes a strange high-kicking move somewhere between an Irish jig and a whirling dervish.

The last person to realize what Todd Pratt has done is Todd Pratt. He rounds first, his eyes shut, grimacing. He has no idea what has transpired until the crowd's window-rattling screams mingle with "mojo risin' . . ." blasting through Shea's PA system. Only then does he raise his arms in triumph and begin running around the bases. And he is running, as fast as a backup catcher's knees will allow. As Pratt's teammates wait for his arrival at home plate, the catcher finds himself choking back tears and slowing his run to jog. He's in no hurry for this to end.

CHAPTER 8

The March to Atlanta

THIS WAS SUPPOSED to be about disease. First Lady Hillary Clinton is visiting a biological field station in Westchester County, in the hopes of promoting a nationwide network to track emerging health crises, and to raise her profile in New York's senate race, her candidacy as-yet unofficial though all but assured. But with the Mets and Yankees both one step away from facing each other in the World Series, the question everyone wants to ask Clinton is, "Who ya got?"

There is little distinction between the sport and political beats at the moment, as local reps talk of nothing but baseball. José Serrano, congressman from the Bronx, reluctantly agrees to attend a House subcommittee meeting, on pain of losing his chairmanship, but only if he can keep one eye on the Yankees game while doing so. Gary Ackerman, Democrat from Queens, shares a party with Serrano but not rooting interests. "There are some things upon which we can compromise and agree. This is not one of them," says the Mets fan with deathly seriousness. After Boston overcomes an 0–2 deficit to take their division series against Cleveland, Vito Fosella, Republican from Staten Island, spends much of the next week needling a colleague from New England over the Yanks' presumed impending victory over the Red Sox in the upcoming American League Championship Series.

Hillary Clinton still has not officially announced her candidacy for New York's Senate seat, but her declaration of "lifelong" Yankee fandom in June essentially made that announcement already. The *Times* was polite compared to most when it deemed this move "politically inartful." Now in October, she straddles the middle. "I am for a Subway Series!"

she declares. "I can state that without fear of any contradiction. I think it would be great for New York and hope it comes to pass." She is then hustled off from the press conference by her press secretary, who hastens to mention that he is a Yankees fan, even though no one asked.

"Real" Subway Series fantasies are more pronounced than ever now that both the Mets and Yankees have dispatched their first-round opponents. (The Yankees swept the Rangers in the division series for the second straight year.) "If there really is a baseball god," insists Tom Keegan in the *Post*, "then all seven games of the final World Series of the millennium will be played within the boundaries of New York City." Keegan's *Post*-mate Joel Sherman writes, "We have not had an exclusive Big Apple World Series in 43 years. It is time." The staid *New York Times* gives over space in its op-ed section to wax poetic about the possibility. "It's not too early to dream about a Subway Series, as every Noo Yawker worth a MetroCard is doing," sayeth the Old Gray Lady.

It would be good for the city. Clinton says it. Both of New York's current senators, Chuck Schumer and Daniel Patrick Moynihan, each of whom profess allegiances to the Yankees, say it. Mayor Giuliani, biggest Yankees fan of them all, has said it more times than can be counted. All the while, the press continues to publish "good for the city" bromides even as they capture comments from fans that boil over with undisguised contempt.

"I really saw the Mets bandwagon take off in the 1980s, and that flew in the face of the history and tradition of the Yankees," one Bronx Bombers fan sniffs. "It was demeaning to baseball."

"I want to put [Mets fans] in their place, sweep them, and get them out of my hair, once and for all," says a man who paid playoff ticket prices to attend game three of the division series at Shea while draped in Yankees gear, for the express purpose of shouting insults at his upper-deck neighbors.

From the other side: "They just are so arrogant," says one Mets fan of the Yankees partisans. "You've got all your Wall Street boys with cigars and suits, bragging like they've been fans for life. And they don't even acknowledge that other teams exist."

Another derides the lot of Yankees fans as "too easy." "Five-nothing, six-nothing, seven-nothing—it's boring. With the Mets, there's always an uh-oh."

For most Subway Series skepticism, you have to look out of town, where the prospect of an all–New York World Series fills people with dread. Leigh Montville of *Sport Illustrated* writes about a Subway Series as if it were an approaching hurricane. "The rest of America had better make preparations," he warns. "Plywood should be nailed over all windows. Sandbags should be placed around all walls. Provisions, food and water should be assembled. This could be the worst sports storm of hype and sentimentality of the entire sports century."

* * *

Once Todd Pratt's home run eludes Steve Finley's glove, the Mets have two days before the National League Championship Series begins at Turner Field on October 12. They take the energy they would have used to play and channel it into forty-eight hours of fightin' words against the Braves, who will be their opponents by virtue of defeating the Astros in four games. When last the two teams met, Atlanta was sure they'd buried New York once and for all, and reveled in the thought. And now here the Mets are, back from the dead and believing the Braves' attempts to kill them have only made them stronger.

"I thought I had heard that [the Braves] were shocked and surprised that we weren't in," Al Leiter says in the champagne-soaked clubhouse following the division series clincher. "They must be really shocked and surprised now." Turk Wendell has the nerve to say, "I think it'll be more special once we beat the Braves," avoiding the cautious preposition "if." Regarding Chipper Jones's now infamous remarks ("go home and put their Yankees' stuff on . . ."), Wendell says, "All I have to say is he stuck his foot in his mouth. He's going to have to deal with it every game. He's going to have to deal with the fans." Darryl Hamilton has worn a Mets uniform for a mere two months and change, but he's packed a lot of resentment into such a small space. "One thing that we've got to remember is the fact that they are supposed to beat us. And *they* said that."

To the surprise of no one, the loudest, angriest darts come from Bobby Valentine's quiver. "We were supposed to be dead, right?" he sneers. "Our fans were supposed to change gear . . . I think he was very confident he wouldn't have to deal with the fans again this year. Guess what, he's going to have to deal with them again this year."

"I'm the guy with the big mouth," Valentine says, "but they're the ones playing ghosts."

The Braves don't need ghosts to spook them. The Houston Astros gave them enough of a fright for one October. Atlanta was shocked in game one of their division series when Greg Maddux was outpitched by Houston starter Shane Reynolds at Turner Field. After tying up the series the following day, the Braves endured an extra-inning nail-biter in Houston in game three, a contest they came within a hair of losing numerous times before eking out a win in the twelfth inning. Then, they took a comfortable seven-run lead in game four before a late Houston onslaught brought the home team within two runs. John Rocker logged a four-out save to conclude the final baseball game ever played at the Astrodome.

Bobby Cox can't let Valentine's words go unanswered. "That's a joke, a joke, the lack-of-respect angle," Cox says, referring to Bobby Valentine's contention that the Braves had been not-so-quietly dismissing the Mets for years. His charges soon chime in, chief among them John Rocker. "I'm really shocked to see how they had to squeak into the playoffs with a one-game playoff," the Braves' closer says with mock concern. "I thought they would beat us out for the division, just looking on paper, at talent, theirs versus ours." And slugger Brian Jordan, who has not been quiet about his antipathy for New York, retorts, "We're not at this level for nothing," while dismissing any effect keyed-up Mets fans might have on the series, "unless you jump out on the field and hit one of us."

For the most part, however, the Braves stick to gracious nods to the opposition or silence. Chipper Jones stays quiet about the Mets and directs his ire at Braves fans instead. While Mets fans camp out overnight at Shea Stadium to purchase championship series tickets, Atlanta has more than six thousand unsold seats for the first game one day before the series begins, with another nine thousand seats unclaimed for game two. "This is an exciting team, a blue-collar team," Chipper gripes, "and this team deserves to have the backing of its fans." Having said his piece on this subject, he refuses all interview requests prior to game one.

When the rematch begins, rain that cut short batting practice earlier in the day has dissipated, though the first pitch is delayed by four minutes while the grounds crew dries up the field. The crowd at Turner Field is charged up, even if the announced attendance is 44,172, or roughly six thousand short of capacity. New York reporters can't conceive of a city where playoff games aren't a hot ticket, but one local sportswriter blames the start of hunting season for interfering with the Braves' postseason attendance numbers. "How can New Yorkers complain about no-shows," reasons the *Post*, "when we've never had to choose between supporting our team or killing defenseless animals?"

Greg Maddux climbs the mound for Atlanta in game one and once again suffocates the Mets lineup with brutal efficiency, working his way around what little trouble he finds and accepting gifts when the Mets make his job easier. After Roger Cedeño leads off the top of the third with a double and moves to third on an error, Rey Ordóñez hits a weak dribbler that becomes out number one when, rather than run, he stays in the batter's box to argue that the ball had rolled foul. Then Masato Yoshii botches a suicide squeeze attempt by bunting right through a Maddux fastball, rendering Cedeño dead on arrival as he sprints home.

Masato Yoshii draws the game one start for the Mets based on his strong September and serviceable performance against Arizona in the division series, but little signs of these outings are in evidence as he puts the Mets in an immediate hole. Atlanta's leadoff man Gerald Williams singles on the first pitch Yoshii throws, then steals second and scampers home on a Bret Boone single. Yoshii escapes the first with no further damage, however, and keeps Atlanta off the board over the three innings that follow. The Mets tie the game in the top of the fourth on an RBI grounder. This comes off of the compromised bat of Mike Piazza, back in the lineup but still in obvious pain from his thumb injury, wincing on every swing.

The Braves strike back in the bottom of the fifth with a leadoff double into the right-field corner by Walt Weiss. When Maddux attempts to bunt the runner over, Yoshii turns his left ankle as he fields the ball. Though Yoshii argues he should be allowed to stay in the game, despite his injury his very next pitch to Gerald Williams is zipped through a drawn-in infield, scoring Weiss and giving the Braves the lead. Yoshii is removed with two outs in the inning and storms into the visiting clubhouse, where he breaks a bat and tosses chairs in frustration.

The Braves tack on in the sixth on a solo shot by catcher Eddie Pérez—who surprised everyone with a strong performance at the plate in the division series as a replacement for the injured Javy López—and add another run on a Walt Weiss RBI single. All the while, Maddux contains the Mets and barely breaks a sweat in the effort. In the top of the seventh, Rey Ordóñez hits a screamer right up the middle that Maddux spears for the third out of the inning. As he heads back to his dugout, he flicks the ball at the mound behind him, as if disposing of a bug that had been pestering him.

When the Mets push a baserunner to third base with two outs in the top of the eighth, John Rocker sprints from the bullpen to fan an overmatched John Olerud and extinguish any thought of a rally. The Mets receive some hope in the ninth when pinch hitter Shawon Dunston reaches on a two-out error by Chipper Jones, moves to second on a wild pitch, and scores on a single from pinch hitter Todd Pratt. That brings the tying run to the plate, but it brings it in the person of Rey Ordóñez. With no one left on his bench who can play shortstop, Bobby Valentine is forced to place his hopes in Ordóñez, and he watches him ground out to third for the game's final out, as the Braves prevail, 4–2.

The failure was a true group effort. Yoshii pitched poorly and botched a squeeze play attempt. Leadoff man Rickey Henderson was held hitless, as were Robin Ventura and Mike Piazza. Runners were stranded in scoring position in the fourth, sixth, eighth, and ninth innings. The Mets' vaunted defense committed two errors. And when Rey Ordóñez came to the plate as the tying run in the ninth inning, Bobby Valentine had no viable option to bat for him, having outfoxed himself with too many substitutions earlier. "It felt as if the Braves had beaten the Mets more thoroughly than the score indicated," Judy Battista wrote in the *Times*, "and pushed the recent upstart just a bit farther down the hill."

* * *

The Mets' loss in game one has many authors. The result of game two will be ascribed to one man's decisions, or lack thereof.

Conditions for game two are almost identical to those of the opener. Once again rain threatens for much of the day, and once again it clears in time to allow the game to start as scheduled at 4:00 p.m. Once again, the Turner Field crowd is short of a sellout by about six thousand paying customers.

Fresh off tossing a one-hitter against the Astros in the division series, Kevin Millwood takes the mound for Atlanta. The Mets work quickly against the young righty, opening the top of the second with a walk and two consecutive singles to plate a run, giving them their first lead of the series. With runners at the corners and nobody out, they are poised to score more until Rey Ordóñez inexplicably attempts to bunt his way on base with the pitcher's spot due up next. His bunt pops weakly into the pitcher's glove for out number one, and the Mets fail to score any more runs in the inning.

Rickey Henderson exits the game after that frame, dealing with a flu bug he can't shake, and Melvin Mora takes his place in left field. The health-necessitated move pays dividends as Mora is the far superior defender, holding batters to singles where Henderson might have conceded doubles. Mora even chips in some shocking offense, clubbing a

Millwood fastball into the left-field bleachers for his first major league homer to put the Mets up 2–0 in the top of the fifth.

That lead is entrusted to the unsure hands of Kenny Rogers. The Gambler's start against Arizona in the division series made no one forget his previous struggles in the playoffs, nor does this one. Rogers allows many baserunners in the early going but skirts trouble with a pick-off move that nails two would-be base stealers. Protests from the Braves that Rogers balked fall on deaf ears. When Andruw Jones hits a one-out single in the fourth, he is so traumatized from being picked off earlier that he stands with both feet on the first base bag as if he were a sprinter waiting to hear the starter's pistol. Through five innings, Rogers has what NBC's Bob Costas terms "one very ugly shutout going."

In the bottom of the sixth, the ugliness continues while the shutout does not. First, the lefty walks Chipper Jones before Brian Jordan dings one of his fastballs off the right-field foul pole for a game-tying homer. Then he allows a single to Andruw Jones, bringing Eddie Pérez to the plate. Pérez is coming off a great series against the Astros and belted a home run in game one. He is also a right-handed batter who would hit well against the lefty Rogers. Turk Wendell, a righty, is ready in the bullpen. Any of these reasons alone are sufficient to give Kenny Rogers the hook. Bobby Valentine acts on none of them and leaves Rogers on the mound. His very first pitch to Pérez is hammered into the seats in left field, putting the Braves ahead, 4–2. In the span of seven pitches, the Mets allow a two-run lead to become a two-run deficit. The manager tears his cap off his head and slams it into everything at arm's length in the dugout before tossing it to the ground.

Turk Wendell and Armando Benítez combine for three scoreless innings, a strong relief effort that makes Valentine's failure to yank Rogers even more damaging in retrospect. The same goes for the Mets' brief flirtation with a comeback in the top of the eighth. After Melvin Mora hits a one-out single under the unsure glove of Chipper Jones, Edgardo Alfonzo belts a long double that scores the speedy Mora and puts the tying run at second base. But unlike his counterpart, Bobby Cox has no trouble recognizing when his starter is gassed. He removes Kevin Millwood and turns to John Rocker, who fans John Olerud swinging on a breaking pitch, the bat flying out of the hitter's hands as he does so for an added layer of humiliation. After an intentional walk of Mike Piazza, Rocker strikes out Robin Ventura on another devastating slider in the dirt to extinguish the Mets' threat.

In his team's last turn at bat, Bobby Valentine is bamboozled once again. Expecting Rocker to return, he sends up right-handed pinch hitter Shawon Dunston to counter the lefty. Bobby Cox counters with a right-handed reliever and shocks everyone by choosing John Smoltz for the job. Scheduled to start game four, Smoltz has never made a relief appearance in his major league career. Prior to the game, he told his manager he could chip in an inning if needed, never suspecting he'd get the call in the ninth. "I never even got to pick a song," he says, as he is forced to warm up to the cheery lilt of The Monkees' "I'm a Believer."

The move stuns the Mets into submission. Dunston fouls out, followed by a ground out from Roger Cedeño, after which the Turner Field PA system blasts the Braves' celebratory song, "Taking Care of Business," thinking the third out has already been recorded. The mistake is understandable. Any resistance the Mets have offered to this point has been token at best. Down to their last out, Bobby Bonilla is sent up to pinch-hit. He takes a pair of pitches on the outside corner for strikes, stepping out of the box after each one, laughing to himself as these wide offerings are called against him, before watching an even wider one for a called strike three.

After this 4–3 defeat, Bobby Valentine's non-move proves the story of the game, as writers do their best to understand what he could have been thinking. Jeff Pearlman of *Sports Illustrated* sounds more like an aggrieved fan than a sportswriter when he labels it "the worst bit of managerial ineptitude in baseball history." The extremity of his tone differs from that of his colleagues, but his assessment does not. Murray Chass of the *Times* notes, "the failure to remove Rogers at what turned out to be a critical juncture of the game was unprovoked by anything Cox did or did not do." The media's attempts to dope out Valentine's reasoning are thwarted by Valentine's own inability to explain it. "I had no reason to keep him in," he admits later. When prompted to explain why this was a mistake, the manager can only sputter, "because [Pérez] hit a home run and we got down by two."

Even Rogers is baffled. "I'm sure he wishes he pulled me," Rogers concedes. "Me too."

The Mets will return to New York down 0–2 in the series, having looked hopeless in each of the first two games. Robin Ventura finds a perverse bit of comfort in that fact. "We've had our backs against the wall," he says. "We've been there for two weeks. It feels normal to us. You learn until you're dead, you're still alive."

* * *

John Rocker hasn't been himself lately. Though he continues to retire Mets batters with ease, he's kept his histrionics to a minimum, the post-strikeout fist pumps subdued by his standards. "I'm trying to act like not quite such an idiot," he says after game two, in the manner of a prankster who is busy plotting some true idiocy.

Like many products of the Braves' farm system, Rocker is a Georgia native, a small-town kid in both circumstance and state of mind. Nothing in his experience prepared him to warm up in the visitors' bullpen at Shea Stadium while serenaded with a torrent of obscenities. "I heard every mother insult, every sister insult, every family insult a person could hear," he said. "F-you, F-your mother, F-your wife, F-your dog. Horrible stuff." Most visiting players at least pretend to pay no mind to the howls of drunken mooks in the Shea stands, knowing the boo-birds only scream even louder if they know they can get under your skin. Rocker chooses to take it personally.

"To hell with New York fans," he growls when the subject of those fans is raised by reporters after game two in Atlanta. "They're a bunch of stupid asses anyway. They keep saying we suck. If we suck so much, how come they can't beat us? They're a tired act."

Once the Braves arrive in Queens, reporters make a beeline for Rocker in the visiting clubhouse, at which point Atlanta's closer says he will not discuss fans further and proclaims himself shocked—*shocked!*—that they would obsess over his comments when there's a playoff series to be waged. "If you don't have any constructive questions about the series, which is the only important thing, then I have nothing to say," he insists. His comments before leaving Atlanta promised steak to the press corps. Once in New York, he delivers them a plate of cold tofu. He has played both New York's fans and New York's media like a cheap fiddle.

Rocker thrives on the hostility, exploiting it to boost his adrenaline and provide a stepladder to the high ground. In an interview with NBC's Jim Gray prior to game three, he complains about batteries and change thrown his way while in the bullpen, playing the part of a wounded good ol' boy who won't cotton to city slickers. "I just don't think it's right," Rocker says in a tone of faux innocence that would shame Eddie Haskell, "and I think somebody needs to speak out and voice an opinion, that we really don't appreciate hearing those kind of things and being fearful of our safety at a simple baseball game." He points to the five hundred additional NYPD officers on hand for the game—two of them charged with guarding him in the bullpen—as proof of Mets fans' animal nature.

His point is bolstered by the more troglodytic extremes of the media such as shock jock Don Imus, WFAN's morning man, who suggests fans arrive at Shea prepared to whip cell phones at the Braves' heads. It is strengthened further by fans who do everything short of that, proclaiming their hate toward Rocker with angry signs and bellowed obscenities. These fans fall right into his trap, presenting themselves as the animals he says they are. Mets fans are thus singled out for particular vulgarity and unsportsmanlike conduct, all thanks to Rocker's "Who, me?" posturing. The media is less interested in the objective truth of his contentions than they are in the theatrics of it all, and some even proclaim they're grateful for an athlete like Rocker who eschews bland pleasantries and dares to be interesting. Tom Keegan of the *Post* praises Rocker for his gusto and laments the future day when colorful sorts like him will be "beaten into relative silence" by the homogenizing powers of media training. In the same paper, Phil Mushnick places the blame for angry, violent fan reactions to Rocker's words on the media's harping on those words, as if he himself were not a member of that media.

During the game three player introductions, the announcement of each Atlanta player's name is followed by a full house appending it with the word "SUCKS!" Rocker receives the loudest, most prolonged boos of all, shouted with more anger than even those directed at Chipper Jones. Rocker responds by tipping his cap with mock grandiloquence. Once decamped to the bullpen, he points a finger at the nearest fans, then to his temple, silently proclaiming, *I am in your head.* Fans aim singular digits of their own right back at him. He stands safely behind the shield of two of New York's finest, secure in the knowledge that he has accomplished exactly what he set out to do. Chipper may have played villain with his "Yankee stuff" comment, but Rocker is now the Laurence Olivier of heels.

Burly infielder Ryan Klesko attempts to inject some levity into the situation by taking batting practice in Rocker's jersey, offering himself up as a decoy for any projectiles intended for the pitcher. "I'm actually protecting our save guy," he says. "We've got a couple of first basemen." Bobby Cox doesn't find it so funny, saying he doesn't support Rocker's antics and even insists, "If I could apologize to [Mets] fans, I would."

John Rocker may have supplanted Chipper Jones as the main source of Mets fans' ire, but that doesn't mean any of them have forgotten Chipper. At the conclusion of the division series, when the subject of a rematch with the Braves was broached, Orel Hershiser revealed the fact that Chipper Jones hated his given name, Larry, with a passion. Fifty thousand obscene taunts from the Shea Stadium stands didn't bother him half as much as one person addressing him as "Larry." Mike Piazza had taken to greeting Chipper with a pointed "Hey, Larry," whenever he came to the plate, because he refused to address a grown man as "Chipper," and because he knew how much being called Larry pissed Larry off.

Now that Mets fans are aware of this, Chipper's every at bat is greeted with bleating choruses of "LAAAAAA-REEEEE." Homemade signs in the rafters greet him with pictures of his namesake member of the Three Stooges. John Rocker might be adept at transforming hostility into performance, but Chipper Jones is not. The intense focus and volume of the mocking chants unnerves him. He looks lost at the plate in game three and will remain in the same state for the bulk of his time at Shea.

With a loud, raucous crowd behind his team and Al Leiter on the mound, the Mets have reason to believe the bad vibes and poor decisions of Atlanta have been left behind. And then the opening inning unfolds in the same luckless manner as the games at Turner Field. Al Leiter starts his night by walking Gerald Williams, a batter not known for his patience. When he induces a comebacker from the next batter, Leiter wheels around toward second, hoping to start a double play, then changes his mind at the last second and turns toward first, launching a high throw. Only a brave John Olerud leap prevents the ball from flying into the stands. One out later, with Brian Jordan at the plate, the Braves runners attempt a double steal. As Mike Piazza leaps from his crouch to fire a throw to second, his left foot slips on home plate, causing his throw to sail into the outfield. Williams scores while the trailing runner moves up to third.

Minutes into the game, the Braves have a lead without the benefit of a hit. The Mets hadn't committed two errors in the same inning in over a year. Once again, their timing in ending such streaks is impeccable.

The next batter, Brian Jordan, sends a fly ball into shallow center field that Melvin Mora catches easily, positioning himself to fire a throw to the plate. When the runner, Bret Boone, recognizes the ball has beaten him to the plate by a sizeable margin, he barrels into Piazza, shoulder to chin, hoping to dislodge it. He fails. An NBC camera in Piazza's helmet captures the collision, his head slamming to the ground with brutal force. Piazza stares up at the home plate umpire until he sees an emphatic punch-out signal.

The Mets later say Piazza suffers a "mild concussion" on the play, a diagnosis that itself seems far too mild. The catcher receives no more time for recuperation than a few silent moments on the bench in the bottom of the first as he awaits his first at bat. This is not nearly enough time to cure him of the woozy and disoriented feeling that will plague him for the rest of this night, and many nights to follow. When describing Piazza's look after the game, most reporters use the word "glassy."

And yet, Mike Piazza remains in the game. He remains in the game after he lets a third strike get away from him in the top of the second, allowing Andruw Jones to reach base safely. He remains in the game when that inning concludes with a strikeout of Walt Weiss, and the helmet camera captures the disturbing sight of him staring at the ball nestled in his hands, unaware the third out has been made. He remains in the game in the eighth when a backswing nails his glove hand, adding another item to a growing list of maladies.

He remains in the game because the Mets need his bat, and because he wants to prove the doubters wrong. He's done almost nothing at the plate so far in the series, after doing little against Arizona before his thumb knocked him out of action, and the back pages are hounding him for it. "The Roy Campanella of the regular season. The Mario Mendoza of the postseason," the *Post* dubs him. "The way he's going these days, only worms run for cover."

No one else in the Mets lineup has fared any better. The team's big three of Piazza, John Olerud, and Robin Ventura have one hit and one RBI between them in twenty-one at bats in this series. "The middle of the Mets' lineup has made as much noise as Marcel Marceau," quips NBC's Bob Costas. In a desperate attempt to shake things up while also separating his left-handed batters, Bobby Valentine asks Edgardo Alfonzo and John Olerud to swap places (Olerud second, Fonzie third), while placing Benny Agbayani in the fifth slot and the slumping Robin Ventura sixth. The reconfiguring has little effect, save to make Valentine appear desperate. In every single inning they face Atlanta starter Tom Glavine, the Mets put at least one man on base. In every single instance, they are turned away. A one-out walk in the bottom of the first leads to nothing. Consecutive two-out singles in the second do nothing more than clear the pitcher's spot. A leadoff single by Rickey Henderson in the fourth is erased when Olerud bounces into a double play, despite Henderson giving himself a head start and barreling into the shortstop. The double play is followed by a pair of singles to put runners on the corners, but Rey

Ordóñez hits a hard liner right at the first baseman. A two-out Olerud single in the fifth likewise goes to waste.

Mike Piazza begins the bottom of the sixth by pulling a single between short and third, but any momentum the Mets might have gained from this is offset by a stadium malfunction. When Benny Agbayani hits a foul down the right-field line, fans in a temporary seating area lean over an unstable wall to grab the ball and knock over the shaky barrier, sending spectators tumbling onto the field in succession like old luggage spilling from an overstuffed closet. Repair work to fix the structure amounts to several workers hammering the broken wall with wild, unfocused abandon and proceeds at a glacial pace. The slow maintenance work is followed by three swift outs from Glavine. Melvin Mora slams his helmet to the ground as he grounds out to first to end the inning.

The offensive futility becomes more galling as the game goes on, as Al Leiter dominates the opposition and allows no earned runs through seven innings. One could argue that Leiter outpitches Tom Glavine, since the Atlanta lefty allows seven hits to his three. Were it not for the pitcher's own error in the first, the game might have remained scoreless. Leiter remembers a similar game in 1998 when he allowed one run to Glavine's Braves and was bailed out by a Piazza two-run blast. He envisions the same thing happening again, as if dreaming can will it into reality.

When Leiter exits the game, John Franco and Armando Benítez keep the Braves off the board in the eighth and ninth innings, Benítez looking impressive as he strikes out four of the five batters he faces. But even this performance brings pain for the Mets, as Gerald Williams flails so wildly at one Benítez fastball that his backswing smacks Piazza in his glove hand. The catcher then watches a ball off his bat die at the warning track in the bottom of the eighth, leaving him to wonder what he could have done to that pitch if his hand wasn't swelling up from this latest blow. He mutters and kicks the first base bag before returning to the dugout. Another zero is placed on the scoreboard.

The bottom of the ninth brings yet another confrontation with John Rocker, who sprints out of the bullpen to an unbroken shower of boos and more than a few projectiles. The first batter he faces, Benny Agbayani, hits a slow roller up the middle that loses momentum as it passes over the mound, allowing Agbayani to leg out an infield single.

It is the closest thing to a break the Mets have gotten against Rocker so far in this series, and it is the only one they will get. With Robin Ventura slumping and having done literally nothing against Rocker, Bobby Valentine sends Todd Pratt to bat in his stead, only to watch the backup catcher go down on strikes. Melvin Mora follows with a ball hit to deep center field, the best swing anyone has managed against Rocker. It still goes for an out. Finally, Rey Ordóñez swings at the first offering from Rocker and loops it toward second, where it is soon converted into the final out.

All three of the Mets' losses have been heartbreakers, but this 1–0 defeat is the most excruciating of all. Rocker turns toward the third base line and roars at the crowd he manipulated like fifty-six thousand marionettes. "Not only did they have to swallow a defeat," Bob Costas says of the fans, his voice tinged with bitterness, "but they had to watch John Rocker finish it."

The Mets insist they are not dead. Mike Piazza speaks of getting the series back to Atlanta. Al Leiter contends the Mets have the ability pull themselves out of this mess if they take things one game at a time. Though the papers abound with never-say-die quotes from fans, the media's own outlook on the Mets' 0–3 deficit in the series is far less optimistic. Mere days after beating the drum for a Subway Series, they attack the Mets for duping them into thinking it possible. The *Daily News* begins its coverage with a Charlie Brown-like wail of *Arggghhh!* "If in the final week of the season the Mets were trying to stop a plummet off a cliff," says the *Times*, "they are now attempting to climb out of a dark, deep abyss." Wallace Matthews of the *Post* wonders if the Mets might be better giving up altogether, as much of the press has already. "They might wake up this morning and decide that the reward isn't worth the price," he sighs, "that revving it up to win one game only buys them three more opportunities for suffering." Their words echo with the sting of those who have been fooled and vow to not be fooled again.

* * *

As far as NBC is concerned, the Mets are already gone. The network's introduction to game four refers exclusively to the Braves, praising their "talent and professionalism" and proclaiming a trip to the World Series will cement their Team of the Decade credentials. The home team isn't mentioned until the very end, along with footage of a groundskeeper working his broom over the infield onto which a Mets jersey has been superimposed, laying flat, waiting to be swept away.

At least the first three games offered the Mets slight hope when it came to the opposing pitchers—despite their All-Star bona fides, both

Greg Maddux and Tom Glavine have mixed playoff histories, while Kevin Millwood possesses little postseason experience. New York lost all three games anyway, and now in game four they must face John Smoltz, owner of more postseason wins than any other pitcher in baseball history (twelve).

The Mets have little choice but to place their future in Rick Reed's hands, and hope he continues the roll he's been on since the end of September. Believing that any added pressure could cause him to overthink and implode, Reed performs mental gymnastics to convince himself that this is no more important than a mid-season start. When his teammates run onto the field, sporting their black uniforms for the first time in the series, Reed plays things so casually that he stays behind on the dugout bench for a few moments before loping leisurely onto the grass.

Once he takes the mound, however, Reed's pace is much quicker as he throws strikes in rapid succession. The impatient Braves swing at most of these offerings, resulting in harmless tappers and easy fly balls. Reed retires the first ten Atlanta hitters he faces, and when Bret Boone singles with one out in the top of the fourth, he is soon caught stealing. The inning ends on a strikeout of Chipper Jones, pleasing the fans who've hung placards bearing the image of Larry Fine from the rafters each time he goes down swinging.

Reed sets down the Braves in order in the following three innings. Over seven frames, Reed faces the minimum and requires only seventy pitches to do so, a model of efficiency that would do Greg Maddux proud. "He may be good for twelve or thirteen innings tonight," marvels Gary Cohen in the radio booth, "and with the way his offense is going, he may have to be."

Reed must be impeccable because his teammates still refuse to hit. For the second straight game, Bobby Valentine asks John Olerud and Edgardo Alfonzo to bat second and third in that order, reversing their regular season positions in the lineup, and watches his batters continue to produce anemic results. John Smoltz retires the side in order three times in the early going. Twice, Roger Cedeño collects a single but is given no chance to run because the man behind him in the order, Rey Ordóñez, makes an out on the very next pitch.

When Smoltz retires the first two batters in the bottom of the sixth, the Mets have been held scoreless for more than seventeen miserable innings. Then, John Olerud turns on a fastball and rockets it to the base of Shea's big scoreboard for a home run. For a team that has been crawling through the desert, this tiny cup of water has the feel of an ocean. With Rick Reed pitching another gem, perhaps the Mets could reverse last night's result and capture a 1-0 victory of their own.

Then Reed's dominance, and the lead, disappear in the blink of an eye. First, Brian Jordan connects with Reed's first pitch in the top of the eighth and crushes it to left field. Two pitches later, while the TV and radio announcers are still commenting on this development, Ryan Klesko—a bulky first baseman who'd seen little playing time in the series before this game—launches a Reed fastball into the Mets' bullpen. He rounds the bases and scores Atlanta's go-ahead run in front of fifty-six thousand fans so silent the broadcast picks up the sound of each footstep.

Rick Reed's first seventy pitches of the evening result in only one baserunner, only one three-ball count, and a plethora of weak grounders. His following three pitches result in a pair of bombs, and flip the Mets' miniscule lead into a 2–1 deficit. As pitching coach Dave Wallace marches to the mound to remove Reed, and Shea's organist offers a melancholy rendition of the bebop tune "Stolen Moments," demoralized fans wonder how it all collapsed so quickly.

With six outs standing between the Mets and elimination, Roger Cedeño leads off the bottom of the eighth by singling up the middle. Rey Ordóñez's attempt to bunt him over results in a weak pop-up and a torrent of boos from a Shea crowd exasperated by the shortstop's offensive futility. When Bobby Cox replaces Smoltz with lefty reliever Mike Remlinger, Bobby Valentine counters by pinch-hitting with righty Benny Agbayani. The move backfires when Benny strikes out. Valentine, it seems, will be outfoxed again.

The next batter would have been Rickey Henderson, but Valentine has replaced the veteran for defense with Melvin Mora. (And did so at the last moment, sending Mora to chase down Henderson after he'd already taken his position in left field to start the fateful top of the eight inning.) After his speed was stymied all night by Rey Ordóñez's impatience, Roger Cedeño gets impatient himself and steals second, barely beating a throw from the Braves' catcher. With a man in scoring position, Mike Remlinger pitches around Mora and walks him. The reasoning is the next batter, John Olerud, should be neutralized by an appearance from John Rocker. Olerud has faced Rocker twice in this series with a runner in scoring position and struck out on each occasion, swinging helplessly at unhittable balls in the dirt.

The spectacle of Rocker trying to end the Mets' season is so great that few note he is double-switched into the game, with veteran Ozzie Guillén taking over at shortstop for Walt Weiss. Though Weiss is a superior fielder, Bobby Cox is perhaps counting on Rocker to keep Olerud from putting the ball in play, rendering moot any questions about fielding.

While Rocker warms up, Mora and Cedeño conference at second base and decide to execute a double steal. Once the tying run reaches third, they reason, Rocker won't dare throw his curveball for fear of it bouncing away from the catcher, which should give Olerud better pitches to hit.

Rocker takes the mound and stares in hard at John Olerud, not sparing a glance back at the runners. When Mora and Cedeño attempt their double steal, catcher Eddie Pérez doesn't even emerge from his crouch behind the plate. That is how confident the Braves are that Rocker will make short work of the batter.

Somehow, John Olerud gets around on a Rocker fastball, just barely, sending a squib past the pitcher and up the middle. Ozzie Guillén sprints to his left, to no avail. The ball dribbles into the outfield as Guillén keeps running, almost tripping over his own feet. Roger Cedeño scores and Melvin Mora barrels across the plate right behind him to put the Mets ahead, 3–2. The two runners leap and embrace in midair. At the conclusion of the inning, Rocker glares at the fans taunting him as he stalks back to the dugout. He flashes three fingers at the crowd, then makes an "O" with his thumb and pointer. Translation: *We're still up 3–0, dummies.*

Armando Benítez takes the mound in the top of the ninth for his first save opportunity of the series. Though he gives up a long fly ball down the left-field line to Guillén that goes foul at the last moment, causing a momentary wave of agita to wash through the crowd, he retires the side in order and strands Chipper Jones in the on-deck circle. It is only one game, a Mets win that could easily have gone the other way but for a few fortunate hops. Everyone in the Mets' clubhouse speaks of this as a mere baby step, saying nothing of the journey ahead. None will say out loud they dream of climbing out of an 0–3 hole, because that is a feat no team has yet accomplished.

Valentine comes the closest. "Someday, someone's going to do this," he says. What *this* represents remains unsaid.

* * *

A storm is coming. Hurricane Irene makes landfall on October 16 and slowly works its destructive way up the Eastern Seaboard. By nightfall the next day, whatever's left of Irene will appear over Long Island. Game five of the National League Championship Series, scheduled for a first pitch time of 4:09 p.m. on October 17, should proceed unimpeded by weather, provided it proceeds at a tidy pace.

There is a minor storm in the Mets' clubhouse as well, stirred up by Rickey Henderson, who was so insulted when Bobby Valentine sent Melvin Mora to take his place in left field during game four that he left the stadium before the end of the game. Henderson makes some noise about not showing up for game five at all, though he turns up at the last moment. If Bobby Valentine has any thoughts of not starting Henderson as punishment for his defiance, these thoughts are dashed when Roger Cedeño arrives at Shea complaining of back spasms. Valentine also has to deal with new anonymous sniping, as a nameless "prominent Met," as Bill Madden of the *Daily News* puts it, intimates there is some resentment in the clubhouse against Valentine for pinch-hitting for Robin Ventura against John Rocker in game three. Teammates see it as "a slight to the player who has carried the team much of the season and is playing on guts and a torn-up knee."

Valentine's response to the strife? "Just business as usual around here."

Ventura says nothing ("characteristically," in Madden's words), because what could he say? His sole contribution in this series came before game four, when he told his teammates he'd woken up that morning serenaded by his daughter singing, "The sun will come out tomorrow . . ." If it was condescending to say this provided the necessary mojo for John Olerud's game-winning dribbler against John Rocker, Ventura would take it, since he had been incapable of providing anything else. Through game four, he'd gone hitless in twelve series at bats, with five strikeouts.

As for Rocker, the blown save in game four grants him no perspective or humility. He calls the John Olerud single that beat him "one of the cheaper hits I've ever given up in my entire life." During batting practice, he feigns tossing souvenirs to fans but makes sure they land short of the seats. He also mimes spitting on the ground near fans down the left-field line, shoots a middle finger to the crowd watching batting practice, and scales a bullpen camera to give the paying customers in the nearby bleachers a piece of his mind. Braves pitching coach Leo Mazzone, tasked with shadowing Rocker, can do nothing to corral his reliever. This is how John Rocker chooses to celebrate his twenty-fifth birthday.

Masato Yoshii attempts to alleviate concerns about the ankle he sprained in game one with a series of thirty-yard dashes on the Shea grass to prove his mobility. Orel Hershiser, sparingly used in the playoffs so far, is ready to jump in should Yoshii falter. When asked which other hurlers are available for the game, pitching coach Dave Wallace answers "everyone but Rick Reed." Hearing this, Reed protests that he too is available despite his seven-inning outing last night.

Clouds gather but do not threaten as Yoshii takes the mound, with temperatures mired in the comfortable mid-sixties, for the moment. He uses a sharp splitter to negotiate the first three innings with little trouble, while the Mets offense gets off to a quick start with a first-inning two-run homer by John Olerud. After enduring this indignity, however, Greg Maddux returns to his old self and bedevils Mets hitters, while Yoshii's flirtation with dominance comes crashing down around him in the top of the fourth as he allows three consecutive doubles that tie the game at two.

In steps Orel Hershiser, who hasn't pitched since a mop-up appearance in the ninth inning of game three of the division series. With rust and age working against him, Hershiser's most effective weapon is his opponents' impatience. He steps off the rubber between pitches, tugs at his cap, fires pick-off throws, stares in at his catcher, using every possible tactic to delay his offerings to the batter. The infuriated Braves scream at him from the bench to throw a damn pitch already, then swing wildly when he does. His procrastinating efforts keep the score tied.

Thus begins a cold war. Each team threatens action but never quite progresses to actual hostilities. In the top of the sixth, after the Braves load the bases with one out, Greg Maddux—normally an excellent bat handler—botches a squeeze play by bunting through a strike three, dooming the runner charging down the line. Such a crowd-pleasing screw-up could inspire a home team to rally, and it nearly does so when the Mets load the bases with one out in the bottom half of the inning on a series of fielding miscues by Atlanta. Then they too come up short, as Rey Ordóñez bounces into a double play.

The strangeness of the sixth is exceeded in the top of the seventh, which begins with Hershiser barely grazing Bret Boone with a pitch, if he grazed him at all. Bobby Valentine employs three more pitchers to negotiate a scoreless frame. The oddest moment of all comes when he summons Dennis Cook mid-at bat to complete an intentional walk, then subs for Cook when a right-handed pinch hitter is announced. It effectively robs Valentine of his best lefty reliever, but it also accomplishes the goal of keeping the Braves off the board. As Pat Mahomes records the third out, a light rain is falling.

Greg Maddux works between the raindrops and departs after seven innings, but the Mets fare no better against his replacements. The eighth inning ends with Robin Ventura bouncing into a double play, drawing scattered boos from a Shea crowd that was serenading him with chants of "M-V-P" a few weeks ago. Fans groan louder when he mishandles an infield single in the top of the ninth, though it results in no damage. No allowances are made for a playing surface that grows muddier by the minute. The precipitation progresses from harmless drizzle to gentle but steady rain. The infield dirt turns a slick dun color while the warning track gathers puddles. The grounds crew speeds onto the field between each half inning to soak up the water with Diamond Dry, then watches helplessly as new pools quickly bubble up.

The game staggers into extras. Armando Benítez allows an Atlanta hitter to reach base for the first time this season in the top of the tenth but strands him, while Kenny Rogers makes his first relief appearance since his Yankee days and contributes two scoreless frames. The Braves' relievers are equally stingy, as lefty Mike Remlinger puts up zeroes in the tenth and eleventh and seldom-used knuckleballer Russ Springer follows his lead in the twelfth.

Having failed to score yet again, the Mets are all but forced to ask Octavio Dotel to start the top of the thirteenth. Dotel hasn't appeared on the mound since a shaky outing in game two of the division series, but with only Al Leiter and Rick Reed left in the Mets' bullpen, Dotel will have to take the mound for as long as he can manage. In his first inning of work, he receives an assist from Melvin Mora, who slogs his way through the drenched outfield to scoop up a Chipper Jones hit and heave it homeward well in time to catch an Atlanta runner trying to score. As Mora jogs back to the dugout, he exchanges high fives with fans congratulating him for what teammates later testify is the play of the game.

In the bottom half, John Rocker tosses yet another scoreless frame that includes a strikeout of Mike Piazza on a high, hard fastball the slugger never even sees. In June, Piazza would have sent such a pitch to the parking lot. Here in October, the mere act of moving his hands gives him an unsettling tingling sensation in his fingers. When he grips a bat, his hands feel like they're being scored by a blowtorch. He returns to the dugout bench and can rise no more. Octavio Dotel will throw to Todd Pratt the rest of the way.

Dotel tosses a scoreless top of the fourteenth, the conclusion of which is followed by the thumping of "Y.M.C.A." from the Shea PA system and invitations for the crowd to stand for the fourteenth-inning stretch. Up in Boston, game four of the American League Championship Series has already reached the third inning, with the Red Sox and Yankees deadlocked in the same score, 2–2. Game five between the Mets and Braves is now officially the longest game, in terms of time, in championship series history. The rain remains stubborn in its refusal to abate or increase, dripping at the same dull pound it has maintained for hours.

John Rocker returns for the bottom of the fourteenth and gets Robin Ventura to fly out to the warning track, the first time Ventura has so much as put a ball in play against Rocker. A small victory. Then Kevin McGlinchy takes the mound and repeats the same act as all his predecessors by stifling the Mets, sending the game lurching into the fifteenth.

Walt Weiss begins the inning by lofting a single into shallow left, the sound of his bat hitting the ball less a crack than a damp *squish*. Called on to bunt Weiss over, McGlinchy strikes out looking but Weiss compensates by swiping second base. One out later, Keith Lockhart turns on a low, flat fastball and rockets it toward right-center field. Earlier in the game, Darryl Hamilton had been playing center field. An excellent glove man, Hamilton might have had a chance to catch the ball, even on the slick Shea grass. Now, in the fifteenth inning, the puddling outfield is patrolled by Shawon Dunston. The ball drops in and Dunston's momentum carries him past as it bounces toward the wall. Weiss trots home and continues on his way into a Braves dugout that now stands three outs away from a trip to the World Series.

When Dotel strikes out an overanxious Brian Jordan for the third out, the remaining crowd erupts as loudly as if the score were reversed. The roaring continues and is still present when the bottom of the fifteenth inning arrives. The fans have seen this act many times in the last month. The Mets are only comfortable with a knife at their throat. Now the fun can start.

The Mets could use a long ball or a baserunner. Shawon Dunston, who will lead off the bottom of the fifteenth, is not a good bet for either outcome. He has neither homered nor walked since his trade to New York. And yet, as he strides to the plate, he hears no booing, only encouragement—"Shawon, you can do it!"—and defiant chants of "Let's go Mets!" These maniacs who should be mourning the season are screaming as if it's only just begun. *If they think I can do it*, thinks Dunston, *maybe I can.*

His at bat does not begin with promise, as a few feeble bunt attempts put him behind in the count. Then Dunston watches a pitch go wide for ball two, and another sail even wider for ball three. The crowd, staving off the rain with hoodies and ponchos and sombreros fashioned from empty popcorn buckets, rises to its feet.

McGlinchy challenges Dunston with a high fastball. Dunston fouls it off. The pitcher throws another high fastball, and Dunston fouls off that one too. A third challenge fastball meets the same fate. So does a fourth. And a fifth. And a sixth. Dunston can barely keep up with McGlinchy's heat, but he does keep up with it. He stays alive, and so do the Mets.

Twelve pitches and nine minutes into the at bat, with all of the remaining fans standing, with both last night's starter Rick Reed and Al Leiter warming up in the bullpen as if they can will another inning for the Mets, McGlinchy throws yet another fastball. This one, Dunston sends skipping straight up the middle for a single.

With the pitcher's spot up next, Bobby Valentine turns to Orel Hershiser, who has served as his brain trust since he left the mound, and asks if he should bat for Dotel even though he has no pitchers left but Al Leiter and Rick Reed. Hershiser reminds him there's no tomorrow. With your season on the line, you have to send up Matt Franco, an actual hitter, your best bat off the bench, and let the chips fall where they may. With a bullpen phone receiver pressed to his ear, gathering intelligence on the respective states of Leiter and Reed, Hershiser assures the manager that "he can go one inning." In the heat of the moment, Valentine doesn't ask for clarification about who *he* refers to. All he knows is *someone* can take an inning, if there is an inning to take.

When Matt Franco steps in the box, Dunston makes a bold break for second. His speed is not what it used to be, and is compromised further by soggy infield dirt, but the catcher's throw is far off the mark. Unnerved, McGlinchy loses the plate and walks Franco. Edgardo Alfonzo then lays down a perfect bunt toward the mound. McGlinchy's only play is to first. The tying run is ninety feet away, the winning run in scoring position.

With first base open, John Olerud receives an intentional walk to load the bases. Normally, this would invite a confrontation with Mike Piazza, but pain drove Piazza to the bench, so Todd Pratt bats in his stead. Roger Cedeño scrambles out to second to pinch run for Franco, gritting his teeth through the back spasms that prevented him from starting.

With each pitch, McGlinchy looks more and more like the twenty-two-year-old rookie he is. His first two pitches to Pratt are far from the plate, and his third is even farther. John Franco steps out of the Mets' dugout, flailing his arms overhead in a *get up!* gesture toward the crowd. He needn't have bothered. Everyone is already standing, screaming themselves hoarse.

After a generous strike call, McGlinchy's fifth pitch is far too wide to benefit from such pity. Ball four. Pratt jogs to first as Dunston jogs home with the tying run. Journey's "Don't Stop Believing" pours from the speakers.

And Robin Ventura will bat with the bases loaded once more. *Dumb luck.* Again.

Ventura takes a pitch down and in for ball one and fouls off the next one, barely putting the bat on the ball. The next offering sails so far outside that the catcher has to stretch far to his left to prevent a wild pitch. Then, McGlinchy throws a pitch right down the heart of the plate. And for one moment, the beautiful swing Ventura showed all summer is back. He hits the ball so deep so quickly that by the time the NBC cameras pick up its trajectory, right fielder Brian Jordan is already running back toward the dugout, headed toward a visiting clubhouse where attendants are hastily ripping down the plastic they'd hung to protect against a champagne-spraying celebration that will not come tonight. Jordan knows the ball is over his head and therefore the game is over. He doesn't stop to watch it sail over the 371-foot mark on the outfield fence in right-center field, rustling a tarp at the base of Shea's big scoreboard.

On television, NBC's Bob Costas calls Ventura's hit a grand slam, and an on-screen graphic flashes a final score of 7–3, accordingly. On the radio, WFAN's Gary Cohen also calls it a grand slam. The red home run apple pops up beyond the outfield fence. Anyone watching from the drenched stands or the dry comfort of their homes would call it a grand slam.

Todd Pratt is one of the very few people at Shea Stadium unaware that Ventura's knock left the yard. Like Brian Jordan, he observes the hit only long enough to see that it is a game winner. As Roger Cedeño sprints home to score the only run that matters, and John Olerud follows close behind him, Pratt advances as far as second base before pivoting on the bag like a runner's block. He wants to be the first to give Ventura a rib-crushing bear hug.

Robin Ventura allows himself a pained smile as he puts his head down and jogs toward first. He raises his gaze as he rounds the bag and sees Pratt advancing on him. He waves Pratt along, but Pratt's nickname is Tank for a reason. He cannot be moved by mere mortals. The catcher grabs Ventura by the waist and hoists him into the air. The rest of the Mets who've spilled onto the field descend on them, mobbing the pair and making triumphant gestures toward the soaked fans who literally shook the rafters of Shea.

And then the players trail off toward the dugout, any thought of completing a circuit around the bases fogged by their delirium, the question of the exact margin of victory unsettled. If Ventura hit the ball over the fence, surely it's a grand slam. Except Pratt went no farther than second, and he made sure Ventura didn't even make it that far. So the score is . . . what?

The official scorer for game five of the league championship series is Arthur "Red" Foley. Queens born and bred, Red Foley is an old-school sportswriter out of central casting, cigar permanently clamped between his teeth, able to swap stories about the Good Old Days with the best of them. If someone in the press box ever has a question about the rules or history of baseball, the response is "Ask Red," because Red was always there and Red would always know. Red Foley has scored every postseason game in the five boroughs in the previous three decades. He surely thought himself inured to all manner of playoff craziness. Now this.

As the Mets leave the field, a puzzled Bob Costas scans the field, looking for umpires to impose direction on this joyful anarchy. They are all gone. Home plate umpire Jerry Layne sticks around long enough to make sure Roger Cedeño touches home plate to score the winning run before fleeing. The question of the final score is confused further by crew chief Ed Montague, who says he saw Olerud cross home plate before Ventura was tackled by Pratt, in which case the score should be 5–3.

So we have to ask Red once more: How to score this insanity?

Ten minutes after the conclusion of the game, Red rules thusly: Robin Ventura will get credit for driving in the winning run, and no more. Though his hit cleared the fence, he advanced no farther than first base and so will be credited with a one-bagger. The final score will be 4–3, and Ventura will be the owner of baseball's first grand slam single.

Red was always there and Red would always know.

Little thought is given over to official scoring in Shea's home clubhouse, where the Mets are happy enough to know they will play again this year. "If you don't like this fucking game," pitching coach Dave Wallace proclaims, "you don't like Christmas."

As for Robin Ventura, artist in the medium of self-effacement, he insists, "I didn't want to run that far anyway."

* * *

It is all too imperfect.

The Grand Slam Single, as it comes to be known, is a uniquely Mets-ian piece of serendipitous magic to rival the shoe polish play in 1969, the ball on the wall in 1973, game six in 1986. The self-styled cynics of the New York sports press, capricious as ever, fall deeply in love yet again. A mere forty-eight hours before the grand slam single, the Mets were presented as dust under the Braves' feet. A pair of insane wins flip the script, daring people not to believe in the team again.

Where the papers were once filled with forlorn "wait 'til next year" sighs, they are now filled with defiant projections of victory. "Only someone who had not paid attention for the last month could doubt that the World Series was still beyond their reach," proclaims the *Times*. "Count the Mets out and watch them soar back," marvels the *Post*. "It's been that way all year." The *Daily News* declares, "Just because no team has lost a 3–0 lead doesn't mean a team can't be beaten four in a row." So many in the press turn from skeptics to true believers that some of their constituent members suggest this can't be good for the Mets' chances. If we really want them to succeed, goes the logic of one *Post* writer, better to write them off. This team only thrives when dismissed.

Now the Mets, not the Braves, are the team of destiny. Now Bobby Cox, not Bobby Valentine, is grilled by the press corps over his questionable decisions, such as keeping Kevin McGlinchy on the mound the bottom of the fifteenth. The Braves' skipper managed the first three games of the series with an almost brutal competitiveness, asking John Rocker to toss multiple innings, using John Smoltz as an ambush closer in game two, negating every appearance by the Mets' best pinch hitter, Matt Franco, with a slew of lefty relievers. And then, three outs from the World Series, he took his hand off the throttle and allowed an untested rookie to melt down, when he could have used a starter like Smoltz or Kevin Millwood to seal the deal. His failure to do so not only cost his team the game, but gave the Mets a dangerous ray of hope. Cox was rarely so careless. It defied explanation—unless you believed in mojo.

Murray Chass peers into Atlanta's clubhouse and decides the Braves have "the look of a loser." Vegas puts the chances of New York winning both games in Atlanta at 5–1, the odds of an underdog with a creeping chance. Yankees manager Joe Torre, who'd played for and managed both teams, and whose team is awaiting the winner of this series, expresses his belief that "the Braves look a little on their heels at this point."

In game six, the spooked home team will be opposed by Al Leiter. The lefty pitches best when he gets extra time off, but he will have to take the mound on only three days' rest. This could be called a risky move if Bobby Valentine had any choice, but after the game five marathon, Leiter is his freshest starter. Leiter spends the day before game six eating a leisurely breakfast of Belgian waffles while he reads his newspaper, followed by a stroll along Peachtree Street, confident in the knowledge no one will harass him in a town where playoff enthusiasm seems luke warm at best. "You've got to believe something crazy is happening," he says, recalling Tug McGraw.

Things are so crazy, in fact, that the locals gobble up three thousand empty seats in time for the first pitch, giving the Braves their first sellout of the postseason. A loud and lively crowd is on hand the evening of October 19 to greet Leiter when he climbs the mound in the first inning, some waving signs that read "THAT'S MR. LARRY TO YOU" and "MASSACRE THE METS," some waving foam tomahawks along with the stadium organist's rendition of the pseudo-Native American "war chant" heard in a million outdated black-and-white oaters.

Leiter's evening begins ominously as he nails leadoff hitter Gerald Williams in the back. A walk of Bret Boone follows, and when the two runners attempt a double steal, Mike Piazza's throw to third base hits the ground before it can reach Robin Ventura. The ball bounces out of the third baseman's glove and toward the Mets' dugout while Williams scampers home, an unsettling replay of the first-inning debacle in game three. In that game, Leiter settled down after early struggles. He will not have the fortitude to do the same tonight.

Leiter hits Chipper with his very next pitch. The following hitter, Brian Jordan, is the first Braves batter to swing at a Leiter pitch, and he zips a single past a diving Ventura. Boone races home from second without a throw. Three pitches later, Andruw Jones taps a ball right back to Leiter. A sure out is waiting at first base. Instead, Leiter spins and heaves a wild throw toward second, pulling Edgardo Alfonzo off the bag. The bases now loaded, Leiter allows a line drive up the middle to Eddie Pérez, driving in two more runs.

By the time NBC cuts back from its replay of Pérez's single, Leiter is already slinking off the mound toward the visiting dugout, serenaded by tomahawk chops. Pat Mahomes takes his place and allows an inherited run to score on a sac fly before inducing an inning-ending double play, closing the books on the worst outing of Leiter's career: five runs allowed, not a single out recorded.

The Mets' season might appear to be over at this point, but Mahomes and Turk Wendell keep the Braves off the board through the fifth inning, and the Mets break through against Kevin Millwood in the top of the sixth. After Mike Piazza drives in a run with a sac fly and Darryl Hamilton knocks in two more with a single, a 5–0 game has become a 5–3 game and Millwood, who'd dominated opposing batters for months, is told to hit the showers.

Shaken out of complacency, the Braves do their best to destroy the rebellion once and for all in the bottom of the sixth, when pinch hitter José Hernández, a backup infielder who'd made few appearances in the postseason thus far, hits a back-breaking two-run single. With the Braves enjoying a healthy four-run cushion to begin the seventh inning, surely the Mets are buried for good The NBC booth praises Bobby Valentine for his moves in game five. Braves radio play-by-play man Skip Caray likewise insists that the Mets are not chokers, that they battled the whole way. This is all said in the manner of requiem, a tip of the hat to an able foe who is no longer a threat.

With three innings separating Atlanta from the pennant, Bobby Cox does what he declined to do in game five and turns to a well-rested starter to shut the door. John Smoltz, whose surprise relief appearance in game two stunned the Mets into submission, takes the mound to do the same thing again in the top of the seventh. Despite the eulogies and Cox's show-no-mercy move, Matt Franco belts a pinch-hit double over the head of Andruw Jones. Rickey Henderson follows with his own double, chasing home Franco.

After a long fly out allows Henderson to tag up and move to third, the Braves concede a run by playing their infield back for John Olerud. The first baseman defies the strategy with an RBI single that scores Henderson and brings Mike Piazza to the plate representing the tying run, a situation that once held far more promise than it does now.

Already hobbled by a season filled with injuries, the concussion Piazza suffered during a home plate collision in game three has rendered him a virtual nonentity at the plate ever since. During game four, Piazza had difficulty seeing the fastballs sent his way by the pitcher he faces now, John Smoltz, and could only hear them whiz by his punchless bat. When relating the extent of his pain to reporters, he could barely turn his head to address them due to an aching neck. Another home plate collision late in game five forced him to exit after the bottom of the thirteenth inning, when his last futile swing made his fingers tingle and his forearms burn beyond anything he felt before. The same tingling and burning continues to plague him throughout game six, even when not gripping a Louisville Slugger. Shots of the Mets bench during tonight's rallies show the whole team on their feet, cheering and screaming, save one member. While his teammates cheerlead, Piazza sits on the bench, staring straight ahead, his face unmoved, his eyes glazed over. Moments ago, in the bottom of the sixth, Brian Jordan slid in hard against him, taking his legs out from under him even though a force out had long since been recorded at the plate. Jordan concedes no ill will toward Piazza per se, but he'd been hit by a Turk Wendell pitch earlier in the inning, and, well, someone had to pay the price. So Piazza paid the price, as he had over and over again, for weeks, for months.

He is barely Mike Piazza now. But John Smoltz is barely John Smoltz either, as both his velocity and his location have gone missing. The pitcher falls behind in the count before finding his control, firing a perfectly placed pitch on the outside corner. Mike Piazza finds himself at the exact same moment. He wheels on the fastball and fires it toward right field. It is an old Piazza specialty, an opposite-field laser beam. The moment before he hits the ball, he looks spent. The moment after he hits the ball, he looks even more exhausted. But freeze the exact nanosecond when he makes contact and he looks like the man who terrified pitchers all season long. He looks like Mike Piazza again. The ball sails a hair over the 390-foot marker in right, leaving the yard in the blink of an eye. The game is tied at seven runs a side. The requiems are torn up yet again.

The Mets get right back to work in the top of the eighth. Benny Agbayani hits a leadoff single, Rey Ordóñez finally lays down a successful sac bunt (a simple task he'd failed to accomplish multiple times in the series), and Melvin Mora continues his puzzling success against Atlanta pitching by hitting a single to drive home Agbayani. The Mets are now ahead, 8–7. "It really does make almost no sense," is all Bob Costas can manage to spit out. In the dugout, Orel Hershiser begs to take a peek at a reporter's scorebook. He knows that his team has scored but needs independent reassurances that the events unfolding before his eyes are real.

John Franco is asked to protect the Mets' first lead of the night, his team six outs away from forcing a game seven, something no baseball team has accomplished after being down 0–3 in a playoff series. He records the first out easily, but the rest is vintage Franco. Eddie Pérez, a thorn in the Mets' side all series long, singles. When pinch runner Otis Nixon attempts to steal second, Piazza's attempt to throw him out falls short and skitters into the outfield. Nixon continues right on to third, then scores when Brian Hunter extends his bat over the plate and pokes a breaking ball into the outfield.

His advantage squandered, Franco logs the last two outs and keeps the game tied, offering up his teammates to John Rocker in the top of the ninth. The Mets' dramatic game four rally, such as it was, marks their only measure of success against Rocker to this point. He dominates them again by setting down Piazza, Ventura, and Hamilton, but after Armando Benítez throws his own scoreless frame in the bottom of the ninth, Rocker returns in the tenth to find real trouble for the first time.

Benny Agbayani starts the inning by working a walk. One out later, Rocker catches Agbayani making a break for second, but a relay throw from the first baseman nails him in the back, allowing the runner to slide into second safely. Then a sharp single by Mora puts runners on the corners, bringing up Todd Pratt (now catching in place of an exhausted Piazza) with yet another chance to play substitute hero. Tank delivers with a fly ball hit to shallow center field. Agbayani tags up and challenges Andruw Jones's arm, an unwise move, but lucks out when Jones's throw is well up the line and bounces out of the catcher's glove. Agbayani slides in headfirst and lays there for a moment before daring to rise. The Mets are ahead once again, 9–8. They are three outs away from a game seven.

But when the Mets fail to score any more runs in the inning, it's Benítez's turn to lose his powers over the opposition. He logs a full count against Andruw Jones before allowing a leadoff single. Bobby Cox begins to empty his bench, desperate to avoid a game seven at all costs. Pinch hitter Ryan Klesko works a one-out walk before another pinch hitter, Ozzie Guillén, laces a single to right that sends Jones barreling around third for the plate. Advancing on the ball, Melvin Mora has a choice: Go for a play at the plate, which has a limited chance of success, or gun down Klesko as he lumbers toward third. Mora chooses the latter. Klesko is thrown out easily, keeping the winning run from reaching third base with only one out, but the tying run has scored, yet again, and though Benítez keeps the game knotted for the moment, the Mets have already tossed aside two leads. They do not produce a third in the top of the twelfth, as Russ Springer sets them down in order.

The Mets tempt fate further by asking Kenny Rogers to hold down the fort in the bottom of the twelfth. After two quick strikes to the leadoff batter, he hangs a pitch that Gerald Williams laces down the left-field line, fair by inches. Williams cruises into second with a double. A sac bunt places him ninety feet away from ending the Mets' season.

Bobby Valentine sends the signal to intentionally walk Chipper Jones, then makes a rare trip to the mound to discuss strategy. Upon his exit, Rogers fires two wide pitches to the next batter, hoping to sniff out a botched squeeze or steal attempt. When neither materializes, Todd Pratt puts his glove out for two intentional balls. A force at any base. A chance for an easy out at the plate. A chance for a double play to end the inning. A chance.

Octavio Dotel is up and ready in the Mets' bullpen, but Valentine sticks with the lefty against the next batter, preferring Kenny Rogers's experience to Dotel's fire against Andruw Jones, a renowned fastball hitter. Dave Wallace, mindful of the three innings Dotel tossed in game five, believes Dotel could face little more than a batter or two anyway. So Rogers it shall be.

The Greatest Infield Ever defiantly plays back, eschewing a play at the plate for a double play. They can turn one more in 1999. They are sure of this.

Rogers's first pitch is low and away, a curve that bends out of the strike zone. Pratt and the pitcher can't agree on the next pitch and conference at the mound for a moment to get their signals straight. Rogers's second pitch lands in the same place as the first for ball two. Rey Ordóñez and Edgardo Alfonzo hedge on their earlier tactic and position themselves a shade closer to the plate, playing halfway.

Jones swings at the next pitch, a sinker that hangs, and sends a slow dribbler up the third base line. Williams darts for the plate. No chance for a hobbled Robin Ventura to get to the ball in time and heave it home. The Mets have to hope it kicks foul. It does. A break.

The fourth pitch tails far too high. Ball three.

The fifth pitch catches the outside corner by a hair in the estimation of home plate umpire Jerry Crawford. Another break. Crawford doesn't want this to end on a walk. Bob Costas and Joe Morgan in the NBC booth each say they'd hate for it to end on a walk. And though the Braves want to finish this game and this series right now, they would probably hate for it to end on a walk too. It goes without saying the Mets do not want this to end on a walk. If it must end here, let it end on a clean single, a grand slam, even an error. To chase away death for weeks on end, only to welcome winter with a bases-loaded walk . . . it simply can't end that way.

Then Kenny Rogers's sixth pitch sails toward the plate, a sinker that refuses to sink, ticketed for a spot well high and wide of the strike zone, so high that even Jerry Crawford won't give the call to the pitcher. The man who threw that pitch watches it rise as his head swims with visions of future decades of goat horns. *Everything you do in the past, they'll forget about and remember this*, he thinks.

Maybe it has to end this way. So much of this was so ridiculous. Let the ending be ridiculous too.

Todd Pratt rises from his crouch to grab the ball before it sails past him. At least he can prevent a wild pitch. One last stab at dignity before the curtain is drawn.

In center field, Darryl Hamilton crumbles to his knees, going fetal, crawling into himself. Rey Ordóñez stands arms akimbo, beside himself with disbelief.

On the other side, Andruw Jones raises his arms in the air, bat still in hand, like a little kid playing airplane, before flinging the lumber toward his own dugout. Gerald Williams jogs home. His teammates mob him at the plate. The Mets are finished.

* * *

But we are not finished with the Mets.

NBC spares some shots of the triumphant home team, but the attention paid to the Braves is, at best, cursory. The camera wants to linger on the despairing Mets dugout, to the expense of the victors. Even when the scene shifts to a champagne-drenched Atlanta clubhouse, the announcers can't stop talking about the Mets. "Seldom has a losing team in a playoff series emerged with such enhanced regard as have the Mets," Bob Costas says. "They have made fans not just in New York, but all around the country with the wild ride they took us through in late September and early October."

Sideline reporter Jim Gray's first question to Bobby Cox is, "Boy, the Mets just wouldn't die, would they?" When Eddie Pérez receives the series MVP award, he too is forced to field questions about the Mets' resilience. The Braves are treated as bit players in their own pennant celebration.

The scene then shifts to a deathly silent hallway outside the Mets' clubhouse. Sideline reporter Craig Sager asks Bobby Valentine what he told his players in the moments after the game. "I told them they played like champions and they should feel like champions," he says. At times, the manager grasps his throat, as if holding back a flood of tears.

"Turn off the television tonight," counsels the *Times'* George Vecsey after game six. "There will be nothing worth watching. There may never be anything quite as compelling as what transpired in recent innings." He also wonders if we're better off without a Subway Series (the Yankees had clinched the pennant the night before game six), wondering how it could possibly have measured up to what preceded it. "As remarkable a team as has ever played a post-season game," says Murray Chass, so overwhelmed with feeling that he can forget his burning antipathy for Bobby Valentine. The *Post* calls game six a "jewel" and places it alongside the glorious sixth games the Mets played against the Astros and Red Sox in 1986, the fact that the Mets lost rendered an afterthought. "Winning without struggle, without resistance, is not entertaining," proclaims Wallace Matthews. Longtime *Daily News* scribe Pete Hamill still marvels at the forty thousand-plus who endured all fifteen rain-soaked innings of game five. Nowhere else could it happen, he says, still wanting to believe, as many of his contemporaries do, that New York is a city of strivers, of strugglers, of belief in lost causes.

The Mets themselves don't feel any nobility in their loss, not at first. As reporters descend on Turner Field's visiting clubhouse, the team can barely respond when asked who they'll root for in a World Series between their crosstown rivals and their divisional ones. Mike Piazza speaks for most when he says he won't watch, not caring who wins now. Al Leiter pretends he doesn't hear the question. He swears he can pitch tomorrow. He still thinks there is a tomorrow.

With the room threatening to descend into bitterness, Shawon Dunston speaks up. When he was traded to the Mets in July, he'd considered retirement a more attractive option. Now he considers his decision to continue playing the best one he ever made. He recounts the litany of pains they've all played through. Not only the wounded warrior Mike Piazza and the hobbled hero Robin Ventura, but the players whose woes never even made the papers. Armando Benítez, who stifled the Braves time and time again until tonight, despite a wreck of a left ankle, who—despite his reputation for histrionics and immaturity—spoke not a word of this injury to anyone outside the clubhouse. John Franco, who'd been taking regular cortisone shots to keep his shoulder in one piece for another few days. Kenny Rogers, who pitched through hamstring woes for months. Six Mets will have MRIs in the next few days. Another will soon go under the knife for knee surgery. To witness all of them fighting through so much, to not hear one word of wanting to retreat for home or the golf course or the fishing hole . . . it moved Dunston. When Piazza hit his home run to tie the game at seven, he jumped up and down like a child and declared, "We're going to the World Series!"

"You guys made me believe again," Dunston says. "You made baseball fun for me. I will never, ever forget what this team did."

He cries. His teammates cry. Then they crack open a few beers, and the sobs turn to laughs, and before they leave Turner Field they make sure to ask the video room for copies of the last two games they played, because they know they will want to watch them again, even the loss in game six. To feel this awful is wonderful, because it means that it mattered.

In his series post-mortem for the *New Yorker*, Roger Angell counsels as much to Mets fans who spend the next few days calling in sick, taking the phone off the hook, pushing away dinner for lack of appetite. He eyes them not with pity, but with envy.

> [O]ne really should be sorry for everyone else, all the rest of us, who can't think of anything to care about on anything like this scale, and might not have the nerve to hang in there, against such odds, even if we did.

CHAPTER 9

Intermission

THOUGH IT IS touted as a battle for the Team of the Decade title, the 1999 World Series between the Yankees and Braves—the two dynastic teams of the 1990s—is no more than a skirmish. Owning as they do the title of team of the twentieth century, the Yankees downplay the importance of the decennial crown. The Braves do the same, but their protests of apathy prove less than convincing. On the eve of the Fall Classic, Atlanta general manager John Schuerholz is spotted wearing a large, championship-style ring engraved with the phrase "Team of the '90s."

As the World Series begins, the press once again harps on the Yankees for failing to be the unbeatable squad of 1998. Words like "strife" and "discord" mark their descriptions of a team that won ninety-eight regular-season games and breezed through the first two rounds of the playoffs. Some signs of "discord" mentioned by the back pages are personal losses, such as a sudden epidemic of players' fathers passing away. When backup infielder Luis Sojo's father dies, it causes him to miss the first two games of the series while he tends to funeral arrangements. This also leaves the Yankees feeling bereaved because it forces them to lean heavily on Chuck Knoblauch, whose fielding abilities have mysteriously deteriorated. The commissioner's office rejects the Yankees' appeal to add a last-minute replacement for Sojo, prompting self-righteous harrumphing from George Steinbrenner. "We feel strongly that the young man's place right at this time is with his family," sniffs The Boss, an attitude that surprises those who remember the time Steinbrenner fired his publicist for daring to fly home for Christmas.

However, most of the blame for discontent among these Yankees is again pinned on Roger Clemens. The cover of a *Sporting News* playoff preview issue asks the question, "Can the Yankees Trust Roger Clemens?" (The even harsher article on The Rocket is entitled "Bombing in the Bronx.") Joe Torre implicitly answers *no* by putting Clemens in the third slot of his playoff rotation and keeping him there despite a strong performance in the division series clincher against the Rangers. "In the game of who you trust, Clemens . . . has not earned his pinstripes," declares the *Post*. Clemens's loss in Boston during the American League Championship Series—in which Clemens is clubbed around by the Sox, unsettled by the jeers he suffers at the hands of fans who once adored him—confirms this assessment. When the Yankees advance to the World Series despite him, Torre drops him to the fourth spot.

Despite all this "discord," the Yanks triumph yet again, as the Braves put up little resistance to their hegemony over all of baseball. New York takes the first two games in Atlanta in front of crowds full of Yankee fans, who are able to snag tickets for Turner Field with little issue. In game one, John Rocker gripes about the strike zone when a series of close pitch calls goes against him, allows a two-run single, and walks in another run in a disastrous eighth inning that dooms Atlanta to a 4–1 defeat. Yankee Stadium's transplanted Bleacher Creatures pride themselves on being able to "tame the beast the Mets couldn't." Bobby Cox looks panicked when he shuffles his lineup for game two and watches it get no-hit by David Cone until the eighth inning, by which point most Braves fans have found their way to the exits.

Cox flubs further when the series shifts to the Bronx for game three. His starter, Tom Glavine, is still recovering from a bout of the flu and the Braves' bullpen is well rested, so Cox should have no compunctions about pulling the lefty when he begins to show signs of fatigue. And yet, Atlanta's manager curiously allows Glavine to continue pitching long enough to allow a game-tying blast to Chuck Knoblauch. The Yankees go on to win on a tenth-inning walk-off home run by benchwarmer Chad Curtis. Bobby Cox's attempts to defend his moves later sound an awful lot like Bobby Valentine's prevarications about Kenny Rogers.

Every shot of Yankee Stadium's visiting dugout during game four shows a demoralized, defeated team. When Roger Clemens pitches well into the eighth inning to ensure a Yankees sweep, the papers congratulate him on finally reaching the finish line but grant him little agency in his team's championship. "Not the overpowering Rocket," declares one writer in his series wrap-up. "Good enough," says another. Clemens dares to utter the words, "I think I finally became a Yankee." In the afterglow of victory, it would be uncouth to argue otherwise, but no one hurries to second his motion.

Once the demolishing of the Braves is complete, the celebration that follows feels, at best, perfunctory. In 1998, police had to shut down the frat-like stretch of bars on Amsterdam Avenue due to the jubilant fans pouring out into the streets. In 1999, no barricades are necessary on Amsterdam, or anywhere else it seems. Cops characterize the night of the Yankees' triumph as "quiet for a Wednesday." "In 1996, winning was like a religious experience," proclaims one fan, suggesting that 1999 is anything but. Another regards this latest victory as "more businesslike" than those in the past. Yet another laments the outcome as "anticlimactic" because it came against the Braves instead of the Mets.

The press agrees. Unimpressed by the bloodless atmosphere of Turner Field, George Vecsey of the *Times* ponders what might have been. "I can't help thinking the Mets would have given the Yankees a better fight in those first two games in a pumped-up Shea Stadium," he writes.

Before the National League Championship Series began, Bobby Valentine taunted Atlanta with the idea that they would have to play "ghosts." The prophecy came true when the Braves played their World Series like haunted men, committing physical and mental errors they rarely did all season. The *Post* contends "the Braves were too busy thinking about their Near-Baseball-Death-Experience against the Mets" to do anything against the Yankees. Before the series even began, John Rocker admitted he was exhausted and, even more shockingly, "tired of talking." One reporter characterizes the mood in their clubhouse after the game four loss as "more tired than upset."

We won more games in the 1990s than any other team, the Braves tell themselves. You have to be great to reach to the World Series at all, the Braves tell themselves. We endured so much to get this far that the journey is enough, the Braves tell themselves. Then the Braves depart for Atlanta, where such perspective from a baseball team is permissible, and leave behind New York, where it is not.

* * *

On the eve of his first victory parade, Roger Clemens suggests his team deserves a ring that not only celebrates their World Series victory, but the Yankees themselves. On his suggestion, they design a platinum behemoth with the team's logo comprised of twenty-five diamonds, signifying the number of championships the team won in the 1900s. It will be inscribed with the words "TEAM OF THE CENTURY," a clear response to John Schuerholz's bragging bling, and will set back their bearers $40,000 a pop. The rings are so huge that one writer compares them to doorstops.

It is telling that the rings are made on the suggestion of Roger Clemens, who is judged not quite yet a Yankee. There is something un-Yankee-like about them, especially for the Yankees of 1999. They find little worth in declaring themselves the team of a century about to end. Put a hundred years in the rear view. Prepare to conquer the next.

* * *

Another flight might kill me.

This is Mike Piazza's belief at the end of the National League Championship Series. The thought of cramming himself into a plane seat for the trip back to New York is too much to bear. So as his teammates board the team charter for the long flight back to Queens, Piazza heads to the rental counter, grabs the only available car (a Ford Escort), turns off his cell phone, and makes his way home slowly and circuitously. He first drives west toward Vicksburg, Mississippi, to indulge his love of Civil War history. Vicksburg was the site of a crucial battle that ultimately gave control of the Mississippi River to the Union, cut off the Western rebel states from the Confederacy, and spelled the beginning of the end of the whole bloody enterprise. Piazza admires the tenacity of the troops who held out for forty-seven long days, the doomed men who charged General Grant's troops despite being outnumbered two to one.

He proceeds at a snail's pace, resting at truck stops, eating at diners, drawing little attention to himself as he makes his way through Dixie. He treats himself to a lunch of crab legs on a beach in Pensacola and eats them sitting in the sand, watching the surf roll in. No teammates, no screaming fans, no manager. Not a thing to answer to through the long winter to come, save his aching body.

* * *

On the frigid morning of November 16, some thirteen hundred Mets fans are summoned to Queens Criminal Court in Forest Hills to pay fines for various offenses incurred during the National League Championship Series. Most received open container violations, a shock to those who'd enjoyed a parking lot beer all season without so much as a warning from the police. Others were nailed for scalping tickets. The fined fans total more than twice the court's average daily case load. An extra judge is called in to process them all.

One fan, embittered forever by the experience, swears he'll never return to Shea. Another plans to exact revenge in a different way.

"I'm voting for Hillary," he says.

* * *

Arrests have been made. Several suspected terrorists who planned to attack Americans around New Year's Day were apprehended in the Middle East, but the State Department cautions that these arrests do not mean the threat is extinguished. The suspects have ties to a "Saudi-born militant" named Osama bin Laden. *Stay away from large gatherings*, the State Department warns.

Security is stepped up in all major cities planning giant celebrations for the impending new millennium. Despite the historic nature of the event, attendance at New Year's festivities across the country will be significantly depressed due to the terrorism scare and lingering fears over the potential chaos brought on by Y2K (the nightmare computer glitch warned of by scientists for years that might render all digital technology useless at midnight on January 1, 2000). Flights are canceled when millions decide to pop champagne in the safety of their homes rather than travel. Seattle—still smoldering from riots during the recent World Trade Organization meetings and spooked by the arrest of an Algerian national who attempted to smuggle dynamite into the city via the nearby Canadian border—cancels its New Year's party altogether.

No thought is given to cancellation in New York. The FBI urges people to stay away, but Mayor Giuliani does not, believing such discouragement would allow the terrorists to claim a victory without detonating a single bomb. He calls on more than eight thousand NYPD officers and orders manhole covers bolted down. He can't ensure perfect safety for everyone. No human can do that. *Life means risk*, the mayor reminds his city.

In the end, close to two million souls gather in Times Square on December 31, 1999, more than four times the size of average New Year's crowds, and yet only fourteen arrests are made, most for minor charges. City emergency rooms report the night passes quieter than usual.

The crowd in Times Square gazes upward, gawking as the nines turn into zeroes and one millennium gives way to the next. They stand in a city without worry, without danger, without a hint of the strife of decades past. The changes of the Giuliani years have taken on the feeling of permanence. At the dawn of the twenty-first century, New York is safe. They believe it has always been this way. They believe it will always be this way.

PART 2: 2000

CHAPTER 10

The Man in the Shogun Helmet

THE STING OF Kenny Rogers's bases-loaded walk is still hanging in the air when the question is raised: What's to become of John Olerud? His arrival in Queens in 1997 was the first step in the Mets' return to relevance, but now free agency calls the first baseman, and it takes a strong man to resist the allure of free agency at the end of the millennium.

"We've made it clear we want to bring him back, and we'll push aggressively to do that," Steve Phillips says within hours of the Mets' defeat at the hand of Braves. But if the general manager is eager to see John Olerud signed as soon as possible, John Olerud is not. The first baseman left a lot of money on the table when he signed an extension with the Mets two years ago. Now thirty-one years old, this might be his last chance to sign for big money.

It's an open secret that Olerud, a native of Washington state, would love to play for the Seattle Mariners, even if that team is shopping its two biggest stars (Ken Griffey Jr. and Alex Rodriguez) to save payroll. Olerud agonizes over his decision for weeks, waffling between his love of New York and the pull of his hometown team, signing a three-year, $20 million deal with Seattle on December 7, 1999.

For the entire six weeks between the end of the World Series and the day Olerud leaves the 7 train behind, the Mets make no deals of note. Their inability to multitask, or to plan for worst case scenarios, leaves them in quite a pickle. With no other first base options immediately apparent, the possibility of moving Mike Piazza to first base is mentioned but soon dropped as impractical, at least for the year 2000.

Instead, the Mets pounce on free agent Todd Zeile, who knocked in ninety-eight runs for Texas in 1999 but felt slighted by the Rangers' lack of urgency in attempting to re-sign him. The drawbacks of asking Zeile to take John Olerud's place are many, the biggest being that he is primarily a third baseman and has never started more than thirty-five games at first base in a season. This alone would make him a defensive downgrade from Olerud, but there is also the matter of him being righthanded. This would not be the first position change of Todd Zeile's career, nor the most dramatic, as the Cardinals moved him from catcher to infield early in his career. He once imagined he'd be a Cardinal for life, but a contract squabble with team management led to a trade to Chicago in 1995, and he's been well traveled ever since. The Mets will be his sixth different team in eight seasons. If nothing else, Zeile is far more vocal and outgoing than John Olerud, quicker with quotes and quips in a way that soon endears him to the New York press corps. He does resemble Olerud in his love of the city and swears he too will take the 7 train to the games at Shea in the upcoming season.

Todd Zeile will accept the comparisons to John Olerud, and the pressure inherent in trying to replace him, because the Mets will offer a chance to play deep into October. His prior postseason experiences have always met an abrupt end against the most immovable object of this era. He's reached the postseason three times this decade with the Orioles and the Rangers. Each time, his team was eliminated by the Yankees.

* * *

Steve Phillips breezes into the winter meetings in Anaheim in December and proclaims he has his eye on more deals to improve the Mets. A torrent of desired players rolls forth from his lips as if he were leafing through the FAO Schwarz catalog before Christmas. *Manny Ramírez. Jim Edmonds. B. J. Surhoff. David Wells. Jason Schmidt* . . . He leaves the winter meetings without making a single deal of note, however, and the press wonders if he's lost the magic touch he displayed last off-season. Stung by the criticism, a defensive Phillips responds by making a very public play for Ken Griffey Jr.

Long regarded the best player in baseball, Griffey turned down an extension from the Mariners during the 1999 season, all but guaranteeing his imminent trade to a big-spending team this winter. The Mariners had eyed the Mets and their deep pockets as trade partners for a while.

In late September, Seattle scouts were spotted at Shea more than once, leading to rampant speculation a deal was in the works for either Griffey or shortstop Alex Rodriguez, who has broadcast his desire to play in New York at every opportunity.

By mid-November, Seattle lets it be known they've received an intriguing offer for Griffey from an unnamed team assumed to be the Mets. New York's sportswriters at once insist—as they had when Mike Piazza became trade bait in 1998—that the Mets *must* acquire Ken Griffey Jr. "Only one baseball player could come to the Mets," insists the *Post*, "and make them so much bigger they wouldn't need a slingshot to fight the Yankees—so much bigger you wouldn't need a magnifying glass on the map dominated by the Yankees."

This chatter reaches a fevered pitch, then is cruelly silenced when Griffey announces he will not accept a trade to the Mets. The news is so sudden and shocking to the team that Steve Phillips is forced to prohibit his players from making any more recruitment calls to Griffey, lest they be hit with tampering charges. Even Bud Selig seems a bit miffed about this development, telling reporters, "In a perfect world, I think it would be great for Ken Griffey Jr. to be in New York."

The story of how the Mets lost Griffey, or if he was ever theirs to lose, takes on *Rashomon*-like duality. One report says that the Mets were once one of Griffey's acceptable destinations, but he soured on the team when his agent was informed the Mets had "other priorities" (the doomed re-signing of John Olerud, presumably, which occupied them for all of November) and was further told that Fred Wilpon preferred to trade for Alex Rodriguez instead. Based on this intelligence, and the fact that the team blew him off for weeks, Griffey was cool to the sudden interest that followed Olerud's departure. Another report insisted the Mets' efforts to acquire Griffey were sabotaged by hurry-up tactics from the Seattle front office, who came to Junior with a deal that would send him to New York but gave him only eight minutes to make up his mind.

Like John Olerud, Ken Griffey Jr. feels the pull of home and accepts a trade to the Cincinnati Reds, the team his father played for during the Big Red Machine era of the 1970s. The Mets and Bobby Valentine are left to wonder what might have been. "I could tell you that I did write out a lineup with him in it, and it did look pretty good," the manager sighs.

* * *

After missing out on both Olerud and Griffey, for a while Steve Phillips finds it difficult to make any deals at all. With free agent pickings much slimmer this winter than last, impact players must be acquired via trade, putting the Mets and their lowly regarded farm system at a disadvantage. It's not until December 23 that Phillips finally brings a deal to the finish line, acquiring pitcher Mike Hampton from the Astros.

The lefty starter was a Cy Young Award contender in 1999, winning twenty-two games and pitching to a 2.90 ERA. The Mets are impressed by Hampton's 13–1 record in his last eighteen starts, which suggests he is immune to the late season swoons that have consumed them in recent years. At five feet, ten inches, Hampton is on the short side for a pitcher, so assessments focus not on overpowering speed or wicked "stuff," but athleticism and toughness. A late selection in the amateur draft (sixth round) and a low signing bonus placed an outsized chip on his shoulder at the start of his professional career. He vowed to "outwork" the competition to make his way to the big leagues, and did. His maniacal competitiveness is on display in every aspect of his life, including at home, where he cannot stand to lose in Nintendo to his four-year-old son. "My dad never let up on me," Hampton explains. "I'm not letting up on my son." The Mets choose to view this behavior in a positive light. *He can't stand to lose.*

But Hampton comes at a steep price. The trade costs the Mets Octavio Dotel, their promising young pitcher, and Roger Cedeño, base-stealing revelation of 1999. The Mets are also forced to take off Houston's hands the hefty contract of aging outfielder Derek Bell. Once a feared run producer, Bell is coming off his worst offensive season to date. Asked what he thinks about the idea of being booed by the vocal Shea faithful, Bell responds, "Try living in the ghetto." Anything Mets fans can dish out is child's play compared to a hardscrabble youth spent in the same rough Tampa, Florida neighborhood that produced Dwight Gooden and Gary Sheffield. Other kids dubbed the young Bell a "monster" for growing to almost six feet tall and sprouting a mustache by the age of twelve.

So the Mets have dealt away two of their best young players and taken on Bell's onerous contract, and all for the promise of no more than one season of Mike Hampton, who is due to become a free agent following the 2000 season. After some discussion of signing a long-term deal with the Mets, Hampton declares he will not discuss a contract during the season. Mike Piazza took the same stance after his own trade in 1998 and returned to New York anyway, but something about Mike Hampton's manner suggests he will be harder to convince. Perhaps a native of Homosassa, Florida—a town where the local economy hinges on offering manatee encounters to northern tourists—might not be a good fit for Gotham. Or perhaps that sixth-round chip on his shoulder compels him to play hard to get.

The Mets are willing to take this risk because they have few other avenues for improving their starting rotation, given the plethora of off-season defections, some more lamented then others. Both Kenny Rogers and the Mets make awkward gestures toward a reunion until the team abruptly rescinds its offer of salary arbitration over an "ambiguous" clause in Rogers's contract. When the Mets also fail to offer salary arbitration to forty-one-year-old Orel Hershiser, he departs for one last hurrah with the Dodgers. Then Masato Yoshii, at times the team's best starter in 1999, is traded to Colorado for Bobby M. Jones (not to be confused with Bobby J. Jones, the longtime Met), a twenty-seven-year-old lefthander with a great deal of potential but few big league results. The newest Bobby Jones is touted as a fifth-starter candidate, but he is also recovering from his own shoulder problem that throws his viability for the starting rotation into question. (The loss of the dependable Yoshii will thus be invariably mentioned any time a Mets starter struggles in the season to come.) And so Mike Hampton, all five feet, ten inches of him, will have to anchor the Mets' rotation in 2000, because the Mets have no other candidates for the position.

* * *

Mets fans didn't think much of Bobby Bonilla to begin with, but Bonilla found a way to make them think even less of him during game six of the 1999 National League Championship Series. While the Mets were attempting to stave off death in Atlanta, Bonilla retired to Turner Field's visiting clubhouse after a pinch-hitting assignment to play cards with Rickey Henderson. They'd played cards together during games all season, but it apparently occurred to neither of them that it might be seen as disrespectful to play cards while their teammates were fighting for their playoff lives.

The Mets are fully aware bringing back Rickey Henderson will invite more of this behavior in the year to come, but Roger Cedeño's departure in the Mike Hampton trade leaves Henderson as their only viable leadoff man. Through gritted teeth, management lets the lingering issue of Card-gate slide for Henderson. They are not so forgiving when it comes to Bobby Bonilla, and even less forgiving after hearing comments the outfielder makes during his charity bowling tournament in early December. Cornered by reporters, Bonilla makes public demands to play regularly in 2000 or else "there will be some fireworks." Then, as if rubbing his defiant act in the Mets' faces, he uses a playing card metaphor to describe his role, comparing himself to a joker in a deck. "You can decide whether you want to play with them or you can discard them, but you do have that chance to play with them," he says.

Bonilla's bowling alley rant initiates divorce proceedings. Shortly after the new year arrives, the Mets announce they've come to an agreement that will make him a free agent and defer his remaining salary far into the distant future. The Mets agree to pay Bonilla close to $1.2 million a year for twenty-five years beginning in 2011. At the moment, 2011 seems impossibly far down the road, and the deferment a small price to pay to be rid of the man. Given his release, Bonilla pokes the Mets in the eye one last time by signing a minor league deal with the Braves. "They explained my role with me and I'm comfortable with that," Bonilla insists.

The trade of Masato Yoshii and deferring the money owed to Bonilla for another decade-plus allows the Mets to shed close to $10 million in salary, leading to speculation that they will use such largesse to pursue a big-ticket player. In truth, the Mets completed all of their big deals before Christmas and possess virtually no trade chips after the Hampton deal. The remainder of the winter is spent handing contract extensions to players like Armando Benítez, Rick Reed, Todd Pratt, and Rey Ordóñez, whose contract's lack of a no-trade clause is taken as a sign the team still intends to pursue Alex Rodriguez.

Other Mets of 1999 are allowed to drift away quietly. Shawon Dunston, both goat and hero of the Grand Slam Single game, expressed an interest in coming back to the Mets, but when his phone doesn't ring, Dunston returns to St. Louis. Billy Taylor, disastrously ineffective as occasional closer, is granted free agency and sent on his merry way.

Compared to the blockbuster trades and bank-breaking deals before the 1999 season, the moves that precede 2000 are much lower in number and much less prestigious in the names involved. St. Louis acquires some protection for Mark McGwire by trading for Jim Edmonds from the Angels. Looking to rebound from a disappointing 1999, the Dodgers snag slugger Shawn Green from the Blue Jays. Desperate to contend again, the Tigers sell the farm to the Rangers for masher Juan González. After rejecting all trade offers in 1999, Angel ace Chuck Finley hits free agency and signs with the Indians. The Red Sox grab Carl Everett from the payroll-shedding Astros. Greg Vaughn, who powered the Reds into wild card contention last year, takes a chance on Tampa Bay. Beyond these moves, very few off-season trades and signings appear likely to have much impact on the upcoming schedule, and none approach the record contracts of last season. If the game's landscape has shifted at all, the movement is glacial.

"Glacial" might also describe the pace of contract negotiations for Bobby Valentine, as far as the manager is concerned. For most of the winter, he sounds hopeful about the possibility of a new pact with the Mets, as his contract is set to expire after 2000. When February arrives and no extension has come, however, Valentine lashes out. "Shame on somebody if they think they need another year to study and analyze me," he harrumphs on the eve of spring training. "If they don't know by now, then they'll never know."

The *Times* fears the story of Valentine's status "will hound the Mets just as Bobby Bonilla's saga dogged them throughout most of 1999," but Fred Wilpon remains unmoved. "The organizational belief is that you sign a contract and then you honor it from the beginning to end," he insists after Bobby Valentine's latest outburst. Reporters point out that Valentine's current contract had been given to him in the middle of the 1997 season. "Policy changes," Wilpon grumbles.

Translation: In 2000, just as it was in 1999, the Mets must win or else. "Like all potential free agents, Bobby Valentine needs a big year," Joel Sherman writes in the *Post*. "You wonder if his bosses want him to have it."

* * *

In 1999, the Mets' arrival in Port St. Lucie was overshadowed by the Yankees' ambush acquisition of Roger Clemens. In 2000, the Mets overshadow themselves by inviting country music superstar Garth Brooks to attend camp as a benefit for his charity, Touch 'Em All. Steve Phillips proclaims he is excited to have Brooks with the team, even though, as he makes the announcement, he must consult some shrink-wrapped CDs to name any of the singer's tunes.

Todd Zeile allows no questions about his work ethic by arriving to camp early and working with Mets legend Keith Hernandez on his first base fundamentals. Despite Zeile's diligence, his nervousness at the new position is betrayed when, during his first intrasquad game, he prevails on Hernandez to stand nearby and remind him where to position himself. Robin Ventura arrives in Florida on the heels of a surgical shoulder "clean up," which keeps him off the field until mid-March, though he swears he will be ready for the regular season regardless. Up the middle, Rey Ordóñez shrugs off his manager's public wishes for an improved offense ("He can say what he wants," the shortstop grumbles) but also follows Bobby Valentine's advice by belting a staggering three home runs in spring action. As for the pitchers, Al Leiter arrives fresh off his own knee surgery, and having shed a few pounds. He declares the Mets starting corps could boast four twenty-game winners now that they have Mike Hampton, Rick Reed, the righty Bobby Jones, and himself. John Franco proclaims this is the "hungriest" group of Mets he's ever seen, an unfortunate word to use when closer Armando Benítez arrives at camp so visibly out of shape that the wags at the *Post* dub him "Armandough."

Benítez's weight issue is quickly forgotten when Rickey Henderson ambles his way to Florida, the last player to arrive at major league camp. When the Mets were holding their first voluntary team workout, Henderson took the word "voluntary" at face value and treated himself to a little R&R. He was spotted in Vegas—playing cards, of course.

Pressed by the media about Card-gate, Henderson's unwillingness to provide a straight answer only invites further interrogation. He ends his first press conference in the town he calls "St. Port Lucie" by proclaiming that he doesn't like how he was used last season and contending he is grossly underpaid at $2 million a year, two proclamations he'd made many times in 1999. With rumors abounding that the team is desperate to trade Henderson, a summit is called between Henderson and Bobby Valentine, just as many summits were called during similar flare-ups last year, and an uneasy détente is reached. One of the newest Mets, Derek Bell, does his part for peace by inviting Henderson on a fishing trip on his yacht-cum-houseboat (the same one Bell plans to dock in Flushing Bay once the season begins). They find they are kindred spirits who both look upon the sport primarily as entertainment. Mere days into camp, Bell's signature call of "yo, yo" echoes loudly in a clubhouse where exuberance was once in short supply.

The coverage of Henderson's outburst highlights the main difference between 1999 and 2000 for the Mets. A year earlier, Henderson's near mutiny would have engendered an avalanche of doom-and-gloom predictions. In 2000, the Mets are coasting on the goodwill they accumulated through their unlikely playoff run in 1999. If turmoil preceded that magical postseason, then surely turmoil was a virtue. Even the *Post*'s

Wallace Matthews, perpetual wet blanket, praises the Mets by saying they make for much better copy than the Yankees.

As the Henderson controversy fizzles out, the biggest question facing the Mets is who will earn the fifth starter's slot. At the start of camp, the job seems Bobby M. Jones's to lose, if for no other reason than to justify the trade of Masato Yoshii, but this hope fades when the lefty's Grapefruit League ERA climbs to the uncomfortable height of seven. Jones's competition hardly fares better. The Mets reacquire Bill Pulsipher, one-third of Generation K, in a trade with Milwaukee to compete for the fifth spot, but he collapses one afternoon due to a combination of dehydration and the accumulated side effects of antidepressants and must be rushed to the emergency room. Though he recovers, his hopes of making the rotation all but end there. Paul Wilson, another Generation K survivor, shows some promise but is nonetheless one of the first players optioned to minor league camp. Hopes that twenty-two-year-old prospect Grant Roberts might step up and grab the brass ring are dashed by indifferent starts and an apparent lack of work ethic. John Franco attempts to shame Roberts by chastising him in the locker room for all to hear when he departs early—"Last one here, first one to leave, huh?"—but the elder statesman's half-joking jibes have little effect.

No one appears to be qualified until the emergence of Glendon Rusch. The southpaw was acquired in a trade with Kansas City at the tail end of last season on the urging of assistant general manager Omar Minaya, who saw him as having the potential to be another Jamie Moyer, textbook example of a crafty lefty. After Rusch contributes a few decent performances in spring action, fellow lefty Al Leiter gives him some unfriendly advice: *Be meaner*. Rusch's stuff is where it needs to be, but Leiter recognizes him as too gentle a soul. (The *Times* describes Rusch as owning "the chipper disposition of the hero in a children's sports novel.") By adding a modicum of meanness to his demeanor, Rusch steps into the breach left by the failures of other comers and throws to a 3.24 ERA in nearly seventeen innings of spring work. *Good enough for us*, say the Mets. Rusch admits he learned his two-seam fastball and honed his ability to induce ground balls from fellow lefty Kenny Rogers during his time as a September call-up in 1999. The team thanks him for taking what he could from Rogers and prays he never mentions *that name* again.

* * *

Coming into the spring, the Mets' bullpen is overflowing with viable lefty arms, leading to wide speculation that one of them will be dealt. Dennis Cook is so sure he'll get his walking papers that whenever he calls his wife, she answers with, "Have you been traded yet?" ("Not even a hello," he says.) Cook remains in New York, however, and the lefty who winds up being dealt is the Mets' newest and oldest southpaw, Jesse Orosco. The forty-two-year-old reliever who once closed for the Mets' 1986 championship team was acquired over the winter from the Orioles and pitches well enough in Grapefruit League action to draw interest from St. Louis. In return, the Cardinals send back Joe McEwing, a pint-sized utility man. McEwing is an earnest, jack-of-all-trades type, so beloved by his manager in St. Louis that, when news of the trade with New York comes down, Cardinals skipper Tony La Russa inserts McEwing in his afternoon's lineup anyway, so he can watch him play one last time (a touching if ethically questionable move). La Russa even asks McEwing for a pair of his spikes as a keepsake before he departs for Port St. Lucie. When he arrives, Bobby Valentine all but assures McEwing he will start the year in triple-A. "Sometime during the year, I want to be part of the puzzle," McEwing says, all smiles, betraying not a trace of disappointment as he is sent to Norfolk.

The newcomer handles the news far better than a teammate who seems likely to join him in the minors. A fan favorite in the summer of 1999, Benny Agbayani cooled down considerably by the end of the season. When he is outhit by younger outfielders in spring training action—especially Jay Payton, long a prized Met farmhand who is finally healthy after years of freak injuries—Agbayani asks his agent to seek a trade rather than face a return to triple-A that appears inevitable.

The only thing working in Agbayani's favor is the fact that the Mets won't need a fifth starter until April 9, and so they can function with only ten pitchers on their roster until then. Management has extra time to ponder his fate because the Mets will begin their season much earlier, and much farther from home, than any American team has before.

Last summer, MLB announced its intention to begin the 2000 season in Japan, with major league games that would count in the standings. The Japanese organizer of the series, Yomiuri Media, desperately wanted a Cubs vs. Cardinals series, which is to say a Sammy Sosa vs. Mark McGwire series, but public griping from McGwire quickly put an end to this fantasy. "Major League Baseball belongs in the United States," the slugger harrumphed upon hearing of the plan. "The Japanese have Japanese baseball, so there's no reason for us to go over there." McGwire continued to grouse in this vein until long after it was assured he would not have to make the trip.

Initially, the Japanese baseball establishment is on Mark McGwire's side. Yoshiaki Kanai, Nippon Professional Baseball's equivalent to Bud Selig, almost didn't allow MLB to start its season in his backyard. For one thing, a series with tickets costing up to $120 seems tone deaf, given the brutal recession Japan is enduring. For another, the defection of stars like Hideo Nomo to America has robbed NPB of its marquee players and driven down revenues across the league. To some in the NPB, allowing American teams to play in Japan is tantamount to an admission of defeat. Eventually, Kanai relents, acknowledging, as Selig implicitly has, that globalization is a force he cannot fight.

To Fred Wilpon, longtime Bud Selig ally, the Japan trip represents less a statement on twenty-first-century globalization than an opportunity to insert his team into baseball history. So when McGwire's objections remove the Cardinals from consideration, Wilpon volunteers the Mets as a worthy substitute. The official announcement of the Japan trip in October of 1999—which will involve two exhibition games against NPB teams and two more regular-season games against the Cubs on March 29 and 30—goes largely unnoticed, coming as it does during the Mets' playoff series against the Arizona Diamondbacks.

Bobby Valentine says he won't sleep until the flight back, not wanting to miss a single moment of his triumphant return to Japan. The Mets manager is truly in his glory from the moment he steps off the plane in Tokyo, showing off his command of Japanese at press conferences and holding forth to the American press on which players could make the transition from NPB to MLB. He places his bets on slap-hitting shortstop Kazuo Matsui and slugging outfielder Hideki Matsui.

The Mets might tell themselves they're not a consolation prize for Mark McGwire, but the preponderance of local advertisements that tout Sammy Sosa, and fail to mention them, indicates otherwise. When the team makes a goodwill trip to a United States military base, the longest tenured Met is introduced as "Scotty Franco." Few Mets are even approached when several players brave a trip on the Tokyo subway after an exhibition in the suburb of Seibu. This is not a contrived meet-the-locals stunt, but an organic revolt against the terror of a two-hour bus trip in Tokyo traffic, an ordeal they now dread after enduring it several times in their first few days in Japan.

The Mets take the field as the home team for the first regular-season game held outside of North America on March 29, 2000, the first pitch coming at 5:08 a.m. Shea Stadium time. Some early risers line up at four in the morning to cram into Times Square's ESPN Zone and witness all the action with a breakfast beer. Among the bleary-eyed Mets fans is at least one interloper who gained entry despite sporting a Yankees hat, which one angry Mets partisan compares to wearing a Saddam Hussein T-shirt to a Desert Storm victory parade. Al Leiter, who exercised his veteran prerogative to stay in the States, watches from the comfort of his home, his three-year-old daughter leaving no need for an alarm clock to wake him up at the crack of dawn.

The contest unfolds in front of a crowd of fifty-five thousand that includes the crown prince of the Japanese royal family and his wife. Though located in a hyper-futuristic megalopolis, the Tokyo Dome looks like a throwback to American eyes, its pale artificial turf closer to multipurpose 1970s facilities like Veterans Stadium than the new spate of cozy Camden Yards-inspired ballparks. Batting helmets feature the logo of the series' sponsor, a corporate intrusion that alarms those who fear a future where baseball players are covered in ads a la European soccer kits or NASCAR vehicles.

The game also marks the Mets debut of Mike Hampton, an event of far less historic import but of great concern to New York. The dirt used on the Tokyo Dome infield, imported from America, is a bone of contention for many players, but no one is more upset by it than the Met lefty. Though he refuses to blame the mound itself after the game, Hampton is visibly uncomfortable while pitching from it, kicking at the dirt and harrumphing at close calls that go against him. Though he allows only two runs, Hampton logs a staggering nine walks and fourteen baserunners over five innings. His plethora of free passes inspires some in the crowd to boo, an exceedingly rare act for a Japanese baseball audience. At least some of the booing is caused by walks of Sammy Sosa, since locals paid through the nose to watch Slammin' Sammy swing the bat, not earn free passes. The lone Mets highlight comes when Mike Piazza belts a 450-foot two-run bomb in the bottom of the eighth to make the game close, but bullpen struggles have already put the game out of reach for New York by the time his homer is launched, and the Mets fall by the score of 5–3. Numerous fans leave after Piazza's blast, as if this were all they came to see and could depart happy.

The series concludes the following night with a pitcher's duel between Rick Reed and Chicago rookie Kyle Farnsworth. The score stays knotted at one until the eleventh inning, when a single and two walks load the bases for the Mets. With the pitcher's spot due up next, Bobby Valentine turns to Benny Agbayani. His future is no brighter at this moment than it was when he left Florida. This is his first at bat in any game in Japan, including the meaningless exhibition tune-ups. It remains a virtual lock that he will move on to Norfolk when the Mets need room for a fifth starter.

Before this game, in a desperate bid to change his luck, Agbayani and his wife took part in *omikuji*, a fortune-telling ritual at a Shinto shrine. He tells reporters the fortune he received, *daikichi*, means "great good luck," the best fortune you could receive. He won't say exactly what the fortune promised, though. Much like mojo, such fortunes must remain secret or they will never come to pass.

Agbayani will say that what he does here means little, really. It's only one game, nothing like "doing it over fifty games." Fifty games was roughly the length of his hot streak in 1999, those glorious days when he hit homers left and right and the Shea stands sang along to "B-B-B-Benny and the Mets . . ." But it sure looks like it means a lot to Agbayani when he eyes a fat 1-0 fastball, raises his left leg in the acrobatic kick he modeled after Japanese home run champ Sadaharu Oh, and knocks the ball to straightaway center field for a game-icing grand slam, leaping like a Little Leaguer and pumping his fist for his entire trip around the bases. The blast secures a 5–1 Mets victory and earns him the trophy for game's best player, a replica shogun's helmet.

Bobby Valentine refuses to get his outfielder's hopes up, offering no more praise than, "I'm glad he's here with us today." Once the team returns to the States, however, injuries pile up that create unexpected openings in the Mets' outfield. The call to death row never comes. Agbayani will remain on the roster for the rest of the season. A banged-up veteran ballclub is the real reason his once certain demotion never comes, but the grand slam in Tokyo will forever be named his redeemer. As the *Times* puts it, "How can you farm out a player with a shogun helmet?"

CHAPTER 11

Jet Lag

THE METS SPIN their Japan trip as an overwhelmingly positive experience, perhaps sensing that their adventures east will catch the blame should they struggle after returning home. To prove they're experiencing no jet lag, the Mets play themselves to a tidy win in their home opener on April 3. Though gray skies hang over Queens the afternoon of April 3, rain does not materialize and all else proceeds in a sunny manner. Al Leiter tosses eight excellent innings against the San Diego Padres (who project to be no better in 2000 than their "Marlins West" campaign of 1999), while a Derek Bell solo shot in the bottom of the eighth scores the winning run, earning the outfielder a thunderous curtain call from the Shea crowd. Armando Benítez earns the save in the ninth and expends only seven pitches to do so. Per the tradition set in 1999, the Mets' 2–1 victory is capped by playing the "mojo risin' . . ." coda of The Doors' "L.A. Woman." *See? Nothing has changed*, Jim Morrison assures everyone.

The promise of opening day dissipates in the days that follow, as temperatures plunge and the Mets' bats are chilled. The righty Bobby Jones, making his first start in almost a year following an injury-plagued 1999, fails to make it out of the third inning in a shutout loss. The next day, Mike Hampton coughs up four runs in less than six innings while his teammates commit unsightly blunders on the basepaths and in the field. Following the two losses to lowly San Diego, they split two games against the Dodgers before a freak snowstorm cuts the series short. Bobby Valentine proclaims the snowy weather to be a portent of "another regular, wacky, abnormal season" and thanks it for giving a day of rest to an already overtaxed bullpen.

Once the Mets hit the road, the climate improves somewhat, but the results are no better. A three-game set in Philadelphia begins on April 10 with two unsightly losses to a Phillies team that is again rumored to be shopping all of its stars. Even when the Mets move on to Pittsburgh and claim their first series of the season, the victories are not without pain, as both Bobby Jones and Rickey Henderson are lost to injury. Soon afterward, Al Leiter complains of a sore groin, and Darryl Hamilton hits the disabled list with a toe injury so troublesome it shelves him for several months and prompts him to seriously consider retirement.

Then it's Bobby Valentine's turn to injure himself with a new controversy. During the Mets' series in Philadelphia, a student invites him to speak at the Wharton School of Business, followed by a Q&A on the current state of the Mets. That state being rather precarious at the moment, and Valentine being Valentine, the manager answers with an unwise level of candor. He admits he didn't like the signing of Todd Zeile to play first base and confesses he's just as baffled as anyone about why Masato Yoshii was traded away. Worst of all, he contends he only slots Derek Bell into his everyday lineup because of pressure from the front office.

These off-the-cuff remarks might have died in the lecture hall, if not for one attendee who posts his notes from the Q&A to an online message board. When the press calls on the manager to explain himself, Valentine calls the controversy "ridiculous," yet denies none of his reported remarks. A spooked Steve Phillips intercepts his team at their next stop in Pittsburgh and attempts to hash things out with Valentine in person. At first Phillips casts aspersions on the source of the comments, sneering, "I don't know what sort of credence to lend to some sort of posting on the internet." But it sure looks like Valentine must have said something damaging when Wharton's student newspaper (*The Daily Pennsylvanian*) reports the manager contacted one of their reporters to request she destroy her tape of the talk. Wharton later reveals that, yes, they do have a tape of the event and, no, they don't plan on releasing it to the public, a revelation that only causes the press to clamor for the smoking gun.

As a halfway compromise, *The Daily Pennsylvanian* produces a partial transcript of Valentine's talk based on a reporter's personal audio recording of the event. The remarks it captures—which include Valentine's prepared talk and exclude the Q&A—are mostly innocuous. The student who set off the controversy in the first place, referred to most newspapers by his message board username (Brad34), muddies the picture further when he contends his recollections of Valentine's answers weren't meant to represent direct quotes.

Coverage of "Wharton-gate" eyes Steve Phillips the harshest, his mad dash to Pittsburgh to "discuss" the controversy seen as the move of a paranoid executive defensive about the team he assembled, which has underperformed so far. "He could have talked to Valentine over the phone and, if he was satisfied with the manager's explanation, informed the media of that and said the matter was closed," Bill Madden insists in the *Daily News*.

Fears that this chaos will engulf the Mets fade once they return to Queens for a lengthy homestand beginning on April 18 and settle into a groove. First, they sweep three games from the overmatched Brewers, as Mike Hampton earns his first win as a Met in the series opener and declares, "I kind of felt like me again, for the first time in a while." Then, after batting below the Mendoza line as a team for the first few weeks of the season, the Mets pound out thirty runs against the visiting Chicago Cubs in a series beginning on April 22 and sweep three from them as well. Continuing his hot spring and showing no ill will from the (alleged) aspersions cast on him by Bobby Valentine, Derek Bell goes 10-for-12 against Chicago pitching. When the Dodgers swing back into town on April 24 for a makeup of the game that was lost to a snow day, the Mets eke out a 1–0 walk-off win. They then cap a nine-game winning streak with a victory against the Cincinnati Reds on April 25 that includes some sweet revenge. Ken Griffey Jr., booed in every at bat for his off-season rejection of the Mets, strikes out to end the game.

Unfortunately, this is the last sustained cheering Mets fans will exhale for some time. The latest downturn begins when the Mets drop the final two games against the Reds to end an otherwise triumphant 8–2 homestand on a sour note. Spirits are further dampened by a grueling thirteen-game road trip beginning April 28 that zigzags through Denver, San Francisco, Miami, and Pittsburgh, in that strange order—the first of several bizarrely plotted road trips imposed on the Mets by cruel schedule makers, after the extra burden of a trek to Tokyo. Dennis Cook labels the unknown sadist who charted this season's course for the Mets "a moron." Robin Ventura, who normally keeps quiet about personal discomfort, points to the schedule and exclaims, with disgusted disbelief, "Just look at it."

Though the Mets take two of three games from the Rockies in their initial stop in Denver, each game is an unsightly slugfest, with one or both teams scoring double-digit runs each night. Bobby Valentine says he finds the city itself beautiful but is grateful his team will make no more trips there this season. The Mets are perhaps eager to get a look at San Francisco's brand-new stadium, Pacific Bell Park, where they'll play four games beginning on May 1. The Giants' new bayside home is a jewel by any measure, but especially when compared to the drafty heap that was Candlestick Park. To a man, the Mets pronounce themselves impressed by the new facility with its crowd-pleasing concessions, quirky dimensions, and scenic overlook on an inlet newly dubbed McCovey Cove.

Distracted by Pac Bell's combination of beauty and quirk, the Mets are swept right out of the Bay Area. In the opener, Bill Pulsipher is recalled to take a start in the place of the injured Bobby Jones and is pummeled in a loss that features the first home run ever hit into McCovey Cove, a 418-foot moonshot off the bat of Barry Bonds. The following night, Glendon Rusch puts a wrinkle on an otherwise spotless spring in an ugly defeat. The fourth and final contest concludes with a bullpen meltdown that turns a winnable game into a lopsided loss.

The third game of the series is the most disturbing of all, as it features another troubled outing from Mike Hampton. Wild yet again, Hampton coughs up three separate leads and barks at the home plate umpire over close calls that go against him. After Jeff Kent hits a walk-off homer, the lefty leaves the stadium on his own and walks the several miles back to the hotel. "It seems like everything's going against me," Hampton sighs, a sentiment many of his teammates share at the moment.

Despite an all-night cross-country flight, the Mets snap their losing streak by winning the opener of a three-game set against the Marlins in Miami on May 5 behind Al Leiter. Hopes of getting back on track are dashed when they proceed to drop the next two tilts, scoring a grand total of one run in both games. They stumble into Pittsburgh on May 9 and win two of three from the Pirates to conclude their first "moronic" road trip of the season, then sift through the wreckage for any signs of life. Pointing to stellar performances in the wins against the Pirates from Al Leiter and Mike Hampton (who gutted out 8 1/3 shutout innings in the opener despite taking a line drive off his wrist), Todd Zeile dares say the team will have momentum going into their much-awaited homestand.

Overjoyed to be back in Queens, the Mets celebrate their return to Shea on May 12 with a loop of Judy Garland from *The Wizard of Oz* on Diamond Vision, repeating "There's no place like home . . ." They proceed to look a lot like the team that struggled on the road, dropping the opening contest against the Marlins and the next one for good measure.

It escapes no one's notice that as the Mets' season threatens to crumble around them, Rickey Henderson is jackhammering the team's fragile foundation. When the Mets come to Shea for their first team workout after the trip to Japan, Henderson again intimates that stress over his contract will be a distraction all year. "I want to leave this game happy," he says. "I don't want to leave the game fussy and mad." After the Mets win their stateside opener on Derek Bell's crowd-pleasing home run, the sole sourpuss in Shea Stadium is Henderson. "I just ain't into it right now," he says. Scarcely a day goes by in the season's initial weeks without another meeting between Henderson and Steve Phillips, or Henderson and Bobby Valentine, or the complete troika to address the latest bruise to the star's ego. Henderson places a month-long moratorium on talking to the media, a ban he refuses to break even on a snowy afternoon when he has a minor car accident while driving to Shea. "Y'all went to school," Henderson reports to the reporters. "You know what a month is."

Many a general manager has been willing to exchange the occasional public spectacle of Rickey Being Rickey for the numbers produced by baseball's greatest leadoff hitter. Steve Phillips held his tongue about his complaints in 1999 when Henderson was a surprising sparkplug for the Mets' lineup, but whatever fountain of youth he drank from last season has run dry in 2000. In Henderson's first thirty games, he bats .220 with one extra base hit and two RBIs, while swiping only five bags. He also insists on sounding alarm bells about a lack of team unity that none of his compatriots have expressed. In sharp contrast to 1999, so far this season no Met is making noise about clubhouse turmoil, on or off the record—except for Henderson. "If it ain't family, it's hard to win," Henderson says after the Mets drop two of three in Miami and blames the team's mediocre play thus far to "a lot of I-don't-knows, a lot of switching, a lot of everything." Translation: *Rickey needs to play more.* When Henderson makes his demand for more playing time, he has appeared in all but seven of the Mets' games.

By early May, signs begin to emerge that the Mets have reached the end of their rope. Some are subtle, such as Henderson being the only unused position player during a rough extra-inning loss in San Francisco. Some are quite obvious, as when the club places him on outright waivers. Any team willing to pay Henderson's remaining salary for 2000 could walk away with a future Hall of Famer, but no one takes the bait, due to a combination of Henderson's hefty paycheck, his recent poor behavior, and the widespread belief that the Mets will release him. Steve Phillips proclaims this last option is not an option at all. "If we wanted to release Rickey, we would release Rickey, or any other player," Phillips insists.

The general manager reverses course in a hurry after the Mets' first game back at Shea against the Marlins on May 12. Henderson leads off the bottom of the first by clubbing a long fly ball to left field. He's so sure he's connected for a longball that he puts his head down and breaks into a slow home run trot. By the time he looks up, the ball has bounced off the outfield wall, and his lack of hustle holds him to a single. Henderson endures angry boos from the crowd for the rest of the night. When a furious Bobby Valentine chastises him in front of the press corps ("Hit it four hundred feet before you do that"), Henderson responds with defiance. "I'm going to do it again if I hit one like that," he insists. "I've been doing it all my life. Ain't nothing going to change about it." When questioned about his play the following day, Henderson curses at a reporter and launches into a rant about a story in the paper he feels misrepresented him.

On May 13, the team gives Henderson his unconditional release. "We were at the point where we were having to compromise our ideals too many times," Steve Phillips says and calls the move "addition by subtraction." Though no player has anything bad to say about Henderson on the record, Valentine indicates players had come to him in private to voice concerns about his incessant complaints and shoddy play.

Henderson has few parting words for the media. "I didn't cause them to lose," he insists. "You better look someplace else. I've got to boogie." When he makes a surprise return to the Mets' clubhouse three days later to pick up a few pieces of equipment, a cynical Bobby Valentine guesses that Henderson came back to pick up his final paycheck. A few days later, Henderson joins John Olerud as he signs a contract with the Seattle Mariners, a team in desperate need of a leadoff hitter.

His Mets career began as a charming comeback story, the crafty veteran still able to ignite a rally at the age of forty while mentoring young speedster Roger Cedeño. It ends with him looking very much his age in play and temperament. Rickey Henderson was a major player in the amazing Mets' story of 1999. Unfortunately, his bitter final act leaves behind a deeper impression than all that preceded it.

* * *

Rickey Henderson had not been much of a leadoff hitter during his brief time with the Mets in 2000, but his departure opens the uncomfortable question of who will bat first in his place. Initially, the answer is leadoff by committee, as Bobby Valentine gives the slot to rookie outfielder Jay Payton, Melvin Mora, Joe McEwing (a recent recall from triple-A), and even Derek Bell, who has leadoff experience from earlier in his career. In the coming weeks, Mets lineups appear to be assembled by grabbing names from a hat, with concomitant results. Though they salvage the finale of the Marlins series that was Henderson's last hurrah, they split a rain-shortened two-game set with the Colorado Rockies on May 16-17. Forty-one games into the season, the Mets' record stands at one game over .500.

The Mets follow these disappointing results by sweeping three games from the Arizona Diamondbacks, edging them out by one run in each contest, giving hope that their ship is finally headed in the right direction. The most satisfying of these wins by far is the Sunday matinee on May 21, when the home team hangs a crooked number on Randy Johnson, who entered the game with a miniscule ERA of 0.97. What makes this result even more remarkable is the fact that much of the damage is done by Joe McEwing. The scrappy utility man, who stands a full foot shorter than Johnson, belts a home run and two doubles off The Big Unit, his second two-base knock coming at the tail end of an epic twelve-pitch at bat. With the score tied at six in the bottom of the ninth, McEwing works a walk, steals second, and comes around to score on a Derek Bell single to complete a walk-off win and cap a fairytale day. "When you see Johnson at a baseball game, you figure he is a powerful athlete," marvels the *Times*. "When you see McEwing, you feel like asking for two with mustard. McEwing would probably fetch the hot dogs, too."

Then the Mets set off on another one of their circuitous road trips, a nine-game sojourn that begins on May 22 in San Diego, heads halfway home to St. Louis, and then U-turns back to Los Angeles. Joe McEwing's mojo misses most of these flights. The Mets drop two of three in San Diego to the middling Padres, an extra-inning win sandwiched by a tough-luck 1–0 loss, and another ghastly performance by Bobby Jones in a spring full of them.

The poor showing in San Diego against a rebuilding team portends doom for the Mets' next stop in St. Louis, as the Cardinals are a far improved team in 2000. With the addition of Jim Edmonds providing protection for Mark McGwire, Big Mac comes into this series belting long balls at the rate of every 5.5 at bats. The pitching staff has been helped by the acquisition of Darryl Kile from the Rockies and veteran hurlers Andy Benes and Pat Hentgen. The Cardinals appear to be a lock to return to October, given their upgrades and weak divisional competition.

And yet, the Mets sweep the three-game set from the Cardinals that begins on May 26, stifling McGwire at every turn and even winning the series finale against Kile, who has worked like kryptonite on New York bats his entire career. But whatever good feeling might be gleaned from the sweep in St. Louis is soon wiped away by the series in Los Angeles. The Mets drop two of three to a low-octane Dodgers team, and even these defeats are not as disconcerting as the other losses they suffer at Chavez Ravine.

It has been a year to forget thus far for Rey Ordóñez. The anxiety that plagued him on and off the field in 1999 should have been assuaged by a four-year contract extension, and yet, if anything, the shortstop is more nervous than ever. When the Mets arrive in Los Angeles, Ordóñez is batting .188, unacceptable even for him. In the season's opening weeks, Bobby Valentine described himself as disappointed in the shortstop's lack of production and plate discipline. The shortstop responded, "So am I." Once again, he entertains the conspiracy theory that Valentine singles him out for ridicule. "Nobody is hitting good right now," Ordóñez pouted after the manager called him out in public. "Why do you always look at me?"

Ordóñez compounds matters by taking his problems out with him onto the field. In 1999, he pulled together a streak of over one hundred games without booting a single ball. In 2000, he commits three errors within a week of returning from Japan. By the end of April, he adds three more. Injury may be to blame, as Ordóñez spends some time on the shelf in May with shoulder inflammation. He confesses he took the field in Pittsburgh with his arm aflame, praying to the baseball gods, *Please, no ground balls hit to me.*

The team is so desperate for Ordóñez to improve his offense that any production is hailed as the precursor to a renaissance. A 2-for-4 night at the plate on May 18 against the Rockies prompts Steve Phillips to insist, "Rey should be able to hit, *will* hit." The general manager's proclamation proves more pipe dream than prophecy. Less than a week later, with the Mets in St. Louis, Bobby Valentine pinch-hits for Ordóñez in the sixth inning, a point so early in the game it seems calculated more to embarrass the shortstop than improve his team's chances. Back in 1999, when Valentine chastised him, Ordóñez could point to his fielding and a respectable batting average as counterargument against any attempt to bench him. This season, he hasn't either leg to stand on. "I want to hit, but I can't," he sighs after being pinch-hit for in St. Louis. He prescribes himself more hard work as the solution.

The elbow-grease cure is given no time to take after the series opener in Los Angeles on May 29. In the bottom of the first, as a Dodger sprints to avoid a pick-off throw, first baseman Todd Zeile whips an off-target throw toward the second base bag. In a move more ballet than baseball, Ordóñez leaps to keep the ball from sailing into the outfield, executes a flawless 180, and slaps the runner with the back of his glove before he reaches the bag. Only Rey Ordóñez could make that kind of play, Edgardo Alfonzo marvels later. However, while crafting this artwork, Ordóñez slams his arm into the runner's batting helmet and falls to the ground in a heap. The resort is a broken ulna, an injury with a recovery time of at least six weeks.

Flash forward to June, when a medical exam dashes hopes for a speedy recovery, as it reveals discomfort Ordóñez had been feeling in his elbow was caused by the broken bone setting on an odd angle. To correct this, plates and screws will be required, a procedure that will remove him from action for the rest of the season.

When Ordóñez's absence is still assumed to be temporary, the Mets believe they can make do at shortstop with a platoon of Melvin Mora and veteran utility man Kurt Abbott, signed as bench fodder during the off-season. Once Ordóñez is lost for the season, however, these are no longer judged viable solutions. Abbott is a light-hitting journeyman without the glove to compensate, and the Mets as yet consider Melvin Mora's viability as an everyday player an open question. Though Mora was the surprise star of the 1999 playoffs, and Bobby Valentine has always gone out of his way to praise him (as when he heaps plaudits on him for earning him a bases-loaded walk that starts a rally during the team's only win in Los Angeles), this love does not extend up the corporate ladder. Steve Phillips makes no bones about his fear of Mora as an everyday shortstop. Team brass is so unsure of what to make of Mora that they consider giving him a trial as a catcher while he spends time in Norfolk rehabbing an injury—a proposal Mora only learns of when reporters ask him about it upon his return.

As if the loss of Ordóñez wasn't enough, the Mets absorb another blow on May 31 when Mike Piazza suffers yet another catching-related injury, nailed in the head by a Gary Sheffield backswing. The shot opens a grisly gash on the catcher's head, blood gushing down his scalp as he receives on-field treatment before heading for the safety of the clubhouse. The sight of a gore-drenched Piazza is not half as scary as the postgame diagnosis that he has suffered yet another "mild concussion." Desperate to reassure panicked Mets fans, Steve Phillips plays doctor and therapist at once. "No one on the medical staff has given us any reason to be worried," he insists of the Piazza injury. For those who want to compare this injury to the terrifying blows he sustained during last year's playoffs, Phillips insists, "The thing he had last year was called a concussion and it really wasn't," though he offers no evidence of why the diagnosis has changed seven months after the fact. Strapping on their own pairs of rose-colored glasses, both Bobby Valentine and team PR flack Jay Horowitz insist Piazza could start the opener of the Mets' next homestand, an outlook that takes into account zero medical advice and also puts the pressure on the catcher to suit up or once again take on the "soft Californian" reputation he's worked so hard to shed.

* * *

Despite the coveting of shortstops and the fragile state of their catcher, the month of June begins with a pair of small moves that address neither issue. On June 2, Steve Phillips trades with the Diamondbacks for Lenny Harris, who impressed as a clutch pinch hitter for the team in 1998. Arizona receives Bill Pulsipher, made expendable by his ineffectiveness in spot starts and minor league assignments. "Billy had his struggles up here," Phillips shrugs. "He didn't put it together down there either." Because the Generation K debacle did not happen under his watch, Phillips has no ties of sentiment or responsibility to its victims. One day later, outfielder Jason Tyner, last year's first-round draft pick, is called up from the minors with an eye toward being the spark at the top of the lineup that's been missing since Rickey Henderson griped his way out of Gotham.

With this new personnel in place, the Mets take care of business against their opponents on the homestand that begins on June 2, winning two of three in an interleague matchup against the stingless Tampa Bay Devil Rays, then doing the same to the flailing Baltimore Orioles. Thus, the team builds up some much-needed momentum right before the Bronx leg of this year's Subway Series.

In 1999, complaints about the Yankees were more about process than performance, a feeling that the team had lost some ineffable something that had propelled them to greatness. That note is sounded again in 2000, and at the start of June, the reasons are as nebulous as they were a year ago. When the Yankees win eleven of their first fifteen games to start the regular season, they are faulted for *barely* winning these games. Joel Sherman of the *Post* notes that the Yanks scored only eight more runs than their opponents over that stretch, and that the big three in their starting rotation—Roger Clemens, Andy Pettitte, and David Cone—had earned one W between them. In Sherman's view, the Yankees were winning "in spite of themselves."

Some of the criticism is as unfair now as it was last season, but it is true enough that the Yankees have had their struggles. The starting rotation has sputtered. The lineup is prone to prolonged slumps and takes a huge step backward when Chuck Knoblauch begins to carry anxieties about his fielding yips into the batter's box. Starving for runs, the Yankees attempt to add speed to their repertoire, swiping an astonishing (for them) twenty-four bases over a twenty-one-game stretch to close out May and begin June. Such moves smack of desperation, but desperation may be called for when the Yankees begin the Subway Series standing a mere half game ahead of the Red Sox in the American League East standings, a stunning closeness compared to the team's recent division dominance.

As in 1999, Roger Clemens receives the lion's share of the blame for the deficiencies of 2000, his mediocre 4.16 ERA judged a dire sin by fans who expect elite performance. If Clemens had any illusions about where he stands in the hierarchy of New York sports heroes, they are shattered the day he and his teammates receive their 1999 World Series rings. The joy of the moment fades when he notices the number engraved on his ring's side: 33. Clemens's number is 22. Number 33 belonged to David Wells, the man he was traded for, the man to whom he is constantly compared, the man whose departure is still rued by many Yankees fans for who they lost and who they received in return.

Roger Clemens is still seen as a player ill-suited for New York, someone incapable of handling the big stage of the big city, and in this regard is often compared unfavorably to Mike Piazza. Both times Piazza faced Clemens in 1999, he knocked The Rocket off the mound with towering, game-changing homers. Clemens knows that when he takes the Yankee Stadium mound against the Mets on June 9, a strong outing would do wonders to change the way he is perceived. At the end of the day, all he does is reinforce the doubts of all those who fear he'll never earn his pinstripes.

In the top of the third, Jason Tyner initiates Clemens's demise when he bunts his way on base. The pitcher is unnerved by the speedy Tyner dancing off of first and walks Derek Bell, who came into this game in a dreadful slump. He then loses Edgardo Alfonzo to another walk, loading the bases with no outs. Up steps Mike Piazza, bringing alternating squeals of anticipation and groans of impending doom from the mixed crowd. Wary of throwing him a fastball, Clemens opts for a first-pitch slider, low in the zone. Piazza wheels on it and parks the ball over the 408-foot mark in dead center for a grand slam, adding a tidy bat flip for good measure. When Clemens stalks off the mound at inning's end, he is pummeled by boos from disgusted Yankee fans.

Clemens proceeds to allow single runs in the fourth and fifth before losing it altogether in the sixth. Tyner tortures him further by zipping a seeing-eye single past first base, then prompts the pitcher to bounce a pick-off throw into the stands beyond first base. Bell follows by belting a double that hugs the right-field line to drive in the rookie. Pitching coach Mel Stottlemyre emerges from the dugout to gauge his hurler's temperature. In the eyes of anyone watching the game, Clemens is pitching on fumes, but he lobbies for a chance to end the inning as a matter of pride. Stottlemyre surmises that Clemens has earned this right. The Rocket rewards his coach's faith by allowing a two-run bomb to Alfonzo that zips over the center-field fence in the blink of an eye. The ball has scarcely left the yard before Joe Torre bounds up the steps to remove his pitcher. As Clemens leaves the mound, the manager assures him, "We'll get this thing figured out." The unbroken chorus of boos accompanying his trudge back to the dugout indicates Torre is in the minority on this point. A disgusted George Steinbrenner leaves the stadium well before the final out, as do most Yankee fans, unwilling to witness the ugly conclusion of a 12–2 drubbing at the hands of the Mets.

After the game, Clemens's excuses are all over the map. He suspects he may have been tipping his pitches, and also fears the extra day of rest he received before this game made him too strong. Then he confesses to feeling tired, making it unclear if he felt too strong or not strong enough. He counters charges that he can't deal with the pressures of New York by saying he's more concerned about the pressures of living up to himself. One anonymous Yankees exec whispers the pitcher's issue is largely mental, the sign of an aging athlete who refuses to adjust because he can't accept he is not the same pitcher he once was. "He has to accept winning without dominating," says the nameless suit. "He has to learn to handle being hit."

Cut to the visiting clubhouse, where a glowing Mike Piazza admits his success against Roger Clemens is as much a mystery to him as it is to Clemens himself, and he has zero interest in solving this puzzle. He proclaims how at home he feels in New York. "I love it here," he says. "I love nights like this." As if there were any doubt. Mike Lupica of the *Daily News* compares the slugger to The Rocket and declares, "Only one of them has been made bigger by the stage. The other has been made smaller by it, sometimes nearly invisible."

Many accounts of the Subway Series opener describe the Yankees as *dead*. As game two unfolds on a sweltering afternoon, no Lazarus act is apparent in the early going, with Andy Pettitte coughing up two leads and the fielders behind him making awful errors. The Yankees finally break through with a vicious crooked number in the bottom of the fifth, then sail on to a 15–5 beatdown. (The bludgeoning is so bad that Mets starter Bobby Jones is all but forced to accept a humbling trip to the minors to work on his mechanics, out of New York's glaring spotlight.) But the decisive Yankee victory does nothing to erase the memory of Clemens's putrid outing, or the ugliness of the first four innings of this game. It feels less like the Yankees exacted revenge than they held serve, especially when their players admit to nervousness over the prospect of being swept by the Mets. Joe Torre confesses he and his team looked at game two as a must-win. Andy Pettitte shudders at the idea that a loss could have put the Yankees in a position to be swept by the Mets at the House That Ruth Built. When Jorge Posada hits a game-changing upper-deck shot, he punctuates it with a Piazza-esque bat flip and a high five so hard it almost takes his first base coach's hand off.

This sets up a Sunday night rubber match between Mike Hampton and David Cone, but the fates intervene by sending a torrential downpour upon the Bronx. While the teams wait out the rain hoping to play, Robin Ventura splashes onto the field to entertain the soaked crowd. A fake Fu Manchu applied with eye black and his body rattling around in a spare Piazza jersey, Ventura stands at the plate and imitates his slugging teammate's batting rituals: the bat waggle, the casual flick of the wrist used to call for time, the contemptuous scowl toward the pitcher. Ventura has Piazza nailed, from his violently kinetic swing to his wild arm-pumping while baserunning, his legs charging up and down like a child pedaling a Big Wheel with worn plastic tread. Ventura legs out an imaginary trip around the bases, sliding across the tarp into each bag in succession, a Shamu-sized wake trailing him.

The rainout will force a doubleheader later this summer. That day will prove fateful for Clemens, Piazza, and both teams. For the moment, though, they can all laugh through the raindrops.

* * *

Back in April, Mayor Giuliani attended the Mets' home opener at Shea. When featured on Diamond Vision, his image was booed by the sellout crowd. In years past, this response was little more than a knee-jerk reaction to the mayor's renowned Yankee fandom and offset with a healthy number of bipartisan cheers. In April 2000, the boos at Shea have an edge to them, for Giuliani's popularity is at its lowest ebb.

The year begins with the verdict in the Amadou Diallo shooting trial. Diallo, a Guinean immigrant living in the Bronx, was shot forty-one times in February of 1999 by four plainclothes NYPD officers who mistook him for a rape suspect and further mistook his wallet for a gun. The shooting set off citywide protests that were exacerbated by the mayor's unquestioning defense of his police department. All four officers are acquitted, creating a tense atmosphere in the city that is still present in March when another unarmed black immigrant, Patrick Dorismond, late of Haiti, is killed by undercover cops. Officers saw the man outside an Eighth Avenue bar, took him for an easy drug bust, and shot him when he responded with anger. The police once again claimed to see a gun where there was none.

As the shooting sparked protests around the city, the mayor ordered the release of Dorismond's arrest records, including sealed juvenile records, to combat what he saw as the media's agenda to paint the victim as "an altar boy." When advisers and political allies urged Giuliani to click his rhetoric down a notch, he released even more records. Protests during the victim's funeral in Brooklyn saw mourners clash with police officers, the scene degenerating into a full-scale riot. Now that both he and Hillary Clinton had officially declared their candidacies for the Senate, polls showed the mayor trailing the First Lady by double digits.

By all rights, Giuliani should easily beat Clinton, whose early campaigning combined carpetbagging cluelessness with head-scratching gaffes such as referring to the Diallo shooting as a "murder," a categorization that rankled the NYPD and, in the eyes of the police, tainted the jury pool for the officers' impending trial. There were smaller oversights too, like the time she stiffed an upstate waitress on a breakfast tip, then returned to apologize but failed to leave a gratuity for a second time. Clinton is campaigning in earnest, however, making good on a promise to visit every county in the state. That is much more than can be said for her opponent, who believes he can capture the Senate seat from the bully pulpit of city hall, seemingly unaware that upstate voters, always wary of New York City politicians, see him as no less an outsider than Clinton. When Giuliani shows little interest in setting foot north of the Bronx, it leaves a wide-open space through which Clinton can charge. While she hits the road in a conversion van, Giuliani no-shows a pricey upstate fundraiser in his honor because it conflicts with the Yankees' home opener.

The mayor's lethargy baffles and infuriates his GOP supporters until April 26, when he calls a press conference to announce he'd been diagnosed with prostate cancer and would suspend his senate campaign (such as it was) while he mulled over treatment options. The immediate response in the press was sympathetic, remarkable given how little sympathy the media had shown him in recent years.

Whatever advantage the mayor gathered from his cancer diagnosis evaporates a week later, as the *Daily News* reports that the mayor has had a woman named Judith Nathan on his arm at official functions for months, and has done little to combat the impression that the two were an item, which they were. It's an open secret that Giuliani has been estranged from his wife, Donna Hanover, but the media had to this point refrained from asking awkward questions about the status of the mayor's marriage and were willing to adopt a nigh-Gallic attitude toward his personal life as long as he was discrete about things. The public revelation that Giuliani was shamelessly attending official events with a mistress was a bridge too far for Hanover, however, and she emerges from public exile to inform the press that she will seek a legal separation.

Following these revelations, state Republican leaders assume Giuliani will attempt to patch things up with his wife or at least demonstrate a modicum of discretion. They also beg him to make a more definitive announcement about the status of his campaign. Giuliani reacts with his usual defiance by both continuing to arrive at social functions with Nathan on his arm and refusing to say whether he is in or out of the senate race for several excruciating weeks. The *Post*, normally a bastion of pro-Giuliani sentiment, labels him "a slow-motion Hamlet."

Finally, on May 19, Giuliani abruptly calls a news conference, at which he announces his decision to drop out of the running for senate. He appears far more humbled and contrite—and far grayer and older—than he ever has before, his speech sounding the notes of a man set to leave public life. One observer compares it to Lou Gehrig's farewell speech.

Faced with a thin pool of alternatives, state Republicans turn to Rick Lazio, a little-known congressman from Long Island. Lazio's official announcement of his entry into the race plays up his local-boy-made-good bona fides by harping on his orange-and-blue fandom. "I put on my Mets hat when I was six years old," he says, drawing a clear contrast with his "lifelong Yankees fan" opponent and perhaps distancing himself from the man whose place he has taken. In his official campaign announcement, Lazio opens by offering best wishes to "the other Republican" who had run for the Senate. Giuliani's name is mentioned once, quickly, so that Lazio can move on.

* * *

By the time Robin Ventura does his Piazza slip-and-slide routine, more than a third of the 2000 baseball season is in the rear view. The Giants and the Tigers have christened new stadiums. Ken Griffey Jr. belts his four hundredth homer, as does Fred McGriff. Mark McGwire breezes past Mickey Mantle on the all-time home run list. Cal Ripken collects his three thousandth hit. Relocated to Seattle, Rickey Henderson logs his ten thousandth at bat and, less than two weeks later, his two thousandth walk.

Even compared to the power surges of recent years, the rate at which balls are leaving the yard is breathtaking, adding fuel to the conspiracy theory that the ball has been juiced. Playing detective, Turk Wendell subjects baseballs from both seasons to X-rays and declares the 2000 specimens are more dense, and hence able to travel faster and farther than they did in 1999. Wendell has also dissected a few baseballs and compares the cork center used now to a superball. He has not offered his findings to the league because he doesn't expect them to cop to any wrongdoing, no matter how definitive the evidence.

In May, the league's vice president of baseball operations, Sandy Alderson, conducts a public tour of the Rawlings factory in Costa Rica where baseballs are assembled by hand and publicly declares there's nothing to see here, folks. Not willing to take his word for it, the *Sporting News* sends a reporter to the same factory, who concludes that if any shenanigans are going on, they're not going on at Rawlings. The factory's top stitcher swears on the record that there is no difference in the way baseballs are assembled between this year and the last. For the record, he also declares his allegiance as a Mets fan.

As for the Mets themselves, emboldened by a Subway Series split and the belief that 1999 inured them to all manner of pain, they dare imagine what it might be like to face the Yankees again in October. "If we had to write a perfect season," Bobby Valentine declares, "I think everyone in the organization would have the opponent be from the Bronx."

The Yankees feel something very different. The word Joe Torre uses to describe such a World Series matchup is "torture." Given no slack by the press, they are surrounded by the desperate, toxic "DO SOMETHING!" atmosphere that goaded their owner into so many disastrous trades in the 1980s. All year, Sammy Sosa has been feuding with his manager in Chicago and made no secret of wanting to play in New York, the reception he received at Shea Stadium last year still ringing in his ears. For a few fitful weeks, the stars appear to be aligning for George Steinbrenner to pull off a blockbuster trade for the slugger. In the end, however, The Boss develops a rare case of cold feet. The chatter about the Yankees trading for Sosa, or someone in his class, fades out not long after the conclusion of the Subway Series.

The Yankees do, however, swipe a middle infielder from under the noses of their crosstown rivals, a career backup who toiled for the mediocre Mets squads of the mid-1990s, and who Steve Phillips had eyed as an insurance policy for his unsure shortstop situation before the Yankees beat him to the punch. The veteran benchwarmer could not be happier, as he's been pining to play a game at Yankee Stadium just once before he retired. As a thirty-two-year-old utility man, he knew his chances to do so were dwindling fast. Now he will get that opportunity. His name is José Vizcaíno.

CHAPTER 12

Inciting Incidents

THE DATE HAS long been circled on their calendar. Ever since the Mets lost the 1999 National League Championship Series in excruciating fashion, they've eyed their next confrontation with the Braves, and for the second season in a row they've had to wait until late June to face Atlanta for the first time. The contests that lie between their last game in the Bronx on June 10 and the first against the Braves matter only in the sense of what they portend for the rematch to come. After going 3–2 on their road trip to Chicago and Milwaukee, the Mets return to Queens for a thirteen-game homestand that commences on June 20 and will culminate in four games against Atlanta. The series begins poorly, as the Mets lose the first two games against Philadelphia, but they recover to take the final game against the Phillies and proceed to sweep the Pirates and Marlins in succession. It is the kind of hot streak a team wants to be on when its most hated rivals are about to roll into town. And it's not just the Mets who are anxious for this Braves series to start, but an entire nation, thanks to a certain mouthy reliever.

John Rocker grabbed headlines in 1999 by taking over Atlanta's closer role and driving both the Mets and their fans to distraction. He was a spectacle, and could be an entertaining one if you didn't have to face him. Such a personality demanded a *Sports Illustrated* profile, and writer Jeff Pearlman drew this plum assignment during the offseason. The reporter was treated to the harrowing experience of sitting in the passenger seat of Rocker's Chevy Tahoe as he sped through his native Georgia, cursed at other drivers, and unleashed a torrent of bile toward the Mets and the city they called home. Pearlman did his best to steer the conversation toward any other subject in the hopes that Rocker would reveal a softer side. Deaf to Pearlman's cues, Rocker crafted every response, no matter the question, into a reflection of his hatred of New York and every conceivable group that called it home.

Pearlman's profile was published in a year-end double issue of *Sports Illustrated* intending to celebrate the best athletes of the twentieth century. The magazine's ambitious (and somewhat unwieldy) attempt to produce articles about the greatest sports personalities from each state drew little notice as Rocker's comments sounded alarms in all fifty of them.

Asked how he would deal with being traded to a New York team, Rocker's response was *retirement*. "Imagine having to take the 7 train to the ballpark, looking like you're [riding through] Beirut next to some kid with purple hair next to some queer with AIDS right next to some dude who just got out of jail for the fourth time right next to some twenty-year-old mom with four kids." Asked to explain his burning antipathy for New York, Rocker's response was *foreigners*. "You can walk an entire block in Times Square and not hear anybody speaking English. Asians and Koreans and Vietnamese and Indians and Russians and Spanish people and everything up there. How the hell did they get in this country?" Rocker was not prejudiced, he insisted, it was simply that "certain people bother me." He then labeled a black teammate (unnamed by Pearlman) a "fat monkey."

Last season, Rocker goaded Mets fans into vulgar counterreactions that only bolstered his claims about how gross they were. The voicing of a racially charged anti-New York screed to a reporter was another calculated step in this program, a means to up his villain quotient a few ticks further. His fatal error was to expand his vitriol to New York in general.

In 2000, New York is hardly a post-racial paradise. The strife of ethnic riots in neighborhoods like Bensonhurst, Howard Beach, and Crown Heights during the pre-Giuliani years is recent enough for its scars to still be visible. The anger engendered by the Amadou Diallo and Patrick Dorismond shootings—and Mayor Giuliani's defiant reactions to that anger—showed how close to the surface those fissures remained. But there is also a collective New York of the mind, where every New Yorker believes in his or her own tolerance and the concept of hating *foreigners* is itself foreign. John Rocker assailed New York's idea of itself and did so in a deep Southern accent that made him sound like the porcine small-town sheriff in a civil rights drama. The loudmouth lefty could have screamed at Bobby Valentine and the Mets until he was blue in the face and half the city would have nodded in agreement with him. Instead, he went after the city itself. Now, everyone across the five boroughs—and many outside it—knows his name and wants his head.

Bud Selig hands the reliever a seventy-three-day suspension, an unprecedented punishment for off-the-field comments that is eventually bargained down to fourteen games. When Rocker checks in at spring training in Orlando, he is subjected to a closed-door "intervention" by his fellow Braves, during which he must give an accounting of his "true" feelings about minorities. Pitcher Tom Glavine swears Rocker displays humility during this confrontation, but catcher Eddie Pérez tells the press, "The only thing I know is he wanted to have that meeting done as quick as possible." Rocker doesn't improve his standing in the clubhouse by refusing all media requests during Grapefruit League action, forcing teammates to answer constant questions about his effect on Atlanta's morale.

At Turner Field for opening day, Rocker receives a hearty ovation when accepting his National League Championship ring. The first time he jogs out of the Atlanta bullpen after serving his suspension, the roars from the Atlanta stands are even louder than last year's. Then he starts to pitch, whereupon the cheers lose volume in a hurry. In his first twenty-one appearances of the 2000 season, Rocker walks an astonishing twenty-five batters and allows almost three baserunners per inning. When Atlanta hits the road, the angry boos greeting his appearances are deafening. Despite his tough talk, the laser-focused hatred of every opposing crowd wears on him. It wears on his teammates too, who must fear for their own safety if they dare stand too close to him. After Kevin Millwood is pelted by an angry fan while sitting in the visiting bullpen at Dodger Stadium, he refuses to be anywhere near Rocker for the rest of the season. In Montréal, the Braves arrive at Olympic Stadium's visiting clubhouse to find several letters missing from their lockers and rearranged above Rocker's locker to spell out a homophobic slur.

No tears would be shed in the Braves' clubhouse if Rocker were cast aside. He gift wraps the team a handy excuse to do just that on June 4, when he confronts Jeff Pearlman before a game against the Yankees at Turner Field. In their first meeting since the incendiary profile was published, the closer verbally harasses the reporter and launches vague threats—"This isn't over between us"—before commanding security guards to keep him out of Atlanta's clubhouse, unaware that players don't have the king-like power to expel credentialed press from the premises.

The following day, with a mixture of embarrassment and relief, general manager John Schuerholz fines Rocker and demotes him to the team's triple-A squad in Richmond, Virginia, to work on his pitching mechanics. It is assumed the lefty will either be traded or kept down on the farm until after the Braves complete their first trip to Shea Stadium, but the Braves' respite from strife is short lived. Rocker has only spent a week at Richmond and made a mere three appearances when an injury to the team's relief corps forces his recall. Schuerholz insists he sent Rocker to triple-A as a means to regain his form, not as a punishment for his reckless speech, but the miniscule amount of time Rocker spends in Richmond proves too brief to serve as either rehab or punishment.

The Mets have been preparing for Rocker's return to Queens for months. After conferring with Major League Baseball on the issue as early as March, the team constructed a special "Rocker Roof" on top of the visiting bullpen to shield Braves relievers from hurled projectiles. To cut down on the influence of Dutch courage, beer sales will be cut off during the sixth inning of the Atlanta series instead of the seventh. The Mets must begin their preparations early because fans have been prepping for even longer. Leaflets handed out near Shea before a Mets-Dodgers game on April 8 encourage fans to celebrate "John Rocker Battery Day" when the Braves come to town, with instructions on where D-cells could be purchased. (The Mets are forced to disavow any connection with this "event.")

Rocker himself complicates matters by proclaiming he will travel to Shea via the 7 train, the mode of transportation he disparaged in his infamous profile. The NYPD swears it can handle whatever John Rocker can throw their way, but with the mayor having already dedicated seven hundred NYPD officers to the job of keeping peace at Shea Stadium, Rocker's hotel, and all approaches between them Rudy Giuliani would rather not call on even more policemen to patrol the 7 train. The peacekeeping force at Shea will include rooftop sharpshooters and horseback patrols in the parking lot, a level of protection normally reserved for visiting heads of state, and omnipresent law enforcement will grant the entire series an unsettling vibe that Bobby Valentine compares to a police state. The same mayor who refused to make any public concessions to terrorist threats at millennial New Year celebrations all but begs the reliever to not use mass transit. In a rare moment of restraint, Rocker backs out of his threat.

On the afternoon of June 29, with his plans to take the 7 train dashed, John Rocker leaves the Braves' Manhattan hotel by a side entrance and is transported to Shea Stadium via unmarked police van for the first game at Shea. A small protest gathers outside the stadium to denounce him, but it escapes his notice and the notice of most fans arriving for the game. Before first pitch, Rocker delivers a short statement to the press that is filmed and later rerun on Diamond Vision for the benefit of fans. It's billed as an apology, yet offers few pleas for forgiveness, and is suffused with heavy doses of self-pity and desperate ploys to portray himself as the real victim. He begins by addressing his "presumed hatred for the people of New York," as if his words in *Sports Illustrated* left any room for ambiguity. When Rocker dares to utter the words "I apologize," it is for statements "many people perceived . . . to be malicious," pinning the blame not on what he may have said, but public interpretation thereof. He concludes his statement by insisting, "I am not the evil person that has been portrayed," underscoring that Rocker's goal is not to show remorse but to generate sympathy. The Shea crowd greets his words with boos and yawns.

In 1999, when injuries and struggles from the Braves' ace starters made Atlanta appear vulnerable, the Mets indulged fantasies that Atlanta could be caught. They were harshly disabused of this notion when the Braves took five of six games from them in late September, nearly crushing their playoff hopes altogether. As if the Mets hadn't learned any lesson from this at all, there is again talk in 2000 that the Braves are vulnerable. Under the strain of the unceasing questions about Rocker, the Braves play a lackluster 12–14 ahead of their first trip to New York and arrive at Shea with a mere two-game lead in the division. Before the games leading up to their arrival in Queens, the Braves sequester themselves in visiting clubhouses like informants hiding from the mafia, refusing all press queries. For a few blessed days, they betray nervousness about the New York series and their situation in general. When the Braves emerge from their cocoon to speak to the media, however, they do not sound panicked in the least. Chipper Jones, Tom Glavine, and Greg Maddux all concede their team has not played well lately but assign no blame to injuries or John Rocker, who none of them mention by name. Maddux professes to be excited to start at Shea, which might be the worst omen New York could hope to hear.

And so, for all the talk that the Braves are vulnerable, that Rocker's mouth has driven them to distraction, that, *No, really, this time we can take them*, the series opener fits into the same template as most Mets-Braves contests of the last three seasons. Atlanta plays flawlessly. New York plays anything but. Strange plays and bad luck abound, all of it conspiring against the Mets. A first-inning error by center fielder Jay Payton gives an RBI triple to Andrés Galarraga (back in action after missing an entire season to receive cancer treatment). Rick Reed's head is nearly taken off by a line drive he can't see due to a blindingly white advertisement behind home plate. The ball bounces off of his non-pitching hand, but when he attempts to work through the pain, Reed allows a three-run homer that all but puts the game out of reach. (A postgame exam of Reed's injured hand reveals a broken bone that will land him on the disabled list.) Mike Piazza suffers a strange brain cramp when he begins marching to the dugout after a strikeout that marks only the second out of the inning, which allows an Atlanta baserunner to swipe third and score on a single by the next batter. The Braves commit three errors and are forced to scratch Greg Maddux from his start due to an illness, but the Mets waste all of these opportunities.

When Bobby Cox turns to his bullpen, each pitching change prompts chants of "WE WANT ROCKER!" from the Shea crowd. Fans get their wish when Rocker sprints out from his sheltered bullpen in the eighth to face the heart of the Mets batting order. He proceeds to retire them in short order and retires to the visiting dugout, not with the fist pumps and crowd taunts of last year, but with subdued high fives for his teammates. The Mets go down in order in the ninth to cap a deflating 6–4 defeat.

For most of the following night, June 30, the Braves are in a prime position to crush the Mets' hopes yet again. Called on to deliver a counterpunch to the visitors, Mike Hampton looks like the pitcher who was utterly lost in April as he walks in a run in the top of the first inning, then loads the bases in the third and allows all three runners to score. An RBI groundout in the top of the seventh hangs a fifth run on Hampton's ledger, at which point his night's work is finished. The Mets get a run back in the bottom half, only to watch Brian Jordan belt a three-run homer in the top of the eighth to make the score 8–1 in favor of Atlanta. Grasping for a term to describe the Mets' feelings at this point in the game, Todd Zeile chooses "wafflestomped." The stands remain packed, however, for this is Fireworks Night, even if it is eerily similar thus far to the last Fireworks Night at Shea, when the Braves crushed the Mets 16–0, John Franco hurt his finger, and utility man Matt Franco did mop-up duty as a reliever.

With a seven-run lead to his credit, Atlanta manager Bobby Cox first turns to little-used reliever Don Wengert to pitch the bottom of the eighth, and Wengert performs adequately in mop-up duty at first. He allows a pair of singles and a Robin Ventura grounder that drives in a run, but this grounder also results in the second out of the inning. Then

Todd Zeile knocks in another run with a hit, and Jay Payton reaches safely after him.

His seven-run lead trimmed down to five, Bobby Cox decides to pull no punches and calls on Kerry Ligtenberg—who reclaimed the closer's role this season when John Rocker faltered—to douse this brush fire. Ligtenberg proceeds to walk three consecutive batters, forcing in two runs. Atlanta's lead, a towering seven at the start of the inning, is now a surmountable three.

Ligtenberg is yanked in favor of veteran Terry Mulholland, but he too loses the strike zone and walks Derek Bell to force in yet another run. That once mighty Atlanta lead is down to only two runs. With a packed house on hand, each pitch a Brave reliever throws out of the strike zone causes the crowd noise to tick a bit higher. By the time Bell walks, that noise is at jet engine levels. The game now has the feel of unstoppable momentum, the Mets a boulder cascading down a mountainside, the Braves an ant in its path.

Mulholland backs his next batter, Edgardo Alfonzo, into a two-strike count, but Fonzie fouls off a tough pitch before pulling another offering wide of a diving third baseman. Two runners dash home to tie the game. The Shea crowd erupts in earsplitting screams. It could not possibly get louder.

And yet, that crowd does get louder when Mike Piazza leaps on Mulholland's first pitch—a pitch in the running for the worst thrown in his long career, Mulholland concedes later—and sends a laser beam down the left-field line, banging the ball off the retired numbers above the left-field fence to give the Mets an 11–8 lead, their eventual improbable margin of victory. "There was no doubt it was going to stay fair," Todd Zeile remarks later. "It was just whether it was going to hit the wall or go through the wall." Piazza pumps his fist as he rounds the bases, his stride so long and charged his feet barely touch the ground.

If there is anything disappointing about witnessing such a violent outburst against the Mets' most bitter rivals—ten runs, a franchise record for one inning, all but one of them scored with two outs—it is that none of the damage is inflicted on John Rocker. Unbeknownst to them, Queens's Public Enemy Number One is unavailable after opening up a callous on his pitching hand. He calls his left hand "one open wound" and shakes his head while his teammates stumble around the clubhouse after the game, shell-shocked, mumbling words like "embarrassed" to describe their feelings when they can produce any words at all. Rocker had disappointed the team with his runaway mouth and his ineffectiveness.

Now when they actually needed him, Rocker was nowhere to be found. Though the Mets and their fans would have loved to see Rocker take damage along with the rest of Atlanta's bullpen, perhaps this is far better revenge, clobbering his fellow pitchers as he sits alone in the bullpen, feeling useless.

There is no need for John Rocker the following night, as the Mets execute another furious two-out rally that begins with a Benny Agbayani solo shot and ends with another exclamation point bomb from Mike Piazza—and all of this damage inflicted against Greg Maddux. Al Leiter fans twelve Atlanta batters as the Mets cruise to a 9–1 victory that brings them within a game of first place and leaves the Braves in utter shock. The word "embarrassed" is again invoked in the visiting clubhouse, this time by Maddux himself. Brian Jordan dares speculate that perhaps the momentum between the two teams has shifted. "The only thing I hate," Jordan rues, "is that we gave them life."

The natural order of the universe is restored when Atlanta takes the finale by the commanding score of 10–2, with the Mets again committing a number of costly errors. Nonetheless, the Braves series produces a palpable feeling that something has changed. Witness Tom Glavine's concession that a split of the four-game series is good for Atlanta from a psychological point of view, an admission that one cannot imagine being uttered by the quietly confident Braves teams of old.

As for John Rocker, he departs with no serious incidents committed against him or in his name. His well-being was purchased with hundreds of thousands of dollars in police overtime, which only ensures the same effort will be required when he next ventures north in September. Richard Hoffer of *Sports Illustrated* marvels at how the city of New York, which prides itself on its toughness and might, could possibly let "a hillbilly from Atlanta" bend its every citizen out of shape. Someone like Rocker might laugh at how New York's dedication to tolerance dictated it must spare no expense to ensure the safety of someone who hated tolerance. He might sneer that the need for such security measures showed that, when push came to shove, this bastion of liberalism was not liberal at all.

New York could do no more than what it expected of itself. Namely, to protect the detestable loudmouth as it would anyone else, and hope he spent his next trip to New York how he spent most of this one, riding the pine.

* * *

The rainout of the final Subway Series game at Yankee Stadium presented the Mets and Yankees with a logistical conundrum: When to make up one of the biggest games on the New York sports calendar, and how? The solution they devised was a two-stadium doubleheader, to take place on July 8, a day originally slated for a Subway Series tilt at Shea. The two teams would do battle in Queens in a 1:15 game, then decamp for a rematch in the Bronx beginning at 8:05. Such a stunt has not been attempted in almost a century, since the New York Giants and Brooklyn (then known as the Superbas) hosted one another for a two-borough doubleheader in 1903.

As the date nears, and the prospect of tons of fans of both teams riding the subway from Queens to the Bronx together looms, the newspapers downplay any chance of violence between the camps by publishing heartwarming profiles of fathers and sons with opposing loyalties. They share these alongside accounts such as that of one 7 train conductor who suspects that Mets fans will literally be set on fire by Yankees partisans once they head into enemy territory. A Yankee fan insists taking the train to the game would be a good way to catch a good fight or two.

Most of the Mets players profess they are looking forward to this unusual event. Meanwhile, the Yankees behave even more put out than they would for a "normal" Subway Series. For the first time in the brief history of interleague play, the Yankees will face the Mets at a time when their crosstown rivals have the better record, and from a position other than atop their division. (The surprising Toronto Blue Jays are currently in first place, albeit by the slim margin of half a game.)

The last time the two teams crossed paths, the Yankees' pitching situation was troubled. Now it is a disaster. David Cone, who started the rain-stopped game in the Bronx, has been removed from the starting rotation altogether. The offense has sputtered all season, with the latest and deepest slump being suffered by Tino Martinez, the veteran first baseman who has looked so lost at the plate in the past month that Joe Torre speaks openly of benching him, for his own good and the team's. Following their failure to trade for Sammy Sosa, the Yanks attempt to shore up their lineup with a deal for Juan González, the former Rangers slugger now with the Tigers, but Juan Gone rejects their offer, hoping for a big payday when he hits free agency after the season.

Since June 2, the Yankees have played two games under .500, their place near the top of their division maintained solely by the relative weakness of the competition. George Steinbrenner lunches with Joe Torre and general manager Brian Cashman after the Yankees drop some frustrating games to Cleveland in early July, a red flag if you know The Boss only calls working lunches for ultra-serious business. The owner later contends he has a good relationship with both men, and, "If you got questions about this or that, you've got to ask Torre or Cashman." New York media fluent in The Boss's idiom know that when Steinbrenner is not pleased with you, he addresses you by your last name. (If he only uses your title—*the manager*—start checking the want ads.)

A slim 2–1 Yankee win in the first game at Shea on July 7 is not enough to quell the critics. The Yankee offense is able to scratch out no more than a pair of runs against Al Leiter, and only then after the lefty melts down following a check swing call that doesn't go his way. Orlando Hernández pitches brilliantly, but he also gives up a good amount of hard-hit balls that find gloves. The consensus after the game: the Yankees *barely* won.

The two-stadium doubleheader begins with a homecoming for Dwight Gooden, who pitches at Shea Stadium for the first time since he left the Mets after the strike-abbreviated 1994 season. It was seen as a sign of pure desperation when the Yankees inked a minor league contract with Gooden, as he'd already been let go this season by the Astros and the Devil Rays, two teams desperate for pitching. Gooden earns the start against the Mets only because a doubleheader stretches the Yanks' pitching depth a bit too thin. "Can't be any worse than what's out there already," shrugs former teammate John Franco, echoing the thoughts of many a Yankee fan.

Gooden experiences flashbacks of his glory days as he warms up in the visiting bullpen and spies a packed ballpark buzzing with anticipation. It was a scene he'd taken in many times before, from the opposite end of the stadium. The Doc Gooden of 2000 can hardly be called even a shadow of Doc Gooden of 1985, his once-blazing fastball now averaging 86 mph. The pitching-poor Yankees will accept what he can give them, however, and what he can give them is an average-for-2000 performance: six hits and two runs in a tidy five innings of work. He exits the game to a polite ovation from all partisans: Mets fans still willing to cheer what was, Yankees fans appreciative of the stability that might be.

Thanks to a Tino Martinez home run in the top of the sixth, Gooden earns the win in the Yankees' eventual 4–2 victory, but the game unfolds tense and strange. Something odd is in the air, with Todd Zeile called twice for interference (first as a fielder, then on the basepaths) and Bobby Valentine ejected for arguing that the first interference call only came after Yankee first base coach Lee Mazzilli screamed at the nearest umpire, a recent minor league call-up, to make the call.

The tension and oddness carry over into the nightcap in the Bronx, where Roger Clemens draws the start. From pitch one, Clemens is pitching angrier than he has in months, years maybe. The Rocket has always relied on intimidation, throwing up and in to spook batters, but even by his own standards he looks to be out for blood on the night of July 8.

After Clemens fires his first pitch of the night, the umpires ask for the ball so it can be saved as a souvenir from the historic doubleheader. The umpires fail to make this request before the ball can be relayed back to Clemens, however, and this oversight irks the pitcher. His very next pitch misses Lenny Harris's head by centimeters. "A guy could lose his career," a spooked Harris muses later. Then he whizzes a purpose pitch near Derek Bell's head. And these are mere appetizers for Clemens's main course.

When Mike Piazza leads off the top of the second inning, the Mets catcher watches a fastball for strike one. Then he watches another fastball scream toward his head. Piazza does his best to duck, but there is only so much evasive action possible against a 92 mph fastball. It nails Piazza above his left eye. The sharp crack of ball connecting with his batting helmet resounds throughout the stadium. Piazza crumples in a heap and stares up into the stadium lights.

Trainers and coaches burst from the dugout to attend to the catcher and slowly help him to his feet. John Stearns—the Mets' cantankerous bench coach—screams at home plate umpire Doug Eddings from that same dugout and flashes two fingers repeatedly. Translation: *He nearly beaned two of our players and now look what happened.* Piazza walks off the field under his own power, his steps unsure and halting, before heading to a hospital to receive precautionary X-rays. Per his custom, after the game, Steve Phillips won't even rule out Piazza for the Subway Series finale the next day, and insists the ugly plunking isn't as serious as the concussion he suffered in Los Angeles—an injury Phillips had downplayed as being *barely* a concussion when it happened.

Meanwhile, Piazza's teammates are left to feel like losers on every conceivable front—losers of another game by the score of 4–2, losers of their best hitter for who knows how long, losers on the scales of baseball justice. Mets starter Glendon Rusch hits Tino Martinez to start the bottom of the second, prompting a warning to both benches from the umpiring crew, but when Clemens throws another inside pitch to Derek Bell, he does not earn an ejection, as an umpires' warning should demand. Bobby Valentine fumes after the game about how the Yankees got a three-for-one deal on brushback pitches and rolls his eyes when referring to Rusch's "retaliation"—a leisurely curveball that grazes the batter's posterior, hardly revenge at all.

To the Mets, it is clear that Clemens's beanball was no accident. The team is convinced Roger Clemens meant to hit Mike Piazza, and its members say so repeatedly. Piazza's backup, Todd Pratt, is virulent in his denunciations, calling the beanball one of the worst things he'd ever seen in baseball and proclaiming he's lost all respect he once had for Clemens. Bobby Valentine lays out his case against Clemens succinctly. "We've handed his lunch to him every time we've played him," Valentine grumbles, "so the first hitter he throws at his head, the third hitter he throws at his head, and . . . my player who had pretty good success against that pitcher got hit in the head." To him, Roger Clemens's actions leave little room for doubt. "You throw someone here when you're trying to brush them back," Valentine notes, drawing an imaginary line across his chest. "And you throw them here when you're trying to hit someone in the head," he says, pulling his hand up to his temple.

Exhibit B: Roger Clemens's seeming lack of remorse. After the beaning, Clemens paced around the infield while Piazza was attended to, making no effort to offer apologies or even inquire about his condition via an intermediary. Al Leiter recalls accidentally hitting Manny Ramírez in the head five years ago and apologizing even as Cleveland's slugger lay dazed on the ground. It would have been awkward for Clemens to do the same, he concedes, but it would have shown his purpose pitch was unintentional.

Prior to the final game of the series, Piazza adds fuel to the fire in remarks that he says will be his only comment on the matter. "I wish I could remember him as a great pitcher, a Cy Young Award winner," he says, "but I know I can't do that." Piazza could have accepted a brushback pitch or even a plunking in a less vital area, an effort to back him off the plate. What he can't accept is that Clemens's seeming intent was to injure him, if not end his career. "He's got no remorse," Piazza insists. "I'm kind of flattered, in a weird way, because he's trying to tell me the only way to get me out is to try to hurt me."

Mike Piazza and the Mets have the circumstantial evidence, but Roger Clemens insists the beanball was an accident, and it's impossible to prove the man is lying. This is the leg that Clemens and his team stand on when questioned by the press. Called on to defend his pitcher, Joe Torre insists no Yankee would intentionally hit a batter in the head.

("We don't do that.") But Torre also admits he'd gotten mad at Clemens for pitching up and in to Yankees when managing against him. He also recalls a spring training game in which an amped-up Clemens plunked Derek Jeter, and how enraged he was at the time. "I'd be mad too, if I were him." Torre says of Bobby Valentine, words that could be read as a tacit admission of Clemens's guilt, painting him as some rogue elephant that snapped its tether.

The New York baseball day of July 8 begins in Queens at 1:00 p.m. with a former Mets ace returning to Shea to stifle his old team. It ends in the Bronx after 10:00 p.m. with the game's best-hitting catcher nailed in the head by one of its hardest-throwing pitchers. Vic Ziegel of the *Daily News* compares this nine-hour span to the Woody Allen short story "Death Knocks," in which a man who must defeat the Grim Reaper in a game of pinochle to save his life asks if they can put money on each hand to make things interesting. "This isn't interesting enough for you?" Death responds.

The following day, the Yankees arrive at Shea Stadium for the series finale to find themselves banned from the weight room and indoor batting cage. Shea has a single weight room, one that is more or less an extension of the Mets' clubhouse but which is made available to visiting players. When Steve Phillips finds out some Yankees are using that weight room, he informs the team's strength and conditioning coach that maybe it's best if they skip the bench presses today.

It is a petty move and serves as woefully inadequate payback, as even Steve Phillips admits. ("It's a far cry from their pitcher throwing at our catcher's head.") It also transforms the Yankees' feelings about the incident. Following the doubleheader, not one Yankee player or coach had officially inquired about Piazza's condition, not even the pitcher who beaned him. Once the weight room ban is announced, however, they become quite concerned about how they're being treated. "I was disappointed that it happened . . . We like to conduct what we do with class," says Joe Torre, sounding a moment away from dropping his monocle in disgust.

Addressing the media via telephone, George Steinbrenner insists the only reason the Mets are making a big deal of the beaning is because they've lost four of five games to the Yankees so far. "They had to take the focus off the fact that they got their fannies handed to them this time . . . I'm not sure it wasn't a very wise public relations move for them to take the focus off the way they were beaten." After voicing some token concern for Piazza's health, Steinbrenner urges the Mets to deal with the blow and move on. "If they don't get over this," he says, "I feel sorry for them."

"That's a heck of a PR stunt," says Mike Piazza upon learning of George Steinbrenner's remarks. "Next time we're going to pull a stunt like that, I'll volunteer not to be the guinea pig." The Boss's words enrage Bobby Valentine even further, dredging up memories of a scary beaning he endured as a minor leaguer. "Unless you've been looking down at someone who's been hit in the head or looking up at people looking at you," the manager says, "you shouldn't have anything to say about that arena, because you don't know anything about that arena."

Thus, there is every reason to fear fireworks in the final game. Reporters ask various Yankees point-blank if they fear getting hit. Derek Jeter would have to be a prime candidate for retaliation, but when asked if the tit-for-tat ended after the final pitch of the doubleheader, the shortstop counters with lawyerly aplomb. "Why wouldn't it be over?" he queries. After all, he and his teammates believe Clemens's pitch was merely a fastball that got away. *The Mets don't see it that way*, reporters remind him, *and their manager* really *doesn't see it that way.*

"So what does that mean?" Jeter asks, prompting reporters to supply the answer he dares not say. *It means someone might get hit, and that someone might be you.*

"That would be stupid," Jeter says. Reporters press on: Couldn't Roger Clemens have defused the situation by showing some kind of contrition? "No," Jeter responds, "because you guys would have thought of a way to blow it up still." A short while later, Joe Torre accuses the media of "fanning the flames" of this controversy. To hear Torre and Jeter tell it, the press and the Mets receive equal amounts of blame for ramping up tensions before the final game, while Roger Clemens, the man who hit Mike Piazza in the head with a fastball, deserves no blame at all.

This is a bit much to many sportswriters, such as Mike Lupica of the *Daily News*. "A few years ago the Yankees acted as if Armando Benítez had robbed a church when he stuck a fastball in Tino Martinez's back," Lupica says, recalling the brawl at Yankee Stadium in 1998. He also recalls that "[w]hen Clemens was picking off Yankees in the old days, people like Derek Jeter screamed bloody murder." Jeter, he of the torturously noncommittal comments to the press, had no compunction saying Clemens "throws at everybody" when The Rocket plunked a teammate two years ago. "Now," Lupica notes of Jeter's change of heart, "he's just establishing himself on the inside of the plate."

To Lupica and most of the New York sports press, the Mets are well within their rights to hit Derek Jeter, Bernie Williams, or whoever else, in their estimation, would balance the scales of justice. But for all the chest pumping and finger pointing, the finale unfolds as a pitchers' duel that leaves no room for retaliatory chin music. The Mets capture a 2–0 win when Mike Hampton tosses seven shutout innings on short rest and Armando Benítez guts out a two-inning save. The tough talk of the previous twenty-four hours is shelved. "Unless Roger was back on the mound and held a bat in his hand," Todd Zeile insists, "I think that incident was behind us."

Zeile says this, so the papers print it, but few believe it. For the first time, the city's media allows that perhaps these teams, and their respective fans, do not like each other. Mark Kriegel of the *Daily News* writes of "actual animosity" between the Mets and Yankees with open-jawed shock, as if it had burst forward suddenly this weekend and had not been simmering for years.

For the most part, though, the papers speak of this beaning in the context of what sort of intrigue it would add to a "real" Subway Series in October. When queried, few players from either team rise to the bait, not even Mike Piazza. Asked what he might do if Roger Clemens tries to contact him, Piazza is as noncommittal as possible. "If I run into him down the line," he says, "we'll see what happens."

CHAPTER 13
Facilities

THE 1999 ALL-STAR Game is a hard act to follow. That edition of the midsummer classic was held at historic Fenway Park and boasted pregame ceremonies honoring baseball's All-Century Team. The 2000 All-Star Game unfolds in the sterile confines of Atlanta's cavernous Turner Field, est. 1996, with many of the starters unavailable due to injury. Mike Piazza is forced to sit out thanks to his Roger Clemens-induced concussion. Cal Ripken misses his first All-Star Game in seventeen years with a back injury.

On the American League side, the New York sports press is captivated by the uncomfortable sight of Joe Torre handing the ball to David Wells to start the game. The former Bronx Bomber earned this honor with a brilliant first half for the Blue Jays while the Yankees' starting rotation fell into tatters. A glowing pre-All-Star Game *Sports Illustrated* profile by Jeff Pearlman lists all of Wells's purported weaknesses (his fondness for fried foods and beer, mainly) to prove they matter not a whit, while Roger Clemens—as devoted to core conditioning as Wells is to Coors Light—is a shell of his former self. "The Rocket's air of invincibility is gone," concludes Pearlman, who wonders, as many fans have, if the devil-may-care Wells is what's missing from the "stoic, uninspired Yankees." "There isn't a Yankee fan who wouldn't send Roger Clemens back to Toronto for him tomorrow," insists Mike Lupica.

Prior to the game, Al Leiter is a dark-horse candidate to draw the National League start for his own excellent half-season, though NL manager Bobby Cox opts instead for Arizona's Randy Johnson. Leiter does make an appearance, though at game's end he may have wished he hadn't.

When he takes the mound in the top of the fourth, Leiter loads the bases, then allows a two-run single to Derek Jeter that proves the margin of error in the American League's 6–3 victory. Jeter, who reports the recent Subway Series prepped him to tackle Leiter, takes home MVP honors. The Met lefty takes home the L.

* * *

In the season's first month, jet lag from the trip to Japan was blamed for the Mets' lethargic performances. In the weeks following the All-Star break, the Mets are mired in a similar torpor, and this time the trauma of the last Subway Series is blamed for causing a hangover effect worse than that of an eighteen-hour flight.

The Mets feel they had not simply been defeated by the Yankees, but humiliated, while the player who bullied them thrives. Roger Clemens's July is easily his best in pinstripes so far, as he wins five games and pitches to an ERA under two. If his rep had suffered outside the clubhouse because of the Piazza beaning, within it his standing had never been higher. He praises his teammates, who have told him to continue to be aggressive as ever because they've got his back, no matter what (a retroactive endorsement of the beaning, it seems). Thus emboldened, the pitcher discusses the incident, expressing some regret over what happened but coming across as more disturbed about his depiction in the press. "Some guys that don't know me write about it," he sighs, "and portray you in the media as someone you're not."

This becomes the tack taken by all Yankees when forced to address the Piazza issue. Some of Joe Torre's initial comments about the beaning almost verged on an admission of guilt, but in the weeks following the Subway Series, he couldn't be more supportive of Clemens and even echoes his pitcher's criticism of the press. "I thought he was unjustly accused," Torre says, as if there were any doubt about who hit Piazza in the skull. "Everywhere you go, people were looking at him as if he was some kind of ogre."

Torre also lays out the Yankees' final word on the incident, and a perfect summation of Yankee philosophy at the dawn of the new millennium. "The bottom line, not to disrespect anybody," Torre boasts, "is the fact that he won." To Torre and the Yankees, victory justifies any means.

Clemens may be able to thrive on the adversity, but the Mets cannot, as they spend the first week after the All-Star break in the same type of malaise that marked their post-Tokyo April. The second half of their season begins with a lengthy eleven-game road trip, the first six of which are interleague matchups in Boston and Toronto. This gives Bobby Valentine ample opportunity to use Mike Piazza as his designated hitter, but Piazza insists on catching all nine innings of the first game, and three of the six games overall, seemingly to demonstrate that Roger Clemens has not broken him. The three homers he hits in the series in Boston beginning on July 13 speak volumes about his resilience, but the Mets lose two of three to the Red Sox regardless.

Then they slink north of the border on July 16 for three games against the Blue Jays, who are hanging tough in the American League East. Some of the Mets beat reporters, unfamiliar with Toronto's home ballpark, are preoccupied with the SkyDome's built-in hotel and the sights on display therein during games, such as several strippers advertising their wares, or the couple in one of the rooms who can be seen in flagrante delicto until they exercise discretion and pull the blinds. During the Toronto series opener, Al Leiter wonders if the home plate umpire is distracted by these exhibitions, because as far as he's concerned, the ump exhibits "the most inconsistent umpiring I've ever had in my twelve years in the big leagues." The strike zone doesn't seem to affect Toronto's pitcher, a young hurler named Roy Halladay, who comes into the game with an ERA of 11.68 but stifles New York nonetheless. The Mets had complained of spotty umpiring during the Subway Series, so Leiter's complaints come across as residual resentment from the beaning incident, if not conspiracy theorizing. Lenny Harris suspects his teammates are "getting used to losing," while Bobby Valentine cryptically says that his team has been obsessing on "a lot of thoughts that are not thoughts of reality." The manager calls a team meeting to clear the air and inject some life into his lethargic squad. This spurs the Mets to win the last two games in Toronto, but they can only manage a split of the two games that follow in Montréal against the lackluster Expos.

Even more disappointing than these results is the loss of half of their infield. Robin Ventura lands on the disabled list with shoulder pain that has plagued him all season, despite receiving off-season surgery to clean up the troublesome joint. Then Edgardo Alfonzo is felled by a sore hip flexor, exacerbated by five games on the unforgiving artificial surfaces found in Toronto and Montréal. Though he stays off the DL, a cortisone shot knocks Fonzie out of action for a few crucial games.

The final stop on the Mets' grueling post-break road trip is Turner Field, their first visit to Atlanta since Kenny Rogers's ball four handed the Braves a pennant. A few short weeks ago, the Mets split four games with the Braves at Shea, results that suggested the Mets might challenge the Braves for the division crown. The starting nine Valentine is forced to assemble for the first game in Atlanta on July 21 suggests something else entirely. Utility man Joe McEwing bats leadoff and plays second base. Lenny Harris, whose best position is pinch hitter, is installed at third. This move proves crucial in the series opener, when Harris fields a grounder and lobs a throw home to prevent a run from scoring but tosses it straight into the runner's path instead of the catcher's glove. The runner in question, Andruw Jones, barrels through Mike Piazza, giving him a slight case of whiplash—one that draws only glancing mentions in the papers, given the litany of injuries he's endured of late—while scoring the tying run. The Braves pull ahead on an RBI groundout shortly thereafter, then cruise to a 6–3 victory.

The second game at Turner Field is the obligatory tease giving the Mets a sliver of hope before crushing it in cruel fashion. Rick Reed—fresh off the disabled list from the broken wrist he suffered during his last outing against the Braves—pitches brilliantly and outduels Greg Maddux in a 4–0 blanking of Atlanta. Reed's fine performance is followed the next afternoon by an excellent one from Bobby Jones. Returned from a trip to the minors to work on his mechanics, Jones scatters seven hits, most of them harmless. Unfortunately, the one that isn't harmless is an RBI double from veteran Wally Joyner—boy-faced wunderkind for the Angels in the 1980s, now filling the Braves' Phenom In Winter role—that plates the only run Atlanta scores in this game, and the only run they will need.

There is, of course, one faint stab at overcoming this small deficit. In the ninth, Jay Payton reaches on a throwing error and advances to second to start the inning. With the Mets' big bats to follow, New York seems poised to tie the game, at least. Then Mike Piazza grounds out to third and Todd Zeile lines a ball straight into the shortstop's glove. The Mets' last hope, Benny Agbayani, misses a game-tying double by inches before grounding out to end the game. Atlanta wins 1–0. The team that looked like it could topple the Braves at the start of July is six games out of first place as the month concludes.

The final loss at Turner Field is indicative of the state of the Mets on all fronts. They are injured, they are frustrated, and they are not able to take advantage of their opportunities. The defeat stings even more for coming at the hands of Andy Ashby, late of the Phillies. A solid veteran pitcher with playoff experience, Ashby struggled in the first half of the season and was anxious to leave behind Philadelphia's tiny payroll, incessant losing, and constant boos. The Braves saw in Ashby a back-of-the-rotation innings eater who could compensate for the loss of John Smoltz (felled by Tommy John surgery), mediocre performances from veteran fifth starter Terry Mulholland, and a regression from last season's promise by youngster Kevin Millwood (ERA of five and climbing). So far, Ashby has been a godsend to Atlanta, which only serves to remind the Mets that they have not yet acquired any pitching help of their own for the playoff run.

As the trade deadline looms, Steve Phillips's every attempt to make a deal has blown up in his face like Wile E. Coyote beta-testing another Acme product. The most embarrassing misstep comes as the Mets are in Atlanta, when it's reported that the team has a deal in place to acquire longtime Red and perpetual All-Star Barry Larkin, who could fill both their shortstop and leadoff man holes, both still lingering after the respective losses of Rey Ordoóñez and Rickey Henderson. The hangup is Larkin himself, who has a no-trade clause and must consent before the pact can be consummated. On July 21, Cincinnati general manager Jim Bowden flies to Houston, where the Reds are playing at the moment, to inform Larkin of the deal in the hopes he will accept it. Larkin storms out of the meeting when Bowden refuses to tell him who Cincinnati would receive in exchange.

There are abundant reasons why Barry Larkin might want to leave Cincinnati. Ken Griffey Jr. struggled mightily in the season's initial weeks, and though he recovers his All-Star form by midseason, by that point the young team around him is in the midst of a collective slump, chafing under the stern yoke of manager Jack McKeon, and mired ten games out of first place. A hideous 1–11 skid to start June and a 2–4 record against St. Louis to end it all but concedes the National League Central division to the Cardinals. Even the resolutely upbeat Larkin calls this season "a very, very negative experience."

Despite all of this, Larkin is a native of Cincinnati who's played for the Reds his entire career and shows little enthusiasm for moving elsewhere. The Mets don't do themselves any favors by sounding lukewarm to the idea of giving Larkin an extension beyond this season, or by their apparent desire to pursue Alex Rodriguez in the upcoming off-season. Steve Phillips offers to fly to Cincinnati with a contingent of Mets and make an appeal to Larkin in person. Larkin's agent tells Phillips to save his frequent flier points.

That is the last Steve Phillips hears about his proposed trade until the announcement that Barry Larkin has signed a three-year contract extension with Cincinnati. Phillips might accept the news more graciously had the Reds informed him ahead of time, and he walks away from the experience feeling used. "I guess we helped Barry Larkin get a contract," the embittered GM grumbles. "I should call [his agent] back and see what kind of cut I get out of his fee."

Last season, Steve Phillips was able to add key pieces at the trading deadline at relatively little cost (the exception being Jason Isringhausen, who departed in the flop deal for Billy Taylor and has now emerged as a top closer for Oakland). In 2000, however, Phillips is the little engine that can't. When calling a press conference to update the press about the status of the Barry Larkin trade—a concession of defeat, really—one reporter asks Steve Phillips for his name, unaware of who he is. A stunned Phillips responds, "Babe Ruth." How soon they forget.

Smarting from the Larkin humiliation, Phillips makes some defiant noise about signing another starting pitcher. There is also talk of inserting pitching prospect Grant Roberts into the rotation, echoing what the team did with Octavio Dotel in 1999, but when Roberts receives a call up to start the first game of a rain-necessitated doubleheader on July 27, the nervous youngster allows seven runs in less than two innings to the Expos and is headed back to triple-A before the nightcap starts. As for other starter options, Bobby M. Jones (the lefty) pitches poorly in a handful of opportunities, is demoted to the bullpen, and earns a one-way ticket to Norfolk by calling Bobby Valentine "a joke."

By the time the Mets return to Queens for their first homestand of the second half on July 25, Phillips must explain why he failed to trade for yet another starter when Philadelphia's ace Curt Schilling is dealt to Arizona. At another dour Shea Stadium press conference, he reveals that the Mets' chances to land Schilling were never more than a "long shot"—true enough, but not what the press, or Mets fans, want to hear. He spends much of the press conference leaning against a wall, as if he doesn't have the strength to stand up, suggesting that if he isn't discouraged by the outcome of his trade deadline deals, he is surely exhausted from all the fruitless phone calls of the last week. To hear Phillips tell it, the Phillies were wary of trading with a team inside their division. A fair excuse, but one that didn't prevent the Braves, also in the National League East, from acquiring Andy Ashby. The back pages wonder how Steve Phillips couldn't have assembled anything better than the Arizona package, which the *Post* labels "a quartet of stiffs" (an unkind characterization, but not far from the truth). Phillips's reluctance to part with the jewels of his farm system comes under more fire when his rumored pursuit of Milwaukee's closer Bob Wickman, a possible insurance plan against a taxed relief corps, goes nowhere. "The perception being created is that the Mets weren't crafty or inventive enough to get the deal done," says one of the writers responsible for creating that perception.

Meanwhile, Phillips's counterpart in the Bronx has no trouble making lemonade from lemons. After multiple big deals fall apart for the Yankees, general manager Brian Cashman is still able to work a trade for David Justice, a veteran slugger made expendable by a disappointing year in Cleveland. Then Cashman shores up the Yanks' rotation with a deal for Cincinnati's Denny Neagle. If these moves are hardly blockbusters, they're still more than Steve Phillips has been able to accomplish.

Phillips finally makes some headway when he acquires Bubba Trammell and Rick White from the Tampa Bay Devil Rays on July 28. The former will dispense right-handed power off the bench, while the latter is a workhorse reliever. In exchange, the Mets part with Jason Tyner and Paul Wilson and, in one fell swoop, wave good-bye to both 1998's first-round draft pick and the last Generation K man standing in the Mets organization.

Still left open: the glaring shortstop question. After Rey Ordóñez was injured, Melvin Mora drew most starts at shortstop, but he has never looked comfortable at the position, and his fielding has devolved from adventure to nightmare. He misplays several balls during the otherwise promising series hosting the Braves in early July. A Fourth of July tilt in Miami goes to the Marlins after multiple Mora miscues. In the first game after the All-Star break at Fenway, Mora flubs a potential game-ending double play, opening a window for the Red Sox to manufacture a walk-off win. Giving Mora time off to clear his head might be called for, except that Kurt Abbott, one of the few qualified shortstops on the Mets bench, is on the disabled list with a bulging disk. Injuries to Robin Ventura and Edgardo Alfonzo force Bobby Valentine to cobble together a makeshift infield, and also ensure that a rattled Mora must play his way through the struggles. When he bungles another easy grounder during the series in Montréal in late July, Steve Phillips—who has never made a secret of his desire to replace Mora at shortstop with a veteran—pointedly mutters to the press, "He's played about how I expected he would."

Had Mora succeeded in his leadoff hitter auditions, the errors might be forgiven, but though he draws the bulk of the leadoff assignments from May 29 (the date of Ordóñez's injury) through the end of the series in Atlanta, Mora posts a subpar .310 on-base percentage and walks a mere eleven times while racking up thirty strikeouts. And even when

Mora does get on base, he tends to be reckless. See the finale of the Braves series at Shea on July 2, when he runs the Mets out of a potential rally by inexplicably attempting to go from first to third on a comebacker. "My job is to take the other team out of concentration," he says by way of explanation, even though he is the only person whose concentration appears to be broken.

When Mora first took over at shortstop, Bobby Valentine protected him with maternal fervor. The more he struggled, however, the more the manager's affections waned. He experiments with batting Lenny Harris first, essentially benches Mora once his infield begins to heal in the latter half of July, and acknowledges that asking Mora to tackle both shortstop and leadoff duties may have been asking too much. When the Mets make their bid for Barry Larkin, Valentine all but buys him a plane ticket to Queens. ("If he was our player, he'd be in uniform right now.") Some Mets pitchers share with Valentine (and the press, anonymously) their belief that Mora's confidence is shot. They say this not for Mora's sake, but their own. An unsure shortstop is not a shortstop that any pitcher wants playing behind him.

Bobby Valentine speaks to Mora privately as a combination pep talk/kick in the rear and tells him that there is no time for on-the-job training with the Mets. When Mora wonders aloud why the team was patient with Rey Ordóñez, Valentine reminds him that Ordóñez debuted in 1996, when the Mets had the luxury of low expectations. He counsels Mora that "our life in baseball is not always fair, and don't always expect it to be fair," a lesson Valentine knows as well as anyone, though he leaves the meeting feeling that the young man hasn't quite taken all of this to heart.

And so Steve Phillips has his manager's tacit blessing when, on the same day as the deal with Tampa Bay, he trades for shortstop Mike Bordick of the Orioles. A veteran of the Oakland A's glory days of the early 1990s, Bordick has put up some remarkable offensive numbers this season for an overpaid and underachieving Baltimore squad, clubbing sixteen long balls at the tender age of thirty-five. He has none of the eye-popping defense the Mets lost with Rey Ordóñez, and his graying temples make him more resemble a middle manager than a ballplayer, so the word Steve Phillips uses to describe what he brings to the Mets is "stability." This stability—plus impending free agency that will allow the Mets to pursue Alex Rodriguez next winter—makes him an ideal stopgap measure.

Baltimore isn't just giving away shortstops, however, and the man the Mets send down the turnpike is Melvin Mora. When announcing the deal, Phillips cruelly refers to Mora, who'd served as his starting shortstop for almost two months, as a "utility infielder."

When the Barry Larkin trade appeared imminent, Melvin Mora greeted the news with a degree of relief that this would move him out of the shortstop spotlight. "I'll play right, center, left, short, second, third," he declared. "I'll be there for them." Then the Bordick deal moves Melvin Mora out of town altogether, away from the only organization he has ever known, and the suddenness of it shakes him to the core. Reporters who seek Mora out for comments find him holding up a wall in the clubhouse, on the verge of tears. "I wasn't ready for this," he says, if the shell-shocked look on his face didn't say it already. "You play more and more and more, you're going to get better, better, better." Mora may still believe that. The Mets do not.

"Melvin did the best he could," Steve Phillips says, giving him a verbal pat on the head as he leaves. And that is that. Phillips and the Mets have moved on.

* * *

In his continuing hunt for reinforcements, Steve Phillips makes some noise about possible trades for sluggers like Milwaukee's Jeromy Burnitz, relievers like Tampa Bay's Roberto Hernández, and starters like San Diego's young star Matt Clement. The general manager spends so much time on the phone in the days leading up to the trade deadline that his voice goes hoarse, a condition exacerbated by the fact that Phillips must deliver separate daily briefs to Nelson Doubleday and Fred Wilpon. (Any deal must be approved by each co-owner, but neither man can stand to be in the same room with the other.) Lisa Olson of the *Daily News* expects Phillips soon will have glow-in-the-dark hair and a calloused index finger from prolonged cell phone use.

In the end, all the dual briefing and cell phone minutes go for naught. The trades with Tampa Bay and Baltimore are the extent of the Mets' deadline dealing. Some in the press praise Steve Phillips for the stability provided by the moves he's made, and for resisting the temptation to acquire rent-a-players, such as a trade for Cleveland's superstar Manny Ramírez, set to be a free agent at season's end, that would have decimated his farm system. Bill Madden declares Phillips "the executive of the trade deadline" for his judicious deals. Lisa Olson wonders if Phillips deserves a Nobel Prize for steering his team's ship through such choppy waters.

The praise for Phillips dissipates quickly once the Braves add B. J. Surhoff to their lineup. Late of the payroll-shedding Orioles, the slugging outfielder was for years a trade target of every team in search of a power bat. His geographic origins—born in the Bronx, raised in Rye, New York—made him a natural mark for both New York teams. (The Yankees were so anxious to acquire Surhoff they offered Tino Martinez in return, and for a time Martinez even spoke to the media of his time in New York in the past tense.) In the end, Surhoff heads to Atlanta, and once he does, the press that once praised Steve Phillips wonders why he opted for mere *stability* when the Braves went for the throat. "The Mets were second to the Braves last season," notes Mike Lupica, "and they were second to them in the National League Championship Series . . . They are second now . . . The team that needed help the least got as much as anybody." Asked if they can beat the Braves now that they've acquired reinforcements, the Mets put on a brave face and say of course they can, some louder and more forcefully than others. "Healthy, yes," says Mike Piazza, adding a qualifier that applies as much to him as it does to the team as a whole. John Franco does not equivocate. "Fuck 'em," he says to a clubhouse watching news reports of Atlanta's latest trade, "we'll beat 'em with Surhoff."

The Mets do receive reinforcements of a kind as their collective health slowly improves. Robin Ventura comes off the disabled list. Edgardo Alfonzo's hip heals well enough for him to return to everyday action. Darryl Hamilton, who'd missed most of the season with a foot injury, is available off the bench once again. Thus reinvigorated, the Mets finish July strong and tear through August of 2000 in a manner that plays out as a carbon copy of August of 1999, their most dominant month of the season.

It begins when the team returns to Shea on July 25, at home for the first time since the final game of the Subway Series, and appears to be overjoyed to be back in Queens when they sweep three games from both the Expos and the red-hot Cardinals. Mike Bordick arrives on July 29, is welcomed into the fold with a helpful name tag from Robin Ventura ("Hi, my name is Mike, but you can call me Bordy"), and belts a home run on the first pitch he sees as a Met. In the same game, Rick White contributes a scoreless eighth inning and earns the W in the Mets' come-from-behind victory. The following afternoon, Bubba Trammell mimics Bordick by clubbing a three-run shot in his first Mets at bat to help complete a sweep of the Cardinals. Bobby Jones helps even more by going the distance in the finale, bringing his ERA in the starts since his minor league demotion down to a shade over three.

The homestand ends with a satisfying series against the Reds. After being spurned by both Barry Larkin and Ken Griffey Jr., neither the Mets nor their fans are in much of a charitable mood toward Cincinnati. (Steve Phillips jokes that the visitors "won't be using our weight room.") With bitter boos ringing out each time Larkin strides to the plate, the Mets exact the best kind of revenge by winning two of three. The victories come on stellar performances from Mike Hampton and Al Leiter and cap a triumphant 8–1 homestand. And they're only getting started.

* * *

This torrid stretch in Queens is followed by a seven-game road trip beginning on August 4 in Phoenix against the scuffling Diamondbacks. Despite the addition of Curt Schilling, Arizona has lost its grip on a division lead and are now the Mets' primary competition for the wild card spot. The Mets make a statement by taking two of three in the desert and roughing up Randy Johnson for the second time this season, with pint-sized Joe McEwing again one of the key contributors in the Mets' victory over The Big Unit.

The trip concludes with four games at Houston's brand-new downtown ballpark, Enron Field, the contrived quirks of which—artificial incline in center field dubbed Tal's Hill, claustrophobically close Crawford Boxes in left field—are labeled "zany" by one charitable beat writer. The injury-wracked Astros put up little resistance as the Mets take three of the games in Texas, though Derek Bell feels stung by the torrent of boos that greet his every at bat. *Fuck 'em*, the former Astro says, both to the press after the first game on August 7 and with his bat during the game when he clubs a game-tying homer in the ninth against Octavio Dotel, the young fireballer Steve Phillips used to bring Bell and Mike Hampton to New York. In the third game, Piazza belts his thirtieth home run of the season, and Darryl Hamilton mashes his own homer in his first return to action since early April.

All is well and remains so when the Mets return home for eight games beginning on August 11. The first four are against the San Francisco Giants, whose second-half surge has vaulted them to first place in the National League West. When the Mets went west at the start of May, it marked one of the valleys of their early season, as the Giants swept a four-game series and a discouraged Mike Hampton walked off his frustrations by trudging back to the team hotel on foot. The Mets exact a measure of payback by taking three of four from San Francisco, while also producing one of the season's more memorable moments. In the game on August 12, with the bases loaded and the Mets clinging to a 1–0 lead, Hampton induces a lazy fly ball to shallow left field. Benny Agbayani catches the fly and hands it to a pleasantly surprised young fan in the nearby stands. Everyone else in the stadium is less pleasantly surprised because the ball Agbayani caught was only the second out of the inning, not the third. A pair of runners take advantage of the gaffe by sprinting for the plate. Agbayani is forced to retrieve the ball from the disappointed boy's hands, but the go-ahead run scores regardless. The Mets eventually win the game anyway, retroactively transforming Benny's boo-boo from an excruciating mental error into a lighthearted blooper, and he receives a hearty reception during his first at bat the following night. Things are going so well for the Mets these days that even when they do err, the miscues inspire more whimsy than woe. Once the Giants vacate the premises, the Mets welcome the Rockies and Todd Helton, who comes to New York flirting with a .400 batting average, and take three of four from Colorado as well.

In 1999, the Mets were able to weather a trio of late-season West Coast trips with little trouble. The trend continues in 2000, when they must endure only one westward swing, beginning in Los Angeles on August 18, and escape it no worse for wear. The trip coincides with the publication of a *Sports Illustrated* cover story on Mike Piazza that dubs him, simply, The Man. When he bats at his old haunt at Dodger Stadium (where the Mets win two of three), he is booed and cheered in equal measure by fans who rue the day he was chased out of town. All the Dodgers can do is sigh at the sight of the one that got away. Though the following series in San Diego goes less well than expected, and includes a 16–1 drubbing on August 22 in which Derek Bell is forced into relief duty (and irks the home team through his insistence on wearing shades on the mound), the Mets escape California with a 3–3 split.

The homestand that finishes out August begins with three more games against the Arizona Diamondbacks, scrapping for a wild card spot that grows more elusive each day. The Mets repeat their performance of a few weeks prior, once again taking two of three from Arizona and serving up another baffling domination of Randy Johnson on August 25. Joe McEwing's continued ownership of the The Big Unit is described in the *Post* as "a tired slingshot reference waiting to happen." "Nothing worked," a haunted Johnson says after his loss, struggling to explain what has happened to him, and to his team, since the trade for Curt Schilling that was supposed to launch them back into the playoffs. They leave New York trailing the Mets in the wild card race by 5.5 games.

For the second season in a row, as summer ends, the Mets have more than the wild card in their sights. After they win two of three from visiting Houston, the Mets are tied for the lead in the National League East with Atlanta, and while they enjoy an off day on August 31, the Braves lose to the Reds. This ensures that the team will begin its next road trip, and the month of September, all alone in first place.

* * *

Minor league baseball has proven a growth industry in the tri-state area at the dawn of the 2000s, with the suburbs attracting several farm teams, and so New York City decides it's high time to get in on the act. When the Yankees propose a $71 million stadium for the Staten Island waterfront to house a single-A affiliate—the most money ever spent on a minor league facility—the project sails through the approval process. The Mets soon follow suit with their own minor league plans, but as with most things Mets-related, their path proves far bumpier.

In 1999, the Mets purchased a single-A team from the Toronto Blue Jays and announced plans to relocate it to Brooklyn as a trial run for moving one of their current minor league squads to the borough. Coney Island is eyed as the team's permanent home, a piece of an overall rehabilitation project for New York's fabled playland. Before a new stadium can be built in Coney Island, Fred Wilpon has his eyes on the Parade Grounds of Prospect Park as temporary digs for his Brooklyn farm team. Once set aside as a spot for Civil War veterans to drill, by the mid-twentieth century the Parade Grounds were the city's premier amateur baseball incubator, the first diamond trod by young Brooklynites such as Phil Rizzuto, Sandy Koufax, and Joe Torre.

The symbolism of placing a minor league squad at the site where so many local major leaguers got their start is almost too perfect. Rudy Giuliani throws his weight behind the idea but is thwarted by Howard Golden, longtime Brooklyn borough president and local Democratic Party power broker, who had allocated city funds to rehabilitate the Parade Grounds for community use before the Mets and Giuliani got minor league stars in their eyes. Long a thorn in the mayor's side, Golden stonewalls Giuliani on the Parade Grounds issue throughout 1999 until the notion of placing a minor league team there is abandoned altogether—yet another sign of Giuliani's waning political clout.

This leaves the Mets only a few short months to find a temporary home for their newly purchased farm team. The solution is to house them on the Queens campus of St. John's University, but attempts to sneak this arrangement past the notice of the locals do not go well. At a public hearing about the temporary stadium that will need to be built on campus, outraged residents of the school's surrounding neighborhood shout about the impact of extra traffic and other quality-of-life issues. Giuliani informs the protesters that the stadium is a done deal, and if they don't like it, "You can vote against me if you want to." This is in reference to his campaign for Senate (still active at the moment), and he says it knowing that in northeastern Queens, firm Giuliani Country, few were likely to take him up on the dare.

Those who feared a minor league team would bring clogged streets and unruly fans had no reason to worry, as the Mets' temporary neighbors, dubbed the Queens Kings, play their first and only season in virtual privacy. For many games, the turnstile count stalls around six hundred, making the temporary confines at St. John's—built to hold thirty-five hundred spectators at a cost of $6 million—appear cavernous. The attendance numbers look even more pathetic when placed next to those of the Staten Island Yankees, who are also playing in makeshift accommodations on a college campus yet manage to average twenty-eight hundred fans per night.

The paltry ticket sales may stem from the fact that few are aware the Queens Kings exist. Once the plan to place a team in Prospect Park falls through, Fred Wilpon and the Mets lose enthusiasm for the scheme and expend almost no effort to promote the team. The few fans who show up are confused as to why they're watching not Mets prospects, but low-level Blue Jays farmhands.

Mets ownership lets the Queens Kings fester and concentrates their energies on the Coney Island ballpark instead. Howard Golden promises to make this process as difficult as the Parade Grounds failure until Rudy Giuliani throws him a bone by including the price of improvements to Coney Island's boardwalk and the surrounding neighborhood in the total stadium costs. These additional expenses push the overall price tag of the project over $60 million, twice the original estimate.

Ignoring the disaster that is the Queens Kings, Fred Wilpon foresees daily sellouts due to the location ("probably . . . the best minor league location for a stadium in the country") and low ticket prices ($6 to $10 per seat). At the groundbreaking ceremony in August, Giuliani plants a shovel in the former site of Steeplechase Park, a classic Coney Island amusement park gone to seed, and proclaims, "This ballpark will do for Coney Island what Disney did for 42nd Street." While everyone is in a celebratory mood, he lets slip that costs for the stadium itself will run to $8 million more than the adjusted cost boosted by neighborhood improvements, due to the need for this stadium to be complete before the start of the 2001 season—and before the end of current mayor's administration. Giuliani has been stymied in his attempts to build a new stadium for either the Mets or Yankees, a failure that rankles him almost as much as his failure to "blow up" the city's school system. He is desperate to inaugurate at least one ballpark, even a minor league one, before he leaves office.

Meanwhile, up in Pittsfield, Massachusetts, the minor league team that will move to Brooklyn in 2001 plies its trade for one last season in cozy Waconah Park. The facility was built in 1913, making it older than every other extant major league stadium save Fenway Park. Future superstars from Lou Gehrig to Greg Maddux have taken this field, as have many current Mets such as Edgardo Alfonzo. All of the quirky charm and old-timey coziness that Camden-clone stadiums aspire to can be found here in authentic form.

There are drawbacks to such rustic authenticity, such as a home plate that faces west, the cause of frequent "sun delays" at twilight. The plumbing facilities also date to 1913, with their attendant discomforts. The Mets pressed the city of Pittsfield for capital improvements, but such money isn't to be found in a working-class town in the shadows of the Berkshires. And so, the Pittsfield Mets will pull up stakes and settle in Brooklyn next season, like so many young people are doing these days. They will play in a brand-new stadium that will be designed to approximate the charm of a place like Waconah Park, constructed entirely at taxpayer expense. Unlike Pittsfield, New York City does not have to worry about where the money will come from, even if some of its pols think the city *should* worry. "San Francisco is considered a small-market team and they managed to put together a stadium in downtown for nothing," gripes one city councilman, referring to the Giants' new, privately funded ballpark. His implicit question—*If they can do it, why can't we?*—is neither asked nor answered.

* * *

If the Mets truly believe they're leading charmed lives in 2000, the month of August would be the reason. It would be incorrect to say that everything goes well for the Mets over this stretch, but they manage to skirt every roadblock and never lose their stride once.

See: Mike Piazza. His grip on health, always tenuous, takes a few hits, yet he emerges unscathed on all occasions. A knee injury suffered in Arizona at the beginning of the month proves harmless. A few weeks later, he crashes into the stands while pursuing a foul ball at Dodger Stadium and shrugs this off as well. Ditto the shot he takes at the plate against the Diamondbacks at Shea on August 26, when Arizona second baseman Jay Bell runs for the plate with both arms held high and braced, as if intending to clothesline him. The collision sends Piazza to the ground, where he stays for a few fretful seconds more than anyone would like, but he remains in the game and belts a home run a few innings later.

Other key members of the team suffer scrapes and bruises, and all of them recover in record time. Edgardo Alfonzo suffers a groin strain in Houston and reports a stiff neck during the Mets' final West Coast trip, but both conditions prove to be minor and Fonzie misses little action. In a game hosting the Astros on August 29, Al Leiter suffers a glute strain and Derek Bell leaves after banging his knee on the outfield fence. Leiter misses no starts, however, and the Mets' bumper crop of outfielders allows Bell time to heal. Mike Hampton exits a start against the Rockies on August 17 after only three innings, feeling discomfort in his ribs, and an X-ray reveals a preexisting stress fracture, which Hampton assumes he suffered while playing high school football. Hampton does skip one start—the ugly loss in San Diego that sees Derek Bell take the mound—but returns to pitch the last game against Arizona at Shea on August 27, tossing eight innings and allowing only three hits in another Met win. He will not miss another start this season.

When the return of Darryl Hamilton at the end of July creates a logjam in the outfield, there is no hint of the personnel issues of 1999. Last year, Bobby Valentine was forced to find playing time for grumbling veterans Rickey Henderson and Bobby Bonilla at the expense of Benny Agbayani and Roger Cedeño, and the resulting game of musical chairs made no one happy. This summer, in the absence of the outsized egos of Henderson and Bonilla, there is no such tension, and each member of the outfield corps performs well when called into action—especially Jay

Payton, the young center fielder putting up a rookie-of-the-year-worthy campaign after several injury-marred seasons in the minors.

Even when outside-the-lines distractions emerge in August, they do not hassle the team for long. A pair of Japanese newspapers publish reports that Bobby Valentine is sought by the NPB's Yokohoma Bay Stars as the team's next manager, but both Valentine and Steve Phillips issue quick denials. This, and the reputation of the sources, known for spreading poorly sourced gossip, cause the rumors to fade away before they can take up much room in New York's back pages.

The Mets do not skirt controversy again until their last game against the Astros at Shea on August 30. After throwing seven excellent innings that day, Rick Reed finds his car swarmed by aggressive autograph seekers as he tries to drive out of the Shea parking lot. One fan bangs his vehicle's side panel, demanding to be heard. Fearing for his family's safety (his wife and baby daughter are in the car with him), Reed bursts out from the car and yells right back at the ruffian. Later, WFAN's phone lines light up with callers who claim both sides of the incident behaved much more aggressively than they actually did. The game of literal telephone over what really happened degenerates to the point that several newspapers report fans rocked Reed's car back and forth, attempting to tip it. Asked to react, Steve Phillips dismisses the worst reports as pure fabrication and labels Reed's behavior as an extreme reaction to a stressful situation. Once it becomes apparent that the exaggerations of the autograph incident are exactly that, the tabloids move on.

In years past, any one of these incidents would have hung over the Mets for weeks, casting a shade on everything they did. In the summer of 2000, none of these potential fiascos persist in the newspapers for more than a day or two. The equity of 1999, a season when strife only seemed to make the Mets play better, remains an inexhaustible source of goodwill, as does the team's place in the standings. Their lead in the National League East entering September 1 is the slimmest possible, a mere half game, but this nonetheless marks the latest calendar date on which they have sole possession of a division lead since 1990. Atlanta is little more familiar with being in second place so late in the season than the Mets are in first; the Braves haven't found themselves looking up at any team this late in the regular season since 1993. This reversal of fortune is caused more by a Mets hot streak than an Atlanta slide, though the Braves oblige by losing three of four to a going-nowhere Cincinnati squad at the end of August.

With an eye on the struggling Bronx Bombers, who also end August in first despite mediocre play throughout the summer, Ken Rosenthal wonders aloud in the *Sporting News*, "What if they threw a Subway Series and only the Mets came?" The Mets play this situation as cool as they can, downplaying their place atop the standings as meaningless until the season ends, jumping through hoops to avoid saying the words "first place." Not even their mouthy manager will speak of taking the division. Though Bobby Valentine is so emboldened he openly talks about a return that his current contract does not guarantee—"I have a good feeling that there's a chance I'll be back with this team next year," he says—his brashness disappears when asked about his team's place atop the division. "Last time I checked we're not even in the last month," Valentine avers.

It's that last month that gives the Mets pause. September of 1998 brought a five-game skid that bounced them out of the playoffs altogether. September of 1999 brought an even worse slide, another catastrophe avoided through a sheer miracle. Though the Mets made the postseason last year, no one wants a repeat of that near-death experience. They can't know what to expect in September of 2000, but the cautiousness they display, despite their sizzling-hot summer, indicates they expect the road to be bumpy.

CHAPTER 14

Staggering

SEPTEMBER BEGINS WITH the Mets in first place and on their way to St. Louis to take on the high-flying Cardinals, who lead their own division by a league-best eight games. They've built up this considerable advantage despite the absence of Mark McGwire, shelved since July 6 by patellar tendonitis. Big Mac's place has been filled ably by veteran slugger Will Clark, snagged in Baltimore's trade deadline fire sale. Though he's no longer the fresh-faced first baseman who dazzled for the Giants in the 1980s, he can still hit like the Clark of old. In his first month in St. Louis, Clark slugs eight homers and drives in nineteen runs.

Before September, the Mets and Cardinals played six games and the Mets prevailed in all six. A correction comes due in this series with the Mets swept out of St. Louis, losing all three games on crushing walk-offs. Frustrating as these losses are, being swept by a red-hot Cardinals team is understandable. It's less understandable to lose two of three to a team that burned out long ago, which is exactly what happens when the Mets move on to Cincinnati. The Mets are so desperate for a victory during the game on September 6 that they engage in the ancient baseball tradition of the Beer Rally, wherein several players run into the clubhouse to chug brews between innings. (Bobby Valentine gives tacit blessing to this activity, noting that only players who were already out of the game were permitted to participate.) The brutal loss that follows is one that could drive a Met to drink, however, as New York's bullpen coughs up a three-run lead, the big blow a grand slam blasted off of Armando Benítez. "Sometimes we're human, no?" the closer shrugs after the game.

True enough, except Benítez had not looked human in months. In his previous thirty-one appearances, he'd allowed exactly one earned run.

Why were he and the Mets only mortal in September? And why were these not mere losses, but gut punches? Darryl Hamilton goes the furthest in admitting this portion of the calendar holds some kind of spell over his team. "September is a bad month for us," he concedes. "I think it's a blessing we're having it now."

As that fateful month plods along, the slide takes on a momentum of its own in a depressingly familiar manner. The déjà vu grows even more frightening when the Mets host the Phillies on September 8. The awful seven-game losing streak at the tail of last September included a baffling sweep by a replacement-level Phillies team. This September, the Phils are even worse, but once again they rise above punching-bag status when facing the Mets, taking the first two games in Queens while holding the home team to three total runs in the losses. After the Mets ruin a Mike Hampton gem in the series opener by failing to score any runs behind him, Bobby Valentine conducts a closed-door meeting with his players. "What could he say: get a hit?" wonders the *Times*.

If so, he might try asking Mike Piazza first, as the catcher is batting under the Mendoza Line for the month and uses the word "numb" to describe his feelings at the moment. Coaches pore over video of Piazza's swing to diagnose his offensive woes, but then proclaim they are as baffled as their patient. His struggles may be due less to his own issues than to those of the man who bats behind him, Robin Ventura. The third baseman had already put up the worst numbers of his career so far this season, then somehow found a way to hit even worse in September. Bobby Valentine sits Ventura down for two games in a row during the Mets' latest homestand, a move the *Post* characterizes as a benching in everything but name.

When the month began, the Mets were all alone in first place. After the second loss to Philadelphia, they trail the Braves by 3.5 games. On the afternoon of September 10, in an attempt to loosen up his team, Bobby Valentine reprises his costumed antics of 1999, patrolling the dugout with sunglasses and an eye-black mustache in imitation of his infamous getup. Al Leiter lightens the mood further by tossing a complete-game shutout against the Phillies. John Franco dubs Leiter "the man who saved Gotham City." For the first time in weeks, the team can share a laugh.

The chuckles die down when the Brewers roll into Queens on September 11. Milwaukee greatly helped the Mets' cause in 1999 by winning two of their last three games against the Cincinnati Reds, enabling the Mets to finish in a tie for the wild card spot. In 2000, they put a hurt on those hopes by punishing Mets pitching in the series opener. Another loss means another closed-door meeting, this one for players only. John Franco calls the conference, as he and the team's veterans speak on the subject of accountability. Order is restored for a moment as the Mets prevail in the last two games against the Brewers.

The team's final road trip of the year begins on September 14 with four games in Montréal, to be immediately followed by three in Atlanta. The *Post* compares the series against the struggling Expos to a boxer's warm-up for a title fight: "spar against some palookas, throw some haymakers, hit them hard and come away with a unanimous decision." At the series' close, though, it's no clearer who is the palooka in this equation. In two of the games, the Mets pummel Montréal pitching and score double-digit runs. In the other two, their bats are held in check by unaccomplished young pitchers. Al Leiter struggles in his latest Canadian outing and calls his performance "pathetic," an adjective that could apply to any other Met at the moment.

Under severe stress for the third consecutive autumn, Bobby Valentine begins to lash out at the press. During the series in Montréal, when Chris Smith of *New York Magazine* approaches the manager for a lengthy profile, Valentine treats him to a tirade about how other skippers aren't forced to endure ink-based psychological examinations each September. "Is there a San Francisco or Seattle magazine that would have the *audacity* to do a story like this at this time of the year?" Valentine spits. "No. Absolutely not!" He evokes the memory of the profile he received in *Sports Illustrated* last September, which contained some of his most unfettered thoughts about his players and hit newsstands when his team was mired in a seven-game losing streak, implying the clubhouse clashes of that period were *SI*'s fault. "The story just about got me fired!" he wails. Valentine fails to mention it was his words about various Mets—phrases such as "losers" and "not real intelligent," for starters—and not *Sports Illustrated*'s publishing schedule that was responsible for the strife.

Smith surmises that Valentine is "descending into the self-destructive verbal twitches of his annual September fever dream." If so, then perhaps it's for the best, since some of his charges believe they can only prevail when facing adversity. Edgardo Alfonzo says the Mets make things tougher on themselves because "that's the way we're used to doing it."

"To be Metsian," concludes Smith, "is to be perverse."

* * *

For the third September in a row, the September schedule has given the Mets low bars to vault, struggling teams like the Expos, Brewers, and Phillies. For the third September in a row, the Mets have played down to their weak competition, and now the schedule that follows will be much less forgiving. As they travel to Turner Field on September 18, they stand three games behind Atlanta in the National League East. Simple math says the Mets can make things very interesting with a sweep. Recent history says the Mets will be fortunate to escape Georgia in one piece. Bobby Valentine seems almost surprised by the advent of another Atlanta series, if his starting rotation is any evidence. Rick Reed, who owns an ERA under three at Turner Field, was not held in abeyance for the Braves but was instead spent in the Montréal series. Thus, New York will send to the mound Mike Hampton, Glendon Rusch, and Al Leiter—three lefties against a team whose hitters have feasted on southpaws all season.

Maybe it doesn't matter who the Mets send to the mound in Atlanta. Maybe they are doomed to play poorly whenever they travel south. Baseball players are a superstitious lot, and none of the Mets can dismiss out of hand the feeling that strange things happen to them whenever they set foot in Turner Field. "We've actually won games against them," Robin Ventura reminds the press, because the Mets themselves seem to forget this whenever the two teams face off. The *Post* refers to the Mets' problems with the Braves as something to akin to Steve Blass Disease, that mysterious sporting dysfunction whereby a talented athlete suddenly forgets the basic mechanics of the game.

It seems that the Braves are in the heads of everyone associated with the Mets, sometimes quite literally. During the first game in Atlanta on September 18, fans who tune into the Mets game on WFAN can hear the radio broadcast for the home team at the same time. The preoccupation even overtakes Mike Hampton, despite the fact that he didn't experience the Mets' tortures at Turner Field in 1999. In the series opener, Hampton allows five runs over six innings, misplays a squeeze bunt, and, just for added Charlie Brown-like humiliation, is hit so hard by an Andrés Galaragga line drive it knocks the glove off his hand. The *Times* refers to Hampton's performance in the inning as the equivalent of dumping the Mets in a ditch. And while Hampton does this dumping, the visitors are given the Vintage Greg Maddux treatment: seven innings of five harmless singles. The ever-efficient Mr. Maddux exits after having thrown only eighty-three pitches, because by this point, the Braves have opened up a 6–0 lead, a gaping chasm these Mets appear incapable of fording.

Still, it would not be a true Turner Field game without a cruel comeback attempt. In the top of the eighth, Derek Bell hits a solo shot. Soon after, Robin Ventura drives in two runs of his own, and Todd Zeile walks to bring the tying run to the plate. The walk also brings John Rocker into the game, however, and though Rocker's season has been horrendous by every measure, he has seldom struggled against the Mets. Tonight, he induces a harmless pop-up to end the eighth, then hurls a scoreless ninth for good measure as the Mets fall 6–3.

The second Atlanta game occurs on the same day the Mets announce a date for division series ticket sales. As if in punishment for their hubris, Glendon Rusch executes an unsightly outing that includes three consecutive extra-base hits, a grounder banked off of Robin Ventura's leg, a wild pitch, and seven runs scoring. Only two of these runs are earned, so Rusch's ERA is spared a blow, even if the Mets are not. Atlanta wins by the unsightly score of 12–4, an embarrassment that leaves fans screaming for the Mets to show some life. One WFAN host suggests their hurlers should throw at Chipper Jones, even though the third baseman has done relatively little with his bat in this series, if only to inject some energy into a team that appears to be running on fumes.

Bobby Valentine calls his team together for yet another closed-door meeting in which he performs the verbal equivalent of flipping the buffet table. It is equal parts tongue-lashing, ass-kicking, and back-patting, delivered with healthy doses of longshoreman vocabulary. Players sum up his comments as, *Get it together, let's go,* and leave out the R-rated words. After his private outburst, Valentine addresses the media in the visiting manager's office, drumming his finger on his desk like a vice principal waiting for the vandals who TP'ed his car to confess. "If someone doesn't think I'm allowed to be ticked off, it's their mistake," he declares. "It's my right and I exerted it." Asked why his team has played so poorly in September, he responds with trademark Valentinean sarcasm. "I just haven't had them ready to play, I guess," he sneers. Does he truly believe the Mets' play in September is a reflection of his managerial abilities, considering this is the third September in a row that his team has wilted? "Oh, sure, let's make it about me!" he answers. "I'd rather have it about me. When the team is going good, I know who it's about and when the team is not going good I know who it's about. I think it's absolutely perfect and justified. So if we come out of this, I want to hear the flip side. I've never heard the flip side."

"What is the flip side?" Valentine's rant continues. "Play it for me, so I can hear the music." At this point, every reporter present starts eyeing the exits for their own safety.

The manager goes on to make the same promise he made last season: If the Mets fail to make the playoffs, he should be fired, though he places the self-threat in more oblique terms than those used in 1999. "If we don't get into the playoffs, I'll gladly take Fred [Wilpon] off the hook." Steve Phillips declines comment on his manager's quotes, presumably because he is hiding in a cool dark room for the sake of his mental health. Wilpon attempts to alleviate the pressure on both men by praising the job each has done, the current slide notwithstanding, though he remains obstinate in his refusal to say if he wants either Valentine or Phillips to return in 2001.

The second loss in Atlanta plunges the Mets five games out of first place with eleven games to play, putting a division title all but out of reach. With that possibility virtually eliminated, the team appears to heave a collective sigh of relief. The Mets pull out a face-saving victory in the final game at Turner Field as Al Leiter outduels Tom Glavine and the bullpen holds off a late charge by the Braves to escape with a 6–3 win. Mike Piazza confesses that his main reason for wanting a win over the Braves was to make annual rookie hazing—a tradition usually staged during a team's final road trip of the season—a lot less awkward.

At first glance, Piazza's confession seems odd for someone who had endured weeks of late-season torment for the third season in a row. All the team meetings and the Valentinean paranoia and the media's squabbling about the same made this September seem like a straight repeat of the last two autumns. The crucial difference this time around is that no one is on their tail. While the Mets struggle through September, the Diamondbacks, their closest pursuers in the wild card race, fall apart completely. On September 20, while the Mets are salvaging their finale at Turner Field, the Diamondbacks lose a 1–0 heartbreaker in Los Angeles. It is their sixth loss in a row, bringing their record in September to a putrid 6–13. Despite their struggles, the Mets own a wider lead in the wild card race than the Braves own in the division.

And so, after weeks of nervous struggle, the Mets begin to relax. As they did in 1999, the Mets follow a disappointing trip to Atlanta with a visit to Philadelphia beginning on September 21, but this time they win three of four from the hapless Phillies, with enough Mets fans on hand to make Veterans Stadium sound like Shea Stadium South. Mike Piazza, MIA at the plate for most of September, blasts several long balls while in

Philadelphia. When one steamed Phillies reliever points to these homers as further evidence the baseball is juiced, a bemused Piazza points to his own biceps. ("Tell him to check these out.")

At series' end, the Mets' lead in the wild card race is six games—now over the Dodgers, who have vaulted over the sleepwalking Diamondbacks—with six games left on their schedule. No one could blow a lead like that, it seems. Except that these are the Mets, and three of those six games are against the Braves.

* * *

Fans who arrive at Shea Stadium for the first of three games hosting the Atlanta Braves on September 26 are handed "rally towels" that say "BATTLE FOR THE NL EAST." An ironic giveaway, considering the Mets threw in the towel on that battle with their lackluster performances in Atlanta. The Braves need win only one of the three games in New York and the division crown is theirs once again, a mathematical fact that robs a good deal of the spice from this series. New York can capture the wild card with one more victory or one more Dodger loss, though no one wishes to back into the playoffs via another team's defeat.

Steve Phillips goes one step further by dictating that the wild card *itself* is backing into the playoffs. He declares that if the Mets claim the wild card, they should not celebrate on the field. In 2000, with the wild card only six seasons old, many smell the hated whiff of "participation trophy" in awarding a playoff berth to a runner-up. "Our goal was to win the division," Phillips says. "The wild card is a fall back." Espousing the same attitude toward frivolity as a seventeenth-century Puritan minister, Phillips says he will suffer his players to smile and hug on the field should they clinch the wild card, but that is it.

The issue does not come up in the series opener, as the Mets sleepwalk their way through a 7–1 defeat that hands the division to the Braves on a silver platter. At the game's conclusion, the Braves mark the clinching with hearty handshakes and backslaps, a muted celebration of which Steve Phillips would approve. In stark contrast to last year, the closest Atlanta comes to gloating is Chipper Jones's admission that "whenever we play [the Mets], a switch goes off in the clubhouse." Chipper surmises that if his team had to play the Mets every day, it might win more games than the 1998 Yankees. Last year, John Rocker told the media he savored his part in eliminating the Mets from the divisional chase. This year, he tells them he won't answer any questions.

The Dodgers do the Mets the courtesy of winning their own game, which allows New York the chance to claim the wild card with a win on September 27. On that night, the Braves field their regular lineup despite clinching the night before, but the Mets prove equal to the challenges as Rick Reed pitches a gem, Edgardo Alfonzo homers, and Armando Benítez strikes out the side in the ninth to cap a satisfying 6–2 victory. Per Steve Phillips's directives, the initial reaction by the team is subdued. Though a near-capacity crowd loudly cheers for their team, the PA system opts to mark the occasion with David Bowie's "Heroes," a thematically appropriate but musically subdued choice. The players walk onto the field and exchange high fives, giving no outward indication this win is any different from the eighty-nine that preceded it. Champagne is poured and sprayed in the clubhouse, however, and even Phillips gets into the act by dumping Freixenet on Bobby Valentine's head.

Clinching complete, the Mets finish their schedule with a flourish, first by taking the final game of the Braves series and ending Greg Maddux's scoreless streak in the process. (The feat is even more impressive for being mounted by a lineup of backups and September call-ups who dub themselves The Terror Squad.) Then they sweep three games from the Expos, ending the season with a thirteenth-inning walk-off win on October 1. The five-game winning streak to close out the schedule stands in stark contrast to the final weeks of the last two Mets seasons.

Once New York clinches the wild card spot at the Braves' expense, Bobby Cox sounds envious of their position. "The Mets can take it easy now," he says. "Everyone else is trying to get the best record." Though Atlanta dropped the last two games at Shea, they remain close to San Francisco and St. Louis, the other divisional champs, for best record in the league and the postseason home field advantage that would come with it. So Cox continues to play all his regulars in the season's final three games, and runs out his best pitchers to boot.

Despite his best efforts, and despite playing those last three games at home against the middling Colorado Rockies, the Braves lose two of these final games. The last contest of the year is a true heartbreaker, as a poor outing from John Rocker and a Chipper Jones error in the ninth brings to the plate slugger Todd Helton, who flirted with hitting .400 during an MVP-worthy 2000 season. Rocker comes achingly close to nailing down this game for the Braves by backing Helton into a two-strike count. Then the slugger wheels on a Rocker fastball and parks it into the bleachers for a crushing go-ahead homer. The Braves go down in defeat, 10–5.

The Giants finish their season with ninety-seven wins, tops in the National League. And while John Rocker and Chipper Jones are gift-wrapping a game for the Rockies, the Cardinals prevail over the Reds for their ninety-fifth win of the year, the same total as the Braves. Because Atlanta lost four of seven games against St. Louis this season, the tiebreaker goes to the Cards. Thus, the divisional series between the two teams will begin at Busch Stadium, the place where, for much of this summer, the Cardinals refused to lose.

* * *

With the Mets capturing a playoff spot for the second season in a row, and doing so in less heart-stopping fashion than last year, their 2000 season can be considered a success. In terms of acquiring a new facility to replace Shea Stadium, however, 2000 represents another year of failure.

Fred Wilpon shared his domed stadium plans with *Sports Illustrated* in 1993, submitted them officially to the city in 1995, and showed off fancy models of his vision—now with a retractable roof—to the press in 1998. Ever since, he has been playing the waiting game, and losing. In 1999, he grew so anxious for any movement on the issue that he entered into serious talks to sell a majority share in the team to Cablevision, just to raise the necessary capital for his dream ballpark. Talks progressed so far that they were said to be a sticking point in the Mets' pursuit of players at the trade deadline. (Exacting a bit of revenge for his first clash with Wilpon in the 1980s, Nelson Doubleday made it known he would not approve the sale at the exact moment when it looked like the purchase was a done deal, killing it in an instant.) As the 2000 season unfolds, there is more talk than ever about the Mets' desire for a new stadium. Unfortunately, there is the same amount of movement as in recent years, which is to say none at all.

When Rudy Giuliani drops out of the Senate race, stadium building rises to the top of the mayor's agenda as a means of putting his imprint on the city before he leaves office. Giuliani not only eyes new homes for the Yankees and the Mets, but also has plans to build a giant domed facility over the West Side railyards which could serve as a new convention center, or new stadium for the Yankees, or the NFL's Jets—or, hell, why not all three?

When Fred Wilpon officially unveiled his plans for a new stadium in 1998, he did so with the diligence of a student who completes his book report a week early in the hope his haste would be rewarded. He was certainly more diligent than the Yankees, who complained often about their stadium in the Bronx yet presented no concrete plans to replace it. The more time passes, the clearer it is that all Wlipon's extra work has brought him is a lengthier period of frustration. Throughout 2000, he clutches his blueprints nervously while the Yankees play Hamlet. No one knows if the Yankees want a brand-new stadium or a revamped old one because the team remains infuriatingly noncommittal. The team's chief operating officer, Lonn Trost, insists the team is making its own study of the West Side option, a survey that is moving at a snail's pace.

In late September, Giuliani begins to sound as desperate as Wilpon feels. He announces the West Side stadium project will be open to any team willing to do business with him, including the Mets, and also ties the project to the idea of an Olympic bid for New York City. The mayor's efforts to loop in other teams to his pipe dreams draws harsh criticism from a state senator representing the West Side district where the facility would be placed, who dismisses the mayor as "obsessed with stadiums," as well as representatives from the Bronx and Queens who fear major league teams could flee their respective boroughs. "Everything I've done they're against," grumbles Giuliani in a Nixonian outburst. "It's almost a signal to me that it's the right idea." Undaunted, the mayor unveils his proposal for financing a new stadium project on the West Side, with costs to be split equally three ways among the teams, the city, and the state. Desperate for any good news, Fred Wilpon declares himself open to the West Side idea if that's what it takes to get his dream house, though it's unclear if the Mets are the mayor's first choice for occupant in the hypothetical West Side facility.

Unfortunately, Giuliani neglects to clear his tripartite financing proposal with the state first. Since the West Side railyards belong to the MTA, a state agency, the governor will have the last word about anything built atop them. And what Governor George Pataki decrees, in no uncertain terms, is that he will not allow a new stadium for the Yankees to be built on the site (though he is open to construction tied to the city's embryonic Olympic plans). The governor's prohibition of the Yankees from the West Side site effectively kills any chance of the Mets playing there either, because that would cause some combination of Yankee litigation and George Steinbrenner's head exploding.

Another damper on new stadium plans comes quickly on the heels of the West Side bickering. As he did last season, Nelson Doubleday again picks the ideal moment to crush Fred Wilpon's dreams. In an interview with the Associated Press, he articulates his preference for renovating Shea over building a brand-new ballpark at taxpayer expense, since a facelift would cost "one-tenth the money or one-one hundredth the money... I think this place can be refurbished and made up to date. We've got all the roads. We've got all the access. Maybe we can even double decker the parking lot." Asked for a response, a gobsmacked Wilpon can only choke out, "If that's what he said, that's what he said."

Doubleday's inconveniently timed comments cause Wilpon's stadium dreams to fade further into the background. Giuliani cites Doubleday's pooh-poohing of a new stadium as a factor in stalled talks over the Mets' new home. And so the mayor moves on, concentrating on Olympic plans for the West Side instead. Rudy Giuliani will remain preoccupied by these schemes for the rest of the calendar year. Nelson Doubleday will remain the X factor, ready to pop his head out of the ground every time a new Met stadium is proposed. And Fred Wilpon will clutch his blueprints for an Ebbets Field 2.0 that remains little more than a nostalgic fantasy.

* * *

September swoons are not in the Bronx Bombers' repertoire, nor do such struggles appear to be in the offing when their early season stumbles are replaced by a summer of brutally effective Yankees baseball. (The brutal effectiveness begins, coincidentially or not, after Roger Clemens beans Mike Piazza.) On September 10, they complete a three-game sweep at Fenway Park so decisive it inspires a *Sports Illustrated* article with a subtitle declaring the Yankees "the team to beat" in the playoffs, the same mantle they'd held every season since 1996. On September 13, the Bronx Bombers own a nine-game lead in the American League East. All is as it should be in Yankeeland.

Then suddenly, it isn't. The lineup that had found a rhythm during the summer goes cold, despite their offense receiving a post-trade-deadline beef-up. Or perhaps because of that addition. The situation is complicated, to put it mildly.

The trouble commences when general manager Brian Cashman spots Tampa Bay's José Canseco on the waiver wire and puts in a claim to prevent a division rival from snatching him. No one else bites on Canseco, however, making the aging masher the exclusive property of the New York Yankees, provided they still want him. When a half-hearted Cashman fails to work out an exchange with Tampa Bay, the trusting Devil Rays send Canseco up north anyway, just to be rid of him and the $1 million he's owed. Even worse for the GM, George Steinbrenner hangs him out to dry in the baffling aftermath. Asked to explain the move, The Boss grumbles, "I think they got caught up in something they didn't think about." Joe Torre plays good soldier about the addition of Canseco, though he suspects the slugger will bring bad vibes with him, suspicions that are proven correct in short order. Within days of arriving in the Bronx, Canseco seethes about lack of playing time, bringing a dark cloud over a Yankees clubhouse in which outsized egos and personality conflicts are rare.

Joe Torre has to deal with many surprises late in the season. For much of the year, he has to juggle the thorny issue of keeping Chuck Knoblauch's bat in his lineup while keeping his glove from doing much damage. A bout of elbow tendinitis sends Knoblauch to the disabled list in August, which should have been a welcome respite for all involved. This ends abruptly on September 1 when Knoblauch is reactivated, despite the fact that the second baseman still contends he is injured, and Torre is more or less commanded to play him. Pressed to explain this, all Torre can say is, "That decision came from Tampa." Much like "the White House" is a stand-in for "the president," "Tampa" is shorthand for George Steinbrenner. Tampa makes matters worse when he insists his "best men" found nothing wrong with the infielder's elbow and compares him unfavorably to other ailing Yankees. "His teammates are gallant warriors," Steinbrenner thunders. "They play tired and hurt . . . I've got millions of players who go out there and play through it. All this started when he couldn't throw the ball to first base."

Knoblauch's response is terse and direct. "I'm fucking sick of it," he says, furious over the implication that he's either a liar or a coward. Eventually, Steinbrenner swallows crow and speaks to Knoblauch in person about the controversy, and though both men leave their talk feeling better, said talk doesn't take place until mid-October. In the intervening weeks, the situation is a giant gaping wound the Yankee owner insists on poking.

Concurrent with this drama, the Yankees' pitching woes return. David Cone is again demoted to relief duty due to ineffectiveness, and Joe Torre admits that Cone's only hope of making his postseason roster might be in the bullpen. Meanwhile, trade deadline pickup Denny Neagle is knocked around to the tune of a 7.52 ERA in September. Hurlers hoping for advice from the team's mound guru are out of luck, as pitching coach Mel Stottlemyre is away from the team receiving cancer treatment.

The Yankees remain in first place throughout September, their nine-game cushion shrinking but never disappearing completely because neither Toronto nor Boston can put together a hot streak capable of deposing them. If the reigning champs are not dethroned, however, September humbles them for the first time in years. This is no more evident than during the Yankees' last trip to the SkyDome beginning on September 19, when they are swept in three games by the Blue Jays. Andy Pettitte and David Cone are shelled in succession in the first two games, but neither defeat is as galling as the 3–1 loss on September 21. David Wells, the one who got away, tosses a complete game to earn his twentieth win of the year and savors every last pitch as if it were a suitcase of Coors Light. When he logs the final out, Wells pumps his fist as hard as he did after the perfect game he hurled in the Bronx. After the game, he brands his former team as "very beatable." This stings, because his ex-teammates know it to be true.

When the Yankees return home on September 23 and watch Denny Neagle get knocked around by the Tigers, it marks the Yanks' sixth loss in a row, their longest losing streak since 1997. They recover to win the following two games against Detroit. Then they drop the final seven of the regular season, concluding a stretch of futility unfathomable for the Yankees of this era.

One sports pundit after another pens his "What's wrong with the Yankees?" column. Their diagnoses vary from a superannuated lineup to a worn-out bullpen to a putrid starting rotation, but all such pieces conclude on a variation of the same thesis: *These are not the old, scary, dangerous Yankees.* This is not a team worthy of mentioning in the same breath as the championship teams of 1996, 1998, or even the lowly regarded 1999 vintage. "The Yankees have been complacent," writes Jack Curry in the *Times*, "a team plodding toward the postseason while the regular season unfolds and they unravel. Did anyone ever speculate that Joe Torre would want to switch places with Bobby Valentine in late September? Yesterday afternoon, Torre would have."

The afternoon Curry refers to is that of September 29, when the Yankees officially capture the American League East. What should be a cause for celebration instead unfolds like a nightmare. In Baltimore, Andy Pettitte and Doc Gooden combine to allow ten runs in the second inning, crushed by an Orioles team that gave up on the season some time in April, en route to an ugly final score of 13–2. The Yankees clinch the division anyway, however, because down in Tampa Bay, the feisty Devil Rays outlast the Red Sox, thus reducing New York's magic number to zero.

The Yankees do what everyone had chided the Mets to avoid at all costs: back into the playoffs. Chilled champagne is available in the clubhouse, but Joe Torre has to beg his players to enjoy it. They pop open bubbly with reluctance and feel obliged to apologize for doing so. "We're not celebrating for the last two weeks," Derek Jeter counsels as he lifts a glass. "We're celebrating something we've worked on since the middle of February."

Most of the media is unsympathetic to Jeter's point of view. "Every time the Yankees would blow a tire, they would go out and buy a new car," Mike Lupica writes of the Yanks' approach to team building. "It's a laugh now to hear them talk of how much they had to overcome to get here." The title of Lupica's column labels the team the "Bronx Bumblers."

With the division clinched, Joe Torre does the sensible thing and gives his regulars some much-needed rest for the rest of the regular season, a major factor in why the Yankees finish with a mere eighty-seven wins. Only four teams in baseball history had won a championship while winning fewer than ninety games. At the close of the regular season, the Yankees haven't led at any point in any game for sixty-two straight innings.

After their final loss of a long, grueling regular season, the Yankees do not yet know where they will begin their playoff run, but they know it won't be the Bronx. Their miserable finish cedes home-field advantage for at least the divisional round, and the rest of the American League playoff picture remains unsettled until late on the last day of the season, October 1. Oakland and Seattle enter the day tied for first place in the American League West, while Cleveland, who reasserted themselves into contention with a hot August and September, trails each team by one game. Should either Oakland or Seattle lose their final game of the year, Cleveland could claim the wild card spot with a win.

The Yankees find themselves in the odd position of rooting for the Indians, the team that dashed their repeat hopes in 1997 by defeating them in the division series. The White Sox, owners of the best record, will play the wild card team unless that team is Cleveland, since squads from the same division can't face off in the first round of the playoffs. If Cleveland claims the wild card, the Yanks will have a short trip to Chicago rather than a trek to the West Coast.

Nothing has broken the Yankees' way for weeks, however, and neither does this. Out in Anaheim, Seattle rebounds from an early deficit and claims their game over the long-eliminated Angels. Meanwhile in Oakland, young A's ace Tim Hudson shuts down the go-nowhere Rangers for eight innings and Jason Isringhausen—the erstwhile Generation K member who blossomed in Oakland this season, becoming one of the game's best closers—records the final out on a strikeout. Seattle and Oakland each finish with ninety-one wins, Cleveland with ninety. Due to tiebreakers, the A's grab the American League West division crown, the Mariners grab the AL wild card, and the Indians grab tickets home, missing the playoffs for the first time in seven years. Much of the 1990s belonged to Cleveland, but it's not the 1990s anymore.

And so the Yankees will have to take a long flight to the East Bay. Oakland does the exact opposite of what the Yankees did this September, racking up a record of 21–7 in the month, and with a payroll dwarfed by New York's, comprised mostly of products of their own farm system. Their lineup is renowned for wearing down opponents with walks before pummeling them with long balls, an approach explicitly modeled on the Bronx Bombers of recent years. "It worked for the Yankees," explains Oakland's wunderkind general manager, a one-time Mets farmhand named Billy Beane, when explaining his true-outcomes-based offensive manifesto. Beane is both explicit about his team-building process—to a degree that suggests he'd be an awful poker player—and brutally honest about its window for success. "The system hasn't allowed any guarantee that we can retain our best players in the prime of their careers," he says, "the system" being a euphemism for the free-agent market that makes the best players unattainable for the likes of Oakland. "These young players are not going to be young and inexpensive for long." Beane's philosophy is, essentially, *Work walks and mash taters, for tomorrow we die.* In Oakland, where baseball is not the deathly important business it is in New York, you can get away with this devil-may-care attitude. In essence, the Yankees will have to play a younger, hungrier version of themselves who have nothing to lose, on their own turf.

Recent results—the seven-game losing streak, the lack of any lead in sixty-two long innings—suggest this will not be an easy hurdle to vault. Many in the press believe the Yankees haven't got a prayer. "The only way the Yankees will get to the World Series," surmises one *Times* scribe, "is if they are mercifully granted a bye through the American League playoffs." The *Post* describes the team as a battered heavyweight champ with eyes bloodied shut and speech slurred, still on his feet, if only for the moment.

CHAPTER 15

A Great Run

THE METS' FINAL weeks of 1999 were so fraught with peril that the team was left with little time to speculate about their first playoff matchup. In 2000, they clinch six days before the playoffs start, leaving them with many hours in which to contemplate such questions. Once it's known that their first-round opponent will be the Giants—a San Francisco win in game 161 assures them the best record in the National League, entitling them to host the wild card winner in the division series—the team can announce its intentions, and the New York press can tout a supposed burgeoning rivalry between the two teams.

The back pagers cite as evidence the series the Mets played in San Francisco in May, when they were swept in four games and the entire team displayed a decided unease. During that disastrous trip to the bay, Todd Pratt accused Giants first baseman J.T. Snow of a "dirty" slide at the plate, Dennis Cook plunked a batter after a balk call (a response that made zero sense unless Cook wanted to incite a bench clearing, which it appears he did), and, most infamously, Mike Hampton pitched miserably and made his lonesome walk back to the team hotel, the nadir of his season. Scribes also cite the fact that San Francisco seems unwilling to extend New York even a modicum of respect. Last season, numerous Giants sour-graped about losing to Mets pitchers they considered lousy. The pattern continues this year when, after the Giants lose three of four at Shea in August, Jeff Kent declares himself unimpressed by his hosts. ("We feel we're a better ballclub than the Mets.")

There is also an assumption of a rivalry between the two teams' managers, which the press has played up during their every confrontation in the past few seasons by emphasizing the differences between the skippers: Dusty Baker, the hands-off players' manager, and Bobby Valentine, the cerebral micromanager. Though both men have contracts that expire at the end of this season, Valentine has often expressed an unrequited desire to return while Baker has played things far cooler, rebuffing preseason contract extension talks. He knows he'll be a prized commodity if he hits the market, especially after the managerial bloodletting that followed the end of the regular season. Pink slips have been handed out to the skippers of the Dodgers, Reds, Phillies, Pirates, and even the Diamondbacks, who canned team architect Buck Showalter.

Most rivalries are borne of familiarity, however, and the Mets and Giants do not play each other often enough to have developed bad blood. When the two teams are viewed with clear eyes, it becomes clear they are more similar than different. Like the Mets, the Giants' starting rotation is not its greatest strength, but it is anchored by an ace; in their case, 1997's postseason superstar, Liván Hernández, who has rebounded from a miserable 1999 with the Marlins in which, among other indignities, he lost to the Mets five times. Behind the Cuban defector are righthander Russ Ortiz and southpaw Shawn Estes, both of whom have benefitted from the tutelage of Giants pitching coach Dave Righetti, mainstay of the Yankee staff in the 1980s. Also like the Mets, the Giants' pitching strength is concentrated in a shutdown bullpen headed by a fireballing closer: Robb Nen, who hasn't blown a save since early July. And again like the Mets, the Giants' lineup is constructed around a few monster bats—Barry Bonds and Jeff Kent, both of whom put up MVP-caliber numbers this season—and a strong support team of role players and super subs.

As the playoffs dawn, Bonds and Kent dominate the New York media's coverage of the impending series. Bonds must once again answer the questions he hates to address: *Why can't you hit in the playoffs?* Previous Octobers have seen few contributions from Bonds, either in a Pirates uniform at the beginning of the 1990s or in a Giants uniform at the end of them. The questions prevail because Bonds is otherwise acknowledged as one of the greatest hitters to ever pick up a bat, a reputation bolstered further by a brilliant 2000 season in which he hit forty-nine homers, a new career high. His new home had little to do with the boost; if anything, Pac Bell Park is far more of a pitcher's park than Candlestick was, but this fact proved no impediment to his power.

The New York scribes are preoccupied with Bonds and his surly reputation, to the point of obsession. They marvel at Bonds's "lair," an entire wing of Pac Bell's clubhouse containing four whole lockers at his disposal and a leather recliner. He removes this last creature comfort before the playoffs began, knowing it will only draw wisecracks from the wisenheimer New Yorkers. Those on the Mets beat write about it anyway to frame Bonds as a pampered diva who folds in the spotlight of October. "Bonds believes that Bonds's postseason failures sell papers," pens Mark Kriegel of the *Daily News*. "If that were only the case, print journalism would find itself in much more favorable circumstances."

Like Bonds, Jeff Kent has little use for the visiting New York press contingent, though for different reasons. He achieved superstar status upon his arrival in San Francisco in 1997, belting twenty-nine homers and driving in 121 that year, has generated comparable numbers ever since, and will go on to claim this year' National League MVP award. His teammates describe him as a "clubhouse leader," the stoic yin counterbalancing the grumbling yang of Bonds.

This assessment astounds New York sportswriters who remember Kent as a petulant brat who whined his way out of Queens. A key return when the Mets traded David Cone to Toronto in 1992, Kent spent his first months in a Mets uniform throwing fits over umpires' calls, bad-mouthing former Blue Jays teammates, and telling the *Toronto Globe and Mail* that his new team was "even worse" than he dared imagine. When team vets swiped Kent's street clothes and replaced them with a humiliating costume as part of end-of-season rookie hazing, Kent dumped the costume on the floor, demanded the return of his civvies, and challenged the entire clubhouse to a fight. When this incident hit the press, it made Kent a target of derision for fans and the media alike. His slightest shortcoming in the field or at the plate inspired cries of "Jeff Can't" from the Shea crowd. Somehow Kent lasted in New York until 1996, though it was clear he hated every minute of his time there.

Kent always pinned the blame for this harsh treatment on Gotham's press—as if the fault was in the reporting, not his behavior—and still refuses to speak with any reporter from the New York dailies. If one of them dares approach with a question, he will pretend as if he can't hear them, acting as if the reporter is a ghost unable to communicate with the world of the living. The antipathy runs both ways. In the days leading up to the division series, Kent is heard swearing that if the Giants win the World Series, he might retire. The seriousness of the second baseman's vow is doubtful, but upon hearing it, one New York sportswriter declares that, if it means getting rid of Kent, then he will root for the Giants to go all the way.

If the New York scribes are not fans of the Giants' two biggest stars, they have fallen completely in love with San Francisco's brand-new stadium, a perfect reflection of its city's quirks and beauty. The Giants struggled there in the first month of the season but soon came to love it and finished with a record of 55–26 at Pac Bell, tied for the best home numbers in baseball. (They are tied with the Mets, though New York has a better winning percentage at Shea since one of its "home" losses came at the Tokyo Dome.) Jeff Kent theorizes that other teams allow themselves to be distracted by the stadium's odd angles and features, which trick them into thinking they have to play *differently* to win there. With the only evidence at his disposal four frustrating games in May, Bobby Valentine still isn't sure he knows what it takes to win in San Francisco. Asked how his team will handle the stadium's odd dimensions, the manager responds, "We've instructed our pitchers to keep the balls in front of our outfielders so that the walls won't come into play."

One thing the Giants never quite figured out in 2000 was left-handed pitching, and so the Mets have the advantage of being able to start southpaws Mike Hampton and Al Leiter in the first two games of the series. The question is which one of them will get the nod in game one, and it is a question Bobby Valentine avoids answering until the final day of the regular season. When announcing his chosen order, he makes his decision sound like the result of pulling a name out of a hat, insisting he'll go with Hampton first and Leiter second for no other reason than it's how the Mets began their season. (Not strictly true, as Leiter did not start until the team's first stateside game, but no one points out the technicality to Valentine.)

As for the rest of their playoff roster, the biggest surprise for 2000 is Joe McEwing, who makes the team by virtue of his versatility. McEwing has played virtually every position on the field this year and thus has value as a late-inning substitution. His addition to the roster comes at the expense of Matt Franco, who never recaptured the status of go-to lefty pinch hitter once it was usurped by Lenny Harris. Franco is also made expendable by the sudden appearance of another lefthanded batter in the Mets' clubhouse.

Prior to September of 2000, few Mets fans would have known the name Timoniel Pérez, unless they also followed the Hiroshima Toyo Carp. The twenty-three-year-old Dominican native spent three middling years in the NPB, but when Hiroshima asked him to start the 2000 season in the minors, Pérez asked for his release. Mets assistant general manager Omar Minaya first ran across Pérez when the outfielder was a seventeen-year-old in the Dominican Summer League, and was so impressed by him that he kept tabs on Pérez's career, watching with great interest as he played in the 1999 Caribbean World Series. When Hiroshima granted Pérez's wish for release, Minaya swooped in to sign him to a minor league deal for the discount price of $85,000, taking a low-risk gamble that the rigorous developmental regimen of Japanese baseball would put Pérez at a distinct advantage over his peers.

By the start of June, Peréz was batting so well for triple-A Norfolk (.350) that the *Sporting News* conjectured he might be "the find of the year." By the end of July, he was mentioned as one of the reasons why the team was willing to part with Jason Tyner, their first-round draft pick only a year ago. At the trade deadline, when the Mets attempted to make deals, Pérez's name was among the dream asks that other teams demanded in return.

Pérez earned a call-up when rosters expanded on September 1 and appeared as a pinch hitter in the Mets' game in St. Louis that very day. Within his first few minutes on a major league field, he displayed all the trademarks of his brand of play. In the top of the ninth, with two outs and no one on base in a tie game, Pérez lashed a line-drive single to center field for his first major league hit. The Mets had a speedy runner on base who could score on a double, and many powerful bats coming up who could supply that double. Pérez didn't allow them a chance to do so, however, as he attempted a steal of second and was thrown out with room to spare.

Communication with Pérez remains a thorny issue. He doesn't speak English well yet, and Bobby Valentine's Spanish is spotty at best. Because both men spent time across the Pacific, they settle on Japanese as their medium of exchange, but Valentine still finds difficulties, since Pérez—recipient of an intensive language course while attending Hiroshima's Dominican academy—possesses a superior Japanese vocabulary.

Most reporters who want to get Pérez's perspective on his storybook rise to the majors must do so through an interpreter. Despite the influx of baseball players from Latin America, relatively few sportswriters have learned their language, believing that players who don't speak English are not unable but unwilling to do so. The belief applies even to players like Pérez, whose path to the big leagues allowed him little time or opportunity to learn English (even if it did allow him to learn Japanese). So while Pérez makes an immediate impression with the Mets, he has no interviews in the press until his team is two games deep into their first playoff series, and even then it comes not with any of Gotham's papers but with a Spanish-speaking sportswriter from the *San Francisco Chronicle*.

The Mets media guide lists Pérez at five feet, nine inches and 165 pounds, generous measurements both. He is a scrappy speedster, a rare breed at the homer-mad dawn of the twenty-first century. The way he runs up in the batter's box and slaps at the ball is a move more befitting the dead-ball era of Ty Cobb than the power surge of the new millennium. Most teams barely know how to defend such hits anymore, a failure that gifts Pérez many a hustle single.

He joins a team that is physically and mentally exhausted from the pressure of a third consecutive autumn chasing a playoff spot. At a time when the Mets hitters are pressing so hard their bats turn to sawdust in their hands, in waltzes this young fresh fellow who makes everything look too easy, beating out infield singles, lining doubles into the gap at will. For a team in need of energy, Pérez proves a godsend. Soon, only the most formal outfits refer to him as "Timoniel Pérez." To fans and teammates, he is simply "Timo," no surname necessary.

Comparisons to Melvin Mora—who joined the team late in 1999 and also injected some life into a flagging team—come quickly. It is a curious reaction, given how unceremoniously Mora was dismissed from New York this season, and perhaps a means of penance for Mora's shabby treatment. Pérez plays all of five games before the *Post* suggests he might be the Melvin Mora of 2000. By the end of the month, the *Times* ditches any hint of equivocation and describes him, flatly, as "a successor to Mora." As he did with Mora last year, Edgardo Alfonzo takes Pérez under his wing, and the young outfielder, per the *Times*, "follows the classy Alfonzo the way a five-year-old trails his ten-year-old brother." Pérez himself invites the comparisons by taking the number 6, the same one Mora sported during his time with the Mets. When the Mets make a trip to Montréal, the PA announcer intones Timo Pérez's name and position even as Olympic Stadium's scoreboard video screen displays Melvin Mora's mugshot.

Pérez's speed should make him a prime candidate to fill the leadoff role, and he certainly looks like more of a leadoff hitter type than Benny Agbayani, who's most often occupied the first spot since Mora's departure. However, Agbayani owns a leadoff-worthy on-base percentage close to .400, while Pérez shows little patience at the plate in his initial weeks in the majors, logging fifty-four plate appearances in September and walking a mere three times. Bobby Valentine only appears comfortable experimenting with Pérez as leadoff man once the Mets' path to the playoffs is assured, placing him in the first spot in five of the team's final six games.

Pérez's presence on the playoff roster is considered little more than insurance, a bet against the need for a pinch runner or the contingencies of an extra-inning slog. For all of his promise, all of his leadoff potential, all of the comparisons to the suddenly lamented Melvin Mora, no one yet dreams they will see much of Timo this October.

* * *

The first division series game in San Francisco on October 4 unfolds on a lovely autumn afternoon, temperatures at sixty-six comfortable degrees. The water in McCovey Cove is gentle enough to accommodate many kayaking souvenir seekers, as well as one brave fan who scales the mast of a clipper so he can catch a glimpse of the action over the twenty-five-foot-tall fence in right field. The game begins at 1:00 p.m. local time to accommodate a prime-time start for game two of the series between the A's and the Yankees across the bay in Oakland.

Liván Hernández draws the start for the Giants. Though the Mets defeated him five times in 1999, four of those starts came for a Marlins team that had thrown in the towel. The Hernández they face now shows a determined cold-bloodedness all afternoon as he picks off Mets batters with ease and efficiency. Mike Piazza, Robin Ventura, and Derek Bell all hit the ball far in the early innings, but inevitably to straightaway center field, the deepest part of the ballpark.

As for Mike Hampton, he allows two hits and an RBI groundout in the bottom of the first inning but redeems himself with a hit of his own in the top of the third that sets up the Mets for a game-tying sac fly. The lefty seems to regain some confidence as he sets down the Giants in order in the bottom of the second and records two quick outs to start the third. Then he allows a single, which ensures he cannot escape the inning before a confrontation with Barry Bonds. On a 2-2 pitch, Hampton places a heater at a perfect spot on the outside corner, but the home plate umpire deems this a ball. Hampton takes a half step off the mound once the ball lands in the catcher's mitt, anticipating a strike call, only to whirl away from the plate and cover his mouth with his glove when that call never comes, like a student afraid of cursing in front of a teacher.

His next pitch is not so perfectly placed, and Bonds smashes it down the right-field line. The ball caroms off the stands that jut out into foul territory, a sudden change of trajectory that assures a run will score all the way from first. When Derek Bell takes a sharp turn to catch up to the ball, he twists an ankle. Though Bell attempts to finish the inning, he is forced to leave the game one batter later. Back on the mound, Hampton loses his command and walks Jeff Kent on four pitches, none of them close. Up steps Ellis Burks, postseason veteran and part-time slugger for these Giants. When Hampton tries to sneak a fastball past him, Burks is fully prepared to wheel on the pitch. His blast is the kind of high-arcing fly ball that usually curves foul, except the batter smashes it so hard that the ball doesn't have time to do so. It bangs off of the left-field foul pole at upper-deck height for a three-run homer, stretching the Giants' advantage to 5–1.

There are six more innings to be played, but Burks's three-run shot is where the action ends, on both sides. Though the Giants threaten in subsequent innings, Hampton and the Mets bullpen prevent further runs from scoring. Unfortunately, Liván Hernández does the same, continuing to frustrate the Mets hitters at every turn. When New York mounts something close to a threat against him, loading the bases with two outs in the top of the eighth, San Francisco calls on hard-throwing righty reliever Félix Rodríguez, and he fans Darryl Hamilton before dancing off the mound in jubilation.

After closer Robb Nen secures the final three outs, the Pac Bell crowd sings along with an ear-rattling blast of "Who Let the Dogs Out?" the earworm mega-hit of the summer. The Mets are surprised to hear this song, and to see many Giants fans brandishing signs referencing it, as they've come to believe this is *their* song. "Who Let the Dogs Out?" was heard thundering through the Shea PA system after Mets wins as early as August, and soon supplanted the "mojo risin'" coda of "L.A. Woman" as 2000's celebratory tune of choice. The Mets are evidently unaware this song has been adopted by almost every other team as well. Even the Yankees, who update their audio fare once every geological era, have begun playing the song during mid-inning breaks.

Picking "Who Let the Dogs Out?" as your signature tune in the summer of 2000 is akin to having picked "The Hustle" in 1975 or "Thriller" in 1984. You need not seek this song out, for it is inescapable. That the Mets would believe this song to be their exclusive property indicates almost as much hubris as a team that believed its path to the World Series would be easy. The Mets almost forgot that they were the Mets. Game one reminds them.

* * *

After the game, the Mets obsess over the strike call to Barry Bonds that wasn't, and the San Francisco rally it sparked. "Ninety-nine times out of one hundred, it's going to the Hall of Famer," Mike Hampton stews. Darryl Hamilton concedes that a hitter of Bonds's reputation "deserves" the call, "But it's the playoffs, and we're trying to win out there. So we don't want anyone given things." In their refusal to let it go, the Mets sound a lot like they did after Mike Piazza's beaning at the hands of Roger Clemens. That incident haunted them for weeks, but they have only twenty-four hours to forget this latest perceived injustice before taking the field for game two. They must also figure out what to do with their outfield, because the ankle sprain Derek Bell suffered will knock him out of action for the remainder of the playoffs. Already, obituaries are being written about the Mets' championship hopes. Murray Chass compares this year's game one to last year's—the exciting win over Randy Johnson in Arizona—and concludes, "The Mets served notice yesterday that their playoff run this year might not be so scintillating."

Game two is therefore a must win for the Mets. Fortunately for them, they will send Al Leiter to the mound, who has prevailed in nearly all of their must-win games of the past two seasons. He will pitch on extra rest, which has always served him well, and will bring to the mound outstanding stats against left-handed batters (only fourteen hits allowed to southpaws all year). The righties haven't had a great time against him in 2000 either. In a pregame interview for Fox, right-handed batter Jeff Kent compares facing Leiter to squaring off against a tennis player, both for his propensity to go right after hitters and for his habit of punctuating each pitch with an emphatic grunt.

Al Leiter is opposed by fellow southpaw Shawn Estes, who possesses an impressive curveball and Leiter-like power over lefties (who batted only .216 against him this season) but who also possesses a less-impressive propensity to lose the strike zone for long stretches. His wildness burns him in the top of the second when he hits Robin Ventura with a pitch and walks two more batters to load the bases with one out. Estes nearly wriggles off the hook by getting Al Leiter to hit a grounder that results in an out at home. This brings to the plate Timo Pérez, drawing the start in right in place of the injured Bell. Pérez looked overmatched in his first at bat, striking out looking on a nasty Estes curve and backing away from the plate as he did so. This time, he golf-swings at the first pitch and lashes it through the infield. Two runs score, stunning the crowd so thoroughly that overjoyed, obscenity-laced cheers from the Mets' dugout can be clearly heard on the television broadcast.

The Giants strike back in the bottom half, beginning when Jeff Kent hits a bloop single, takes second on a stolen base, and scores as Ellis Burks lashes a double down the left-field line. This troubles Al Leiter, who curses at himself on the mound for leaving a pitch up to Burks, but he is even more troubled in the bottom of the third when he walks Shawn Estes on four pitches, and he continues to murmur self-criticism after every pitch to the following batters. Then Mike Bordick handles a grounder poorly and throws too late to second, a small disaster reminiscent of the brain cramps against the Braves in the 1999 playoffs. Estes neglects to slide, however, and he rolls his ankle before staggering away from the bag. An alert Edgardo Alfonzo tags him out before the pitcher can be helped off the field.

Leiter escapes the inning without further incident, while Estes's spot is taken by Kirk Reuter, a right-handed starter relegated to long-man duty in the playoffs. If the Mets hope they will be able to take advantage of a lesser pitcher, they are soon disabused of that notion. In sharp contrast to his predecessor, Reuter is an inveterate strike thrower, and the Mets are unprepared for the sudden shift in strategy. When Reuter leaves the game after 4 1/3 scoreless innings, he receives a standing ovation from the appreciative home crowd.

The Mets' anemic bats seem of little concern, however, for Al Leiter is in total control for most of the game, carving up the Giants hitters in precise, efficient fashion. They seem of even less concern after the top of the ninth, when Edgardo Alfonzo wallops a two-run home run to left center, expanding New York's lead to 4–1. Like his grand slam against the Diamondbacks in 1999, Alfonzo's homer takes much of the life out of the home crowd as it sails through the air. This game appears to be all over but the shouting.

And then Barry Bonds, held in check to this point, greets Al Leiter in the bottom of the ninth with a long leadoff double into the right-center gap. There seems to be no point in pushing Leiter any further, so the Mets summon a well-rested Armando Benítez. The first batter he faces, Jeff Kent, bounces a ball deep in the shortstop hole, another grounder that Mike Bordick cannot quite handle, resulting in an infield hit that brings the tying run to the plate. After Benítez induces a weak pop-up for the first out of the inning, Dusty Baker sends up lefty batter J. T. Snow to pinch-hit.

Distracted by Barry Bonds, who dances off of second begging for a pick-off throw, Benítez falls behind Snow before offering him a blazing fastball right down the heart of the plate. Snow belts it down the right-field line, just high and just far enough to land on the very top of the giant wall in front of McCovey Cove. The home crowd holds its breath until the ball lands with a *clank* on the tin fronting of the wall's summit, ringing with metallic certainty like a double hit off the Green Monster. A three-run homer. A tie game.

This game now seems as firmly in the Giants' grasp as it once did in the Mets'. The home team is so confident as game two hits extra innings that they send Félix Rodríguez back to the mound for the top of the tenth, despite him having surrendered the homer to Alfonzo in the ninth. Rodríguez responds by inducing two quick outs to start the frame before Bobby Valentine sends up Darryl Hamilton as a pinch hitter. Hamilton, an ex-Giant, draws a few spiteful boos and derisive chants of "DAR-RYL" from the local fans and is still stinging from the day before, when he felt shown up by the "little dance" Rodríguez executed after striking him out. He tells himself, *You gotta get this guy after what he did yesterday*, and makes good on his promise by lining the first pitch into the right-center gap and sprinting out of the batter's box, desperate to get into scoring position. Giant center fielder Calvin Murray is stunned to see Hamilton rounding for second, and his throw is a hair too late to nail the runner. Moments later, Jay Payton also swings hard at the first pitch he sees and lines it to center for a single. By the time Murray's throw hits the infield, Hamilton has slid across the plate, giving the Mets the lead once more.

Like the Giants, the Mets tempt fate by bringing back the man who gave up a damaging homer in the ninth to pitch the tenth. Given this shot at redemption, Armando Benítez allows a leadoff single to pinch hitter Armando Rios. His brutal night ends there. Now John Franco, owner of four hundred regular-season saves, will try to earn his first in the postseason. After a sac bunt moves the runner to second, Franco receives an enormous break when Rios attempts to cross over to third on a sharp grounder hit in front of him. Halfway to the bag, Rios stutters for a moment, realizing his grievous error but also realizing he can do nothing but commit to it now, and is tagged with room to spare for the second out.

The Giants are down to their final out, but to secure that out John Franco will need to face Barry Bonds. Franco's first two pitches miss the zone, and though he gets some help when Bonds swings wildly at a high fastball for strike one, he fails to help himself by hurling a slider in the dirt for ball three. Walking Bonds to put the winning run on base and bring Jeff Kent to the plate would be bad. Throwing a get-me-over strike that Bonds could crush to end the game would be worse.

The next pitch catches the knees by the slimmest of margins and is called a strike. An incredulous Bonds throws his head back in disgust at the call. Then, another high fastball that Bonds barely misses, fouling it sharply past first base.

As the clock strikes midnight in New York, Mike Piazza calls for another fastball. John Franco shakes him off. He wants to throw a changeup. "I've been making a living for seventeen years getting people out on my changeup," he says later. "What better time to throw it than that time?" Franco follows his instincts and unleashes that money-making pitch. If strike two was close to the border of the strike zone, this one is even more so. The home plate umpire waits for a half second, one that passes like an eternity to anyone watching, before rendering his verdict: a histrionic punch-out, and a 5–4 Mets win.

Bonds arches backward in agony while Franco pumps his fist and Piazza runs out to the mound with congratulations. They are soon joined by their teammates, who can be heard whooping and hollering over a silent home crowd. Somehow, despite the disaster of the ninth inning and the near-death experience of the tenth, this series is tied at one game apiece.

The method of victory in game two suits this team. "If Armando Benítez had worked out of the ninth inning without incident," writes Tyler Kepner in the *Times*, "and the Mets had taken a tidy victory with them to Shea Stadium—well, they would not be the Mets." But there is a wrinkle to all this jubilation, and T. J. Quinn of the *Daily News* dares mention the elephant in the room. "Whenever a game gets close in the rest of this postseason," Quinn counsels, "the Mets will remember that Benítez, one of the best closers in the game, has blown two saves in his last two playoff games." New York's best chance at advancing far into October this year, it seems, is to give Benítez as little rope as possible.

* * *

The Mets know that when they play their next game on October 7, Shea Stadium's stands are sure to be packed to the rafters with Mets fans ready to explode. Two days at Pac Bell Park make Shea seem even homelier than usual, but defensive New York sportswriters insist its lack of charm works to the Mets' advantage. According to Mark Kriegel of the *Post*, "The Giants are accustomed to good fans. They get loud. But it's a well-mannered sort of loud. It's not the same profane menace you hear at Shea." Most Mets agree with this assessment. "Now they've got to come to the jungle," says Benny Agbayani. Rick Reed, who will start game three for the Mets, remembers the last playoff contest waged at Shea, the Grand Slam Single game, when he watched the entire stadium sway under the thunderous weight of all the fans jumping up and down in jubilation. "I am glad I was on the New York side," Reed confesses, "because that was scary."

Reed and his teammates may count on a wild Shea crowd to upset the Giants, but when the press raises the specter of spooky, shaky Shea to San Francisco's game three starter, Russ Ortiz, he is unfazed. "I like being in New York," the young righty says. "It's the kind of city where the town likes baseball, and they get excited for it. And I think I enjoy that." *But what about New York's famously brutal fans?* reporters ask, as if this were Ortiz's major league debut and not his third full season. "Any time you get a packed stadium, a lot of the time the sounds are muffled anyway," he insists. The media is either ignorant or forgetful of the fact that Ortiz has already won two games in his career at Shea and has yet to lose to the Mets in any stadium.

The Giants' righty throws with the same hand as Rick Reed but otherwise shares little with his opposite number. Ortiz dominates with a boring fastball and sharp breaking pitches, while Reed's offerings top out in the low nineties. Like his injured teammate Shawn Estes, Ortiz can lose the strike zone at times and finished second in the league in walks while also uncorking thirteen wild pitches. Reed, by contrast, is a serial strike thrower who is stingy with free passes; a graphic on the Fox broadcast labels Reed a "poor man's Greg Maddux." Ortiz hails from sunny Van Nuys, California, and sports a never-shaved smoothness, with an almost regal Roman nose. Rick Reed of Huntington, West Virginia, takes the mound with a fair amount of stubble, looking like a beleaguered dad woken up too early on his day off.

The Shea crowd is whipped into a frenzy two pitches deep, but it has nothing to do with the offering from Rick Reed. Fans are reacting to the out-of-town scoreboard, on which a definitive F lights up next to the score of the other National League divisional series: Cardinals 7, Braves 1. St. Louis has completed a three-game sweep in which they utterly embarrassed Atlanta, and Atlanta utterly embarrassed themselves. The news is followed by a mock tomahawk chop, executed by nearly all in attendance in the manner of someone who knows their longtime tormentor is safely behind bars.

Though scoreboard-induced schadenfreude stirs the crowd into a fine lather, their enthusiasm is soon dampened by Russ Ortiz, who holds the Mets hitless through the first five innings. As for Rick Reed, he Houdinis his way out of several jams before his luck catches up with him in the top of the fourth, when he allows four singles that lead to two runs. The crowd, expected to shout Ortiz into submission, instead murmurs to itself, waiting for signs of life from their team. Reed swears he can hear a pin drop as the fifty-six thousand fans behave as if strained quiet will be rewarded.

If this is a strategy, it pays no dividends until the bottom of the sixth, when Ortiz starts the frame by walking Mike Bordick on four straight pitches, none of them close. With each offering out of the zone, the fans tick a bit louder, hoping Ortiz's infamous wildness has caught up with him. Darryl Hamilton, pinch-hitting for Reed, rockets a single between first and second, New York's first hit at last, as Bordick moves to third. Timo Pérez follows by dunking a single in front of Barry Bonds in left to bring home the Mets' first run, and with the crowd in full voice again, they appear to be poised for much more.

They get nothing. After Edgardo Alfonzo grounds out, the Giants issue an intentional walk to Mike Piazza to load the bases and call on lefty reliever Alan Embree to face Robin Ventura. As a frustrated Ortiz throws a glove-tossing tantrum in the dugout, Embree induces an inning-ending double play.

Once again, the Shea faithful slump into disappointed disquiet and remain there as the Mets are turned aside in the seventh. The eighth inning begins with promise as Mike Bordick is hit by a pitch, but this gift is followed by two quick, listless outs. The frame only continues because Lenny Harris is judged to have beaten out the back-end of a potential double play, a questionable call and a break that gives the Mets a slim chance, should they finally be able to collect a clutch hit.

Dusty Baker was criticized after game two for sticking with Félix Rodríguez instead of using his closer to silence the Mets, so with Edgardo Alfonzo due up and the ballpark organ playing its own rendition of the Ramones' "I Wanna Be Sedated," he calls on Robb Nen to secure the final four outs. Nen has numbers remarkably similar to those of Armando Benítez (forty-one saves and ninety-two strikeouts in sixty-eight appearances) and has not blown a save since July 2. He does not hold runners well, however, so when Nen delivers his first pitch to Alfonzo, Lenny

Harris swipes second easily. With the tying run now a hit away from scoring, Alfonzo supplies that hit by leaping on a hung slider and ripping it down the left-field line for a double. Harris races home, high-fiving teammates as he crosses the plate.

After Nen fans Mike Piazza to end the inning, it's impossible to avoid comparisons with the Grand Slam Single game. Conditions are different, to be sure, the pale wind of 2000 far milder than the nagging rain of 1999. But like game five of 1999's championship series, a cloudy October afternoon gives way to a chilly evening, and both teams are frustrated in their every attempt to pull ahead. The Yankees are hosting their division series in the evening, making this the first time that two playoff games are played in New York City on the same day. To mark this historic occasion, Mayor Giuliani attends the Mets-Giants game before leaving to catch the Yankees' fourth game against the A's. By the time he arrives for the first pitch in the Bronx, the end of the game in Queens is still nowhere in sight.

As the game drags on, the Mets and the Giants play a game of "Can you top this missed opportunity?" John Franco and Armando Benítez work around leadoff hits in the ninth and tenth, while Félix Rodríguez starts the eleventh by allowing a pair of singles but retires the next three Mets in order, a sequence that includes an epic at bat from Jay Payton, who fouls off seven pitches and breaks three at bats before striking out.

Due to the flurry of pinch hitters and other subs Bobby Valentine uses in the eleventh, the team he must field in the top of the twelfth is not his ideal lineup. Todd Pratt takes over behind the plate, Joe McEwing takes third, and Robin Ventura moves across the infield for a rare appearance at first base. On the mound, Rick White allows yet another leadoff man to reach, but strands him like all the rest. When the game crawls into the thirteenth, White gives himself a bigger challenge by allowing a pair of singles, allowing Barry Bonds to bat with two out. A warmed-up Glendon Rusch stares in from the bullpen, expecting a call that never comes. Rather than go with a lefty-on-lefty matchup, Bobby Valentine sticks with White, a gut decision that even the manager seems to doubt as he rests his chin in his hand, afraid to watch what happens next. He is rewarded when Bonds swings at White's first pitch, throwing his head back in disgust with himself as he does so, and pops out to second.

In the bottom of the thirteenth, Benny Agbayani steps up with one out and several failures weighing on his mind. On multiple occasions tonight, he was asked to lay down a bunt and failed each time. Had he succeeded even once, the game might have been over already. So when reliever Aaron Fultz throws him a meatball right down the heart of the plate, he crushes it with the anger of someone trying to prove a point. There is little doubt from the moment he makes contact that the ball will leave the park. On the crack of the bat, the entire Mets dugout surges up the steps and onto the field, sure they will be celebrating in a matter of seconds.

Five hours and twenty-two minutes after the first pitch, the man who gave the Mets their first win of the year in Tokyo comes through with one of the biggest home runs in franchise postseason history, the bow atop a thrilling 3–2 Mets victory. "He will be canonized now," declares the *New York Times*, "the hero of one of the greatest postseason games in recent years." And it is the same man who was destined to start his season in the minors before his Japan heroics. "Bobby Valentine told me things have a way of working out," Agbayani recalls of this dark time. "I didn't understand that. Now I do."

* * *

Though the Mets have already announced who they will send to the mound in game four, everyone keeps asking them if they are sure. Faced with a choice between Glendon Rusch and Bobby Jones, Bobby Valentine stuns everyone by going with the aging righty over the young lefty. This is shocking both because the Giants are susceptible to left-handed pitching, and and because Jones seems a gamble at best. Bobby Jones began his year by posting an ERA close to ten and was asked to spend a few weeks in the middle of it at triple-A relearning his craft. Though he had enough major league experience to refuse the assignment—he debuted in 1993 and has toiled for Mets teams that mostly ranged from wretched to mediocre—the ugly first half of his season forced him to humble himself. He pitched well after rejoining the big league club, but he is not the coup de grace a fan wants to see in a potential series clincher. Even after his minor league rehab work, Jones remains a Rick Reed-like control artist whose fastball struggles to break glass on a good day.

In explaining his choice, Bobby Valentine insists Jones is a "pro" who knows how to complement his fastball with an array of breaking pitches. "Look it up in the dictionary and you'll see his picture beside the word 'pro,'" the manager says, as if trying to pad out a book report. ("Webster's dictionary defines 'pro' as . . .") Everyone seems to doubt the seriousness of Valentine's choice. Even Jones's wife, Kristi, asks the manager if her husband will really start game four, as if she herself can barely believe the choice. When Valentine confirms it, she says, "You won't be sorry that he is. He'll be pitching the game of his life."

As Jones climbs the mound at 4:00 p.m., the PA system blares Hank Williams Jr.'s "A Country Boy Can Survive." Temperatures stand near fifty degrees, with a low October sun that will be square in the hitter's eyes until dusk. These conditions will work in the pitcher's favor, as will the condition of his opponents. Following last night's brutal defeat, every member of the Giants says the right things. ("When you get beat like that, you just tip your cap," says an unusually gracious Barry Bonds.) But the deathly silence of the pregame visiting clubhouse, and the haunted looks on their faces before game four, show that the loss took more out of the Giants than they care to admit. Dusty Baker can't even remember what inning it was when Benny Agbayani's homer finally beat him. "It was long," is all he can recall of the game.

If Bobby Valentine draws some raised eyebrows for his choice of starter in game four, the same goes double for Dusty Baker. With his back against the wall, he could have called on Liván Hernández to pitch on short rest, or turned to Kirk Rueter, the lefty who pitched so well in relief of Shawn Estes in game two. Instead, he chooses Mark Gardner, a well-traveled righty who split his season between the bullpen and the back of the rotation. His insistence that Gardner is a "big game pitcher" sounds a lot like Valentine asserting Bobby Jones is a "pro." Jon Miller, calling the game for ESPN, doubts either starter will make it past the sixth inning.

In the bottom of the first, after recording the first two outs easily, Gardner pitches carefully to Mike Piazza before walking him. He has no fear of walking the catcher because Robin Ventura is due up next. The third baseman failed to collect his first hit of the postseason until the eleventh inning of the marathon game three and is coming off the worst offensive season of his career. Gardner is so unafraid of Ventura, his first pitch is a vulnerable get-me-over fastball. The Ventura of 1999 reappears for one glorious moment as he clubs Gardner's gift and sends it over the fence in right-center to a spot not far from where the Grand Slam Single landed.

With a two-run lead on his side, Bobby Jones retires the Giants in order in the first four innings, mostly on grounders. Some of the outs are hit rather hard, however, and his trickery appears to be wearing off when Jeff Kent leads off the top of the fifth with a double just over Ventura's leaping glove. Kent then tags and moves to third as Ellis Burks hits a fly ball to right, missing a home run by a few short feet. But though the Giants load the bases on a pair of walks, they ultimately come up empty, in large part because Dusty Baker allows his pitcher to bat with two outs.

One factor in Baker's decision to let Gardner bat must be his faith that a lineup with Kent and Bonds and Burks will eventually do *something* against a soft tosser like Bobby Jones. The Mets force him to regret his decision in the bottom of the fifth, with a rally that begins when Jones advances to first on a dropped third strike. After Timo Pérez doubles, Edgardo Alfonzo knocks his own double to left center to drive home two more runs and extend New York's lead to 4–0.

Though the Mets score no more in the inning or the game, this doubling of their advantage, coming right on the heels of the Giants' failure to capitalize on Jeff Kent's leadoff double, takes away what little wind remained in the visitors' sails. San Francisco goes down in order in the sixth, and again in the seventh. For the rest of the game, the Giants fail to even come close to a hit. When Jones records the first two outs with ease in the eighth, the Shea crowd begins to chant "BOB-BY! BOB-BY!" before every pitch, a level of enthusiasm the longtime Met has never experienced before. When Jones bats for himself in the bottom of the eighth, having earned the right to finish what he started, the fans reward him with a standing ovation, and continue cheering even as he strikes out.

In the ninth, with the stands pounding out a steady chorus of rhythmic applause, Jones again retires the first two batters with minimal effort. The last man standing for San Francisco is Barry Bonds, and he sees no reason to prolong the suffering. Swatting at Jones's first pitch, Bonds skies it to deep left center, where Jay Payton runs it down for the final out. The Mets dugout spills onto the field for its second dogpile in as many days, this time centered on the man at the mound.

Jon Miller calls this "A masterpiece!" and Jones's performance in the Mets' 4–0 series-clinching win is every bit of that. Eight of nine innings, Jones set down the Giants in order. It is the first one-hit shutout in the playoffs in thirty-two long years, and it was pitched by a man who was an afterthought when these playoffs began, who missed out on the playoffs last year due to a shoulder injury with awful timing, who'd humiliated himself at midseason by accepting a triple-A assignment because his career was hanging in the balance. The *Times* labels Jones's story "too hokey for Hollywood."

While the Mets pop champagne and spray it gleefully at each other, the Giants are stunned into silence, wondering how the team with the best record in baseball could watch their World Series dreams dissolve in less than twenty-four hours, felled first by a rotund Hawaiian who almost began the year in the minors, then by a pitcher who *did* spend part of his season in the minors. "This will definitely eat at us in the off-season," grumbles Jeff Kent, chafing at the thought that Bobby Jones and the Mets were the instrument of his demise. "I believe we were the better ballclub. We'll be asking ourselves, 'Why couldn't we get to the Mets?'"

The Mets make note of Kent's sour grapes. As they prep for the Cardinals and the championship series, one wag clips out the headline "CONFIDENT KENT STILL SAYS GIANTS ARE BETTER." "He might be right," Darryl Hamilton says, "but we're still going to St. Louis."

* * *

Betting men still like the Yankees' chances, even if few others do. The Bronx Bombers ended their season in a tailspin while their first-round opponents, the A's, surged to finish a step ahead of the Mariners in the American League West. And yet, New York is still favored to take the series, according to Vegas oddsmakers.

The bookies are perhaps swayed by the turnaround of Roger Clemens. In 1999, Clemens was relegated to the back end of the playoff rotation, but in 2000 he's pitched so well since the ugly beaning incident that he earns the game one start on October 3. The *Post* captures the consensus when it judges Roger Clemens the second-half MVP for the Yanks for the pitching performances that followed the fastball he hurled toward Mike Piazza's skull. ("He came. He beaned. He conquered," says Kevin Kernan.) Clemens subdues the A's for four innings, allowing no more offense than an infield single over that stretch, while his teammates build a 2–0 lead—the first time the Yankees have held an advantage at any point in seven full games' worth of innings.

"Being on top on the scoreboard obviously gave the Yankees vertigo," quips Ira Berkow in the *Times*, commenting on how quickly the lead is lost. Undone by wildness and shoddy fielding behind him, Clemens allows four runs over the fifth and sixth innings, the bullpen allows one more, and Jason Isringhausen sets the Yanks down in order in the ninth as Oakland prevails, 5–3. Paul O'Neill compares the momentum of the A's to a runaway train.

Searching for any kind of formula that will kick-start his sputtering offense, manager Joe Torre drops a slumping Paul O'Neill—number three batter in perpetuity—to sixth in his game two lineup, replacing him with

David Justice. The reconfigured offense collects a pair of two-out hits that plate three runs in the top of the sixth, while Andy Pettitte throws almost eight brilliant innings en route to a 4–0 Yankee win.

Back in the Bronx for game three, the Yankees execute a tidy 4–2 victory behind the pitching of Orlando Hernández, with an assist from a few errors and mental blunders from the A's. The immortal ghosts of the House That Ruth Built are invoked as the reason for the boo-boos, Oakland's youngsters unprepared to combat the weight of history.

With a chance to wrap up the series at home, the Yankees go for the jugular. Rather than pitch a well-rested but shaky Denny Neagle, Joe Torre opts for Roger Clemens. Though The Rocket would pitch on only three days' rest, he is opposed by rookie Barry Zito. The twenty-two-year-old lefty confesses the biggest game he pitched previously was the Cape Cod League championship. He also proclaims he won't get more geared up to pitch this game than any other. The pressure and majesty of Yankee Stadium had eaten up many a young whippersnapper who told himself the same thing. It had eaten up many of his teammates the night before.

When game four is played, however, it's Clemens who melts down early, surrendering a three-run homer in the opening inning and six runs overall before exiting in the sixth to a chorus of Bronx cheers. One of the greatest strikeout pitchers in baseball history heads to the showers after watching only seven of his ninety-three pitches go for swings and misses.

Though Oakland wins by the unsightly score of 11–1, Clemens had pitched on short rest to give his team its best shot to wrap up the division series at home. He surely thought that this effort, plus the great second half of his season, would buy him some equity with the press. If so, he thought wrong. "The Yankees' most notorious mercenary . . . kept intact his reputation for routinely failing to deliver in must-win games," scolds the *Daily News* in a typical postmortem.

In failing to win the series in four games, the Yankees force themselves to not only fly cross-country to play a do-or-die game five the very next day, but to start Andy Pettitte on short rest. The *Times* dares compare Joe Torre's desperation lunge at two short-rest starts in a row to the 1964 Phillies, the gold standard of chokers, who pitched their aces every day in an ultimately futile attempt to stave off a historic collapse.

Everything is unraveling for the Yankees, including their manager's unquestioned authority. Chuck Knoblauch begins the series as a designated hitter but is removed from the lineup due to Joe Torre's offensive finagling. At first, the troubled second baseman sounds all the right notes. ("I'll do whatever I can off the bench," Knoblauch says, though "through clenched teeth," in the description of one reporter.) When the series shifts to New York, however, Knoblauch refuses to take grounders during warm-ups and is summarily benched in games three and four. Knoblauch adopts the defiant Eminem song, "The Way I Am," as his personal anthem, blasting it in the clubhouse like a sullen fifteen-year-old drowning out his nagging parents.

The bleary-eyed Yankees land on the West Coast on October 8 at 6:30 a.m. New York time and arrive at Network Associates Coliseum right before pregame warm-ups, desperate for anything to open their eyes. On cue, the opposition provides them with some emotional caffeine. Prior to the game, when reporters ask Oakland third baseman Eric Chávez about the possibility of ending the Yankee dynasty, he beams at the idea. "It's time for some other people to have some glory here," he says. "But no, they've had a great run." None of this would have reached Yankee ears until after the game, except that for some reason the Chávez interview is broadcast on the titanic videoboards beyond the outfield fences. The Yankees can scarcely believe their ears at the sound of a twenty-two-year-old infielder referring to their run of domination in the past tense.

With Chávez's words acting like a double shot of espresso, the Yankees give Pettitte as much help as possible by scoring six runs in the top of the first. Reinserted in the leadoff spot by a pride-swallowing Joe Torre, Chuck Knoblauch collects two hits in the frame as the Yanks bat around. But a gassed Pettitte falters, allowing two runs in the second, one in the third, and two more in the fourth before getting the hook. Somehow, the bullpen holds feisty Oakland at bay, though the A's bring the tying run to the plate in sixth, eighth, and ninth innings. Mariano Rivera toughs his way through a five-out save to seal the 7–5 Yankee win and the series.

"Who says we're too old?" bellows reliever Mike Stanton in the triumphant visiting clubhouse. "We're just old enough!" This is the tone of the Yankees' celebration after the win in Oakland: joyous but defensive. Jack Curry of the *Times* compares this team's on-again, off-again daring to a toddler standing on a beach, deliberating if he wants to get splashed by the waves or not.

It escapes no one's notice that the two losses in the series came on starts from Roger Clemens. He'd pitched so well in the second half of this season, yet no one forgot his checkered postseason history. No one forgot how much he still had to prove. And no one would let him forget.

CHAPTER 16
The Spotlight

THE NATIONAL LEAGUE Championship Series matchup between the Mets and Cardinals brings with it memories of the 1980s, a time very much in resurgence at the moment. The two teams traded National League East crowns toward the end of that decade, St. Louis eking out titles in 1985 and 1987, New York dominating in 1986 and 1988. The Cardinals won on speed and defense, the Mets on pitching and slugging. The Cards' stars were speedster Vince Coleman and glove wizard Ozzie Smith, while the Mets boasted the arm of Doc Gooden and the bat of Darryl Strawberry.

The two teams, and their fans, could not have disliked each other more if they tried. The overloaded Mets hated to be thwarted by the Cardinals' slap hitters and speed demons, while the Cardinals couldn't stomach a Mets team that embodied every stereotype of arrogant folks Back East. Their fans referred to the Mets as "Pond Scum," an epithet coined either by late-night host David Letterman or a St. Louis DJ, depending on who you ask, and which endures into the new millennium.

This rivalry tapered off when the Mets and Cardinals each fell on hard times in the early 1990s, then disappeared altogether when the divisional realignment of 1994 removed St. Louis from the National League East. There's little hint of the 1980s-style Cardinals in their current incarnation, who rely on the slugging of Jim Edmonds, Mark McGwire, and Will Clark. In the division series, St. Louis pummeled every Atlanta hurler they faced and swept the Braves three straight, an outcome that stunned their manager. Asked if he thought his team would sweep, skipper Tony La Russa said he wouldn't have bet so much as a dollar on that proposition.

La Russa came to the team in 1996 with an impeccable résumé, having piloted the Oakland A's of Mark McGwire and José Canseco to three pennants and a championship. Like Bobby Valentine, La Russa is often taken to task for his cerebral style of managing. Unlike Valentine, La Russa has been rewarded for it with many prominent admirers in baseball's intellectual class. (Conservative political columnist and baseball writer George Will penned a tome, *Men at Work*, partially dedicated to proclaiming La Russa's unqualified genius.) When first hired in St. Louis, La Russa was put in the awkward position of quietly shunting Ozzie Smith—the team's beloved but aging shortstop—into a part-time role, an unpopular move that one local writer compared to "demoting the pope." Despite the controversy, La Russa led the Cardinals to the playoffs that first year in St. Louis, where they breezed through the divisional round and took a three-games-to-one lead on the Braves in the National League Championship Series. Then Atlanta won three games in a row, the final two by blowout margins, to swipe the pennant from their grasp. This, residual resentment from the Ozzie Smith benching, and the three mediocre seasons that followed put La Russa in the hot seat, but the success of 2000 has been so resounding that the Cardinals faithful are reconsidering their opinions of George Will's genius.

If there is any true animosity between these squads, it comes between La Russa and Bobby Valentine, who share a genuine dislike that each does little to hide. The last straw for Valentine came after the 1988 World Series, when he was still managing the Rangers, and La Russa chastised him with the officiousness of a Victorian schoolmarm for the crime of cheering for the Dodgers (captained by his mentor, Tommy Lasorda) rather than exercise American League solidarity and root for La Russa's A's. Even Valentine had to marvel at the chutzpah of these objections.

Mere minutes after dispatching the Giants, the Mets pronounce themselves excited to take on the Cardinals. These preferences are couched in the team's elation at not having to face the Braves, and are peppered with praise for Cardinals fans and their intense enthusiasm for their team (with digs, both implicit and explicit, of Braves fans for their lack of the same). Bobby Valentine says, "I think the crowd [in St. Louis] is much more supportive than the crowd in Atlanta, and so there might be some more emotion here in this series." But the Cardinals sense disrespect in the Mets' professions, an implication that they are an inferior opponent to the Braves. The New York media add fuel to this fire when they pen condescending reports portraying St. Louis as a Podunk backwater, mocking the *gee-whiz* civic enthusiasm that inspires a city to dye fountains red (or pink, really, once the dye is diluted by running water). "Ask any local what there is to do here and you'll earn a blank stare or hear laughter," snickers one *Daily News* writer. A colleague characterizes the uniform sea of red in the Busch Stadium stands as more pep rally than baseball crowd. If the Cardinals read the New York papers, they would also have cause to feel woefully underestimated as a baseball team. One *Post* scribe sees the Cardinals as "a straight, belt-high fastball splitting home plate in half. All [the Mets] have to do is make solid contact." In the eyes of Gotham's newsmen, St. Louis is flyover country before landing in an all-New York Fall Classic. New York is already looking beyond them to a Subway Series—looking beyond St. Louis to better admire themselves.

The Cardinals' resentment toward this apparent dismissal is evident in every response their players offer to even the most innocent of press queries. Asked how he will handle Al Leiter and Mike Hampton, Jim Edmonds shoots back, "How good is [Tom] Glavine?" Edmonds and his team hung seven runs on Glavine's ledger in game two of the division series. Hadn't the New Yorkers watched that series? Or were they too busy counting Subway Series chickens before they hatched?

The Cardinals take the collective refuge of the Little Team That Could. A squad that boasts an All-Star lineup now acts as if it's a plucky sandlot team taking on the rich snobs from New York City. "There are glamour cities people are talking about and a little team from the Midwest has come in there a bunch of times," Tony La Russa proclaims of his team's history. "Nobody's talked about us all year," insists veteran outfielder Eric Davis.

Davis's wounded comment is not true by a longshot; the size and virulence of the Cardinal fan base, combined with their hot play in 2000, has forced baseball writers to talk about them all season. The Cardinals persist in saying they're being ignored and disrespected anyway, in part because this allows them to mask some unpleasant truths. New York media provincialism may inspire many observers to pick the Mets as the favorites in the series, but St. Louis has enough issues to draw that conclusion regardless.

The Cardinals' most glaring issue is the near absence of Mark McGwire. After patellar tendonitis knocked him out of action for much of the summer, McGwire was well enough by September to swing a bat but still in no shape to field first base. St. Louis chose to carry McGwire on its postseason roster as a not-so-secret weapon, and this paid a dividend when he belted a huge pinch-hit homer in game two of the division series. However, his knee remains in such bad shape that he must be swapped for a pinch runner if he reaches base on anything other than a home run, a two-for-one contingency that puts a strain on St. Louis's bench. The issue of when to use this special arrow in La Russa's quiver will loom large throughout the championship series.

The Cards' lineup is further compromised by the loss of catcher Mike Matheny, one of the better defensive backstops in the game, who cut his hand in a freak knife accident and will miss all of the playoffs. To compensate, the Cardinals are carrying three catchers on their roster, but none of them measure up to Matheny either at the plate or behind it.

There is also the state of the starting rotation, which suffered multiple setbacks during the division series. During game one against Atlanta, rookie Rick Ankiel experienced a baffling loss of control that called his future effectiveness into question. Then Garrett Stephenson was forced to leave the game three clincher due to elbow tendinitis, making another start from him unlikely. These calamities have stretched the Cardinals' pitching staff dangerously thin.

Even so, most observers predict a hard-fought series. Keith Hernandez, who won a World Series ring with both St. Louis and New York, predicts the National League Championship Series will go seven games, though he hesitates to say who will come out on top, while the pregame crew on Fox (broadcaster of the NLCS) assumes it will last at least six games. Part of the reason for believing this, despite the Cardinals' handicaps, is the fact that the Mets seldom make anything easy on themselves in October.

* * *

Bobby Valentine will again start Mike Hampton and Al Leiter, in that order, to begin the championship series. Once more he explains his reasoning no more than to say, "It was the way we started the season." In game one, Hampton will be opposed by Darryl Kile, a pitcher who has dominated the Mets for years. Kile no-hit the team as for Houston in 1993 and, before losing a decision to them at Shea Stadium last season, had not taken a loss in New York in eight seasons. He spent one miserable year in Colorado, where his trademark curveball refused to break at mile-high altitudes, before a trade to St. Louis helped him recapture his ace-like form. Tony La Russa has already discussed starting Kile on short rest in game four—a risky move, but one that must be considered given the unsure statuses of Garrett Stephenson and Rick Ankiel.

Game one unfolds on October 11, a warm but breezy autumn evening in St. Louis. Gusting winds will have their way with fly balls all evening. Batting leadoff, as he had for much of the division series following Derek Bell's injury, Timo Pérez belts a stand-up double off of Kile and soon scores on a Mike Piazza two-bagger. In the dugout, the sight of Piazza's first RBI of the playoffs inspires bench coach John Stearns to yell, "The Monster is out of the cage!" After the game, he explains "the Monster" is his nickname for Piazza, his cheer a prediction (or hope) that the Mets' catcher has shaken off the funk that gripped him since early September. (When Fox shows replay video of Stearn bellowing this phrase, his odd outburst provides the team and its fans with a rallying cry for the remainder of the playoffs.) Shortly after Piazza's monstrous RBI, Robin Ventura knocks in another run on a sac fly. In the blink of an eye, the Mets are up 2–0.

The unanimously red-clad Busch Stadium crowd, quieted by this outburst, perks up in slow increments when Mike Hampton takes the mound in the bottom of the first, falls behind each hitter he faces, and loads the bases. Though the Cardinals walk away empty this time, they continually threaten in most of the innings that follow. It seems only a matter of time before they break the fragile lefty over their knee.

Somehow, they never do. Hampton dances around a two-out walk in the second and a one-out single and wild pitch in the third. He sidesteps an error from Benny Agbayani in the fifth and a Will Clark double in the sixth. In the seventh, Jim Edmonds goes the other way on a Hampton fastball and comes within inches of blasting a game-tying homer. Hampton is so afraid Edmond's belt will leave the yard that he refuses to breathe, fearing the slightest breath might push the ball over the fence. Agbayani scrambles back to the left field wall as autumn gusts toss the ball to and fro and makes an awkward shoulder-high catch for the final out of the inning. Calling the game for Fox, Tim McCarver compares the Cardinals' offensive futility to "a football team that's only good between the twenty and twenty." The St. Louis offense racks up plenty of yardage on Hampton but cannot punch the ball into the end zone. The Mets, meanwhile, make the most of their opportunities. Though Darryl Kile pitches better than Mike Hampton most of the game, when Hampton legs out an infield hit in the top of the fifth, Edgardo Alfonzo knocks him in to expand New York's lead.

Bobby Valentine turns to John Franco to handle the eighth inning and the lefty allows a two-out single. Thus is the Great Mark McGwire Conundrum faced for the first time in this series: to bat or not to bat? Fox's cameras show McGwire in the dugout, batting helmet on his head and bat in hand, but La Russa holds Big Mac in abeyance until he can represent the tying run and sends up Shawon Dunston—goat-then-hero of last year's Grand Slam Single game—as a pinch hitter instead. Franco induces an easy fly out from Dunston to keep McGwire on the bench, all dressed up with no place to go.

This is the last opportunity the Cardinals receive, as the Mets make their lead McGwire-proof in the ninth. Todd Zeile starts off the frame with a line-drive homer over Dunston's glove in center field. Moments later, Jay Payton zips a fastball down the left-field line for a two-run homer to extend New York's lead to six runs, the nail in the coffin that sends many of the locals scurrying for the exits. Though Armando Benítez allows a pair of runs in the ninth after a few errors, the tallies are both unearned and harmless. The Mets prevail 6–2, their pitchers having held the vaunted Cardinals offense hitless with men in scoring position, even in the sloppy ninth inning. Tim McCarver places the Mets "right in the driver's seat." Each of the last seven teams to win the first game of the National League Championship Series has gone on to capture the pennant.

* * *

Going into the National League Championship Series, the entire St. Louis starting rotation beyond Darryl Kile is considered questionable, but no one is more questionable than Rick Ankiel.

A week earlier, Rick Ankiel was the greatest rookie pitching sensation since Hideo Nomo. The lefty possesses a blazing fastball and knee-buckling curveball that each draw comparisons to another southpaw of note, Sandy Koufax. Everyone agrees Ankiel's arm is special, and the Cardinals have gone to great lengths to preserve it, keeping his pitch counts reasonable at a time when most teams have yet to take such care with any of their pitchers. During spring training, St. Louis pitching coach Dave Duncan worked with Ankiel to adjust his footwork so he wouldn't throw across his body, believing this would prevent future arm injuries. The adjustment led to increased wildness, as evidenced by the ninety walks and twelve wild pitches he collected during the regular season, but these were far overshadowed by a K-rate higher than anyone in the league not named Randy Johnson.

This is what inspired Tony La Russa to name Rick Ankiel his game one starter for the division series—an announcement he sprung last minute on both the Braves and the media, going public with his choice immediately after reporters had left a press conference with presumed game one starter Darryl Kile. In the end, however, it was Ankiel who appeared ambushed. In the third inning of game one, the lefty walked four batters and uncorked an astonishing five wild pitches. A pitcher who looked like the second coming of Koufax all season suddenly couldn't toss a straight fastball to save his life. Ankiel's historic wildness led to four Atlanta runs and nearly brought a demoralized Braves team back into the game.

After St. Louis held on to win, La Russa insisted he would still start Ankiel in a hypothetical game four against Atlanta. A series sweep prevented him from making good on his promise, but there is nowhere to hide Ankiel in the series against the Mets. Any thought of skipping him, or burying him deep in the rotation, was eliminated when Garrett Stephenson went down with an elbow injury.

Sending Ankiel to the mound is nearly as much of a gamble as the lineup La Russa assembles for game two, which includes five left-handed batters against Al Leiter, who has been virtually unhittable for lefties this season. It is a La Russian move in the extreme, demonstrating his compulsion to do the opposite of what is expected as a means of baffling the opposition and perhaps show everyone how *hard* he is managing. Remarking on this counterintuitive gambit, and other curious decisions the skipper will make this evening, one *Times* writer heads his game two recap, "Tony La Russa played manager tonight . . ."

The sellout crowd at Busch Stadium greets Rick Ankiel's appearance on the mound with supportive cheers. It is hoped their encouragement can will away the butterflies that are surely churning in Ankiel's stomach and correct whatever mechanical errors have infected his windup.

And then the lefty launches his first pitch of the game over the batter's head.

The crowd lets out a sickly groan, as if they all are witnessing a horrible accident. For his part, Rick Ankiel retains the same calm mien he displayed against the Braves, peering over his glove with an Andy Pettitte-like scowl. Even when the wild pitches fly from his hand, the look on his face is impassive. He alternates well-placed pitches that pick off the corners with others that seem to explode out of another dimension. There is no pattern to any of this, no inciting incidents for the wildness and no soothing signs that bring a return of his precision. Ankiel is more victim of these events than its author.

For a few moments, such unpredictability seems to work to his advantage. Despite the scary start to the at bat (or perhaps because of it), Ankiel strikes out Timo Pérez looking at a curveball on the outside corner, then backs Edgardo Alfonzo into a two-strike hole. He airmails his subsequent pitches, however, walking Alfonzo, and uncorks his first official wild pitch to Mike Piazza, moving the runner to second. After a mound conference, the southpaw regains his composure for a few tantalizing moments and goes full to Mike Piazza before unleashing his second wild pitch, walking the batter and moving Alfonzo to third in one fell swoop. The next pitch he manages to throw over the plate is lofted for a sac fly by Todd Zeile. The crowd cheers anyway, as this marks the second out, which means a third one is close.

But Ankiel walks Robin Ventura on four pitches, none of them wild but none of them close either, and falls behind Benny Agbayani before the batter splits the left-center gap with a double to score Piazza. Ankiel throws one pitch to Jay Payton (high, outside) before Dave Duncan leaps out of the dugout and puts the pitcher out of his misery. He receives a subdued, nervous reception from Cardinals fans as he walks slowly off the field.

With Al Leiter on the mound, a 2–0 lead on their side, and the young hurler's failure weighing heavily on the opposition, the Mets have every reason to feel confident. But the visitors make baffling errors all night that force Leiter to labor more than he should, bringing St. Louis right back into the game. After the Met lefty works around a rare Robin Ventura error in the first, he can't quite sidestep trouble in the second, when a Benny Agbayani misplay puts runners on the corners and a run scores as a tailor-made double-play ball bounces off of Edgardo Alfonzo's chest.

Leiter negotiates around more baserunners in the third and fourth innings, but his teammates hardly fare better against Britt Reames, the first line of defense out of the St. Louis bullpen. Though Reames allows a laser-beam homer to Mike Piazza in the top of the third to expand the Mets' lead to 3–1, he too works around his own teammates' poor defense, and thwarts several attempts to salt this game early for New York. In both the third and fourth innings, a Mets baserunner reaches on a miscue yet is stranded, and in the fifth an Edgardo Alfonzo triple goes wasted.

Through the first thirteen innings of the series, the Cardinals failed to collect a single hit with runners in scoring position. Considering their myriad of opportunities and the talent of their lineup, this tally has to improve at some point, and that point arrives in the bottom of the fifth. After Leiter mishandles a bunt attempt to put a man on base, the Cardinals reach him for a pair of doubles to plate two runs, tying the game at three. Muttering self-deprecating expletives to himself on the mound, Leiter stops the scoring there, then executes his first clean innings of the night by setting down the Cards in order in the sixth and seventh.

The Cards put up zeroes of their own thanks to hard-throwing righty Matt Morris, who keeps the game tied despite a two-out walk in the sixth and a leadoff Todd Zeile double in the seventh. He then returns to retire the first two batters in the top of the eighth before Timo Pérez swings at the first pitch he sees and laces a single to left. Edgardo Alfonzo follows by working a full count, which allows Pérez a head start when he lines a hit into the left-center gap. Jim Edmonds tracks down the ball and heaves it home, but Pérez beats the throw to score the fourth Mets run while Alfonzo takes second on the throw.

The Cardinals intentionally walk Mike Piazza and summon closer Dave Veres from the bullpen, but Todd Zeile defies the gambit by singling to left. Alfonzo scores on the hit, and though Mike Piazza is tagged out while attempting to take third on the play, the Mets boast a 5–3 lead and a well-rested bullpen to protect it as they head into the bottom of the eighth. If New York's relievers can keep the basepaths clear, it will prevent St. Louis from sending Mark McGwire to the plate as the tying run. It will also put Al Leiter in a prime position to win his first playoff game as a Met, and to grab a 2–0 lead in the series.

The world of the Mets is rarely so simple, however, and the same can be said of most appearances by John Franco. After retiring MVP candidate Jim Edmonds with ease (an ease abetted by Edmonds's strange failure to run out a grounder), Franco commits the baffling error of walking light-hitting catcher Carlos Hernández. Will Clark follows by lashing a single into the right-field corner, and though Timo Pérez does an excellent job of cutting the ball off in time to hold Clark to a single, Franco undoes his fine work by bouncing his next offering past Piazza, a wild pitch that scores Hernández and puts Clark on second base as the tying run. Hoping to spur the Mets lefty into a full meltdown, the Busch Stadium crowd serenades him with a mocking chant of "FRAN-CO,

FRAN-CO," with the ballpark organist providing the proper notes for accompaniment.

Now, it seems, is the ideal time to use That Big Redhead sitting in the dugout who was spotted readying himself during a few potential rallies already tonight. But Tony La Russa notes that Turk Wendell, a righty with some history of success against McGwire, is warming up in the bullpen. So after Shawon Dunston makes the second out of the inning, La Russa pinch-hits not with McGwire, but with the right-handed infielder Plácido Polanco. This prompts Bobby Valentine to grab his righty from the bullpen, at which point La Russa replaces Polanco with lefty-batting outfielder J. D. Drew.

This matchup—J. D. Drew vs. Turk Wendell—is the one La Russa has been angling for all along, and Valentine falls right into his trap. Drew fights his way out of an 0-2 count and slashes a single to right center. Jay Payton attempts to pick up the ball with his glove, but the leather can't grip the horsehide, and he overruns it for one costly moment.

Payton's bobble is a disaster and a savior all at once. The bobble is a disaster because it allows the slow-footed Clark to rumble home to tie the game at five and Drew to dash to second as the go-ahead run. The bobble is also disaster because it all but ensures that Mark McGwire will enter the game to pinch-hit for the pitcher's spot, due up next.

And yet, the bobble is a savior, in a perverse way, because Drew's advance to second base opens up first. Now the Mets can safely walk McGwire and instead face a much poorer bat in his place. Some of the Mets are shocked that McGwire would still be sent to the plate to pinch-hit in an obvious intentional walk situation. ("I give Tony La Russa a lot more credit than that," says Turk Wendell later.) Having spent his bench to tie the game, however, La Russa's only available hitter apart from McGwire is Rick Wilkins, a third-string catcher who is a bat in name only. So the earsplitting cheers of Cardinals fans at the sight of McGwire striding to the plate soon become boos as Wendell throws four wide to put him on base intentionally. McGwire performs the perfunctory jog to first and leaves for a pinch runner (last night's starter, Darryl Kile). The local fans are disappointed further when Wendell ends the inning without further incident.

So the eighth inning ends with the Mets having suffered a mere disaster instead of a catastrophe, leaving them in prime position to benefit from a Cardinal calamity in the top of the ninth. It begins with Robin Ventura swatting a hard grounder toward first base. The hit clanks off one of Will Clark's cleats, the ball's carom so long and slow developing that even the snaillike Ventura is able to beat it out for an infield single. Benny Agbayani, who failed in several sacrifice bunt attempts during the division series, executes one here to move Ventura to second, where he is removed in favor of pinch runner Joe McEwing.

Jay Payton follows by dunking a single into center field. If the ball was fielded cleanly, McEwing may not have tried to score on the hit, but Jim Edmonds is not his usual Gold Glove self at the moment. The center fielder fouled a ball off his own foot in the previous inning and has played in obvious pain ever since. (His curious failure to run out a grounder in his last at bat was the most blatant sign.) This blow comes on top of a tailbone injury he suffered in game one when he tripped while fielding a fly ball. So when Payton's hit bounces high off the Busch Stadium carpet, Edmonds can only make a feeble half jump to keep the ball in front of him. It ricochets off his glove and slips behind him, rolling all the way to the wall. He compounds the miscue by jogging after the ball at a pace more befitting a charity fun-run than an outfielder whose team is in danger of falling behind in the ninth. As Edmonds chugs, Joe McEwing scores easily and Payton races all the way to third.

A pair of weak grounders fails to bring home an insurance run for the Mets, but this time it proves of little consequence. The Cardinals bench is depleted, Mark McGwire is in the showers, and his teammates' ability to put a fight in this ugly game has been fully exhausted. Armando Benítez enters in the bottom half for the save and completes his task with little hint of drama.

It is a brutal, interminable mess of a game, full of head-scratching mistakes and bushels of missed opportunities on both sides. At just shy of four hours, it is also the longest nine-inning championship game ever played, and at times it felt twice as long. To the victors, however, who blew two leads and lived to tell the tale, the ugly 6–5 win enters the annals of October Mets magic. "They have come back so often to win so many dramatic October games that the thrilling has become almost routine," says the *Times*. The team itself begins to agree. "Every day!" a triumphant Bobby Valentine yells in the victorious visiting clubhouse, emerging from his office with a beer in his hand, a peppy disco soundtrack trailing him.

Valentine's players own enough confidence in this moment to yell, "Six more, six more," as they run down the tunnel and into the visiting clubhouse, six being the remaining number of victories necessary to capture a championship. The feeling is mounting that this magic will carry them far, that perhaps the Cardinals won't be quite the formidable obstacle some feared at the series outset. Descriptions of the Mets weigh heavy with words like "poise" and "calm," words that, but for brief intervals, have never before been applied to a Bobby Valentine-led team.

History shows that only three times before has a team recovered from losing the first two games of a best-of-seven playoff series at home (the 1986 Mets being one of them, having pulled off the feat in the World Series). At the moment, these Cardinals don't appear capable of executing a fourth instance. "The NLCS is a seven-game series," notes the *Daily News* with a note of hubris, "but last night, as the Mets boarded a plane home with a 6–5 win over the St. Louis Cardinals, it felt as though the whole thing was already over."

* * *

The Yankees' victory over the Oakland A's bought them a date with the Seattle Mariners, who advanced to the championship series with a stunning sweep of the Chicago White Sox in their own division series. Unlike Oakland's baby-faced lineup, Seattle owns a lot of experience between John Olerud, Edgar Martínez, Jay Buhner, and Rickey Henderson, and is helmed by a managerial veteran, Lou Piniella. Once renowned for his epic on-field tantrums—learned at the feet of Billy Martin, who managed him for the Bronx Zoo Yankees of the 1970s—Piniella has mellowed a bit with age, though he still occasionally attacks the umpiring corps with the impetuousness of Bobbies Cox or Valentine.

Piniella's personal evolution is mirrored in the transformation of the team under his wings. Seattle's offense was once built exclusively around the home run, but that was before last year, when they moved midseason from the claustrophobic Kingdome to spacious, open-air Safeco Field, then lost Ken Griffey Jr. and his forty-eight homers to Cincinnati. Piniella placed a new emphasis on speed and defense in 2000, and it paid off handsomely. The scoring lost by Griffey's absence were produced by other means, as Edgar Martínez and Alex Rodriguez combined to drive in 277 runs, the largest total for any two teammates in baseball this season.

The ways in which the Mariners won in 2000 seem magical to their fans, with attendant folkways that would ring familiar to Mets partisans. The juju that powers Seattle to victory is referred to as SoDo Mojo (SoDo being the Seattle neighborhood where Safeco Field is located), while every bit of good fortune exhibited by the home nine is greeted with a brief blast of "Who Let the Dogs Out?", with a full playing of the summer's most infuriating earworm following each victory.

In contrast to their lineup, Seattle's pitchers are a young set, as exemplified by the man they send to the mound to open the series on October 10: Freddy Garcia, who turned twenty-four years old five days prior to game one. As with Oakland's Barry Zito a week earlier, it is assumed Garcia will be spooked by the ghosts of Yankee Stadium, and the unseasonably wintry temperatures (forty-two degrees at first pitch). Also like Zito, none of this bothers him as he tosses 6 2/3 scoreless innings with hardly a peep from the home team. Joe Torre is so desperate to kick-start his flatlining offense late in the game that he pinch-hits for Paul O'Neill (having a miserable 4-for-26 postseason thus far), to no good effect, as the Yankees fall, 2–0. Alex Rodriguez compares Garcia's outing to one of Pedro Martínez's, high praise indeed. "Remember the slump the Yankees supposedly broke out of in Game 5 of the Division Series? Consider them back in." So writes *Sports Illustrated* at the conclusion of game one. The team is exhausted from the battle with Oakland, multiple cross-country trips, and the wear and tear of a stressful season. Even Joe Torre is tired of it all. "To watch Torre before, during, and after Game 1 on Tuesday," continues *SI*, "one is struck more by a feeling of exasperation than anticipation or exuberance."

The Yankees look no less exhausted the following night when the team's batters are shut out for seven more innings, a potential waste of another brilliant postseason outing from Orlando Hernández, as yet unbeaten in October. El Duque allows no more than a run-scoring single in the third, but thanks to the anemic offense behind him, he is ticketed for a tough-luck loss—on his birthday, no less. In the midst of the scoring drought, an exasperated Joe Torre asks his team, "Are you guys trying?" The postmortems in the papers characterize this outburst as a "joke," despite ample evidence that the manager is frustrated enough by a seemingly endless stretch of scoreless innings to mean each word with deathly seriousness.

If anything, the Yankee batters are trying far too hard. Paul O'Neill, dropped down to seventh in the batting order, admits he is perturbed by the angry pleas of fans yelling at him to get a hit already. He compares his efforts to do anything at the plate with learning how to drive a manual transmission for the first time, grinding gears with humiliating ineffectiveness. The fit he throws when he is called out on a close play to end the bottom of the sixth is—even by his own standards as a premier tantrum thrower—an all-time meltdown, as he chucks his helmet and charges at an umpire until he must be restrained by his teammates. His cantankerousness is contagious. David Justice, as cool as any customer on the Yankees' roster, shrieks in disbelief like O'Neill after a check swing call goes against him. When the Yankees load the bases in the bottom of the first on an error and a pair of walks yet fail to score, the Bronx crowd responds with thunderous boos.

The shutout is all the more frustrating for being engineered by John Halama. Apart from owning an underwhelming regular season ERA over five, Halama's stuff appears to be hittable all game long. The lefty makes mistakes with his location that the Yankees should be able to pound, yet snaps off a devastating curveball each time he must, a breaking pitch none of the New York hitters can touch. The Yankees flail wildly at first pitches and fail to go deep into counts, sins they failed to commit even during their worst slumps this season. Calling the game for NBC, Bob Costas refers to the long plane rides of the last round and the superannuated nature of their lineup and concludes, "you have to think this is a tired team." Worst of all, Halama doesn't even appear to be that interested in the proceedings. When reporters ask the Brooklyn-born southpaw how exciting it is for a city kid to pitch in the Bronx in the playoffs, he confesses he never went to Yankee Stadium as a kid and visited Shea only once. "I'm not really a big baseball fan," he admits. When New York media ask which neighborhood he grew up in, he dismisses the query as "irrelevant," making him the only Brooklyn native to ever respond with that answer. Costas wonders aloud if Halama is able to shrug off the aura and mystique of the House That Ruth Built because he simply doesn't care.

With Seattle's shutdown closer, Kazuhiro Sasaki, looming in the ninth and New York six outs away from falling behind two games to none in this series, the jumpy Yankees finally jump all over Seattle pitching in the bottom of the eighth. The Mariners' bullpen, unimpeachable in the playoffs until this point, surrenders eight hits and seven runs, capped by a two-run shot from Derek Jeter after the shortstop had struck out four times in his previous at bats in the series. The Yankees go on to win 7–1, though anyone watching the game would feel the score was surely closer.

The postgame mood in the visiting clubhouse is subdued, the Mariners realizing they've blown a chance to take a commanding lead in the series. But so too is the home clubhouse as they pack for another long cross-country flight in near silence. Their win has engendered not joy or relief, but an unseemly resentment. The Yankees—at least the ones who speak to the press—feel they are not given much credit for their comeback win but are still being shamed for failing to dominate in the first two games. "I think y'all are so spoiled by the Yankee teams of the past," says newcomer David Justice, "that you expect us to just float through the playoffs."

To which the press responds, not in so many words, *Of course we do.* The victory, thrilling and cathartic though it might be, is no less than what the media and fans expect of the Yankees. This is all due to the realignment of expectations that followed the 1998 season, a realignment the Yankees themselves encouraged. The trade for Roger Clemens after that magical season was, in essence, a defiant insistence that the Yankees could and would always attempt to improve on perfection. To watch them fight and claw for every victory over Oakland, to witness them be shut out for their first sixteen innings facing Seattle pitching—this is unacceptable to the media, because the Yankees themselves have declared it unacceptable.

* * *

"Other than the record, how can you be down about this club?" This is Tony La Russa's rhetorical query about his squad prior to game three in Queens, one that unconsciously evokes Bobby Valentine's reaction to similarly dire circumstances early in 1999. (*Other than a victory . . .*) A sunny disposition is his only defense against long odds. The Cardinals land in New York at 5:00 a.m. following their grueling game two defeat and enjoy a few fitful hours of rest before they must be at Shea Stadium for an off-day workout. Still groggy from lack of sleep, they gather in the lobby of their Manhattan hotel to wait for a bus to transport them to Queens. And wait. And wait some more. The Cardinals' bus gets caught in traffic due to a rally at the United Nations, so the team doesn't leave for Flushing until 1:30 p.m., by which point they should have already been on the field, taking their cuts and fielding grounders.

Optimism is admirable, but more than optimism will be required, considering their remaining hopes rest on Andy Benes, shaky ground indeed. A former first-round draft pick and All-Star for the San Diego Padres, the veteran starter logged decent work at the back of the Cardinal rotation until a knee injury knocked him out of commission in mid-August. The halting gait from his knee trouble, combined with his square jaw and weekend warrior physique, gives Benes the look of a former high school quarterback dreaming of past glories. Benes drew only three starts in late September and none in the division series, but thanks to the state of his rotation, Tony La Russa has no choice but to call on Benes in game three, Darryl Kile on short rest in game four, and Pat Hentgen—another veteran question mark—in game five. What he will do beyond that point is a bridge he will cross when he gets to it. If he gets to it

For now, the Cardinals can take solace in the fact that they reached the Mets' game three starter, Rick Reed, for eight runs in two games this season. Prior to the game, Bobby Valentine says he believes Reed's 2.84 career playoff ERA will prevail over his spotty record against this season's Cardinals, but it is evident from the very start of the game that it will not.

When the game begins at 4:00 p.m., there isn't a single cloud in the Flushing sky, temperatures settling in the mid-seventies. Only the shadows cast on the field by the low autumn sun tell the viewer it is October 14 and not mid-May, as it sits right above Shea's upper deck and bounces a distracting glare off the batter's eye beyond center field for much of the early proceedings. In the early going, however, it's not sun-blinded hitters who look distracted, but the Mets starter, as Reed consistently leaves pitches up in the zone and pays for each mistake. In the first inning, Jim Edmonds reaches him for a two-run double. Two more hits, a walk, and a sac fly lead to two more runs in the top of the third. In the fourth, after Mike Bordick makes a poor play on a grounder to allow Andy Benes to reach safely, Reed allows another pair of hits that send Benes chugging home from second, bad knee and all, with the Cardinals' fifth run. When Reed is yanked in favor of Glendon Rusch, who'd been warming up since the first inning due to the starter's struggles, the righty is so furious about his poor performance he struggles to put on his jacket in the dugout out of pure frustration.

The Mets make some noise of their own in the first with singles from Timo Pérez and Edgardo Alfonzo, putting runners on the corners for Mike Piazza, who is greeted by signs bearing a thousand variations on "THE MONSTER IS OUT OF THE CAGE" motif. But Piazza falls behind in the count before chopping a hard grounder to third base, on which the Cardinals turn a deft double play. Though Pérez scores in the bargain, the twin killing dims the Mets rally and sets the tone for their offense—or lack thereof—for the remainder of the afternoon. Hard-hit balls find gloves. Soft-hit balls stay fair, like Mike Bordick's two-out dribbler in the second, which rolls foul down the first base line for a moment, only to trickle back on the field of play and into Andy Benes's glove. In the fourth, when the Mets load the bases with no outs, they manage no more than one run as Jay Payton rolls into a rally-crushing double play.

This is as close as the Mets will get, as Rick White allows three runs in the top of the fifth to put the game well out of reach. Before the game, Tony La Russa confessed he was counting on Benes for no more than five or six "strong" innings, but at day's end he receives eight, and for most of those innings he stifles the home team so effectively that the Shea crowd has no excuse to express its rowdy id. By the time Benes sets down the opposition yet again in the top of the eighth, a steady stream of fans are seen heading up the ramp to the 7 train beyond the outfield fence, not wishing to see the conclusion of an 8–2 Cardinals win.

Last October, after days of must-win games, the Mets' adrenaline ran out in a sloppy, luckless game two of the division series in Phoenix. That pattern seems to have repeated itself in this game three. The Mets concede they were lacking the energy needed to fight back against the early deficit in this year's game three. Jay Payton says, "We didn't have the fire we had in the last two games." Darryl Hamilton describes his team as "flat." Edgardo Alfonzo utters words few athletes ever dare by admitting that once the Mets fell behind big, "after that we gave up."

* * *

Bobby Jones draws the game four start by virtue of the brilliant one-hitter he tossed in the clincher against the Giants. But while that game unfolded on a sunny afternoon, game four begins at 8:00 p.m. on the night of a full moon, and will be marked by many lunatic doings, not the least of which is the disappearance of Bobby Jones's magic. His second pitch of the evening is zipped down the first base line for a leadoff double. His third is converted into a sacrifice bunt. His fourth is crushed to the base of the scoreboard by Jim Edmonds, giving the Cardinals a 2–0 lead in the opening inning for the second straight game. Jones collects the final outs of the inning on long flies to the deepest part of the yard, a disturbing sign for a pitcher who must keep the ball down to be successful. Whatever spell Jones cast over San Francisco has no effect on St. Louis.

The Cardinals' quick start gives Darryl Kile some margin for error, one the hurler returns with interest. Kile is pitching on only three days' rest, a feat he has seldom performed and has performed even less frequently with any success—his career ERA stands at a hair shy of seven in such outings. The state of the remainder of the Cardinals rotation made the decision to throw Kile less a gamble than Hobson's choice. This does not make what transpires any easier for Tony La Russa to swallow.

The bottom of the first begins with Timo Pérez sending a screamer to the fence in right center, where it bounces over for a ground-rule double. Then Edgardo Alfonzo lines the first pitch he sees down the left-field line for his own double, scoring Pérez and cutting the Cards' lead in half. Mike Piazza follows with another double over the head of J. D. Drew in straightaway center, then Robin Ventura crushes a Kile offering for his own, scoring both Alfonzo and Piazza and giving the Mets the lead. One out later, Kile falls behind Benny Agbayani before watching him belt another well-struck hit, one that comes within inches of leaving the yard. Ventura jogs home on the fifth double of the inning, a new championship league record. In the blink of an eye, the Cards' 2–0 advantage has become a 4–2 Mets lead.

Darryl Kile's torment continues in the second, as the Mets load the bases with two outs. Kile nearly escapes this jam by backing Todd Zeile in a two-strike hole but then inexplicably drops into a sidearm delivery to fool the hitter. Zeile rockets the trickery into the left-field corner, driving in two runs with the Mets' sixth double in two innings, and Agbayani singles home another run shortly thereafter. Kile finally exits after issuing a leadoff walk in the bottom of the fourth, having given his team what appears to be an impossible deficit to overcome.

When the Cardinals make some noise on a solo shot from Will Clark in the top of the fourth, Mike Piazza responds by hitting a titanic homer of his own in the bottom half, deep into the visiting bullpen. At this point, the Mets are up 8–3. All the loud outs off of Bobby Jones seem to be of little concern, because he is recording outs, after all.

Then Jones starts the top of the fifth by giving up a well-struck single, followed by another hit that skips right under his glove. Pinch hitter Eric Davis follows with a double down the left-field line, fair by a matter of inches. One runner scores and two more stand on second and third with nobody out. Jones is removed in favor of Glendon Rusch, who allows both inherited runners to score. Now the score is 8–6, much more manageable for the Cardinals and much more nauseating for the Mets.

The Mets regain the momentum, and a wider lead, in the bottom of the sixth against Mike Timlin, a grizzled bullpen vet who took the loss in the sloppy game two in St. Louis. Timlin hurts his own cause by opening the inning with a walk of Mike Bordick, who has slumped all October. After two futile bunt attempts, Glendon Rusch's third try lands near the pitcher's mound. Timlin scrambles for the ball with designs on starting a double play, but the pitcher slips for one crucial moment. By the time he recovers, his only play is to first, as Bordick reaches second safely behind him. Then Timo Pérez reaches on an error by third baseman Fernando Tatís and Timlin hits Edgardo Alfonzo with a pitch to load the bases and bring Piazza to the plate. Though Piazza hits a weak grounder, Tatís bobbles the ball again, and the batter reaches safely as a run scores. Moments later, Robin Ventura brings in another run with a sac fly, expanding the Mets' lead to 10–4 without the benefit of a single hit. Speaking of the patch of grass where Mike Timlin slipped, John Donovan of *Sports Illustrated* writes, "you might as well bury the St. Louis Cardinals—every last one of them—under it."

This inning should doom the Cardinals' chances, but while the Mets go quietly the rest of the way, the visitors mount threats in each of the three remaining innings. In the top of the seventh, the Cardinals are only turned aside when Shawon Dunston is thrown out as he attempts to tag up and move to second on a shallow fly ball, a risky move in a close game and a suicidal one when your team is trailing by four runs. In the eighth, John Franco logs two quick outs before ceding a single and a walk, bringing him one baserunner away from a potential confrontation with Mark McGwire. The next batter dribbles a slow roller toward third base, but Robin Ventura makes a classic Robin Ventura play, running in on the ball, barehanding it, and tossing it to first in time—barely—for the final out of the inning. McGwire is stranded in the on-deck circle once again.

When Armando Benítez enters the game in the ninth, he too places himself into hot water by allowing a leadoff single and losing the next hitter to a walk, a series of events that again brings the Mets one baserunner away from an appointment with Big Mac. The first out is only recorded when Edgardo Alfonzo makes an amazing play on a bad throw from Mike Bordick, diving to catch the ball and kick a heel into the base at the same time. After a strikeout, Benítez gets ahead of Jim Edmonds before losing the strike zone and going full. This time McGwire is not looming on deck because the next scheduled batter is Will Clark, another man the Mets do not want to bat with a chance to tie the game.

Armando Benítez's seventh pitch to Jim Edmonds is a fastball that catches too much of the plate. Midsummer, a healthier Jim Edmonds might have crushed such an offering. In October, with a chill in the air and Edmonds fighting his way through back pain, the batter misses the sweet spot by a few decisive millimeters and lofts a towering fly ball to right field. Timo Pérez holds his glove aloft for a several eons, waiting for it to settle in the leather. Once it does, the Mets have a 10–6 victory, a commanding 3–1 series lead, and a chance to punch their ticket to the World Series the next evening.

In the wake of the Cardinals' loss, Tony La Russa once again comes under fire for the moves he made and the ones he didn't, particularly his failure to use Mark McGwire yet again. In the *Daily News*, Vic Ziegel shares the tidbit that before the game, Cardinal general manager Walt Jockety had visions of McGwire belting a game-winning homer like Kirk Gibson did for the Dodgers in 1988. "He better relay his vision to La Russa," quips Ziegel. "Time is getting short." Given a chance to defend La Russa, Big Mac instead hangs his manager out to dry by refusing to speak to the media after the game.

The Cardinals clubhouse is deathly silent, a postgame repast of chicken barely touched. One of the few Cardinals who speaks at length to the press following their defeat is Pat Hentgen, the veteran who will draw the game five start. Apart from an excess of rest—he has not started in sixteen long days—the former Cy Young Award recipient and anchor of the great Toronto rotations of the early 1990s believes his previous playoff experience will give him an edge. "I've pitched in World Series games before," Hentgen says, reminding everyone of the two championships he won with the Blue Jays.

The man who will oppose him, Mike Hampton, is more guarded in his comments, at least at first. Many of his superstitious teammates refuse to mention the words "pennant" or "World Series"; he follows their lead in fear of jinxing a team so close to the promised land. But then he concludes his comments with words that would be familiar to those who remember Bobby Jones's start last week.

"I'm looking forward to pitching the game of my life," he says.

* * *

When the American League Championship Series relocates to Seattle for game three, the bypassed chances continue to pile up for the Mariners. Though the game is played on an ominous date on the calendar—Friday the thirteenth of October—only the home team is affected by bad luck. Seattle logs ten hits against Yankees hurlers in game three, yet all but one of them are singles. They score one run off of Andy Pettitte in the bottom of the first with a trio of one-out hits, but every other scoring chance is squashed by crafty pitching from the lefty and rotten luck for his opposition. The Mariners bounce into double plays and commit baserunning gaffes all game, as in the bottom of the third, when the slow-footed Edgar

Martínez allows himself to be picked off of first base, nipping a rally in the bud.

Aaron Sele takes the mound for the Mariners, and he gets ahead of nearly every batter, but on each occasion where he falls behind, he pays for it dearly, as in the back-to-back homers he allows to start the top of the second. When Tino Martinez hits a comebacker in the sixth, Sele fields the ball but fails to get it out of his glove in time, a blunder that eventually allows the fourth Yankees run to score. A four-run top of the ninth sends the Mariners faithful fleeing, and the Yanks cruise to an 8–2 victory.

In game four, Seattle squanders no chances because they receive none. For one brilliant night, Roger Clemens looks like The Rocket of the 1980s, an unstoppable strikeout machine. He fans fifteen batters and allows no hits until a leadoff double in the seventh. No more follow that one, and at the end of the night, Clemens has pitched an utterly dominating complete-game one-hit shutout.

From pitch one, Clemens has otherworldly stuff at his command. The 47,803 white-towel-waving fans—including a beaming Microsoft chief Bill Gates in a field-level box—soon realize they will have little to cheer this afternoon. The home team never recovers from the bottom of the first, when Clemens throws a fastball up and in to Alex Rodriguez. The shortstop spins out of the way, lands in a genuflecting pose, and stares out at the pitcher as Seattle fans respond with boos and hisses. Clemens answers them all by throwing his next pitch in the exact same spot.

The Mariners retaliate after a fashion when their starter, Paul Abbott, throws some chin music to Yankee catcher Jorge Posada, while a furious Lou Piniella screams toward the New York bench words to the effect of, "Two can play this game, bud." But a Paul Abbott fastball is no match for a Roger Clemens fastball. It is clear who has the advantage in this arms race.

The Rocket's cause is helped further when the umpiring crew takes more of a boys-will-be-boys attitude toward the situation, at least when it comes to one boy in particular. As Clemens takes the mound for the bottom of the second, crew chief Mike Hirschbeck gives him a stern talking to in the same tone a principal would reserve for a star athlete caught vandalizing school property. *Roger, I'll have no more of that, I've seen it, that's it.* Clemens nods and silently agrees to behave. But when his first pitch of the bottom of the third sails up and over Seattle second baseman David Bell's head, the umpires don't even blink. Clemens pitches the rest of the game knowing that Hirschbeck's tut-tuts have all the weight of a helium balloon. The spooked Mariners, each of them fearing a ball to the dome, flail helplessly at Clemens's pitches for the rest of the night.

Home runs from Derek Jeter and David Justice give Clemens more than enough offense as the Yankees prevail 5–0. For the New York media, it is the signature Roger Clemens game they've been waiting for since he arrived in the Bronx. Reggie Jackson, Mr. October himself, calls it "his graduation."

Seattle's take is quite different. In their view, Roger Clemens's plan was to frighten them into submission, a plan that worked to perfection thanks to complicity from the umpires. Clemens has little to say about the pitch to Alex Rodriguez in his postgame comments except to insist he missed his spot, no harm or malice intended. No explanation is offered as to how he could miss his spot yet throw at the same dangerous spot two pitches in a row, and hit that spot against multiple Mariners batters.

The Yankees' response to such charges are nearly identical to their defensive postures following the Piazza plunking. Think Roger Clemens threw at your hitter on purpose? *Prove it.* Don't like how he's pitching to you? *Do something about it. Get a hit off him. Make him pay that way, or stop complaining.* Clemens himself avoids most comment on the matter, but when asked to respond during a pregame radio interview the following day, he plays the part of an aw-shucks yokel. "I'll defer to my mother," he says of Lou Piniella's accusations that he threw at Rodriguez on purpose, "who said you should never get into a hissing match with a skunk."

Alex Rodriguez exacts the only revenge he can the following day during game five. His two-run single in the bottom of the fifth gives the Mariners the lead and sparks a five-run outburst against Denny Neagle and the Yankees bullpen, leading to a 6–2 Seattle victory and yet another long plane ride to continue the series. After the game, Mariners coach John McLaren gives his lineup card to Rodriguez, part souvenir for a masterful game in the field, part memento of what might be his final game played in Seattle.

The battle between New York and Seattle won't be settled any earlier than game six. The day prior to that will be an off day in the series. This means that the evening of Monday, October 16, is left entirely to the Mets.

* * *

The evening of October 16 is different. After the Mets played most of their playoff games in relative warmth, rain prevails for much of the day of game five. The tarp remains on the Shea Stadium infield until forty-five minutes before the first pitch, bands of mist illuminated by the gargantuan ballpark lights. By game time, the temperatures have dipped into the mid-fifties. Finally, it feels like October.

The two dugouts are different. Tim McCarver reports that he ran into Bobby Valentine before the game, and that the manager "looked more relaxed than I've ever seen him." Cut to the visiting dugout, where the Cardinals look flat. Hitting coach Mike Easler paces the bench, imparting batting advice clichés while his charges pay him no mind at all.

On the evening of October 16, the crowd is different. With the exception of the Mets' disappointing loss in game three of this series, every game played at Shea Stadium in this postseason has been cheered on by more than fifty-six thousand loud and raucous fans. But even by this measure, the crowd on hand tonight leaves the previous attendees in the dust in the categories of volume and enthusiasm. When the series was in St. Louis, Al Leiter could feel the roar of the crowd pressing against him as he stood on the mound, but he figures anything St. Louis can do, New York can do better. Once the series returns to the Big Apple, Leiter and John Franco lobby Mets management for an extra set of giant speakers mounted beyond the center-field fence, the kind normally reserved for rock concerts, in order to blast the opposition into submission. After the disappointing game three left little reason to use them, the new toys were unboxed during the Mets' barrage of doubles in game four. Throughout the broadcast of that game, the Fox crew commented on the extra loudness. But even that was mere child's play compared to the noise that will be unleashed in game five.

Most of all, the evening of October 16 is different because of the man on the mound. So far, this series has lacked a quality starting performance from either side. For the Mets, Al Leiter huffed and puffed through seven innings in game two, while Rick Reed and Bobby Jones disappointed in the two games that followed. Mike Hampton had put up the best line of them all by throwing seven shutout innings in game one, but his outing was less pitching clinic than magic act. No tricks are needed the night of October 16. Hampton promised to pitch the game of his life, and he is true to his word.

The first inning begins with a leadoff single, but Hampton knuckles down to retire the next three Cardinals in order. This marks the first time in the series that the visiting team has failed to score in the first inning.

It also marks the closest the Cardinals will come to scoring at all for the remainder of this game.

Pat Hengten takes the mound in the bottom of the first having not thrown a pitch in anger in over two weeks. The long break since his last outing explains his lack of poise and command on this evening, but it doesn't explain the skittishness and unsure hands of the defense behind him. The frame begins, once again, with a single by Timo Pérez. When Pérez wastes little time in attempting to swipe second, the catcher's throw is several feet short of the bag and skips into the outfield. Pérez scampers to third and scores moments later after an Edgardo Alfonzo grounder zips under the shortstop's glove.

Hentgen pitches carefully to Mike Piazza and walks him, eyeing a double-play grounder from the slow-footed Robin Ventura. The third baseman foils the plot by lining a single to right, scoring Alfonzo and sending Piazza to third. Hentgen nearly produces that elusive double play by inducing a grounder from Todd Zeile, but as the infielders bobble this ball, Piazza trots home with the third run of the inning. The Cardinals are unprepared for the slick field conditions after a rainy day, unprepared for the crowd noise and PA rumble that greets every Mets hit and Cardinal error, unprepared for anything they will face this evening.

Hentgen escapes the inning with no further damage, though he has already allowed more runs than the Mets will need to back up his opposite number. Hampton sets down the Cardinals in order in the second. He cedes a one-out single in the third but shuts the door thereafter. Another one-out hit by Will Clark in the fourth is followed by commanding strikeouts of Jim Edmonds and Edgar Rentería. "Mike Hampton is in total control at this point," says Joe Buck in the Fox broadcast booth. Four innings of work should be too few to proclaim any pitcher is in total control, but it doesn't sound like exaggeration to anyone observing the lefty's domination.

For his part, Hentgen has to feel he's settled into a groove after his rough first inning. He retires the Mets in order in the second and works around a pair of walks in the third. The powerful Cardinals lineup should be more than capable of vaulting a three-run deficit, even if they have looked helpless against Mike Hampton to this point. And then comes the bottom of the fourth, the inning that puts a bow on the conclusion of this series.

It starts with Timo Pérez, as all things Mets do these days. With one out, he hits a sharp grounder that lands one millimeter short of Pat Hentgen's foot and takes a weird bounce off his cleat. Luckily for the

Cardinals, the ball shoots right into shortstop Edgar Rentería's glove. Unluckily for the Cardinals, Rentería's throw bounces short of first. Then with two outs, Mike Piazza belts a double to left, moving Pérez to third. Burned once by Ventura, Hentgen walks him to face Todd Zeile instead. In the dugout, Alfonzo paces the dugout and screams encouragement, demanding that his teammate put the Cardinals away for good. The sight of an emotional Alfonzo is as rare as they come, but the second baseman is haunted by the near miss of 1999. The Mets are so close to taking the pennant, he does not want to leave any scoring chance uncashed. His screams say, in essence, *End it here.*

An RBI hit in game four of this series notwithstanding, Todd Zeile's bat has been MIA for most of the playoffs. Nonetheless, the Cardinals' preference to face him over Robin Ventura strikes him as an insult, as does Tony La Russa's decision to stay with Pat Hentgen, who is nearing the end of his rope, rather than turn his bullpen. To be disrespected in this manner by the team that traded him away as a young player is doubly motivating. "It's the place I grew up in baseball," Zeile says of his years in St. Louis, an admission that makes his desire for revenge sound almost Freudian.

Behind in the count, Todd Zeile goes with an outside fastball and launches it to the base of the wall in right center. Timo Pérez scores. Mike Piazza scores. Robin Ventura scores. Todd Zeile flies to second. The Mets are now up 6–0. The upper deck of Shea literally sways with the weight of fans jumping for joy. The tone of the Fox broadcast booth's reportage on the noise level in the stadium transforms from impressed to terrified, as if Joe Buck and Tim McCarver are war correspondents treading too close to a battlefront.

The only questions remaining in this game are, will the fans pull Shea Stadium out by the roots, and how long will Mike Hampton continue to carve up Cardinals hitters? The answer to the first query is unclear. The answer to the second is: until the twenty-seventh out. The demoralized Cards go down in order in the fifth and manage no more than a one-out walk in the sixth. Hampton sets the opposition down one-two-three in the seventh and again in the eighth. Only duty and the rules of the game bring the Cardinals to the plate. Their hearts are not in the endeavor. As early as the fifth inning, each man Hampton retires prompts Joe Buck to note that he is one out closer to history. As early as the sixth inning, Fox graphics promise they will bring viewers the trophy presentation ceremony that will follow this game, without the caveat of the word "if."

As for the Mets, they do little against the relievers who succeed Pat Hentgen, but this is seemingly by choice. With Hampton cruising on the mound, they are content to speed up the cork popping. And then Tony La Russa steps in to make his final managerial miscalculation of the series by asking Rick Ankiel to pitch the bottom of the seventh inning. The reasoning is that this will allow him an opportunity to draw some positive experience out of this series, so that the last thing he remembers from his season is not his disastrously wild start in game two. In a vacuum, it might be a debatable decision. In the raucous atmosphere of Shea Stadium, with the Mets six outs from a pennant, Tony La Russa is offering his young pitcher up as a human sacrifice.

The first indication that this will not go well comes during warm-ups, when one of Ankiel's tosses almost hits a T-shirt-cannon-wielding stadium worker, who is nowhere near the plate at the time. As he pitches to leadoff batter Mike Bordick, he has trouble finding the zone, leading many in the crowd to chant, "WILD PITCH! WILD PITCH!" A walk ensues. After Mike Hampton bunts Bordick over, Ankiel takes some measure of dignity back by striking out Timo Pérez looking. Then he lets loose a pair of wild pitches to score Bordick, each errant throw drawing a sarcastic cheer from the merciless Shea stands. A wild walk of Edgardo Alfonzo finally brings Tony La Russa out of the dugout to remove the young lefty, his attempt at salving the young man's feelings having produced the opposite effect.

With the game out of reach and their entire roster demoralized, the frustrated Cardinals take out their feelings the only way they can at this point. In the bottom of the eighth, Cardinal closer Dave Veres throws a pair of pitches up and in to Jay Payton, the second nailing him in the temple, opening a gash over his right eye. Payton hits the turf for a moment, then leaps back to his feet and takes a few purposeful steps toward the mound. As the benches clear, Benny Agbayani and Bobby Valentine hold the battered outfielder back. Some posturing and mild shoving ensues, but no true hostilities break out. The Mets realize fighting at this point will only tarnish the victory they are about to savor. Veres later insists the beaning was an accident, and with victory so close the Mets can taste it, Payton is willing to let the matter go. "I'd take a shot in the head every year to get to the World Series," he says.

In the top of the ninth, Hampton makes quick work of two pinch hitters (including Mark McGwire, finally logging an at bat). By this point, the air at Shea is thick with makeshift confetti. Fans rip up any paper they have on hand—programs, soda cups, beer bottle labels—and rain it down on the field. Players from both teams have little room to stand in their respective dugouts due to the NYPD officers preparing to storm the field after the final out and prevent overjoyed fans from doing the same.

Twelve months ago, the Mets lost a grueling championship series, mounting innumerable comebacks only to fall short. They, and their fans, felt they deserved to win that series for all the pain they'd endured. Perhaps this is the delayed make-good on those torturous games with the Braves: a series with the Cardinals that was supposed to be a dog fight and felt, for most of its duration, more like a cakewalk.

Many Mets had endured years of frustration to get here, but in the end, the man who records the final out is the man with the shortest amount of major league service time, though he may have come the farthest distance: Timo Pérez, six weeks into his big league career, with the Mets by way of the Dominican Republic via Hiroshima, who had more impact on this series than anyone dared imagine. The final out is a high, looping fly ball to center field, where Pérez stands now, shifted there due to the injury to Jay Payton. He does not have to move an inch to catch it, but Timo being Timo, he does more than move. The ball is hit so high, Pérez has time to leap for joy twice, land, and ready himself to catch the final out.

The ball settles in his glove at 11:39 p.m. on Monday, October 16, 2000. No other New York team has played all day. Spoilsports say this will not last, insist it cannot last. Realists will offer no break between the capturing of the pennant and the questions about the looming opponent. But on the field at this moment in time, the Mets do not have to care about that, or about anything at all but hoisting Mike Hampton into the air and celebrating and whooping and hollering with all of their fans. All of them have one whole day to savor a trip to the World Series, one whole day to believe this city might be theirs again.

CHAPTER 17

Stand Clear of the Closing Doors

GAME SIX OF the American League Championship Series is waged at Yankee Stadium on the evening of October 17. Less than twenty-four hours have passed since the triumph of Mike Hampton, and so signs abound in the stands with variations on "BRING ON THE METS." The visiting Mariners are deemed a mere trifle due to the tide of destiny and the fact that the Yankees will pitch Orlando Hernández, whose postseason record is stainless.

The Mariners proceed to put their fingerprints all over that record by hanging four runs on him in the first four innings, while John Halama keeps the Yankees off the board for the first three. Nervousness reigns in the Bronx until the bottom of the fourth, when the home team scores three runs against Halama, then takes the lead on a three-run homer by David Justice in the seventh, a long ball that sets Yankee Stadium shaking with pennant-clinching anticipation. Three more runs scored in that inning seem to render the remainder of the game a mere formality.

When Alex Rodriguez leads off the top of the eighth with a solo shot, Joe Torre calls for Mariano Rivera to secure the final six outs of the game. As with El Duque, the sight of Rivera taking the mound is enough to convince fans this game is over. And yet, Rivera allows a pair of runners to score in the eighth, shaving a once mighty lead down to two runs. More struggles for the Yankees where there were none before. More staggering to the finish.

In the ninth, Rivera retires the first two batters before the pesky Rodriguez dribbles a weak grounder down the third base line and beats it out. This brings the tying run to the plate in the form of Edgar Martínez, the absolute last man any Yankee fan wants to see at bat in this moment. It was Martínez who belted a game-winning double in game five of the 1995 division series, the hit that sealed a devastating playoff collapse for New York, and who has continued to kill the Yankees in this series.

On an 0-1 pitch, Martínez sends an easy grounder to Derek Jeter, who tosses to first for the final out of the game and the series. The Yankees have won, 9–7, and are once again headed to the World Series, even if Bronx Bombers of old would blanch at the notes of underdog-ism played by this year's team. "We were written off," David Justice insists. But at least Justice is new to the team and its corporate culture, which cannot be said of Tino Martinez, who proclaims, "Probably the easiest thing we've done this year is get it over in six." The same goes for Bernie Williams, who describes the season as a "struggle" in which "everything hasn't been easy." Yankee teams of the 1990s did not speak of a playoff series as if it were a household chore to be endured, nor did they concede any part of the season was a *struggle* for fear of showing weakness.

And yet, tone does not matter to those who expect the Yankees to prevail no matter what. They prevailed. Case closed.

And so it begins.

* * *

In 2000, no Mets winning streak was too brief that it couldn't inspire a reporter to ask a player his thoughts on a "real" Subways Series. Never, *What would it be like to play in the World Series?* Always, *What would it be like to play the Yankees in the World Series?* Such questioning gained a fever pitch in the triumphant Mets clubhouse following their final victory over the Cardinals. Apart from the assumed inevitability of a Yankee win the next day, it was impossible to avoid questions about facing the Yankees while Rudy Giuliani was in the room, daring to wear a commemorative Mets hat in celebratory solidarity. Forced to reciprocate the courtesy, co-owner Fred Wilpon said he would root for the Yankees in their impending game six and debased himself further by describing the Mets as "the little guy from Queens trying to emulate the Yankees."

Even after the Yankees knock off the Mariners, the Mets field the bulk of the questions about the imminent clash, in large part because they are willing to answer them. Very few men on their roster have ever been to the World Series, and so they express their excitement about this new adventure in a manner that borders on hubris.

Ever since October of 1999, when a series of improbable events propelled the Mets as far as game six in Atlanta, the media has proclaimed them a scrappy, hungry bunch that could do anything through the power of magic. The prevailing wisdom is captured by Murray Chass, who marvels, "Who would have ever conceived of a series where a pestiferous Mighty Mouse of a leadoff hitter named Timo (don't call me Timoniel) Pérez would make a greater impact than a Man Mountain of a home run hitter named Mark McGwire?" After a year-plus of Cinderella fantasies like these, overconfidence abounds in the Mets clubhouse. Todd Zeile professes he has "unfinished business" with the team that has ended his playoff hopes three times before. Jay Payton insists, "This is our chance to get a place on the map." Darryl Hamilton even has the nerve to insist his team's relative lack of World Series experience matters little because "of all the experience the Yankees have, I don't know if any of those guys are prepared for what's going to happen here because playoff experience and World Series experience doesn't prepare you for the Subway Series." When making these statements, Hamilton—like many of his teammates—has logged zero innings of World Series play.

The team's cockeyed optimism is exemplified by Benny Agbayani, another out-of-nowhere type who becomes a very popular man this October. During an appearance on Howard Stern's morning radio show, he steers ably through the shock jock's most R-rated queries without embarrassing himself, but when Stern presses him for a series prediction, he cracks. "Mets in five," Benny boldly says. Later that morning, while appearing on *Live with Regis and Kathie Lee*, he repeats his prediction to the shock of Regis Philbin, avowed Yankee fan.

The inexperienced Agbayani has no idea of the firestorm he has set off. To his surprise and horror, "BENNY: METS IN 5" is blasted across the front pages of the papers. All he can do is walk back his "prediction." He was joking, he says. He pulled the five-game mark out of thin air, he says. But his equivocation can't prevent his words from becoming bulletin board material. The Yankees post those "METS IN 5" headlines in their dugout during batting practice, a silent comment on their displeasure with the Mets' chattiness.

Silent comments are the only kind most Yankees will make. In stark contrast to their yappy competition, the Yankees adopt the same stance they have toward regular-season Subway Series games: pretend it's no big deal and say as little as possible. This is no small feat. An actual, no-joke Subway Series will be New York's biggest sporting event—nay, event *period*—in decades. And yet, somehow they find a way to spend as little time in the spotlight as possible. Derek Jeter shares a few comments about Benny Agbayani's "prediction," but otherwise keeps his own counsel. Hardly a peep is heard from Bernie Williams. Ditto Paul O'Neill, Tino Martinez, Chuck Knoblauch, and Andy Pettitte. The trials of this season—and the hell the Yankees caught from the press for daring to slump—had already made them less forthcoming than usual. Now, on the eve of the World Series, they are all but radio silent. When a Yankee is profiled at length or interviewed in the days leading up to the series, it is inevitably new Yankees like David Justice and Denny Neagle, or bit players like Luis Sojo and Luis Polonia. Former Mets like David Cone and Doc Gooden are once again polled on the differences between the two teams, but the Yankees' other megastars practically go into hiding.

The Mets are therefore painted as the fun team, their gregarious stars granted Good Guy status by the media they supply with endless copy. The Yankees are contrasted as cranky, aloof. "When Derek Jeter answers every question with a snide remark about being old, as he's done ad nauseam for weeks now," writes Lisa Olson, "it makes us wonder what we've done to him, other than write glowing praise about what a great and classy player he is."

Perhaps there are Yankees who wish to counter these unkind characterizations, but their press embargo comes from on high. George Steinbrenner declares of his players, "I want them to be very quiet." Thus, they are. The Boss does enough bragging for the whole team, while also betraying testiness, grumbling, "All you guys have been saying we're tired and they can't do this and they can't do that anymore." But he takes no swipes at the Mets and offers no predictions other than to say, "We'll be there, we'll be ready." Every question directed his way—*How badly do you want to beat the Mets? Is there still bad blood over the Mike Piazza beaning?*—receives a noncommittal answer appended with some variation on, *We'll be there, we'll be ready*, to the point that he resembles a malfunctioning robot.

The *Times* runs a piece entitled, "Teams Cannot Avoid the Subject Any Longer," regarding the looming head-to-head battle for baseball's crown, but its substance belies its own premise, as only one side is speaking. Most of the quotes the piece contains come from Steve Phillips, and the plurality of the rest goes to other members of the Mets. Lou Piniella, manager of the vanquished Seattle Mariners, contributes more verbiage to the article than any Yankee.

Weeks ago, before the swoon of September, Buster Olney of the *Times* observed how well both the Mets and Yankees were playing and mentioned casually to Paul O'Neill that there could be a Subway Series. O'Neill almost fainted. "I just couldn't handle that," he said, shaking his head. "You know, during the year we downplay it for you guys in the interleague series, and say it doesn't mean anything. And that time it would mean something."

* * *

The city's newspapers fill with twinkling reminiscences of the Subway Series of yesteryear, when gods like Mickey Mantle, Willie Mays, and Duke Snider roamed New York's earth. Reams of purple prose flow from the pens of the city's sportswriting doyens. None of these memories have any relation to the World Series that will be played in 2000, a trifling technicality that bothers none of the authors.

"I remember the autumns of a half century ago, when the city was never finer," gushes Roger Kahn, whose 1972 tome about the Brooklyn Dodgers, *The Boys of Summer*, forever cemented the notion of postwar New York baseball as a glorious Camelot. His essay for the *Times* is entitled "A Baseball Town, Again," as if New York had ever ceased to be one. Kahn's recollection, like nearly all of those of his peers, concerns the Yankees and the Dodgers exclusively and relegates the New York Giants—who played in Manhattan for seventy years and were the first professional team to grow the sport in the five boroughs—to the status of also-ran.

It is an article of faith among the scribes who look back lovingly at Eisenhower-era New York—for reasons both baseball-related and not—that New York could not regain greatness until it boasted another Subway Series. Now that it will, the renaissance of the city is considered complete. "New York is back at the center of the baseball universe, where most of its citizens undoubtedly believe it should be," crows the *Times* in an op-ed so municipally self-congratulatory its true feelings would be revealed by striking the word "baseball."

This attitude, deeply ingrained among New Yorkers of a certain age, is foreign to most of the players, as virtually none of them came of age within the New York City area. American-born players have a hard enough time grasping the Subway Series obsession, but those who hail from Latin America understand it even less. José Vizcaíno, part-time infielder for the Yankees, hears the phrase "Subway Series" and asks beat writers to explain themselves. "Why do you keep calling it that?" he wonders aloud, with genuine befuddlement. For someone who grew up in the Dominican Republic, in a rural town where watching the World Series cost a penny a pop on the one TV shared among the villagers, the bygone majesty of an all-New York October means little.

The media sort the two teams into the same roles the Yankees and Dodgers occupied back in the 1950s. The Yankees are the team of excellence, industry, and success, a symbol of the primacy New York once again holds over all cities. "You want to root for a team like the San Diego Padres which holds fire sales of players? Cheap little markets like Milwaukee? Why didn't they make themselves into major metro areas when they had the chance?" So writes legendary New York sports scribe Robert Lipsyte. Like many similarly backward-glancing pieces, this essay's author proclaims Yankee fanaticism, yet mentions current Yankees only in passing, if at all. To the sportswriters of his generation, the Subway Series is a grand stage on which actors like Derek Jeter and Bernie Williams now have their own hour to fret and strut. In their eyes, Mets fandom is a fad, Queens itself a nowheresville of Babbits. Lipsyte looks toward Shea and sees not the real Queens of 2000—one of the most culturally diverse places on the planet—but a collection of sad sacks out of *Marty*. "If we have to lose," he writes, "who better to lose to than the Mets, whose fans so desperately need this pathetic affirmation that they have some brief value in a world they can never own."

On the other side stand those writers who remain heartbroken Brooklyn Dodgers loyalists, who consider the Yankees the team of soulless corporate fealty. More than one press veteran repeats the old saw that rooting for the Yankees is like rooting for U. S. Steel, forgetting that after the collapse of American heavy industry, even U. S. Steel isn't U. S. Steel anymore. To ex-Bums partisans, the Mets exemplify Regular Joe New Yorker-ness lacking in the Yankees. And yet, if writers like Lipsyte seem to know little about the modern Yankees, this crowd appears to know even less about the Mets. The papers fill with pieces like the one from longtime city newsman Denis Hamill, who tells *Daily News* readers that the Mets are the "the true New York team," even while his column mentions many bygone Dodgers and only a single Met, and that one Casey Stengel.

Most of those who reminisce about the glorious year of the last Subway Series have no patience for anyone who highlights 1956 as a more troubled time than popular memory would have it, a time when New Yorkers first began abandoning the city for the prefab comfort of the suburbs, never to return. But there are some who remember the

Subway Series of old quite well, and who dread the coming of the new one. George Vecsey of the *Times*, a Dodgers fan in his youth, recalls the Octobers when the Bums faced off against Yankees teams that would win after some unknown Bronx Bomber stepped into the spotlight long enough to defeat Brooklyn. "We are reminded of Yankee power and Yankee pride and Yankee ingenuity and, most of all, we are reminded of Yankee luck," says Vecsey. "It's not that I root, doctor, but this Subway Series fills me with fear and trembling."

* * *

On October 7—when two playoff games are played in the five boroughs on the same day for the first time ever—the *Times* polled fans on their feelings about a possible Subway Series matchup. The results showed a surprising amount of bipartisanship, with Yankees fans confessing they could possibly root for the Mets, and vice versa. It provided soothing evidence for those who believed a Mets-Yankees World Series would bring people together, not tear them apart.

Once both teams advance to the championship series, however, the tone shifts, and the shift for Yankees fans is seismic. "The Yanks and the Metties make it into a Subway Series," speculates one Yankee fan as he holds court at a sports bar in Bensonhurst. "They square off, but the Yankees lose. You think I'm ever going to live that down?" Quoth another Yankee fan, "The closer it gets, the more afraid I get. I don't want to hear the Mets fans rubbing it in our faces if they win. If it were up to me, I'd rather the Yankees and the Cardinals make it to the Series."

As far as the media is concerned, any differences between the fan bases can be ironed out, but even the question of what these differences might be is complicated. When the press attempts to accumulate data to disprove stereotypes about Mets and Yankees fans, they wind up making the picture of the two fan bases clear as mud. First, a poll conducted by the *New York Times* and CBS last October is dredged up, which shows that Mets fans have slightly more advanced degrees, and those who attend their games tend to hail from the city itself. The poll also shows their fans tend to identify more as Republicans, while Yankee fans identify as either Democrats or unaffiliated liberals. This would seem to run counter to the ideas of the corporate Yankees and the blue-collar Mets. Then the *Daily News* conducts a poll of its own whose tallies say Mets fans support Hillary Clinton over Rick Lazio in the Senate race by a larger margin than their Yankee-rooting counterparts. Per the *News*, almost 20 percent of those polled who proclaim Yankee fandom moved to the city in the last five years. The poll also indicates Mets fans are older on average than Yankees fans and tend to hail from the suburbs.

So, Mets fans are proletarian suburbanites, but are also from the city and vote Republican, except they support Hillary Clinton for Senate, and are also old and have postgraduate degrees. And Yankees fans are better educated and more urbane, except when they aren't city natives at all. Contradictory results, to say the least. Yet even this weirdness is spun as good news by the media, who say the unclear portrait it presents means the fans can't be all that different. Therefore, this Subway Series will be a kinder, gentler affair than those of the past.

Except, didn't the old Subway Series take place in a kinder, gentler world? This question too is given muddled answers. Even idealized remembrances of the old Yankees-Dodgers tilts contain slips that reveal there was bloodshed between fans of rival teams. Rudy Giuliani's fond memories include an incident in which the future mayor dared walk the streets of Brooklyn in Yankees gear and barely escaped with his life. However, these brief glimpses of baseball-inspired mayhem are invariably couched in glancing terms or antiquated slang. The implied difference is that this violence occurred in a largely white ethnic New York and is therefore quainter mayhem than that committed in the browner New York that emerged after Eisenhower. No newsman dares couch it in these exact terms, so self evident does this assertion seem to them and their intended audiences.

However, if there is little demographic difference between the two camps—and the *Times*' and *News*' contradictory polls could be interpreted in this fashion—then surely the hostilities of this latest Subway Series will be subdued. One *Times* writer even pens an entire editorial wishing there were *more* hatred between the two camps ("Can't we not all get along?" its clever coda).

Such contentions ignore the animosity among the two camps right under the newspapers' noses. "They're going to need separate bathrooms," insists one Mets fan from Long Island, unable to imagine the two fan bases that will pack the stadiums in near-equal numbers won't be able to do their business alongside each other without fighting. A married couple from Queens with divided loyalties reports their annual Halloween display includes a dummy corpse on the roof of their house, and tension has already arose about which team's jersey will be placed on it. Asked how they will watch the series, the wife mutters, "In different rooms." The article sharing these anecdotes is entitled "A City Happily Pitted Against Itself," even though it captures little happiness.

The same *Times* article recounting last year's poll results also features less-formal queries of actual fans, whose responses reiterate the stereotypes each side holds about the other, and themselves. "Yankee fans are less emotional about the game, less rowdy and more cultured," says one Bronx Bombers fan from New Jersey. "I believe it's the dignity of the unchanged uniform that correlates into the fans. Upper-class people who enjoy winning and the finer things from life."

This fan must not read the *Daily News*, where all season Filip Bondy has chronicled the folkways of Yankee Stadium's Bleacher Creatures in as much profane glory as print will allow, reporting on their chanting roll calls, the fights (verbal and physical) among their ranks, and, above all, their attitude toward the Mets and their fans, which goes beyond the bounds of contempt and skirts the hem of hate speech. This missive penned during the American League Championship Series is a typical account:

> We will scream this once again, for those of you who are hard of hearing: The Creatures do not want a Subway Series. We are confident that such a contest would be appropriately one-sided, but that is not the point. We do not wish to be associated with the Mets, in any form or on any known planet. We don't want to be seen in public with them, let alone in a World Series. We cannot bear the thought of sharing the same headlines, or even appearing in the same photos with that imposter New York team, its curlicue "NY," or any of its sophomoric fans.

The newspapers can insist they see a city united by sports fandom. What they actually capture is much closer to the assessment of Jon Stewart, *Daily Show* host and professed Mets fan. After his favorite team captures the National League pennant and a confrontation with the Yankees appears imminent, Stewart contends a Subway Series would be "a showdown which would undoubtedly restore New York's fading reputation as a nightmarish cesspool of hate."

* * *

Rudy Giuliani beams. The year 2000 has been a trial for him, but watching Hizzoner in the days leading up to the World Series, one would believe he'd endure all of it twice for the glory of these moments. "You can't believe how long I've been praying for it," he confesses, and this is surely not hyperbolizing.

The Subway Series is also a boon for the spirits of GOP Senate candidate Rick Lazio, who uses his Mets fan bona fides to prove his "real New Yorker" credentials (in contrast to Hillary Clinton, whose "lifelong Yankees fan" claim remains a cringe-inducing totem to use against her). As the Mets progress through the playoffs, Lazio is never far behind, in attendance at Shea Stadium when the Mets take game five from the Cardinals and receiving a healthy cheer from the crowd when introduced mid-game. In the days that follow the Mets victory over St. Louis, his campaign offices are unabashedly exuberant, feeding off of their boss's enthusiasm.

The Mets' run through October is the closest thing to good news the Lazio campaign has received in weeks. The first debate between him and Clinton in mid-September ended on an odd note when the Long Islander marched over to the first lady's podium and requested she sign a pledge, then and there, to not take "soft money." It was an attempt to brand her every bit the slippery political opportunist as her husband but instead came across as bullying. Before the debate, many polls showed the race to be a toss-up. Afterward, Lazio's numbers plunged.

While Lazio takes solace in the Mets, any interest Hillary Clinton might have in the Yankees is kept well hidden. When campaign advisers debate the optics of Clinton attending one of the World Series games in person, Lazio wonders aloud why she should. "The Cubs aren't in it, the White Sox aren't in it," he smirks, referring to the fact that the first lady grew up in the Chicago area.

Those running for national office aren't immune from Subway Series questions either, as the "issue" comes up on the presidential campaign trail. Vice president and democratic nominee Al Gore arrives in New York late on the evening of October 18, ahead of a full day of media appearances and campaigning for both himself and Hillary Clinton. With three days to go before game one, among the first questions he is asked is who he will root for in the World Series. Gore's initial response is to ignore the question altogether, but when pinned down on the subject the following day, Gore quips lamely, "I'm for New York."

After his busy day on the networks, the veep appears at the annual Alfred E. Smith Memorial Dinner, the premier event on New York's political calendar. A long-running New York tradition, the Smith Dinner invites politicians from both sides of the aisle to gently roast one another while feasting on delicacies. Apart from Gore and both of New York's Senate hopefuls, the most notable attendee is Gore's Republican opponent, Texas governor George W. Bush. Each man delivers remarks in which they poke gentle fun, mostly at themselves. Bush's remarks play on his party's well-heeled constituency ("Some people call you the elite. I call you my base."), while Gore's spiel plays off his reputation as a robotic wonk. Hearty bipartisan laughter is exchanged. To the campaign press, this is as reassuring as fan polls are to the sports scribes. Witnessing some lighthearted self-deprecating humor on the part of both candidates, they tell themselves there is no hatred between the camps, no real difference between the two challengers. This reassures them that no matter who wins the office in November, the ship of state will continue on the straight and narrow.

Like Gore, Bush answers the ultimate campaign question of the week with cutesy avoidance. ("I'm for the New York team.") The closest Bush comes to taking sides is when he gives gratitude for the support of Bobby Valentine, who has expressed his preference for Bush whenever asked. The former owner of the Rangers reports, "I appreciate that he's going to vote for me, even though I fired him."

* * *

If there is an official kickoff for Subway Series festivities, it occurs on the afternoon of October 20, when Mayor Giuliani leads a "Pledge Your Allegiance" pep rally at Bryant Park. Despite a chill drizzle turning parkland into mud, summertime ballpark treats of hot dogs, peanuts, and Cracker Jack are distributed freely. The two lions who stand guard at the nearby New York Public Library are fitted with giant baseball caps they will wear for the duration of the series. The lion known as Fortitude wears a Yankees hat. The Mets hat is placed on the lion labeled Patience.

With the first pitch of game one a day away, there is an edge to the proceedings. The fans are segregated by allegiances, split on each side of a DMZ carved through the park with steel police parade barriers. One camp brandishes signs like "HEY PIAZZA, HOW'S YOUR HEAD?" The other chants, "METS IN SIX! METS IN SIX!"

Little prompting is needed to rope Rudy Giuliani into all the cantankerousness. When the mayor is presented with a hybrid Mets-Yankees hat, he flings it across the dais in disgust. "This is what I call the coward's hat," he sneers. "This is a time of crisis and you have to pledge your allegiance. We don't accept any of this, 'I root for the Yankees, I root for the Mets, I root for New York City.' You root for the Yankees, or you root for the Mets. That's it."

There is no argument from the crowd.

* * *

John Franco sees it. Another afternoon in the clubhouse at Shea, in the days before the Series begins. Another phalanx of reporters, local, national, and international, ask him the same questions they've asked a thousand times already in the previous week. Suddenly there it is: a tiny mouse scurrying through them all.

Shea Stadium abounds with critters. Apart from the ubiquitous pigeons found in the city's airspace, those who work at the stadium report encounters with chipmunks, squirrels, and even raccoons that stray into the ballpark from nearby Flushing Meadows Park. The most famous animal visitor of all appeared in September of 1969, when a black cat emerged near the dugout of the visiting Cubs, paused to peer at the batter in the on-deck circle, then ran off and was never seen again. The symbolism could not have been more obvious. The Cubs' thinning playoff hopes crumbled completely while the Mets surged to their first division title, pennant, and championship.

Everyone knows what a black cat means. What of a mouse? Franco tries to follow the tiny thing through the snarl of microphone cables and cramped feet, hoping to save it from an untimely demise under the shoes of the press. But the little guy is too quick. He scampers under the door of a locked office. He is gone.

* * *

When it finally happens, the damp chill of pennant-clinching week is, for the moment, gone. The teams arrive in the Bronx around 5:00 p.m.—the Yankees in their own vehicles, the Mets bounding off a charter bus wielding camcorders like gawking tourists—to a bright and sunny October afternoon. Not a sign of a cloud in the sky. Temperatures of seventy degrees inspire many a sidewalk party near the stadium, as locals drag their televisions to the curb, running extensions cords from the nearest buildings, and enjoy the baseball action *en plein air.*

For those at home, Fox's pregame show begins with a montage of Subway Series past narrated in *dese-dem-dose* New York-ese by Billy Crystal. Pre-taped interviews with Bobby Valentine and Joe Torre devote the majority of their time not to the current teams, but to remembrances of old ones. Torre recalls his attendance at Don Larsen's World Series perfect game in 1956. Valentine recalls the spring training twenty-one years ago when Torre cut him from the Mets.

A special Subway Series train is scheduled to depart Grand Central at 7:00 p.m. None of the old battle-worn Redbird cars—the ones normally seen on the 4 line that serves Yankee Stadium, some of which are only a few years younger than the last Subway Series—will do for this event. This charter train is made up of ten cars of the MTA's latest models, gleaming steel, with digital displays of upcoming stops, and maps that update as the train moves along the line. The inaugural train is trimmed with Yankee pinstripes and arrives a half hour behind schedule. Rudy Giuliani, governor George Pataki, and a slew of city dignitaries, their families, and bodyguards climb into the first car and wait to embark for the Bronx. Eager fans who follow them are eyed by suspicious security details and compressed by a surfeit of TV cameras. The governor deftly signs autographs without holding on to a handrail. The mayor fields questions about new stadium plans for the Mets and Yankees and breaks away for a moment to tell his fourteen-year-old son Andrew not to stand on the brand-new seats.

By the time the train arrives at the 161st Street station at 8:05 p.m., Yankee Stadium announcer Bob Sheppard can be heard on the elevated platform, intoning the names of the visitors in his timeless monotone. Each Met introduced receives a perfunctory boo interrupted by cheering. The pattern is reversed when the home team trots onto the field. The sounds of boos and cheers wash around each other, competing for dominance before settling into an odd olio of mixed emotions.

A moment of silence is observed to honor the victims of the USS *Cole*, a Navy destroyer bombed in the Persian Gulf nine days earlier. Long Islander Billy Joel sings a painfully slow and occasionally off-key national anthem. A bald eagle makes a triumphant flight from center field to the pitcher's mound. Don Larsen, perfect-game tosser in the last Subway Series, throws a ceremonial first pitch to his old battery mate, Yogi Berra. Fox punctuates its last bumper before the first pitch with the tense, minimalist piano music from *Eyes Wide Shut.*

And then, at 8:13 p.m. on Saturday, October 21, 2000, with flashbulbs crackling throughout the House That Ruth Built, forty-four years of waiting and four days of inexhaustible hype give way to the first pitch of the new millennium's Subway Series. It is thrown by Andy Pettitte, who draws the first Yankee start despite a spotty record pitching at home in World Series action. Bobby Valentine flips his October script and hands the ball in game one to Al Leiter, who'd pitched brilliantly in the postseason this year and against the Yankees over the last two seasons. Between his time with Toronto and Florida, Leiter has five World Series appearances to his credit, including two starts, giving him far more experience in the Fall Classic than all other starters on the Mets' staff. Everyone else is tied for second, with zero.

Playing in an American League park, Valentine takes full advantage and uses Mike Piazza as his designated hitter while slotting Todd Pratt behind the plate. Pratt is ecstatic, having logged only one at bat in the division series and none in championship series ("I started getting some spider webs and cobwebs") and owning bitter memories of the 1993 World Series, when he was the backup backstop for the Phillies and rode the pine for all six games. The Yankees choose Chuck Knoblauch as their DH, as they had for much of the playoffs (when he wasn't benched for petulance), hoping to keep his bat in the lineup and his glove off the field. Taking his place at second is not Luis Sojo, who'd filled in ably at the position for much of this postseason, but José Vizcaíno, who the Yankees acquired at midseason right under Steve Phillips's nose. For added Subway Series symbolism, Vizcaíno is one of only two players in baseball history to play for all four teams that have called New York home (the other being Darryl Strawberry).

True to form, Al Leiter overpowers the Yankees in the first five innings. Andy Pettitte is not quite as dominating, but he gets by with a little help from the opposition. The Mets put the leadoff man on base each inning from the second to the sixth but are turned aside each time, mostly due to baserunning blunders. After beginning the fourth with a single, Mike Piazza is picked off first. Todd Zeile follows by hitting a slow dribbler up the third base line that rolls foul before taking a sudden tilt to the right, and is thrown out easily when he fails to run. Despite witnessing this object lesson in lack of hustle, Jay Payton fails to run in the top of the fifth when he taps a ball near the plate that be believes is foul and is tagged out while still arguing the point with the home plate umpire.

The Mets save their most crushing mistake for the top of the sixth. For the fifth straight inning, the Mets put their leadoff man on base when

Timo Pérez singles up the middle. Though Andy Pettitte logs two quick outs after this hit, Todd Zeile makes a bid to redeem himself for his earlier brain cramp by belting a fastball into the left-field corner. Zeile's wallop is a line drive lofted just high enough to give it a chance of clearing the fence. Timo Pérez has never played at Yankee Stadium before tonight, but he is so sure Zeile has hit a two-run homer that he slows down in celebration, his gallop reduced to a mere jog by the time he reaches second base. Zeile trots with a champion's confidence toward first, raising a fist as he reaches the bag.

Zeile was at Yankee Stadium with the Orioles in October of 1996 when a potential fly out was transformed into a home run by a young fan named Jeffrey Maier, who plopped his fielder's mitt over the head of the right fielder and came away with the ball. Baltimore argued it was a case of fan interference, which it clearly was, but received no satisfaction from the umpires. Anyone who has watched a game at Yankee Stadium has seen fans leaning over its low walls in a similar fashion to interfere with a ball in play. So it is not mere hubris that causes the runners to slow down on the basepaths, but the historical record. To believe that no fan will put their hands on a ball hit so close to the left-field stands is to ignore decades of evidence.

That is why it is stunning that when Zeile's blast lands right on top of the outfield wall, *not a single fan touches it*. Every nearby fan recoils as if repelled by an invisible force field. The ball slides across the protective padding and plops down onto the warning track, still in play. It is the longest fly ball one can hit in that direction and *not* be a home run, down the millimeter. David Justice retrieves the ball and heaves it in to Derek Jeter, who then wings it home. Upon realizing the ball has not cleared the fence, Pérez restarts his engines, but Jeter's throw beats him to the plate with plenty of room to spare. Had Pérez been running hard on the play, the Mets would have salvaged one run out of the near miss. Instead, the inning produces nothing more than additional Mets humiliation. Later, Pérez pins the blame on no one but himself. "Those are things that happen to someone with little experience," he admits with a sigh.

The Yankees immediately make the visitors pay for their blunders, as David Justice belts a booming double to drive in two runs in the bottom of the sixth, an outcome that makes the Mets' constant foot-shooting appear fatal. And yet, the Mets are somehow able to shrug off the blunders of the first six innings and fight right back in the top of the seventh, loading the bases and tying the game on a two-run single by pinch hitter Bubba Trammell. Then Edgardo Alfonzo hits a squib down the third base line that does not travel more than forty feet, so softly hit that Yankee third baseman Scott Brosius has no time to field it. A runner trots home on the play, giving the Mets a 3–2 lead.

When Al Leiter records another scoreless frame in the seventh and John Franco does the same in the eighth, the Mets are, almost despite themselves, three outs away from taking the first game of this series and relegating the idiocy of the initial innings to the realm of deep trivia. They even present themselves with a golden opportunity to pad their lead in the top of the ninth by putting a man on third with one out. That runner is the slow-footed Todd Pratt, however, and when he doesn't run on contact on a Timo Pérez grounder, the Mets are turned aside yet again.

Thus, Armando Benítez will enter the bottom of the ninth to protect a mere one-run lead. After he records the first out on a hard-hit fly ball to left center, Paul O'Neill steps up to the plate, though *staggers* might be the more apt verb. He has been missing in action at the plate for more than a month as he battles injuries, chief among them a sore hip, collecting only one extra-base hit since September 6. Benítez quickly gets ahead of him, throwing heat the outfielder should not be able to catch up with.

But Paul O'Neill does catch up to one, barely, and fouls it off. Then he knocks another a few rows deep into the third base stands. Robin Ventura lunges for it, desperate to secure the second out, but it lands a few frustrating feet beyond his reach. Benítez tosses two balls—one wide, one high—to bring the count full. Then another pitch is slapped foul beyond third base. And another. Benítez continues to place heat on the outside black, and O'Neill knocks it foul each time, waiting for a pitch to hit or something he can watch sail outside. He will not allow himself to make the second out.

The tenth pitch from Benítez lands wide, and O'Neill takes his base. It is a prolonged battle of an at bat, a battle won by the hitter. It is the kind of at bat that, in the past, has served as the prologue to a Benítez meltdown.

Joe Torre sends up veteran benchwarmer Luis Polonia to pinch-hit for Scott Brosius. Like O'Neill, Polonia should be no match for a Benítez fastball, but he slashes a single to right field, a few hops short of Timo Pérez. Then Benítez falls behind José Vizcaíno before the second baseman lobs an opposite-field single. Joe McEwing (now playing left field due to a flurry of late-inning substitutions) runs in on the ball and whizzes a throw to the infield to prevent O'Neill from advancing past third. But all the Yankees need now is a fly ball to knot the score, and they get it when Chuck Knoblauch lofts one to deep left. O'Neill tags and scores, sore hip and all. Tie ballgame.

Though Armando Benítez fans Derek Jeter to keep the game tied, and the Mets' Houdinis of middle relief work around many Yankees baserunners in the innings that follow, it is inescapable that the Yankees have these chances because the Mets blew so many of theirs and are presenting themselves no new ones. While Dennis Cook, Glendon Rusch, and Turk Wendell dance between the proverbial raindrops, the Mets fail to collect a single baserunner in the tenth, eleventh, and twelfth innings.

In the bottom of the twelfth, their luck runs out. First Tino Martinez lobs a one-out single to right field, then Jorge Posada lines a ball past a diving Edgardo Alfonzo, and as it rolls all the way to the wall, Martinez dashes to third. Turk Wendell issues an intentional walk to the next batter to load the bases and gets a huge break when Luis Sojo pops out behind the plate for out number two. But in the end, it is not Derek Jeter or Bernie Williams or Paul O'Neill who brings this game to an end but José Vizcaíno, inserted into the lineup on a hunch, playing second only to keep Chuck Knoblauch off the field, a player who might be a Met right now if Steve Phillips had been quicker on the trigger.

Vizcaíno lines Turk Wendell's first pitch up the middle, just beyond the infield. Martinez jogs in with the winning run. At 1:04 a.m., four hours and fifty-one minutes after the first pitch, the first Subway Series game in forty-four years ends just as the last one did, with the Yankees on top.

Turk Wendell is tagged with the loss, though by all rights the L should go to Armando Benítez, whose blown save in the ninth all but assured defeat. Or perhaps it should be shared among the many Mets who forgot how to run the bases during the course of this game. The whole experience is so draining that Wendell can barely muster disappointment. "This is what I always envisioned," he says of his first World Series appearance, "but it usually didn't end this way."

* * *

Postmortems attribute the outcome less to Yankees experience than Mets naïveté, and the fact that the team seemed more concerned with arguing calls than moving on. The day following game one, Valentine spends far too much time in his press conference discussing his belief that the Yankee Stadium grounds crew engaged in landscaping skullduggery (like deliberately dampening the infield turf) that led to the odd bounces and rolls. He sounds uncomfortably like someone trying to lay the blame for his own mistakes elsewhere.

More time and ink would be spent reviewing the Mets' mental errors of game one were it not for the rematch promised by game two. For weeks, before either team was even close to capturing a pennant, questions about a Subway Series inevitably included this puzzler: *What happens when Mike Piazza and Roger Clemens face off again?* If there was any chance that such questions could be avoided, Clemens reminded everyone of his headhunter reputation by buzzing Alex Rodriguez in Seattle.

When the Mets are queried on the subject, it is clear that the Mike Piazza beaning still weighs heavily on all of them. Asked if he and his teammates thought the incident was over, Todd Zeile responds with an unequivocal, "Like hell, it is." Asked how he felt about the Yankees, Todd Pratt says, "We actually like their team. Or at least twenty-four of their guys." No clarification was needed about who Pratt excluded from his list. The only man on the Mets willing to move on, it seemed, was Piazza, who worried aloud that obsessing over it would ruin the hitting mechanics he'd worked so hard to regain.

As for the Yankees, most of them avoid this question along with all others leading up to the World Series. Joe Torre could not duck the press, however, and when he announced that Roger Clemens would start game two in the Bronx—and was therefore unlikely to pitch at Shea Stadium—reporters asked if he was glad to keep Clemens out of the batter's box and away from possible retaliation. The manager snapped back, "Am I glad to avoid what the media has created?" To him, all the blame lay with the press's obsessions over the Piazza beaning, none with Clemens. "Whether you pick up a newspaper or you watch a network," he growled, "that's all you see is Mike getting hit in the head. I would like to believe this World Series is more about competition and fun than it will be about getting even and inciting riots." He later referred to Clemens's beaning of Piazza as "the misfortune" ("in the way people in Ireland refer to the civil wars as 'the trouble,'" quipped Lisa Olson).

If Torre was perturbed by the constant questions, Clemens was seething. "I was as upset as anybody," he said of "the misfortune" and declared it would not alter his intimidating pitching style in the slightest. When reminded that Piazza had said he lost all respect for Clemens after the beaning, Clemens reported the respect of Piazza meant nothing to him. Behind the scenes, his teammates muttered to each other about what effect these queries would have on the pitcher and thanked their lucky stars that *they* didn't have to stand in the box against him.

When Clemens takes the mound on the evening of October 22, the mercury has dropped from game one's springlike temperatures to a more autumnal forty-nine degrees. And yet, the pitcher appears to be overheated. When Timo Pérez fakes a bunt on his very first pitch, a common tactic for the slap-hitting speedster, Clemens takes it as a personal affront, growling a dire "fuck you" in his direction. He strikes out the rookie on a series of fastballs in the upper nineties, then does the same to Edgardo Alfonzo on a splitter in the dirt that clocks in at an astonishing 94 mph.

And then, Mike Piazza. On Roger Clemens's fourth pitch to him, Piazza breaks his bat and sends the ball rolling foul down the first base line. The bulk of what's left of Piazza's lumber spins up the middle, in the general vicinity of the pitcher's mound. If you are watching at home, you see only the briefest glimpse of Piazza's shattered bat twirling toward Clemens, as the Fox broadcast chooses to follow the path of the ball instead. And then you hear 56,069 fans groan in unison.

When the barrel of Mike Piazza's bat tumbles toward Roger Clemens, he picks it up by the fat end and sidearms it into foul territory. The bat crosses in front of Piazza, missing him by no more than a foot. The catcher turns toward the pitcher, his face caught between anger and confusion. "What is your problem?" he yells. No response from Clemens, who refuses to react to the batter. The pitcher pleads for forgiveness—not from Piazza, but from home plate umpire Charlie Reliford, who he fears may eject him. "I thought it was the ball," he insists, avoiding eye contact with Piazza at all costs. Reliford is too busy acting as a human wall between a furious Piazza and a stone-faced Clemens to address The Rocket's excuses.

The entire Mets dugout spills onto the field, and though the Yankees follow suit, no violence ensues, only angry crowding and quick separation. Roger Clemens himself is oblivious to it all, holding his glove aloft in the universal pitcher's request for another ball from the umpire, pleading his case robotically to Reliford, repeating "I thought it was the ball . . ."

He need not worry. This umpiring crew is no more inclined to punish him than the one in Seattle. Crew chief Ed Montague explains later that he considered Roger Clemens's bat chucking "an emotional reaction," one in no need of correction. And so after all this, Piazza is forced to step back into the box against a pitcher who, moments earlier, threw a jagged piece of wood in his direction. He grounds out to second. The inning ends with Clemens again entreating the home plate umpire on his way back to the dugout, begging forgiveness, putting his arm around Reliford. Not a glance or a gesture in the direction of Piazza.

Though the crowd cheers Piazza's inning-ending grounder, it is not with the raucous yells of game one. For the remainder of game two, fans treat all proceedings with oddly subdued reactions. Roger Clemens's bizarre bat-flinging act puts a pall on the proceedings, and fans seem to feel as if they should behave themselves as penance. In the Fox booth, announcers Joe Buck and Tim McCarver debate what they witnessed for several innings, wondering if Clemens would have been ejected if this were a regular-season game (they say yes), characterizing the object the pitcher threw as "a weapon," labeling his act "indefensible." As the game carries on and the crowd continues to react with muted cheering, both Buck and McCarver share their opinion that Clemens is to blame, describing the fans in the stands as stunned. The two announcers harp on this idea so often throughout the broadcast that Brian Cashman barges into the booth between innings to accuse them of painting a biased picture of the game.

The crowd might be cowed by Roger Clemens's act, but no one is more shocked than the Mets, who find themselves incapable of registering anything close to payback. In eight innings on the mound, Clemens allows only two hits, both singles, and four total baserunners while striking out nine batters and walking none. It is utter domination, made all the more painful by the fact that the pitcher certainly could have (and perhaps should have) been sent to the showers after his bat-chucking act. The Clemens who wilted in his previous starts against the Mets is nowhere to be seen.

Also missing is the Mike Hampton who crushed the Cardinals in the championship series. Hampton pitched the game of his life in the pennant clincher, but that pitcher has been replaced by the Hampton who lost the plate in April. In the bottom of the first, after retiring the first two batters, he suddenly tosses eight straight pitches out of the strike zone, setting up the Yankees to collect a pair of RBI singles. In the second inning, he serves up a solo shot to Scott Brosius. (For added pain to the Mets, Brosius's homer drops a few feet behind the spot where Todd Zeile's non-homer landed the night before.) In the fourth, more two-out baserunners and a Paul O'Neill single stretches the Yankee lead to 4–0. After the shaky Hampton departs, the Yankees tack on against the Mets bullpen, scoring single runs in the seventh and eighth innings. As the eighth inning ends, Luis Polonia holds aloft a red balloon for the benefit of Fox's cameras, one that someone has inscribed with the slogan "METS IN 3000." It's unclear if this is a reference to Benny Agbayani's pre-series prediction ("Mets in five") or to a belief that the Mets won't be able to beat the Yankees for another thousand years.

With a 6–0 lead heading to the ninth, the matter of the final three outs appears a mere technicality to the home team. Clemens has departed the game, however, and in his absence the spell he weaved over the Mets' bats dissipates. After Edgardo Alfonzo lines a leadoff single into left center, Mike Piazza crushes a pitch from reliever Jeff Nelson, banging it high off the left-field foul pole for a home run. Robin Ventura follows by lacing a single to center, at which point Joe Torre decides to take no chances and turns to Mariano Rivera to restore order.

The closer records the first out with ease, but then Benny Agbayani sneaks a single through the shortstop hole, and Jorge Posada allows a passed ball to move two runners into scoring position. Rivera secures the second out, but Jay Payton keeps hope alive by lining an outside Rivera cutter into the right-field porch for a three-run homer. After eight innings of offensive blackout, the Mets have erupted to make this a one-run game, and they've done it against the closer who is the surest thing in baseball.

The next batter due up is Kurt Abbott, a late substitute at shortstop for Mike Bordick, who could charitably be called a light hitter. Bobby Valentine could turn to super-sub Joe McEwing to bat for Abbott, and he still has Matt Franco (added to the Mets roster after Derek Bell was lost for the postseason) on his bench, the man who collected a memorable game-winning hit against Rivera last season. Franco's successful history of pinch-hitting and his left-handedness might make him the Mets' best chance to prolong this game.

Valentine curiously chooses to stick with Kurt Abbott, however, and Mariano Rivera shrugs off the struggles he exhibited to the previous batters, striking him out looking on three pitches that pass in the blink of an eye. The Yankees stagger off the field, counting their blessings for this 6–5 win, a laugher that turned squeaker. The Mets sit rooted to the visiting dugout bench, stunned at the near miss, stunned at Roger Clemens, stunned at everything that's transpired in a span of twenty-four hours.

* * *

The Mets have lost a plethora of battles. They lost the game. They lost a chance to retaliate against Roger Clemens. And worst of all, they lost their standing within the baseball community for not fighting back.

It is unlikely Roger Clemens's bat-chucking act involved any level of thought beyond that of lizard-brain reaction. And yet, this move was, in its own way, as brilliant as anything Clemens did on the mound in game two. Mike Piazza encapsulates why in his postgame remarks. "You're damned if you do and damned if you don't," he says. "We punch him, guys get thrown out, we're selfish. We back down . . . we look gutless."

In a tacit way, commissioner Bud Selig abets this line of thinking. He is in the stands for game two and could have made some sort of immediate ruling on Clemens's fate. The commissioner refuses to insert himself into the proceedings because the situation defused so quickly, he says, and because the Mets themselves didn't demand an ejection. It was up to the Mets to protest, apparently, either verbally or physically. But they did not, and will be faulted forever after for failing to do so.

During the broadcast, Fox color man Bob Brenly makes a point that will be sounded again and again in the years to come when he wonders aloud why Piazza "hadn't charged the mound more forcefully." Brenly, and many who share his opinion, are careful to say the Mets shouldn't have started a physical confrontation. Then what *should* they have done? No one has an exact prescription except to say they should have done more than what they did do, which was nothing.

Some say the Mets *should* have thrown punches, consequences be damned, to maintain a modicum of manly pride. Michael Kay, Yankees radio announcer drafted into postgame duties for the MSG Network, touts his team's party line. "For the last two months, all the Mets talked about was how they wanted to get at Roger Clemens, they wanted to get at Roger Clemens to pay him back," Kay fumes. "Every single one of the Mets had a chance at Roger Clemens. They were five inches from him. Mike Piazza could have darted out to the mound quicker than anybody. But they didn't."

Even those who condemn Clemens in the harshest terms save words to tut-tut the Mets for their failure to retaliate. "The Mets can yell about Clemens all they want," writes Mike Lupica, in a column mostly dedicated to lambasting Clemens. "But the Mets had a clear shot at Clemens for seven innings after his Mike Tyson moment with Piazza's broken bat. Only from the Tyson moment on, he seemed to get bigger on the mound."

"They're looking for excuses," sneers George Steinbrenner. "We'll just keep playing; playing and winning." The Boss's statement is a summation of the criticism of the Mets: They lack the heart of a champion. They would rather excuse a loss than prevent it. The Yankees, and Roger Clemens, will do whatever it takes to win. If you are not prepared to do the same, if you are not prepared to fight back with offense of any kind—home runs or haymakers—then you will not win, and you will not deserve to win.

The Mets walk away from game two diminished in many people's eyes, but so do the Yankees. Though no one would expect the Yankees to turn on a teammate, their defense of Clemens is a little too enthusiastic, a little too us vs. them. Every Yankee who takes it upon himself to excuse or dismiss what Clemens did comes away looking at best silly, at worst like a bully. Rudy Giuliani—a Yankee in everything but name—rushes to appear on ABC's *Good Morning America* the morning after game two, where he labels Clemens's act "an instinctual reaction" and refuses to believe that the pitcher would throw at Piazza with purpose, because "he would get himself thrown out of one of the most important games of his career." This is the defense forwarded by the Yankees (and proxy Yankees) in Clemens's defense: he didn't mean to throw the bat, so he shouldn't have to pay for it.

Apart from Roger Clemens himself, no Yankee escapes the incident looking worse than Joe Torre. At the press conference following game two, Torre counsels the press, "Understand that Roger is wearing our uniform, and we're going to go overboard to back him." The media are not surprised by this declaration, but when Torre voices nothing close to contrition or remorse over what was done, they continue to press. *Why did he do it? Did you ask him to explain himself? Are you afraid your players will get hit now?* Torre insists that if he were in the broadcast booth (he had been a color man for baseball broadcasts right before he took the Yankees job) and saw this incident, he would consider it as benign as he does now. Upon hearing this, it's all the reporters can do to not laugh in his face.

A flustered Torre falls back on the "excellence" defense, chalking up Roger Clemens's act as a byproduct of superhuman intensity, a "need to win" that only the Yankees could possibly understand. "If some guys take that competitiveness and put another tag on it, then I can't help it," he sneers at his interrogators. "These guys have a need to win." Torre then threatens to leave the press conference altogether before fuming at his accusers, a petulant move that does him no favors. "Why would he throw at him?" Torre asks. "So he could get thrown out of the game in the second inning of the World Series? Does that make any sense to anybody? Someone answer my question. Why would he do it?"

The reviews of this performance are unkind. "If Torre wants to go into the tank for Clemens because Clemens is one of his own, fine for him," Mike Lupica writes. "But Torre doesn't get to act indignant and nearly storm out of an interview room because everybody won't go along with him." Quoth Mark Kriegel of the *News*, "After three championships, you wonder if the rules are different for him than for other managers." "The Yankees should have condemned what Clemens did last night," writes Jack Curry of the *Times*. "They should have shaken his hand for the splendid game, then shaken their heads and told him that they disapproved of his dangerous behavior. They did not. So, like a bully, they are tarnished, too." Lisa Olson calls on Clemens to apologize to his team "for forcing a proud organization to look shameless and silly as it comes to his defense."

But no apologies are forthcoming from Roger Clemens. Interviewed on the field after the game two win, the closest he comes is to obliquely blame the media for "all the stuff I had to hear in the last week." At the very press conference where Joe Torre is raked over the coals, Clemens stands in the wings, in eyeshot of everyone in attendance, muttering about how unfair this all is—to him. "We win game two in the World Series and all they ask about is this shit," he whines.

This refrain continues the following evening when Roger Clemens appears at a Home Shopping Network event held at the Meadowlands, prior to a Monday-night battle between the Jets and the Dolphins. Peppered with more bat-related posers, Clemens counters, "You got any other questions besides that?"

"I wish it had been somebody else," he sighs as the queries continue. "I wish it had been Mike Bordick's bat."

One of the most shocking outcomes of the incident is that Bobby Valentine says almost nothing about it. When Roger Clemens beaned Mike Piazza in July, he was the loudest voice shrieking in protest. Many insisted The Rocket only acted tough because he never had to step into the batter's box himself, but few said it with the same vitriol as the Mets manager, who growled, "With a DH, you can wear a skirt."

Now, Valentine steers clear of any remotely controversial comment, a stance unknown to him. When told MLB will fine Clemens for the bat hurling, Valentine professes to not care unless the money is going to his favorite charity. When asked to give his opinion about what Clemens might have been thinking when he threw that bat, Valentine plays the "let he who is without sin" card. "I get very, very upset when people see my actions and try to tell me what my intentions are," he says, suddenly flush with monkish magnanimity.

Bobby Valentine's uncharacteristic stance perhaps comes from the recognition of how little good can be accomplished from further protest. It might be unfair that Clemens was allowed to pitch after his lumber tossing, but that won't change the fact that he *was* allowed to continue pitching, nor will it undo eight shutout innings. The more the Mets talk about the injustice of what he did, the more they sound like sore losers.

On the off day between games two and three, Al Leiter appears at the same Monday-night Meadowlands event as Roger Clemens. The two pitchers cross paths. They exchange words. All are civil. It's pointless to argue now. The moment has passed. Clemens has won.

* * *

At a Steiner Sports autograph event at Mickey Mantle's Restaurant, several former players are polled on their opinion of Roger Clemens, the only topic of conversation in the city in the forty-eight hours between games two and three. Vic Ziegel of the *Daily News* surveys the scene at this event and is struck by the sight of Bill Buckner and Mookie Wilson signing autographs on enlarged photos of their moment in history together, that roller along first in game six of the 1986 World Series. Mere feet away, Ralph Branca and Bobby Thomson are doing the same to photos of their own shared piece of baseball lore, the Shot Heard Round the World. Taking it all in, Ziegel wonders how many years will have to pass before Mike Piazza and Roger Clemens will be seen scribbling their names onto photos of a shattered bat and a confused scowl for $50 a pop.

At the moment, the answer appears to be sometime after hell freezes over. The first two games of the series birthed a new wave of animosity between the two camps. See Filip Bondy's Bleacher Creatures column, wherein the author and the fans around him describe the opposition, quite literally, as subhuman. "You try to treat them like human beings," it begins. "You really do. But there is always something very strange about Met fans, something repulsive and off-putting. It is as if they are a mutant race of primates, isolated in a penal colony in Queens so they don't reproduce and overrun the rest of the world." The Creatures chronicled in Bondy's piece recoil at opposing fans who have painted their faces ("That stuff won't come off without gasoline" says one) and wear Mets colors to the Bronx. Spying a Mets fan who wore orange shoes to the game, one Creature wonders aloud, "Is she trying to make it that much easier for me to run her over in my car?"

The atmosphere around Shea Stadium for game three is deemed "sluggish" by one *Times* writer, the spirits of Mets fans tempered by their team's 0–2 deficit, the manner in which they lost those two games, and the arrogance of Yankees fans who storm the gates with brooms in anticipation of a sweep. The NYPD dispatches seven hundred officers to Shea, even more than were mustered at the stadium for John Rocker's return, and the omnipresence of law enforcement dampens the mood even further. One Mets fan confronts a policeman and demands to know who he's rooting for in this game. "I'm a fan of overtime," the officer deadpans.

The scene is also sobered by volunteers for Rick Lazio, who hand out masks of Hillary Clinton wearing a Yankees cap outside Shea Stadium. Lazio attends the game and makes a point of riding the Subway Series special 7 train decked out in orange and blue with Mayor Giuliani and Governor Pataki. "Yankee fans respect real Met fans," Giuliani insists, though a poll of fans these days might contradict this. "[Lazio] became a New York Met fan living in New York, the traditional way," Giuliani continues. Like many of Lazio's moves since his disastrous debate gambit, the mask campaign comes across as tone deaf and uncouth. "Can you imagine Senator Moynihan doing that?" asks a Clinton aide, referring to the bow-tied patrician senator for whose seat they are vying.

Rick Lazio is far from the only person to try and exploit the bat-chucking hype. The opening segment of Fox's game three broadcast is set to the *Sopranos* theme song and features numerous replays of Clemens hurling lumber. The dual hosts of the pregame show, Keith Olbermann and Steve Lyons, both profess they are sick of talking about the shattered bat hurling, then proceed to discuss it for five full minutes. When the coverage switches over to the booth with Tim McCarver and Joe Buck, they play up the incident as a ticking time bomb, describing their sense of "an odd feeling on the field prior to the game" and repeating ad nauseam their belief that the incident is "hanging over the series."

The only way to remove that feeling will be for the Mets to commence winning. Game three is a bad time for them to do that, as the Yankees will send to the mound Orlando Hernández. In the three seasons since he left Cuba behind and signed with the Yankees, his team has not lost a playoff game he has started. In the hours before game three, a rumor emerges that El Duque may be fighting some illness, but the strong performance Hernández puts up provides evidence to the contrary. "If he's not feeling well, I'm going to have everyone catch what he has," Joe Torre says.

Opposing El Duque is Rick Reed, whose right-handedness and inveterate strike throwing are both considered deficits when facing a patient and lefty-heavy Yankee lineup. Working in his favor is a quiet quest for revenge, as he seems personally offended by Roger Clemens. "It's hard to turn the other cheek when a situation like this happens," Reed reports on the eve of his start, adding that "there was no room in this game for what he did." He works against type in the early innings, recording five of his first six outs on strikeouts, though El Duque does him one better by collecting all six outs on strikeouts in the first two frames. However, Hernández has a propensity for giving up long balls, particularly to left-handed batters like Robin Ventura. So when he hangs a slider for his first pitch of the bottom of the second, the third baseman sends it to the base of the scoreboard in right field.

This gives the Mets their first lead in the series since the brief uprising in the eighth inning of game one. Short-lived as that lead was, this one is even shorter, as successive hits by Derek Jeter and David Justice drive home a run to tie the game in the top of the third, and a Paul O'Neill RBI triple in the fourth gives the Yankees a 2–1 lead. Though Reed pitches scoreless ball in the fifth and sixth innings, Hernández does the same, making Reed's effort to right the Mets' ship appear too little, too late. The Shea stands that had literally rocked during the championship series are deathly quiet, silenced by the wizardry of El Duque, the memory of Roger Clemens, and the inability of their team to summon up any hint of a rally.

Even when the Mets do scratch against Hernández, they manage to fall short. Mike Piazza opens the bottom of the sixth by doubling down the left-field line. With Ventura due up next, Hernández pitches carefully and walks him, opting to face Todd Zeile instead. Desperate for offense, Bobby Valentine initially asks Zeile to bunt the runners over, but rethinks when Zeile makes a halfhearted stab on the first pitch, then stares into the dugout and silently begs the manager to call off the bunt. Given the go ahead, Zeile wheels on the next pitch he sees and belts a double into the left-field corner, sending home Piazza to tie the game at two. Benny Agbayani follows with a walk, loading the bases with nobody out.

Here is a golden opportunity for the Mets to grab the lead, if not blow the game wide open. The Mets proceed to pass it up completely. Each of the next two batters—Jay Payton and Mike Bordick—swing wildly at pitches far out of the zone and go down on strikes. Pinch-hitting for Rick Reed, Darryl Hamilton bounces out to shortstop. "You get the feeling that was the Mets' shot," says Tim McCarver. The crowd agrees. Fans who reentered the game for one moment go back into hibernation and stay there when El Duque sets the Mets down in order in the seventh on only nine pitches.

Hernández begins the bottom of the eighth inning with 121 pitches under his belt and not a single sign of faltering. "The number of pitches you make is not important; it's how you feel," he says later, and he feels just fine at the moment if his strikeout of Robin Ventura to open the inning—his twelfth of the night—is any indication. Then, he runs a full count against Todd Zeile before the first baseman bounces a single past Derek Jeter's glove. But with another righty batter due up next, and with all the postseason collateral El Duque has earned, Joe Torre sees no reason to relieve *Señor Octubre*.

Hernández offers that righty, Benny Agbayani, a slider that catches too much of the plate, which Agbayani clubs into the left-center gap. As it rolls all the way to the wall, Todd Zeile shows the hustle he failed to display in game one, sprinting all the way, even if his lack of speed makes the sprint look more like an old truck leaking oil. By the time the outfielders catch up with the ball, there's no play at the plate, and the Mets have the lead once more.

The Mets had a lead late in game one too, but eventually lost that game partially due to their failure to pad that advantage. This time, they make sure to acquire some insurance when a Jay Payton infield single moves a runner to third and pinch hitter Bubba Trammell drives him in with an RBI sac fly.

On to the ninth, where the Mets ask Armando Benítez to collect the save that eluded him in game one. The first man he faces is pinch hitter Chuck Knoblauch, who channels some of his resentment—he'd been promised a start at second base at Shea before Joe Torre pulled a switcheroo—by lining Benítez's second pitch into center for a leadoff single. The Mets fans groan, haunted by visions of the blown save in game one. Edgardo Alfonzo trots to the mound for a moment to offer a brief pep talk. *Don't forget you're the man*, he says.

Benítez gets some help from the next batter, an overanxious Luis Polonia, who swings at the first pitch he sees and sends a fly ball to center field for out number one. Then Benítez freezes Derek Jeter on an outside changeup, the twenty-fifth strikeout of the game, matching a World Series record. The Mets are one out away from victory, and yet Shea is shockingly quiet. Doom is still anticipated, nothing taken for granted until the final out.

It is imperative that Benítez secure that out with the next batter, David Justice, because Bernie Williams—6-for-7 lifetime against the Mets closer—stands on deck. Benítez falls behind Justice 3-1, at which point fifty-five thousand-plus stomachs can be heard churning in unison. Barely a cheer is heard until Justice breaks his bat on a foul ball, bringing the Yankees down to their final strike. The next pitch is popped up just beyond the infield, where Edgardo Alfonzo retrieves it for the last out of the game, a 4–2 Mets victory.

Thus ends the Yankees' World Series winning streak—fourteen games going back to 1996—and El Duque's unbroken string of October dominance. The cheer that erupts when the ball settles in Alfonzo's glove, loud though it is, escapes less as a joyous roar and more like a sigh of relief.

* * *

The magic is back.

The game three Mets win is a godsend not for only the team, but the media as well. The sloppy slog of game one and the ugly controversy of game two had all the scribes fearing this super-hyped Subway Series would be a snooze. Then comes the crisp, well-played pitcher's duel of game three, won by unlikely heroes such as Benny Agbayani and Bubba Trammell, and the press rejoices.

"Strange eighth-inning things happened in the park where Tommie Agee once made a spectacular catch in 1969 and Ray Knight made a desperate romp around the bases in 1986," writes George Vecsey, comparing the rally of game three with Mets postseason glories gone by. "Perhaps, just perhaps, the Mets may have opened the door for sliding, Swoboda-like catches and Dykstra-like home runs that marked their two previous world championships." After two games of being spooked by the ghosts of Yankee Stadium, Vic Ziegel could talk of "the magic of Shea" propelling the Mets to victory, and no one dared laugh.

For the first time in this series, the Yankees look riled in game three. While they warmed up on the field prior to game time, many of the Yankees blanched at the bone-rattling volume of Shea's speakers. Paul O'Neill said he had to plug his ears at times just to hear himself think. "I like rock music, but . . ." he explained, trailing off because whatever he might have said next couldn't have been heard over the noise anyway. The Yankees feel so put out by Shea Stadium, in fact, that George Steinbrenner imports furnishings from their home clubhouse to Queens, a finicky move that allows the Mets to think that maybe, just maybe, they have wormed their way into the opposition's collective psyche. "I never thought we could make the Yankees feel uncomfortable," Bobby Valentine says upon hearing of Steinbrenner's redecorating. "That's an encouraging sign."

The Mets are likewise encouraged by Joe Torre's choice of starter for game four. After holding out the possibility of starting David Cone, he turns instead to Denny Neagle, a shocking decision in that it runs counter to the manager's tendencies. Denny Neagle is not a Torre guy, and it's clear he will never be one. The manager avoided the lefty like the plague during the division series, then called him out for his lack of aggressiveness during two championship series losses. Neagle responded by calling such a characterization of his performances "ludicrous." It's unclear if the two men even spoke between the end of the series against Seattle and the afternoon Neagle finds out he'll start game four. Considering the southpaw's playoff performances to this point, and his manager's lack of confidence in him, the Mets feel as if they're being handed game four on a silver platter.

They feel magic in their own game four starter, Bobby Jones, who spun one of the unlikeliest playoff gems since Don Larsen's perfect game by one-hitting the Giants in the division series clincher, after turning his season around with a humbling trip to the minors. The Mets firmly believe that this, and the admirable performance by Rick Reed the night before—a pitcher similar in stuff and temperament to Jones—spell a good outing for the Mets righty. The Mets believe they now have a firm grip on the momentum of this series and confirm this with a live pregame performance of their personal anthem (and every other team's), "Who Let the Dogs Out?" by the Baha Men.

There are a myriad of reasons why the Mets believe magic is on their side, and plenty of reasons why the Yankees want to disabuse them of this notion. With Chuck Knoblauch still riding the pine, Derek Jeter takes over leadoff duties, and as he strides to the plate to start the game, Knoblauch dares say aloud, "First pitch is going out." He's not sure why he says it, really, except that it would be great for the Yankees if it happens, so what the hell, say Jeter will hit a homer. Maybe Knoblauch will look like a genius.

Between Shea's amped-up PA system and its amped-up crowd, Derek Jeter can't possibly hear his teammate's prognostication. He is, however, well versed in Bobby Jones's repertoire, and knows his first offering is likely to be a get-me-over fastball. When this proves true, Jeter is more than ready to wheel on that pitch and send it soaring deep into the left-field bleachers. His no-doubt home run sucks the life right out of the crowd. Some fans are still finding their way to their seats when Jeter's blast comes screaming across the sky. They never even have a chance to cheer.

It will be that kind of night for the Mets. Bobby Jones's performance in game four is nothing like his masterpiece against Giants, nor is it the near disaster he logged against the Cardinals in the NLCS. It is instead a typical Bobby Jones start, which is to say solid, workmanlike. In August, this might be enough for the Mets to prevail. In October against the Yankees, it is a death sentence. Though Jones is relatively stingy with baserunners after the leadoff solo shot, he does allow a triple in consecutive innings, first to Paul O'Neill in the second (with an assist from Timo Pérez, who overruns O'Neill's hit for one fatal moment, allowing the sore-hipped outfielder to chug all the way to third base), then to Jeter in the third. Both men score, expanding the Yankees' lead to a daunting 3–0.

The third Yankee run scores, in part, because Bobby Valentine does not play his infielders up with a man on third base. Presumably, he believes his hitters will figure out Denny Neagle, just like Seattle's did a week ago, and the amount of loud outs the Mets record against him in the early going would lend credence to this theory. So too would the monster two-run shot that Mike Piazza belts in the bottom of the third, cutting the Yankees' lead down to one run. It seems a mere matter of time before the Mets wear Neagle down.

That time never comes. For the rest of the game, both teams take turns fashioning near misses, creating and wasting run-scoring opportunities as if this were a contest to determine who can produce the most frustrating inning. The Yankees put men on base in every inning after the third and drive home none of them, thanks to nifty fielding by Edgardo Alfonzo and clutch relief pitching from Glendon Rusch. The Yankees even put two men on against Armando Benítez in the top of the ninth, yet somehow do not induce a meltdown from the irritable Mets closer.

As confounding as all this is to the visitors, the Yankees have the lead in the game and the series. The Mets have neither, and so begin to exhibit uncharacteristic anxiousness, as when Benny Agbayani swings on a three-ball count against Neagle in the fourth and pops out, or when Mike Piazza strikes out on a bad pitch to end the fifth against the first Yankees reliever, David Cone. When hope arrives in the sixth via a Todd Zeile leadoff single, it is soon dashed when reliever Jeff Nelson spears a Benny Agbayani line drive, then spins and doubles off Zeile to end the inning. In the seventh, Bobby Valentine sends up a flurry of substitutes to bat for the most struggling members of his lineup, hoping to light a fire under his offense, but it yields no appreciable results. Lenny Harris, batting for the ice-cold Mike Bordick, earns a one-out walk, but that is as close as the Mets come to scratching against the Yankees bullpen. When Valentine counters the appearance of lefty reliever Mike Stanton with the right-handed Bubba Trammell, he is rewarded with a strikeout. Most shockingly, he bats for Timo Pérez—an unthinkable move a week ago but a necessary one for an outfielder who is batting .125 thus far in the series. This alone would signal a sense of panic from the manager. That he pinch-hits for Pérez with the anemic bat of Kurt Abbott signals just how deep that panic goes. Abbott strikes out to end the inning.

A Mets defeat is all but assured in the bottom of the eighth, when Joe Torre makes his own substitution and calls on Mariano Rivera to secure a six-out save. If Derek Jeter's leadoff home run served to take the crowd out of the game at its start, the insertion of Rivera is Torre's attempt to remove any comeback hopes at the end. Having spent most of his best bench players in the bottom of the seventh, Valentine has few reserves to call on in the final two innings, though against Mariano Rivera it may not have made much of a difference anyway. The Yankees are so confident that when Mariano Rivera logs a rare at bat in the top of the ninth, with a man on first and nobody out, they allow him to swing away rather than bunt the runner over. The Yanks fail to score in the frame, yet another blown opportunity that matters little. When Rivera returns to the mound in the bottom half, Benny Agbayani goes down looking, fooled by a cutter that catches the inside black. Jay Payton logs a strong at bat, fouling off a few tough pitches, only to fly out to left.

Matt Franco steps up as the Mets' last hope, and one of the very few men who can claim a big hit against Rivera on his résumé. It was Franco who capped an unlikely comeback against the Yankees last July by driving in the tying and winning runs in a thriller at Shea. It meant the world to the Mets and their fans in 1999. In 2000, the memory does nothing to prevent Matt Franco from being frozen on a Rivera cutter for a called strike three. The Yankees win, 3–2, to take a commanding 3–1 lead in this series.

In Shea's home clubhouse, Robin Ventura says the team has fought its way out of lower spots before. Jay Payton reminds reporters that his team has won three straight games this season, and the opposition has lost three straight games this season. Benny Agbayani again sustains himself with the memory of his triumphs in Tokyo back in March, when a good fortune and a grand slam saved him from a year in the minors.

These words will have to do for solace, because Agbayani and his teammates have little else in the way of comfort. Every attempt to describe what has happened to them in the first four games of this series reveals a lack of self-confidence that would have been unthinkable mere days ago. "They were getting us out, what can I tell you?" is the only explanation Agbayani can extend. Bobby Valentine has little more than shrugs to offer. "We're giving everything we have out there," he says. "They're giving just a little extra."

The biggest symbol of the shift in the team's luck and confidence is Edgardo Alfonzo. After two rounds of playoff heroics, and a ton of big hits last October, Alfonzo is mired in a miserable slump. His one World Series RBI came in game one, on an infield hit that dribbled at a snail's pace up the third base line. He has left ten men on base all by himself. Renowned for his discipline at the plate, he now swings at bad pitches, taking his team's offensive woes all on his shoulders and straining under its weight. "I picked the wrong time to let my team down," he says after game four, sounding a negative, self-pitying note that is not at all in character for him.

In the wake of the game four loss, Jeff Pearlman of *Sports Illustrated* tracks down pinch hitter Lenny Harris. Pearlman recalls that, before the playoffs began, Harris was one of the team's loudest and most raucous cheerleaders, who proclaimed his squad was "a team of destiny." Now, Harris expels tired, perfunctory clichés: *I still believe . . . We've been down before . . . You can't put your head down . . . Give Joe Torre credit.* They're not the words of a man who believes in destiny.

The same can be said of Mike Piazza, whose two-run homer did little more than make game four one long tease. After Matt Franco strikes out to end the game, Piazza remains in the dugout for far too long, unable to bring himself to move. "I'm not in the best of moods," he says once he finally drags himself to the locker room, in a voice a reporter describes as "defeated."

Following their game three win, it was said the Mets had magic on their side. Magic had propelled them in 1999, and for one day it seemed as if it would do so again in 2000. Now, it seems magic has some very hard limits. "Here's the compliment no team wants to hear: The Mets made it close," writes Vic Ziegel of the *Daily News*. Mike Lupica declares, "Game 4 was all the games" in this series: blown chances, near misses, rallies that came up just a bit short, all adding up to a Mets team that is only good enough to barely lose to the Yankees. In game four, the visitors stranded more baserunners than the home team (nine to three), but the Yankees won anyway, because the Yankees win. Mike Piazza marvels at the opposition's depth, wondering how they manage to score just enough to nip the Mets every damn night. "It's frustrating to play them so close and come up with three one-run losses."

Maybe that is the Yankees' unique genius: beating you in the precise way that makes you want to give up trying. Paul O'Neill seems to think so. "This is the time of the year you talk about the New York Yankees," he says. "I don't want to be rude, but that's just the way it is."

One *Times* writer spies a biblical admonition over Edgardo Alfonzo's locker: "Faith is assurance of things hoped for, a conviction of things not seen." That is the difference between these two teams summarized. The Mets have belief, faith, and magic. The Yankees have wins.

* * *

Al Leiter has never won a playoff start as a Met, which is more a reflection of buzzard's luck than anything else. This year, he has the lowest ERA of any pitcher in the postseason (2.86). Between 1999 and 2000, he has pitched five bona fide gems in the postseason and left with a lead on four of these occasions, and yet not earned a single W.

One of those games includes the first contest of this World Series, the one that hurt most of all. During the game-changing ninth inning at bat by Paul O'Neill, Leiter sweated, trembled, and rocked on the visiting dugout bench. When Armando Benítez issued the fatal walk, the lefty allowed himself to hang his head for a moment. He grew up a Mets fan. He had a sense of dread endemic to their kind. He knew what was coming. But when asked if he was frustrated over losing another win to the bullpen, the lefty shrugged. "If you really want to keep it in your hands, you go the whole game," he said.

The message was clear. If he takes the mound again in this series, he will leave nothing to chance. He will stay on the mound until he determines its outcome. The Mets' win in game three ensured he would appear again. Their loss in game four ensured it would be a must-win.

Quoth the *Daily News*, "If there's justice for the cheated, if there's truly a law governing averages, Al Leiter will win Game 5 of the World Series tonight."

The team supporting him in his ride-or-die effort will have a different look than the one behind him in game one. Kurt Abbott fills in at shortstop for Mike Bordick, who has been useless at the plate all October. Benny Agbayani moves into the leadoff spot he occupied for much of the year by default. He does this because Timo Pérez—arguably the biggest reason why the Mets have made it this far—has been benched. Asked if the Yankees are pitching him differently, Pérez just laughs, as if to sarcastically respond, *Gee, ya think?* Called on to elaborate, he places his hands far apart from one another. Translation: *They're throwing pitches outside the zone, and I'm swinging at them.* Timo had stunned the Giants and Cardinals by slapping at pitches, often the first ones he saw in an at bat, surprising oppositions unprepared for his aggressiveness. But the Yankees had two rounds of playoffs to study him, and know not to throw him anything close to the zone. His bat, which propelled the Mets through the playoffs, has disappeared as a result. Bubba Trammell takes his place in right field.

On the evening of October 26, the Mets jog out of the dugout for what will be, regardless of outcome, the final game they play at Shea Stadium in 2000. Fireworks shoot off beyond the outfield wall as they emerge from the dugout, an odd greeting for a team that has produced so few pyrotechnics in this series. The haze from their smoke lingers on the field as Al Leiter takes his warm-up tosses to the tune of "Tenth Avenue Freeze-Out" by his beloved Bruce Springsteen. Counter to his emotional reputation, Leiter appears remarkably calm and focused in the first inning, setting down the side in order while recording a crowd-pleasing strikeout of Derek Jeter.

Leiter has to believe the outs will continue in the top of the second when the first man up is Bernie Williams. The Yankees' commanding lead in this series has been achieved in spite of their cleanup batter, who has literally done nothing with the bat (0-for-15) so far. When he gave the ball a ride a few times in game four, it was as close to a positive sign as he had exhibited at the plate. Williams's struggles at the plate are perhaps why Al Leiter tosses cutters to him on a full count, hoping he will bounce it to one of his infielders. But the switch hitter fouls off several tough offerings before clubbing one into the mezzanine seats in left field for a solo shot.

Leiter betrays little emotion after the home run, displaying none of the glove-barking that usually follows his mistakes. He simply asks for another ball and retires the next three batters in order. An overpowering, nervous silence engulfs the stadium, a reaction befitting fans who've watched their team thrash against one deficit after another and make no dents at all.

It is especially daunting that the Mets must battle from behind against Andy Pettitte, who has yet to allow a run on the road in his considerable body of World Series work. The near pointlessness of trying to score against Pettitte is emphasized in the bottom of the second, when the Mets manage to put two men on base via a Bubba Trammell walk and a Jay Payton hit, and even push them both into scoring position with two out, but are forced to send Al Leiter to the plate to cash them in. On any given at bat, Leiter is a virtually guaranteed out. Against a fellow lefty, there is even less hope. In the WFAN booth, Gary Cohen describes this matchup as "almost a complete give up."

As if acknowledging the futility of his cause, Leiter attempts to bunt his way on, a curious move for someone who is as slow a runner as he is bad a hitter. Except that his bunt is placed exceptionally. The ball rolls past the mound, forcing first baseman Tino Martinez to charge in to field it. Andy Pettitte covers first while second baseman José Vizcaíno scoots to his right to back up the play. Though Martinez bobbles the ball for a split-second, he should have time to nail the painfully slow Leiter at first. Then Martinez's shovel toss clanks off of the pitcher's glove and pinballs off of Pettitte, Vizcaíno, and the first base umpire in quick succession. By the time the ball plops to the ground, Leiter reaches base safely, a runner has crossed the plate, and the game is tied at one.

While the Shea crowd crows over this bit of luck, Benny Agbayani swings at Andy Pettitte's very next pitch and sends a dribbler up the third base line. Scott Brosius runs in on the ball to make a barehanded grab, the kind he has successfully executed hundreds of times before. In the first inning of this game alone, Brosius made two excellent plays on hard-hit balls to rob hits from Mets batters. But this one has too much English on it. The ball skips under Brosius's hand and through the infield as Jay Payton scores, giving the Mets a 2–1 lead, and giving the crowd the first reason to roar in what feels like years.

Al Leiter sustains himself with this advantage for as long as he can. He sets down the Yankees in order in the third, ignores a two-out single from Bernie Williams in the fourth, and sidesteps a one-out Jorge Posada hit in the fifth. He believes he can preserve the lead through sheer force of will. Anyone watching at this point might believe the same. As foolish as it might be to contemplate, perhaps a one-run lead will be sufficient.

It will have to be, because after the Mets take the lead on a "rally" that consists of a pitcher's bunt and a third baseman's error, their hitters log one helpless at bat after another, waiting for some more magic that never arrives. Pettitte picks off Kurt Abbott to defuse a potentially fruitful fourth inning. In the fifth, Mike Piazza belts a long two-out double, but is stranded when David Justice runs down a Robin Ventura fly ball at the warning track.

With one out in the top of the sixth, Leiter's will to keep the one-run lead intact crumbles for one disastrous moment. He falls behind Derek Jeter and leaves a cutter too high in the zone, in almost the same spot where he'd hung one to Bernie Williams. Jeter's swat isn't quite as prodigious as Williams's, but it goes long enough and counts all the same, landing in the visiting bullpen to tie the score at two.

As soon as Jeter connects, Leiter kicks the dirt at the foot of the mound, then turns to watch the ball leave the yard as he stabs the air with barking expletives. The Mets lefty negotiates the rest of the inning with little trouble, but stalks off the mound at its conclusion screaming into his glove. For the rest of the night, the calm, controlled Leiter of the early innings is gone. His delivery is wild, as if he can start his motion but not stop it, giving himself up to gravity mid-delivery.

Meanwhile, Pettitte allows two more hits in the sixth and another in the seventh, yet strands all runners. He stalks off the mound after that frame with a hefty 129 pitches to his credit and a boatload of scoring chances nipped in the bud. His night on the mound is done. Leiter's has hardly begun. Determined to see this thing through to the end, he screams at himself to match zeroes with his fellow southpaw. A leadoff walk of Paul O'Neill in the top of the seventh is followed by pronounced muttering and three quick outs.

When the top of the eighth begins, Al Leiter has crossed the one-hundred-pitch mark. And yet, not only is there no hint of action from the Mets' relief corps, but not a single reliever can even be seen in the bullpen. The place looks as if it has been abandoned for months. Leiter falls behind Chuck Knoblauch—who Joe Torre dares to bat for José Vizcaíno—before retiring him on a pop-up behind the plate. He falls behind Derek Jeter too, almost losing his mind when a close pitch is called ball three instead of strike three. Then he throws a cutter that sails up and in, and the shortstop swings and misses wildly. Leiter almost comes unhinged when David Justice bounces a single past a diving Kurt

Abbott, slamming his glove with his fist. Pitching coach Dave Wallace trots to the mound to calm him down, and he responds by fanning Bernie Williams to end the inning.

The lower third of the Mets' order is quickly retired by the first Yankee reliever of the night, lefty Mike Stanton, in the bottom of the eighth. So Al Leiter is soon back on the mound for the top of the ninth. Still, there is not the slightest stirring in the home team's bullpen, and Leiter gives no cause for any. Sensing the finish line is close at hand, he lets loose on every pitch, heaving, grunting, sweating his way through it all, hoping will alone can push him to the end. He fans Tino Martinez on three pitches. He puts Paul O'Neill in an 0-2 hole and, after a few annoying foul balls, strikes him out too, making the right fielder look bad on a sharp slider.

At a point when he should be completely spent, Leiter has recorded his last four outs via Ks. Get one more, and he will give the heart of the Mets' order a chance to push one across in the bottom of the ninth. A strikeout is not too much to hope for from the next batter, Jorge Posada, owner of the fourth-highest K total in the American League this season. Leiter lets every pitch fly, putting forth max effort as he battles the catcher to a 2-2 count. Then, a foul ball. Then, another. And then a pitch Posada takes on the outside corner. Home plate umpire Tim McClelland deems it a ball. The crowd deems it reason to groan in protest. Then, another long foul ball, followed a by a pitch slightly wider than ball three. Posada takes his base.

Finally, a man is up in the Mets' bullpen. John Franco, of course. In the WFAN booth, Gary Cohen wonders how Al Leiter can possibly "crank it up again" after Posada's lengthy at bat. The answer is fully evident once Scott Brosius sneaks a single past the shortstop, pushing the go-ahead run into scoring position. The answer is, *He can't*. Leiter is exhausted, physically, mentally, emotionally, spiritually. But Al Leiter swore he would see this game to its conclusion. No one is going to keep him from fulfilling that promise.

The pitch Scott Brosius hits for a single is Al Leiter's 141st pitch of the night. Al Leiter and high pitch counts are well acquainted, but this is an ungodly amount even for him. And yet, he does not budge from the mound. No one on the Mets' bench makes a motion in his direction. There is no thought that Al Leiter might not be allowed to face the next batter, Luis Sojo, inserted at second base in the eighth.

The first pitch Sojo sees, the 142nd Leiter throws, is a slider that catches too much plate. The batter swings and sends the ball back up the middle. It takes almost as many hops as pitches Leiter has thrown, skipping across the grass like a flat stone off the surface of a lake. Leiter does not field his position well even when calm and collected. In his agitated, worn-out state, he has no chance of snaring the ball. All he can do is crumble to the ground in a heap and crane his neck in the desperate hope of seeing an infielder behind him grab the thing.

Kurt Abbott is not up to the task, diving and missing as the ball crosses the second base bag. Edgardo Alfonzo, who has made one fantastic play after another in this series even as his bat failed him, cannot make this one. His dive, deep on the outfield grass, comes up empty.

Jay Payton jogs in from center field to retrieve the ball. The Mets' last hope is that Posada's slow wheels will permit Payton enough time to nail the runner at the plate. He scoops up the ball and heaves it home all in one motion, throwing so hard he sends himself tumbling to the turf. His throw is right on target, and arrives just as Posada slides homeward, but the ball caroms off the runner and pings into the Mets dugout. Ground rules send Scott Brosius home as well, and Luis Sojo to third. The Mets are now on the wrong side of a 4–2 score. The Yankees stand three outs away from their third consecutive championship.

As all of this unfolds in front of Bobby Valentine, the manager is strangely unemotional, as if he fully expected this, as if he'd seen it already. When he speaks of the fateful ninth later, he makes it sound like the mistakes were his. "I thought that striking out those first two guys and the pitches he threw to Posada made me think he had plenty," Valentine says. "If I brought somebody else in, they definitely would have gotten the guy out and we'd still be playing." This implies it was Valentine's decision to make. This was Al Leiter's game to win or lose. Everyone knew this. Now they know he will lose.

Bobby Valentine emerges from the dugout, pausing briefly to get the umpire's ruling on why Brosius was awarded home before turning to the mound to remove Leiter. The southpaw receives an appreciative ovation as he slumps toward the dugout with glove shoved under his arm, staggers toward the bench, removes his cap, and runs his hands through sweat-drenched hair. Teammates take turns approaching him in silence, patting him on the back before moving on, leaving him alone in his anguish.

Once John Franco secures that elusive third out, the Mets are once again tasked with rallying against Mariano Rivera. Last night, he was called on to secure the final six outs and did so with little trouble. That provides one sliver of hope, that the Yankees closer might be so fatigued from last night's prolonged outing that he'll be vulnerable this evening. When pinch hitter Darryl Hamilton strides to the plate, however, he's the one who looks tired. Hamilton strikes out on three pitches.

And then, another brief glimmer of a chance, as Rivera's next four pitches sail wide, earning a walk for Benny Agbayani, who soon takes second base on defensive indifference. Rare are the times that Mariano Rivera loses the strike zone. Perhaps he can be had after all. Perhaps Edgardo Alfonzo, due up next, can play hero again.

Then Fonzie falls behind in the count before lofting a lazy fly ball to left field, one that accomplishes no more than allowing Agbayani to tag up and move to third.

The final hope for the Mets is Mike Piazza. As final hopes go, this is a good candidate. A flick of his wrists could tie this game.

Mariano Rivera's first pitch to Piazza dents the lower edge of the zone for a called strike one. On his second, Piazza takes a mighty cut, a Piazza cut, the bat whipping over the plate in one violent split second and rebounding back over the catcher's shoulder. The ball flies to deep center field. In the Yankee dugout, Joe Torre yelps, "No!" thinking the ball will leave the yard and tie the game. Steve Phillips thinks the same thing. He sees Piazza's blast arc into the air and tells himself, *That's supposed to be part of the script.*

It was part of the script before, in a glorious moment in Atlanta when Mike Piazza fought his way through the fog of a concussion, fought his way through a five-run deficit that should have doomed the Mets' chances, and swatted a majestic three-run blast to tie the game. Al Leiter started that night too. You could believe it could happen again.

But that was 1999, and the Mets had lost that game anyway. It only felt like a win because the Mets were allowed to leave Atlanta thinking they'd won, if not the game, then something else important. This cannot be allowed in 2000. Mets fans came to this game armed with signs proclaiming "You gotta believe!" But belief is no longer enough. One Yankees fan spied these signs and proclaimed, "You believe, we know."

Noble defeats were once permitted. Now, it is the twenty-first century. Now, there is no glory in losing. Now, Mike Piazza's fly ball settles in Bernie William's glove, a few feet short of the fence. Now, hope dies on the warning track.

CHAPTER 18

Coda

WHEN THEY FIRST spoke of it, they were kind.

During the fateful ninth inning of game five, Joe Buck announced that Al Leiter had "nothing to hang his head about" (even as the distraught pitcher literally hung his head in sorrow). The newspapers' retrospectives had titles such as, "The Mets Lose Series, But Their Pride Is Intact." One writer insisted, "Unlike after previous disappointments against the Atlanta Braves, there was no sense of devastation. They played great against a great team, and lost." That this was untrue—*No devastation? Played great?*—seemed impolite to point out at the moment. Bobby Valentine said of the Mets, "I think they were the champs of this World Series." Even by Valentine's standards this was a whopper, and yet no one in the press batted any eye.

The soothing was somewhat aided by their enemies, who lauded the Mets as valiant foes. Derek Jeter, crowned World Series MVP, asserted the series losers were "the best team I've seen in five years." George Steinbrenner expressed similar sentiments. "The Mets gave us everything we could want," he said between sobs in Shea's victorious visiting clubhouse. Rudy Giuliani broke away from his beloved Yankees to give a hug of commiseration to Al Leiter, and proclaimed to the pitcher, "You'll be back."

The more verbal salve was applied to the Mets' wounds, however, the more condescending it sounded. George Steinbrenner praised Mets fans at Shea Stadium—"We were treated so well, and our people could walk around by themselves with no problems."—in a manner that suggested this was no virtue. This would become the prevailing thought: the Mets had not put up a fight against the enemy on any front. In choosing to sell World Series tickets via phone, rather than at their stadium as the Yankees had, the Mets made it easier for brokers and scalpers to snatch up tickets for Shea and sell them on the secondary market. This made it easier—in the imagination of one *Times* writer—for "stockbrokers and internet millionaires with personal secretaries" to tie up the lines and buy up all the tickets. And we all know who *stockbrokers* root for: U. S. Steel.

Free-agent-to-be Alex Rodriguez attended all the games in Queens, desperate to attract the attention of the Mets for the upcoming off-season, and came away feeling that the atmosphere was "corporate" and "jaded." Such words had seldom before been attached to the Mets' homely home on Flushing Bay, but that home had also never before hosted a Subway Series where tickets were being sold by scalpers for the same price as an economy car. Shea's seats went to well-heeled Yankees fans and camera-hogging celebrities, creating a sterile atmosphere that favored the visitors.

Regardless of what Derek Jeter and George Steinbrenner said in public, behind the scenes the Yankees eyed the Mets with the seething contempt a gladiator reserves for an inferior foe. The team stung with the memory of all those in the press who doubted them, proclaimed them old and decrepit and no match for playoff competition judged younger and feistier. The Mets weren't responsible for any of this rhetoric but bore the brunt of their rage anyway. Revelers in Shea's visiting clubhouse took time out from champagne spraying to fling a towel at a TV screen that dared show a picture of Bobby Valentine. A sarcastic chorus of "Who Let the Dogs Out?" soon followed. A group of Yankees raised a glass to mock-toast Turk Wendell, the mouthy righty with the shark tooth necklace, and the crow he was surely eating at that moment, though it was unclear exactly what he'd said to earn their ire. Rather than decamp to a club, the Yankees partied well into the night at Shea, knowing the stunned Mets were still in their own locker room trying to numb their loss with silence and Budweiser. Roger Clemens climbed the pitcher's mound with his sons and scooped dirt from it into a plastic bag to take away as a souvenir of war. Clemens hadn't pitched from this mound in the series, but he made sure to plant his flag at Shea nonetheless.

In the end, it came back to Roger Clemens, the man of whom so much was expected, the man blamed for his team's every failing until he engineered its definitive triumph. In 1999, the Mets were able to claim a moral victory in overcoming so much adversity to reach game six of the championship series. Roger Clemens assured no such moral victories could be claimed in 2000 when he flung a bat at Mike Piazza, and when Piazza and his teammates chose not to brawl over the insult. The Mets left themselves open to charges that they were scared, that they were unwilling to stand up for themselves, that they were cowards, that they just didn't want to win as badly as Roger Clemens and the Yankees did. Once reviled as a pinstriped carpetbagger, Clemens thus achieved the acceptance he desperately craved from Yankees fans. Mike Piazza, once said to understand stardom in New York far better than his nemesis, became known less for what he had accomplished on the city's biggest stage than what he hadn't—revenge.

Within days of the series' conclusion, the hearty pats on the back for the Mets disappeared entirely. In their place, Steinbrennerian tough love. "In the end, the Mets were not the Subway Series' Little Engine That Could," wrote Murray Chass. "They couldn't be because the Yankees were the Super Chiefs."

In 1999, the Mets' improbable playoff run was so captivating that Rudy Giuliani offered to honor them with a parade of their own. At the conclusion of the 2000 World Series, Giuliani offered a two-team parade as a healing bipartisan gesture. The Mets might have been able to get away with accepting the offer in 1999 (though they didn't). In 2000, there was no chance in hell they would have. "They deserve the stage to themselves," Steve Phillips said of the Yankees. The offer seemed a trap now, little more than a chance to be paraded as spoils of war in front of an ugly, mocking crowd.

* * *

At the conclusion of the Subway Series, the press proudly declared its "good for the city" predictions had come to pass because it symbolized New York's renaissance. "This city is back, and the Subway Series has been the emblem of that," Pete Hamill, legendary newsman now toiling for the *Post*, proclaimed at series' end. "This has been the cherry on the cake." Writers were correct, after a fashion, in their belief that the Subway Series was a symbol of what New York had become. How that series was won, and how that win was addressed in the years to come, was equally symbolic of the state of the city in the early 2000s.

Beginning with the troubled mayoral administration of John Lindsey in the late 1960s, there had been a great public debate about the "soul" of New York. Could it remain a bastion of tolerance while maintaining safe streets? Could it remain a hub for business while also taking care of its neediest citizens? Then Rudy Giuliani came along, with a Reagan-inspired Manichean view of the world, to essentially say, *We don't have time for this nonsense.* He instituted his budgetary and policing agendas with the drive of a crusader, placing all arguments in with-us-or-against-us terms. Conditions in the city had grown so dire, he felt, that no time was left for complicating *Yes, but* . . . hedging or for that ultimate New York luxury item, liberal guilt.

By the time Rudy Giuliani's administration neared its end, the city was safer and richer than it had been for decades—a transformation that ironically doomed his further political aspirations. It all happened so quickly, and attracted so many out-of-towners to settle in New York, that people forgot the worst of the bad old days, and no longer had any stomach for Giuliani's take-no-prisoners attitude. He lost a great deal of political capital and public support in his final years in office because his combativeness and personal issues prevented him from accomplishing much, and because new New Yorkers didn't quite understand why he was so driven, so *angry*.

The man who succeeded Giuliani in the mayor's office, and would bring his policies to their inevitable conclusion, was Michael Bloomberg, billionaire media mogul turned politician. Bloomberg was no Reaganite, but he did possess a neoliberal businessman's pragmatism and shared his predecessor's belief in Things That Work. Bloomberg's administration continued on the trail blazed by Giuliani, while removing the public fights and pointless vendettas that derailed Giuliani's biggest dreams.

Thus was Bloomberg able to accomplish many of the goals that had eluded Rudy Giuliani, such as eliminating the Board of Education and constructing new stadiums for both the Yankees and the Mets. What Giuliani had sputtered and pontificated about from his City Hall bully pulpit, Bloomberg achieved via the civic equivalent of closed-door boardroom deals. He even repealed mayoral term limits with hardly a peep of protest—another goal that Giuliani couldn't accomplish, not even after the September 11 attacks of 2001, when his popularity rebounded—and won an unprecedented third term.

New York City, supposed bastion of fuzzy-headed liberal ideals, voted for twenty consecutive years of uncomplicated, business-first, law-and-order-oriented Republican leadership. (Though Bloomberg changed his party affiliation from Republican to independent before his third mayoral campaign, he hadn't shifted his views or policies in any sense, and the city's Republican Party put him on their ticket anyway.) At the end of those two decades, there was no longer any real debate about the "soul" of the city. The questions of safety vs. freedom and economy vs. social safety net had been answered in New York, as they had been answered in cities across America since the early 1990s. A new generation of urban voters overwhelmingly chose the former options over the latter.

By the conclusion of Bloomberg's time in office, all those Brooklyn stickball stoops of John Franco's memories were now attached to brownstones with multimillion-dollar price tags, sold to the ultrarich who wouldn't have been caught dead east of Soho twenty years earlier. The entire East River waterfront from Long Island City, Queens, on down to Red Hook, Brooklyn, sprouted one billion-dollar luxury condo after another, most of them empty for much of the year, held as investments or pieds-à-terre by the 1 percent of the 1 percent. Manhattan had taken on the character of a European capital like London or Paris, a place set aside for well-heeled tourists and foreign dignitaries. Or perhaps it felt more like Shea Stadium did during the last World Series it hosted: rendered less noisy and enthusiastic, thanks to a slew of rich newcomers who could afford the tickets the old diehards could not.

The question of what happened to the poor and working-class New Yorkers who could no longer afford to live in their neighborhoods was seldom asked. Nor did anyone much care that a city that was once an incubus for new ideas in all fields was now unaffordable to those who required time to fail in order to figure out how they could succeed. (No room for a Jason Isringhausen or a Melvin Mora here.) Likewise, little thought was given to what happened to a sense of community in a city in which a large, fickle portion of the population would only flit across its landscape for a short while.

This change was nowhere more dramatic than on the Northside of Williamsburg in Brooklyn. Back in 1975, when crime was rampant and the city was on the brink of financial ruin, mayor Abe Beame proposed draconian cost-cutting measures, including the closing of Engine 212, the Northside's local firehouse. Fed-up residents occupied the firehouse for over a year in protest. These were not hardened radicals, but neighborhood families, grandparents, literal Boy Scouts trying to keep a vital piece of their community alive, and they succeeded. When the city caved and agreed to keep it open, Engine 212 was dubbed the People's Firehouse. This didn't prevent the city from trying to shut it down again in 1991, when both the local economy and crime in the Northside were no better than sixteen years earlier. Once more, the locals occupied the firehouse for months until the mayor (David Dinkins this time) backed down.

When the next threat came in 2003, the mayor was Bloomberg. Citing another downturn in city finances, Bloomberg proposed closing six firehouses, including Engine 212. This time, the mayor had no compunction about roughing up the grandmothers and Boy Scouts who tried to keep Engine 212 open, dispatching police in riot gear to seize the company's fire truck, a move one elderly local referred to as "Gestapo tactics." Protests against the closure raged throughout the year. Bloomberg countered by insisting that Engine 212 was one of the least busy firehouses in the entire city and enlisted a former fire commissioner to testify that his cost-cutting measures were, if anything, merciful. ("He probably could have closed a few more," the ex-commish contended.)

It did not seem this fight would end well for Bloomberg. The September 11 attacks had rendered firemen a kind of civic saint in New York, and the mayor dared threaten their jobs. Those with long memories pointed out that, during the 1993 campaign for City Hall, two people were killed by a fire in a neighborhood where David Dinkins had just closed the local firehouse. Rudy Giuliani blasted Dinkins for the shortsightedness and went on to a narrow victory on election day. Bloomberg's opponents foresaw the same outcome for him. "He may never recover," said one City Council member, all but cackling.

Instead, Bloomberg got away with it, in the Northside and elsewhere. After months of rage, the protests fizzled. A year later, there was no hint of the demonstrations of old—and no hint of an anti-Bloomberg backlash either. The Engine 212 building remained shuttered for a decade until it was revived not as a firehouse, but as an arts and performance space—and only then through a Kickstarter campaign.

What had changed? The neighborhood, dramatically. By 2003, the bulk of the old protesters had been priced out of the Northside. The new New Yorkers didn't see Gestapo tactics when police in riot gear broke up a demonstration. They saw police maintaining order, which was no less than what they expected, nay *demanded*. They didn't blanch at Bloomberg's diminishing of the importance of a local firehouse to a community. They wanted a mayor who would make decisions based on data rather than emotion.

Of course, this assumes the new residents noticed the closure at all, which is debatable. It is more likely that they knew nothing of the firehouse protests, either of 1975, 1991, or the ones happening right under their noses. A closed firehouse wouldn't hold the interest of people who didn't intend to put down roots in the city. Those who relocated to neighborhoods like Williamsburg—and then Greenpoint, and then Bushwick, and then Ridgewood, deeper into the former working-class enclaves of Brooklyn and Queens each year—saw the city less as a home and more of a waystation, a place in which to invest for a short while or to have fun while there was fun to be had. When the time came to settle down, or simply find a new location for fun, they would leave these places behind, with no regrets.

New York had always been in a constant state of change. The difference prior to the 1990s is that the change was often the exchange of one community for another. A new group of people would come to New York from elsewhere, build up their pride and power, move through the ranks of city life, and then be replaced by the latest downtrodden. Now, communities were removed altogether. In their place, an archipelago of playgrounds. New York was no longer the place to come to make it, but the place where you showed you'd already made it.

* * *

The baseball narrative that developed after the 2000 World Series paralleled the city's evolution. Before that October, there was a sense that the Mets *could* depose the Yankees as the team of the city. After the 1999 season, the hottest topic of conversation was not another Yankee championship but the Mets' unbelievable year, which seemed so much more interesting than robotic Yankees efficiency. The following year, the media continually wrote of the Mets as a far more dynamic team than the world-weary Yankees. It was less assessment than wish, a wish that the team that had coined the phrase "Ya gotta believe" could somehow prevail. There were also plenty of writers who declared all of this to be nonsense, who held forth that the mighty Yankees and all their history could never be deposed by the Mets. Nonetheless, there was a palpable fear emanating from the Yankees camp that said a loss to their crosstown rivals could perhaps tilt the city in the Mets' direction.

This proposed a complicating question that the outcome of the 2000 World Series seemed to settle for good. *There can't really be two teams in this city, so one must be destroyed.* This is what people meant, consciously or not, when they said the Subway Series was good for the city. It removed this complication and crowned a winner—forever it seemed. The Yankees alone would represent a city in which you had to win to belong. Those who touted the concepts of lovable loserdom and moral victories and *belief* would be priced out of the narrative.

It was a narrative that would obliterate complication for both teams. At times in 1999 and especially in 2000, the Yankees seemed to win almost out of spite for those who doubted them. After defeating the Mets, Derek Jeter declared, "I'd be lying if I said this one wasn't more gratifying. I mean, we struggled this year. We had tough times." New York in the year 2000 had no room for stories of struggle, however, nor did the team that purported to represent that city. The story of a team that struggled is compelling, but it's a story that had no place in the New York of the twenty-first century. That is how the Yankee Dynasty of 1996–2000 came to be spoken of as a monolithic triumph, smooth as glass, precise as clockwork, in which the Yankees beat everyone and that was all that need be said.

The Yankees themselves perpetuated this idea by establishing their own cable channel-cum-propaganda arm in 2002. Dubbed the YES Network, the channel reran playoff victories from these years ad nauseam, with intermittent bumpers advertising upcoming Yankees games set to regal trumpet music, implying an unbroken lineage from those years to the present. This created a paradox that celebrated the team's glorious history yet rendered it meaningless. Each new season, it was said the Yankees not only could reach the same lofty heights as they did in their glory days, but *must* reach those heights, or else they would be judged a failure. Every year was supposed to be 1998, a sameness that flattened out the perspective in all directions, past, present, and future. Repeating a judgment first applied to Roger Clemens, all future wearers of pinstripes were determined to be either True Yankees or not, on a sliding scale of expectations that were frequently adjusted, especially in October.

If this narrative made things very difficult for any Yankee post-2000, it did wonders for George Steinbrenner. In the early 1990s, it was believed that the Yankees would have to win in spite of Steinbrenner, a contention confirmed when The Boss's ban from the game was followed by the team's return to greatness. After 2000, however, Steinbrenner became beloved because he exemplified the idea of doing whatever it took to win, the highest virtue in the new New York. All the things that once made Steinbrenner a punchline—the tantrums, the impulsive firings, his two bans from the game—were now excused as excesses of zeal from a man who wanted to win so much more than any other mortal could possibly understand. When the owner died in 2010, he received a monument in the brand-new Yankee Stadium that dwarfed those dedicated to Babe Ruth, Joe DiMaggio, Mickey Mantle, and every other Yankee immortal.

Few protested this audacity any more than they protested the relegation of his many offenses to the memory hole.

By the end of his life, New York's media accorded Steinbrenner a status close to sainthood. When any local team would try to lure a big free agent to town, the scribes invoked his name and proclaimed, *George could get it done.* Typical of this genre was a cringe-inducing 2010 column by Bill Madden of the *Daily News* in which he imagined Steinbrenner wooing LeBron James to the New York Knicks through sheer force of will. The piece made no mention of any of the economic realities of roster building in the NBA, such as the salary cap, because The Boss could make anything happen, even from the great beyond. The days when Steinbrenner's ban from baseball was cheered by his own team's fans were now excused, if not forgotten altogether.

* * *

If the decade and a half following 2000 were disappointing by the Yankees' uncompromising standards—only one lousy World Series ring, captured in 2009 and curiously unspoken of ever since—the afterglow of their dynasty gave them primacy in New York. Winning would be required to depose them, and this the Mets were unable to accomplish except in brief, tantalizing spurts.

The Mets' 2001 season acted as a mirror image of the ones before it, an ugly first half almost redeemed by a late surge. When Mike Piazza's dramatic eighth-inning home run cinched a win against the Braves at Shea on September 21—the first game played in New York City after the September 11 attacks—brief talk of *magic* emerged for the third September in a row. And then the Mets went to Atlanta, where two gut-wrenching losses at Turner Field all but ended their playoff hopes. The big story of the ensuing postseason became the Yankees and their emotional trip to the World Series, a seven-game loss to the Diamondbacks that was nonetheless proclaimed a healing balm for a still-smoldering city. Mike Piazza's heroics were consigned to the baseball equivalent of a cult classic.

The Mets of this era threw good money after bad, assuming this was how teams were built in the new millennium. In 2002, with the addition of past-their-expiration-date free agents, the team performed badly on the field and off. Accusations of rampant pot smoking among the Mets' minor leaguers were broadcast by gleeful city tabloids, and Bobby

Valentine wrote his own pink slip by treating the affair with a lack of seriousness—an attitude the overblown controversy deserved but one that shocked the pearl-clutching press and infuriated Mets ownership. Valentine was gone at season's end.

After a brief stint at ESPN, Valentine returned to Japan for a second shot at managing the Chiba Lotte Marines. This tenure was longer and even more successful than the first, as he steered the Marines to an NPB championship in 2005. (His roster contained ex-Mets like Benny Agbayani and Matt Franco, Valentine guys still.) Now a celebrity in Japan, his likeness was used to sell burgers, beer, and sake. A documentary crew followed him for one season to produce a film (*The Zen of Bobby V*) that captured his immense popularity with the locals and his impassioned pleas to save Japanese baseball, whose attendance numbers and finances had taken a hit after the exodus of so many stars to America.

Valentine's second Japanese adventure terminated in much the same fashion as the first. Once again, the Marines' front office resented his popularity and waged a vicious campaign to undermine him, employing every tactic from removing his image from team facilities to circulating stories about his alleged racism. (If there was any truth to the latter, considering Valentine's unpopularity with the press, it seems impossible some intrepid reporter wouldn't have discovered this earlier.) Once again, a fan campaign to save Valentine's job collected an impressive number of signatures. Once again, team management fired him anyway, sending him packing after the 2009 season.

Valentine openly pined for another shot at managing a big league club, but when one season skippering the Red Sox in 2012 proved an unmitigated disaster, it seemed this would be his last hurrah. He had reached the latter half of his sixties, an age at which most baseball lifers are shuttled into ceremonial advisory positions. For some reason, an offer for such a post was never extended by the Mets, even though the team continued to greet Steve Phillips—who was fired by the team in 2003, then lost a job with ESPN after having an affair with a network production assistant—with open arms. While Phillips did fill-in radio work for the the Mets and appeared in a host of team-produced documentaries, the closest Valentine came to returning was occasional pre- and postgame analyst work for SNY, the team's cable home, where he could be kept at arm's length.

Following the election of Donald Trump, Valentine's name was forwarded as a possible ambassador to Japan. It made some perverse sense, both for the ex-manager's love of that nation and Trump's love of low-tier celebrity, but the idea progressed little beyond talk. While appearing at the Queens Baseball Conference in early 2017, when asked about the possibility of ambassadorship, Valentine seemed doubtful that such a role would suit him. "Would you have to know where I am at all times?" he had asked during the vetting process. He was told yes, of course the government would want to know the whereabouts of its Japanese ambassador at all times. "Then it's not for me," he answered.

* * *

After 2000, when the Yankees failed to win, no one questioned their methods, only their results. When the Mets failed to win, it was chalked up to some innate Mets-ness to which success was foreign. The Mets aided this perception in the new century by losing in uniquely painful ways. See 2006, when their All-Star-laden team captured a National League East title and executed an easy sweep of the Dodgers in the division series, then were defeated in a seven-game championship series by a St. Louis Cardinals team that won only eighty-three games. The following year, the Mets made the September swoons of the late 1990s look like child's play as they choked away a seven-game divisional lead with seventeen games to play, arguably the worst late-season collapse of all time if you have a stomach for such arguments. In 2008, the Mets not only gagged away another divisional lead late in September but closed out Shea Stadium with a loss to the Marlins that assured they would miss the playoffs by one game yet again.

Shortly after the 2008 season ended, the Bernie Madoff scandal broke. When it was revealed that Madoff's titanic investment returns were actually an elaborate Ponzi scheme, it wiped out billions of dollars of assets overnight, some of which belonged to Fred Wilpon (sole owner of the Mets after buying out Nelson Doubleday in 2002). In the years that followed the Madoff revelations, Wilpon would insist that the financial loss had no impact on team operations. The multiple loans he received from MLB, and the team's sudden lack of interest in free agents, suggested otherwise. With a farm system bereft of talent due to the free-agent signings of the previous decade, the Mets had little chance of winning on the cheap. Brand-new Citi Field—a less ambitious version of the domed Ebbets Field manqué Wilpon always dreamed of building—was rendered a ghost town every August by lack of winning, and a lack of hope that the team would ever compete again.

Over this same period, the nature of the media that covered baseball in New York, and the methods they used, changed dramatically. In 2000, most fans gleaned their information from print newspapers, and from columns written by veteran writers whose interaction with the readers was glancing, at best. This world was dismantled by the emergence of the internet. By the 2010s, fans came to expect immediate breaking news via social media and to dialogue with the beat writers and maybe the players too. Beat writers and opinion columnists no longer needed to interpret a fan base's mood. The fan base told them how they felt, twenty-four hours every day.

In the initial years of sports social media, every fan told these reporters the Mets were a joke. Even Mets fans. *Especially* Mets fans. Every misstep the team made, every PR blunder (and there were plenty), could be posted with no more comment than "LOLMets," and the internet would know another punchline had been written. Every July 1, a website could wring cheap clicks out of the latest $1 million payment in deferred money sent out to Bobby Bonilla and point out how many members of the current no-name Mets he was out-earning. Plenty of teams paid deferred money to retired players each year. Only the Mets could do it to sighs and chuckles of "Only the Mets . . ."

Fumbling mediocrity reigned in Queens for so long that the relative success of the Yankees scarcely mattered. The Mets' little-brother status seemed chiseled in stone. The fact that they'd once come close to challenging the Yankees' supremacy, and that large swaths of the old-school press all but begged them to prevail, was obliterated from public memory.

* * *

But there was one tantalizing blip in this otherwise flatlining EKG. It came in 2015.

During the 2015 season, seemingly out of nowhere, the Mets produced a fearsome, fireballing young pitching staff—Generation K come to fruition for one brief moment. At the trade deadline, they dealt for Cuban slugger Yoenis Céspedes, who powered them into October with one titanic homer after another. For the final months of the season, the Mets were easily the most exciting team in town. Sports coverage in New York centered on the Mets through their long run into October. To many fans, especially the younger ones, the last Yankee Dynasty was as beyond their memory as the Mets' glory years of the 1980s. In a city where only winning mattered, the Mets were winning and the Yankees weren't.

The true victory of 2015 was not in how far the Mets went, but how the Mets went far. Consider the lowest twenty-four hours of the season. On the evening of July 29, with the trade deadline less than two days away, it was widely reported that infielder Wilmer Flores—starting shortstop only because he was the team's cheapest option at the position—would be traded for a veteran bat. Word leaked to Flores in the dugout, and when he took the field again he began to choke back tears for all to see. The Mets were ripped to shreds in the court of public opinion for not shielding Flores from such public embarrassment. Even worse, the rumored trade fell through. The next afternoon, with the Mets one out away from a face-saving win, a rain delay intervened. When the clouds cleared, the bullpen promptly choked away a once-large lead to an anemic Padres lineup. This disaster seemingly sealed another summer of irrelevance. A more "LOLMets" series of events could not have been scripted.

Those who threw up their hands and wondered, *What next?* could scarcely believe what did happen next. The trade for Yoenis Céspedes was consummated at literally the last moment before the trade deadline. Then, the Mets began August by sweeping a three-game series from the division-leading Washington Nationals, overtook them with a blazing-hot month of August, and—perhaps most amazingly of all, given their autumnal history—continued to play amazingly well into the fall, capturing the National League East flag without a hint of a September swoon. In October, they won a hard-fought division series against the Los Angeles Dodgers, taking game five on the road, and then swept a powerful Chicago Cubs team to advance to the World Series. It was as dramatic and improbable a turnaround as any in franchise history. It was mojo reborn.

And then, the Mets went down in defeat in a World Series that unfolded in a fashion eerily similar to the Subway Series of 2000. Opportunities to expand or take a lead were sidestepped. Late advantages were squandered. Errors were committed at the worst possible moments and, in an echo of Timo Pérez, by the same players who brought them so far—the prime example being second baseman Daniel Murphy, who hit homers at a Ruthian pace to propel the Mets deep into October, then turned back into a pumpkin once the Fall Classic began. Once again, a thrilling game three win that seemed to put the Mets back in the series was negated by a crushing game four loss. Once again, the Mets' ace put the team on his back in a must-win game five—Matt Harvey filling the role of Al Leiter—and still it wasn't enough. The only solace was that, unlike in 2000, when the Mets lost to a team whose trophy case was filled to bursting, this time they lost instead to the long-suffering Kansas City Royals.

In three short months of 2015, the Mets had the reality-stretching highs of the Grand Slam Single and the deflating lows of Roger Clemens's bat chucking. The next year, despite a myriad of injuries to their lineup and pitching staff, the Mets went on another late-summer tear and captured a wild card berth. Though they lost the play-in game to the Giants, a new generation of New York sportswriters—more in tune with fan feeling, less inclined to accept established narratives as gospel truth—began to ask if the Mets were about to become the toast of the town, if the era of Yankee hegemony might have crumbled overnight, toppled at the first shove from the direction of Queens.

It was not to be. The Yankees returned to the playoffs in 2017 when a brief selloff of pricey veterans yielded a slew of exciting young players. (Nothing showed how much had changed since 2000 more than the fact that the Yankees were allowed to rebuild.) These were soon supplemented, in classic Yankees fashion, with All-Stars who'd grown too expensive for their small market teams. Meanwhile, the Mets quickly lost many members of that magical 2015 team due to a combination of insufficiently deep pockets, injury, controversy, and uniquely Mets-ian rotten luck.

In his book about the Giuliani-era gentrification of Manhattan, *Vanishing New York*, Jeremiah Moss describes the false hope of viewing a vestigial remnant of the city's radical, rougher past on the street, comparing this to seeing a polar bear "sweating on her chunk of ice, and then denying that the world is cooked because, hey, there's a polar bear." It's possible the 2015 Mets were simply one of those polar bears, nothing more than an anomaly amid the sameness of post-Bloomberg New York City. If you're of a less cynical bent, though, you could believe it was also heartening that the improbable insanity that once served as the Mets' hallmark could emerge anew, as it did in 2015, and bring a whole city along for the crazy ride. Even in the new New York, even on the far side of the year 2000, people still wished to believe in a 1999.

SUPER READERS

The following people went above and beyond the call of duty in the backing of this book and are thus bestowed with the title of SUPER READERS, with all the attendant rights and privileges.

Joshua and Lianne Addington
Christina Ali
Iris M. Alvarado
Nitin Bhargava
David DeGroff
Anthony Del Broccolo
Brian Dermody
Joe Duffy
Joel Hugman Huggins
Stephen A. Kaden
Melanie C. Koch
Lee Kennedy-Shaffer
Frank J. Leykamm
Kevin Marshall
Chris McShane
Louis J. and Stephanie Rebecchi
Austin Robins
Alexander Roche
David Schaefer
Martin M. Tomlinson
Giorgio M. Zeolla

INKSHARES

INKSHARES is a reader-driven publisher and producer based in Oakland, California. Our books are selected not by a group of editors, but by readers worldwide.

While we've published books by established writers like *Big Fish* author Daniel Wallace and *Star Wars: Rogue One* scribe Gary Whitta, our aim remains surfacing and developing the new author voices of tomorrow.

Previously unknown Inkshares authors have received starred reviews and been featured in the *New York Times*. Their books are on the front tables of Barnes & Noble and hundreds of independents nationwide, and many have been licensed by publishers in other major markets. They are also being adapted by Oscar-winning screenwriters at the biggest studios and networks.

Interested in making your own story a reality? Visit Inkshares.com to start your own project or find other great books.

www.ingramcontent.com/pod-product-compliance
Lightning Source LLC
Chambersburg PA
CBHW030106100526
44591CB00009B/292